Beat

BANCHO Otome

2

LOVE'S BATTLE ROYALE

YO
FIGHT
SHISHIKU HIGH
SHISHI

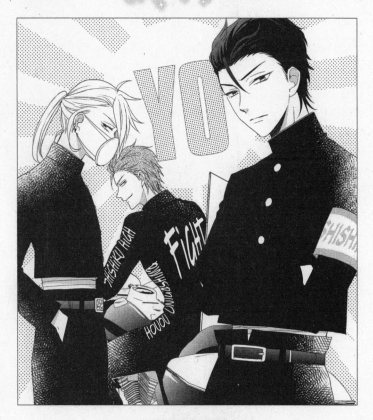

STORY & ART BY

CHIE SHIMADA

Original concept by Spike Chunsoft
Video game developed by Red Entertainment

KENKA BANCHO
Otome
LOVE'S BATTLE ROYALE

2

CONTENTS

I WANT TO RECORD EVERYTHING ABOUT YOU

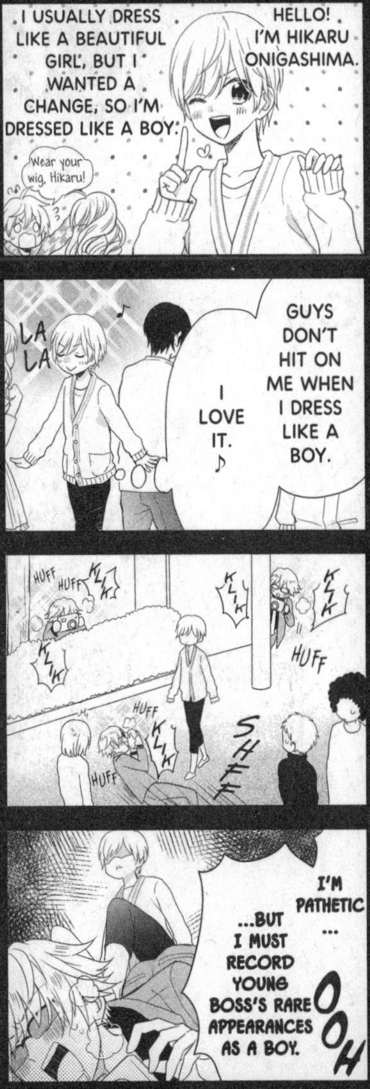
HELLO! I'M HIKARU ONIGASHIMA.
I USUALLY DRESS LIKE A BEAUTIFUL GIRL, BUT I WANTED A CHANGE, SO I'M DRESSED LIKE A BOY.
Wear your wig, Hikaru!
GUYS DON'T HIT ON ME WHEN I DRESS LIKE A BOY.
I LOVE IT. ♪
LA LA
KLIK
HUFF
HUFF
KLIK
KLIK
HUFF
KLIK
HUFF
KLIK
HUFF
SHFF
I'M PATHETIC...
...BUT I MUST RECORD YOUNG BOSS'S RARE APPEARANCES AS A BOY.
OOH

ACT LIKE A BEST FRIEND

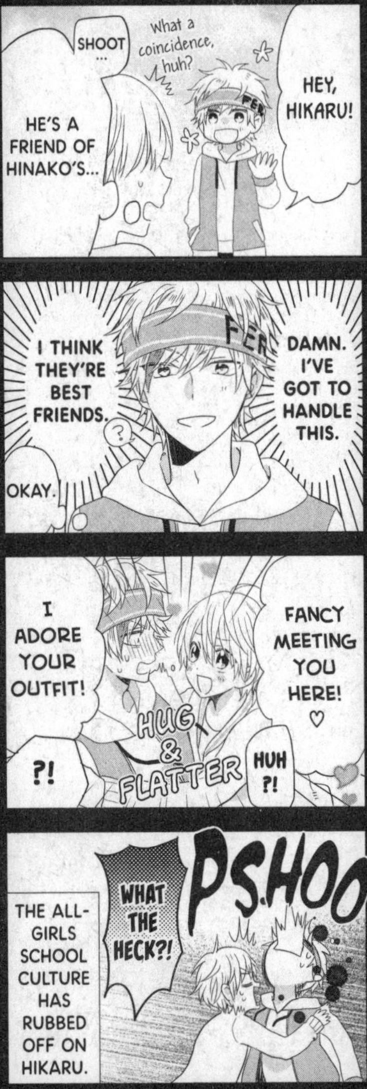
HEY, HIKARU!
What a coincidence, huh?
SHOOT ...
HE'S A FRIEND OF HINAKO'S...
DAMN. I'VE GOT TO HANDLE THIS.
I THINK THEY'RE BEST FRIENDS.
OKAY.
FANCY MEETING YOU HERE! ♡
I ADORE YOUR OUTFIT!
HUG & FLATTER
HUH ?!
?!
PSHOO
WHAT THE HECK?!
THE ALL-GIRLS SCHOOL CULTURE HAS RUBBED OFF ON HIKARU.

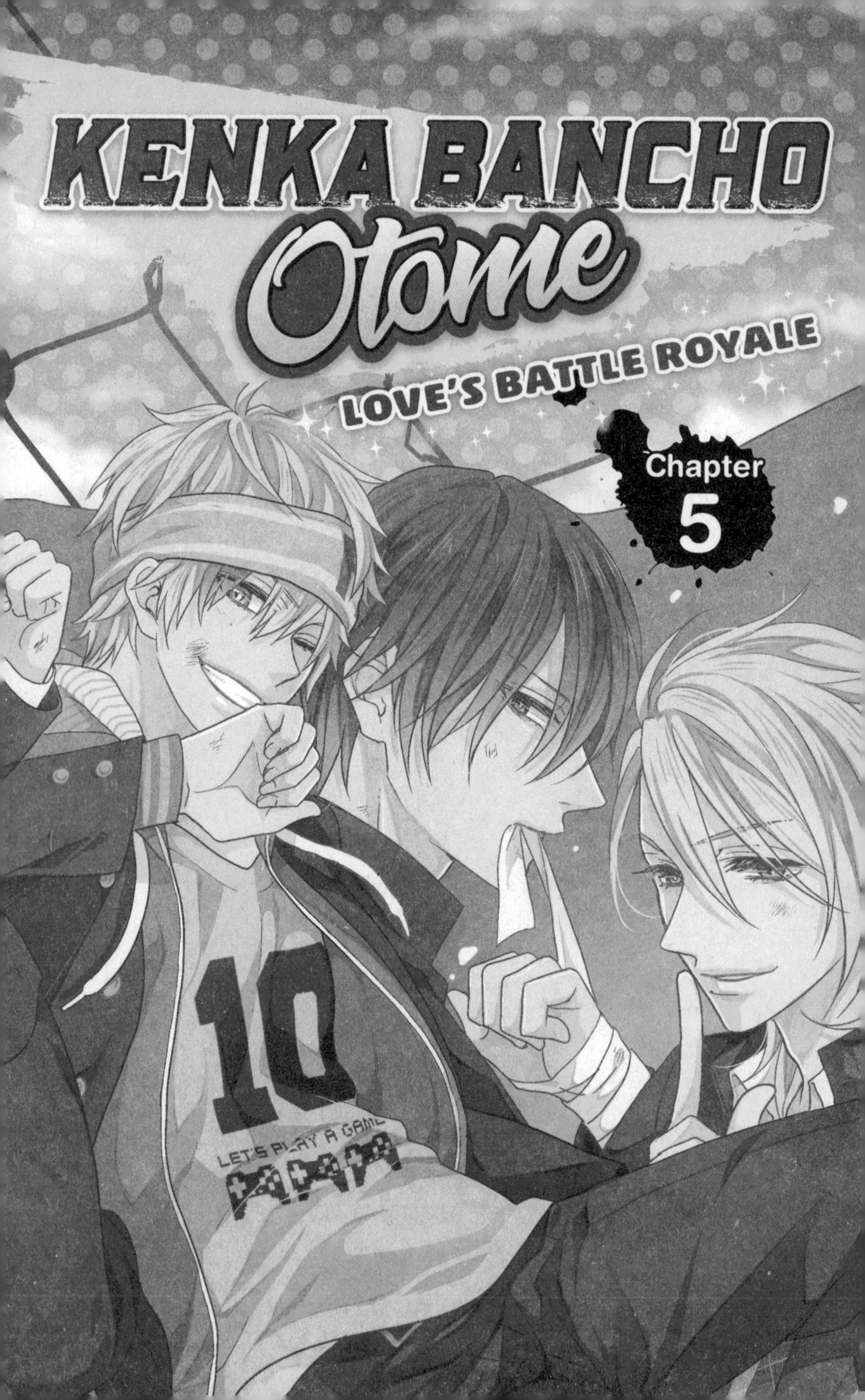
KENKA BANCHO
Otome
LOVE'S BATTLE ROYALE
Chapter
5
10
LET'S PLAY A GAME

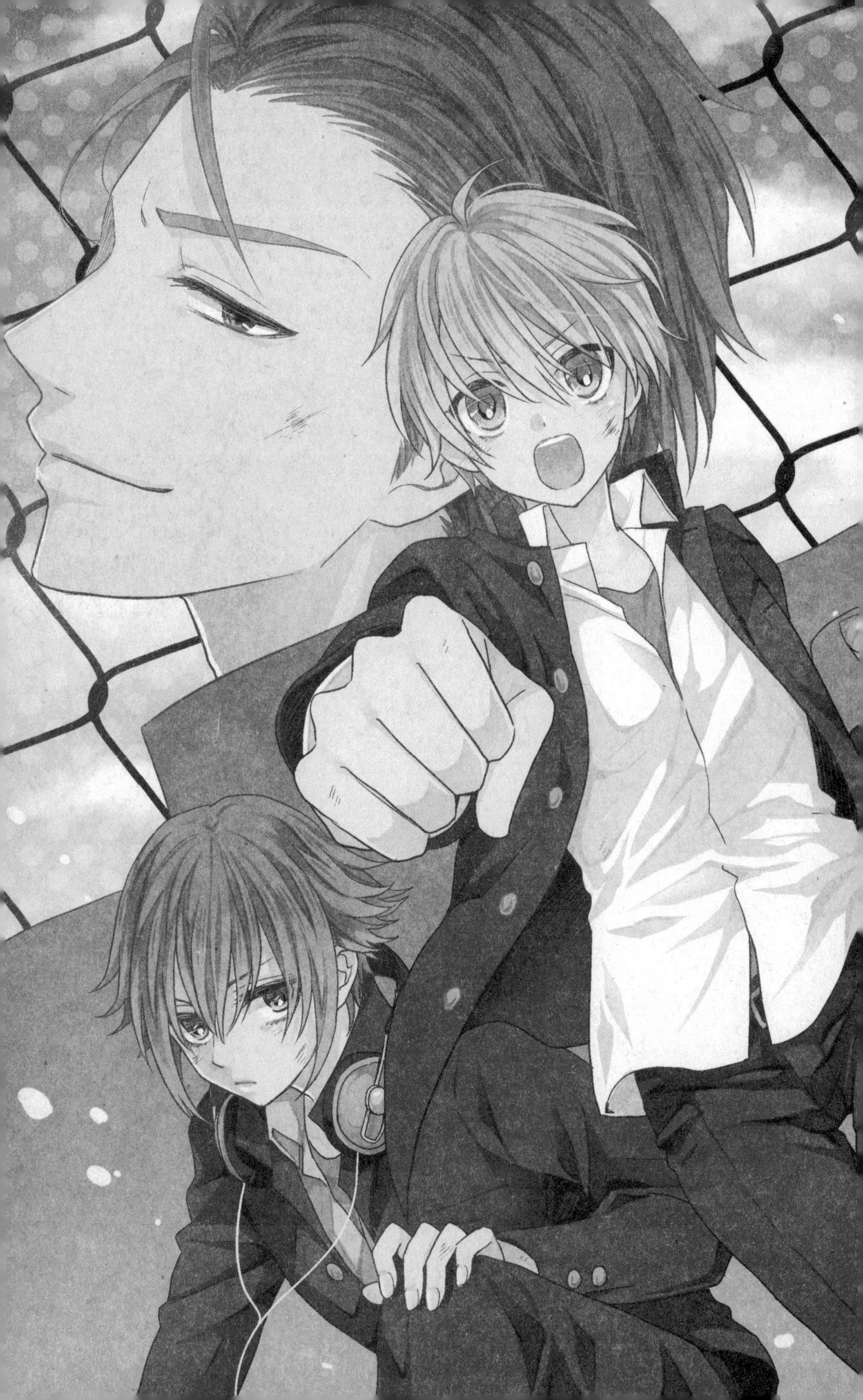

WASH BLOOD WITH BLOOD

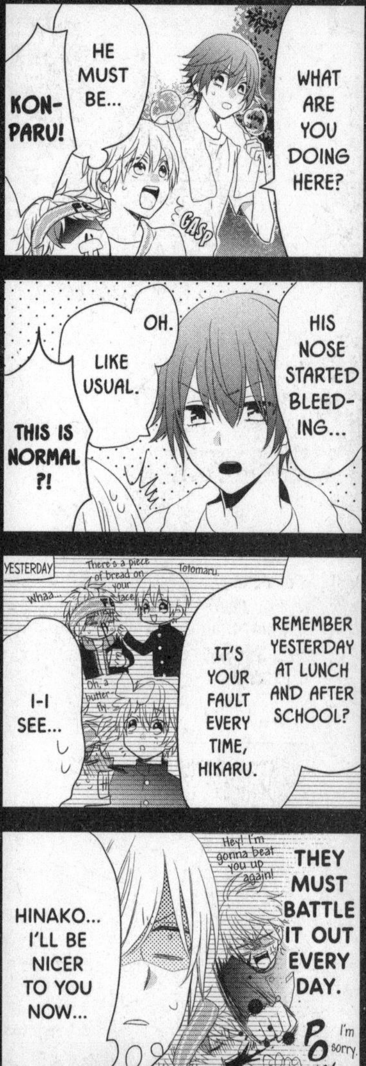
WHAT ARE YOU DOING HERE?
HE MUST BE...
KON-PARU!
GASP
HIS NOSE STARTED BLEED-ING...
OH.
LIKE USUAL.
THIS IS NORMAL?!
REMEMBER YESTERDAY AT LUNCH AND AFTER SCHOOL?
Totomaru,
There's a piece of bread on your face.
Whaa...
YESTERDAY
IT'S YOUR FAULT EVERY TIME, HIKARU.
Oh, a butter-fly.
I-I SEE...
THEY MUST BATTLE IT OUT EVERY DAY.
Hey! I'm gonna beat you up again!
I'm sorry.
POW
HINAKO... I'LL BE NICER TO YOU NOW...

I'M ALWAYS WATCHING OVER YOU

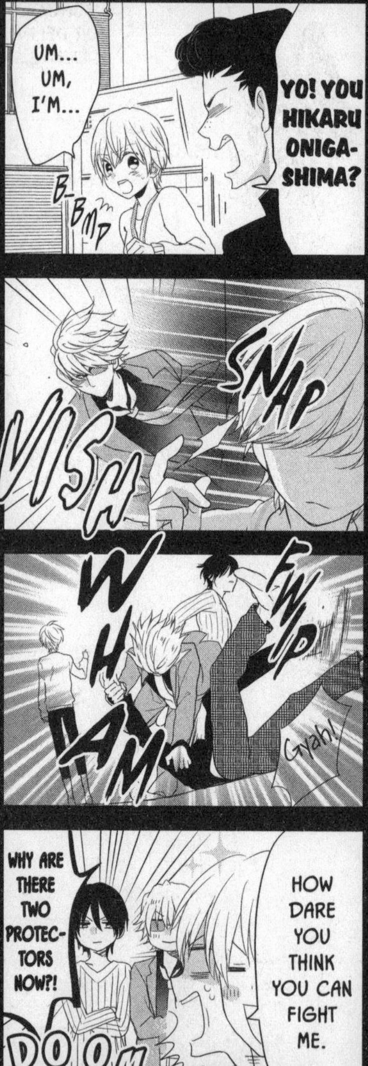
YO! YOU HIKARU ONIGA-SHIMA?
UM... UM, I'M...
B-BMP
SNAP
VISH
FWIP
WHAM
Gyah!
HOW DARE YOU THINK YOU CAN FIGHT ME.
WHY ARE THERE TWO PROTECTORS NOW?!
DOOOM

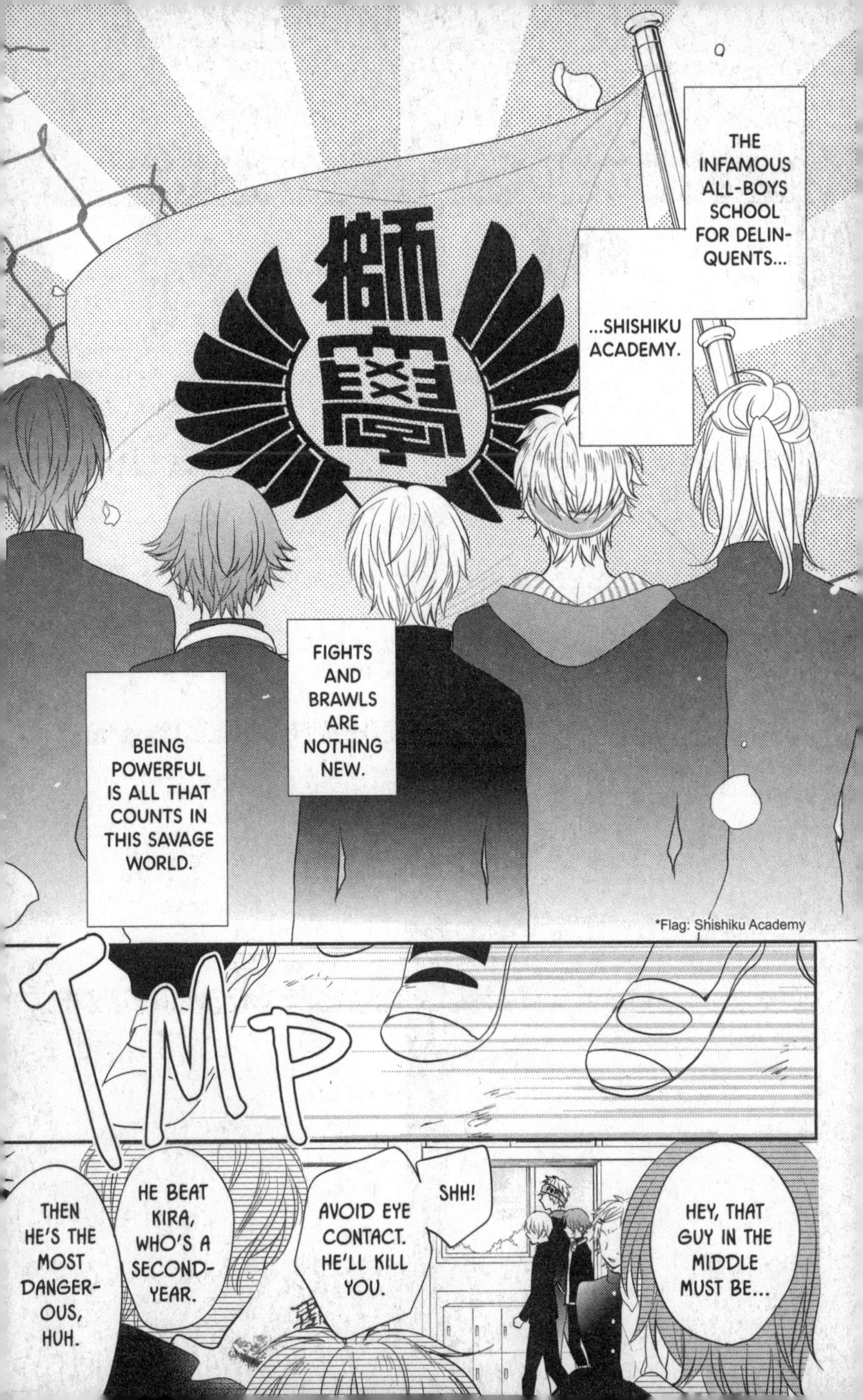
THE INFAMOUS ALL-BOYS SCHOOL FOR DELINQUENTS...
...SHISHIKU ACADEMY.
FIGHTS AND BRAWLS ARE NOTHING NEW.
BEING POWERFUL IS ALL THAT COUNTS IN THIS SAVAGE WORLD.
*Flag: Shishiku Academy
TMP
HEY, THAT GUY IN THE MIDDLE MUST BE...
SHH!
AVOID EYE CONTACT. HE'LL KILL YOU.
HE BEAT KIRA, WHO'S A SECOND-YEAR.
THEN HE'S THE MOST DANGEROUS, HUH.

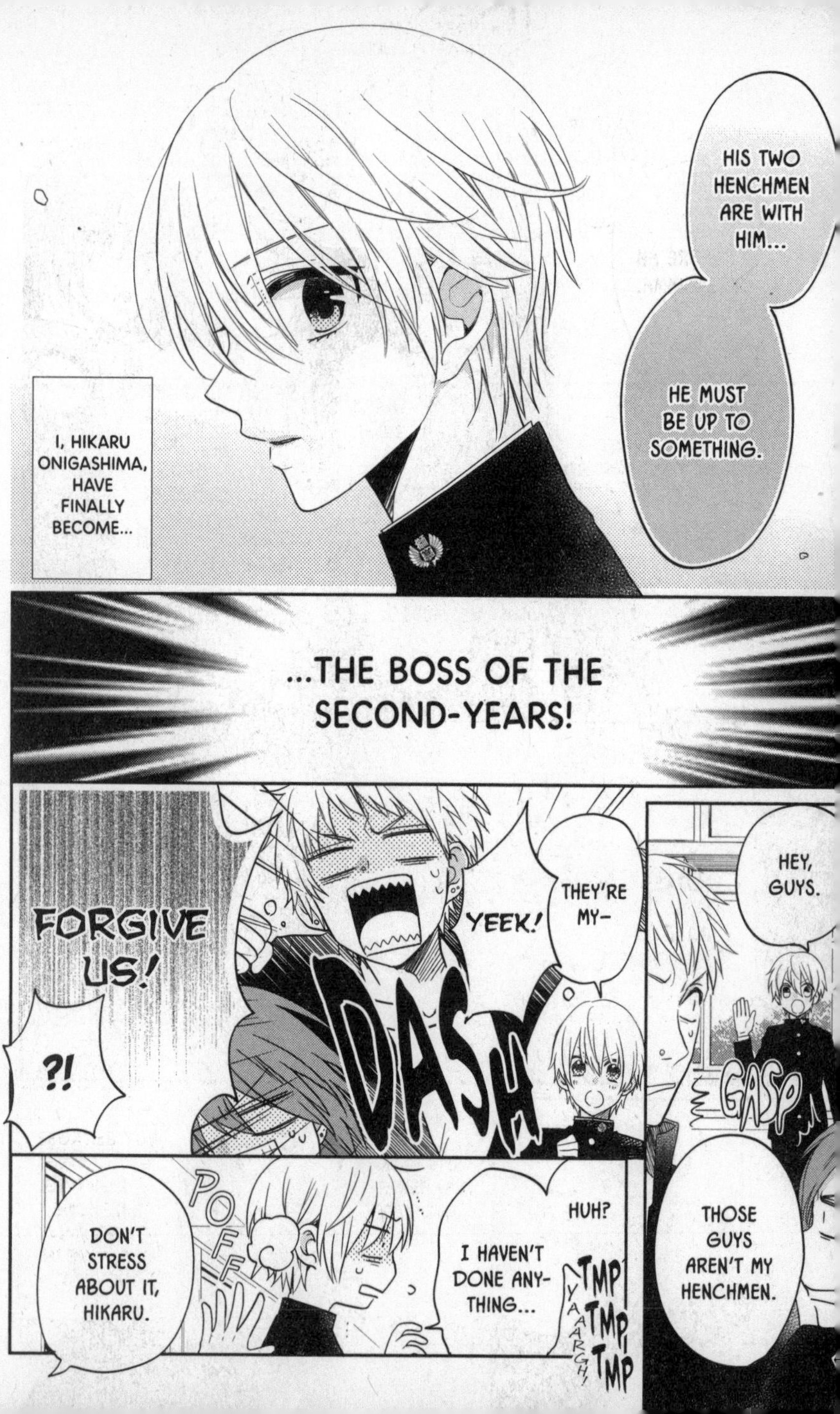
HIS TWO HENCHMEN ARE WITH HIM...
HE MUST BE UP TO SOMETHING.
I, HIKARU ONIGASHIMA, HAVE FINALLY BECOME...
...THE BOSS OF THE SECOND-YEARS!
HEY, GUYS.
GASP
THOSE GUYS AREN'T MY HENCHMEN.
THEY'RE MY—
YEEK!
DASH
FORGIVE US!
?!
HUH?
I HAVEN'T DONE ANYTHING...
TMP TMP TMP
YAAARGH!
POFF
DON'T STRESS ABOUT IT, HIKARU.

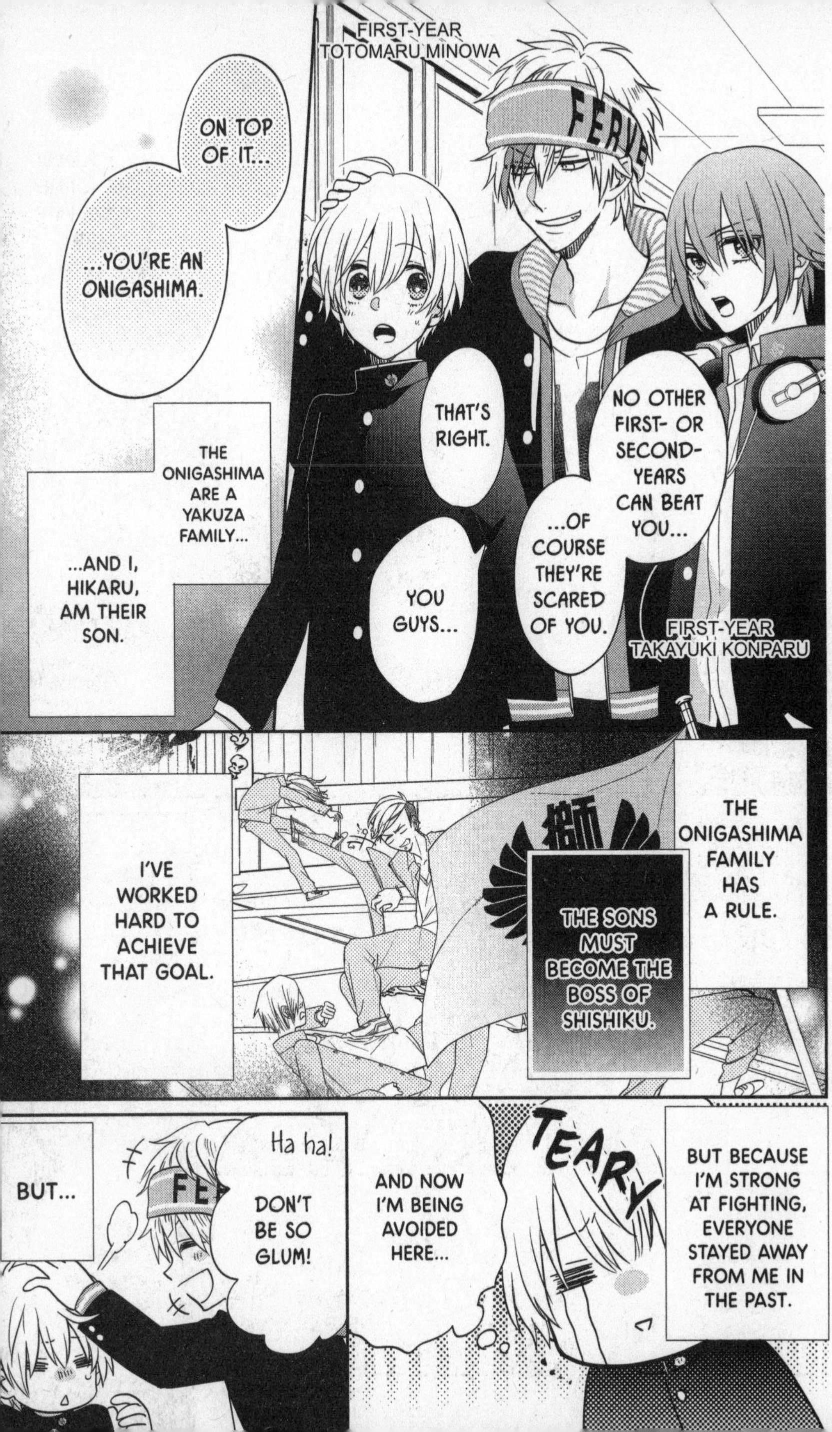
FIRST-YEAR TOTOMARU MINOWA
NO OTHER FIRST- OR SECOND-YEARS CAN BEAT YOU...
...OF COURSE THEY'RE SCARED OF YOU.
FIRST-YEAR TAKAYUKI KONPARU
THAT'S RIGHT.
YOU GUYS...
ON TOP OF IT...
...YOU'RE AN ONIGASHIMA.
THE ONIGASHIMA ARE A YAKUZA FAMILY...
...AND I, HIKARU, AM THEIR SON.
THE ONIGASHIMA FAMILY HAS A RULE.
THE SONS MUST BECOME THE BOSS OF SHISHIKU.
I'VE WORKED HARD TO ACHIEVE THAT GOAL.
BUT BECAUSE I'M STRONG AT FIGHTING, EVERYONE STAYED AWAY FROM ME IN THE PAST.
TEARY
AND NOW I'M BEING AVOIDED HERE...
Ha ha!
DON'T BE SO GLUM!
BUT...

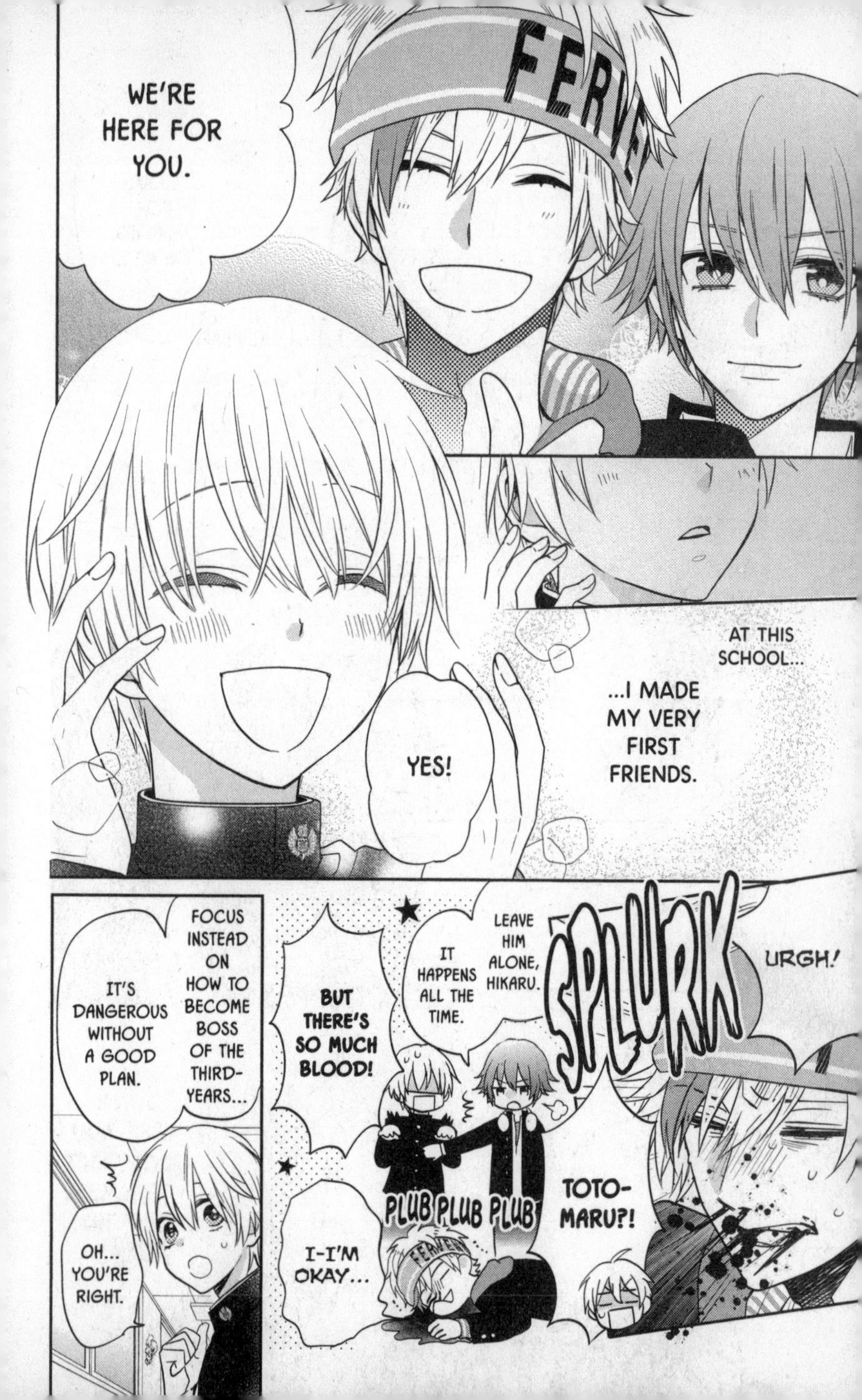
WE'RE HERE FOR YOU.
AT THIS SCHOOL...
...I MADE MY VERY FIRST FRIENDS.
YES!
SPLURK
URGH!
TOTO-MARU?!
LEAVE HIM ALONE, HIKARU.
IT HAPPENS ALL THE TIME.
BUT THERE'S SO MUCH BLOOD!
PLUB PLUB PLUB
I-I'M OKAY...
FOCUS INSTEAD ON HOW TO BECOME BOSS OF THE THIRD-YEARS...
IT'S DANGEROUS WITHOUT A GOOD PLAN.
OH... YOU'RE RIGHT.

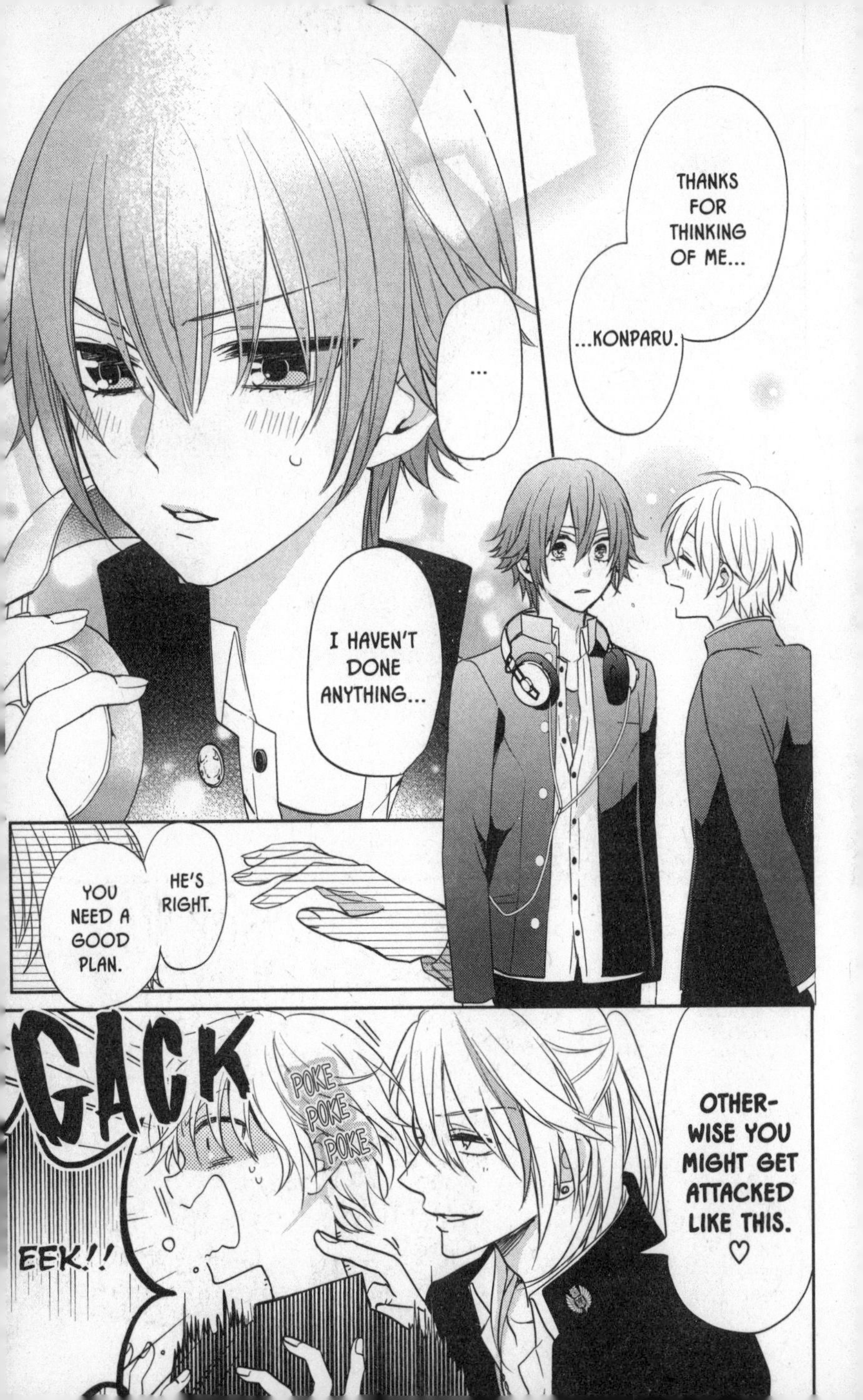
THANKS FOR THINKING OF ME...
...KONPARU.
...
I HAVEN'T DONE ANYTHING...
HE'S RIGHT.
YOU NEED A GOOD PLAN.
OTHER-WISE YOU MIGHT GET ATTACKED LIKE THIS. ♡
POKE POKE POKE
GACK
EEK!!

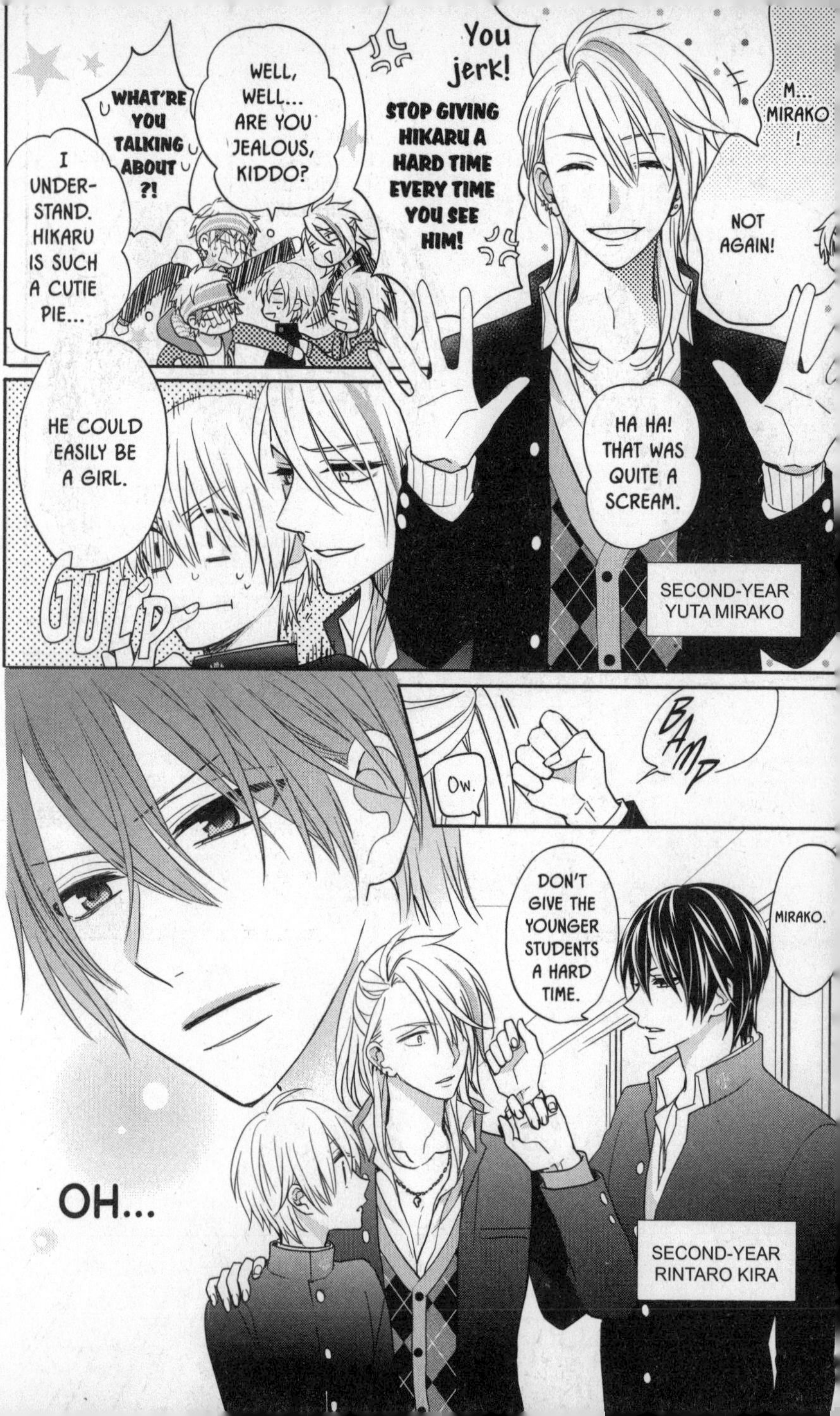
M... MIRAKO!
NOT AGAIN!
HA HA! THAT WAS QUITE A SCREAM.
SECOND-YEAR YUTA MIRAKO
You jerk!
STOP GIVING HIKARU A HARD TIME EVERY TIME YOU SEE HIM!
WELL, WELL... ARE YOU JEALOUS, KIDDO?
WHAT'RE YOU TALKING ABOUT?!
I UNDER-STAND. HIKARU IS SUCH A CUTIE PIE...
HE COULD EASILY BE A GIRL.
GULP
BAM
Ow.
MIRAKO.
DON'T GIVE THE YOUNGER STUDENTS A HARD TIME.
SECOND-YEAR RINTARO KIRA
OH...

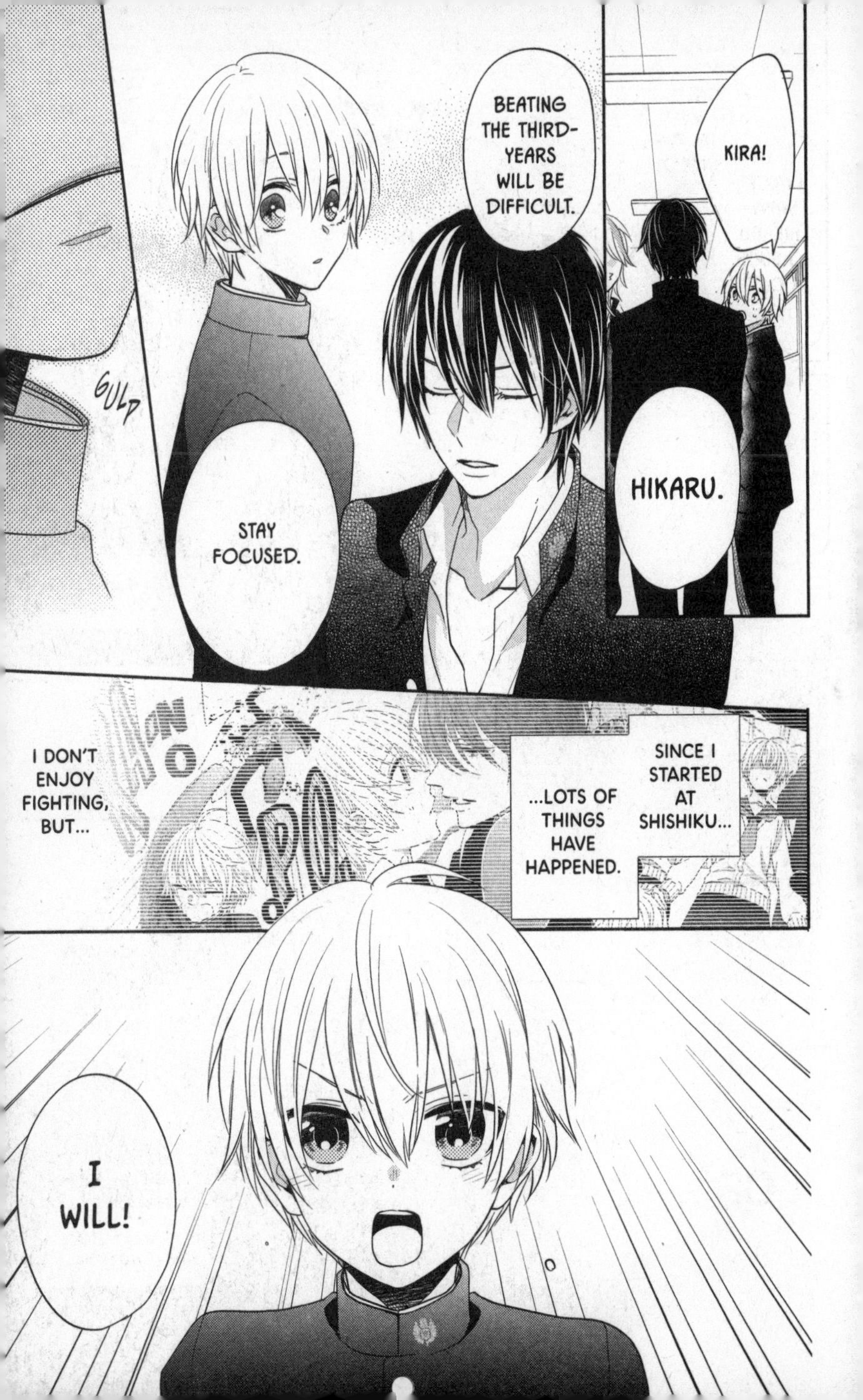
KIRA!
HIKARU.
BEATING THE THIRD-YEARS WILL BE DIFFICULT.
GULP
STAY FOCUSED.
SINCE I STARTED AT SHISHIKU...
...LOTS OF THINGS HAVE HAPPENED.
I DON'T ENJOY FIGHTING, BUT...
I WILL!

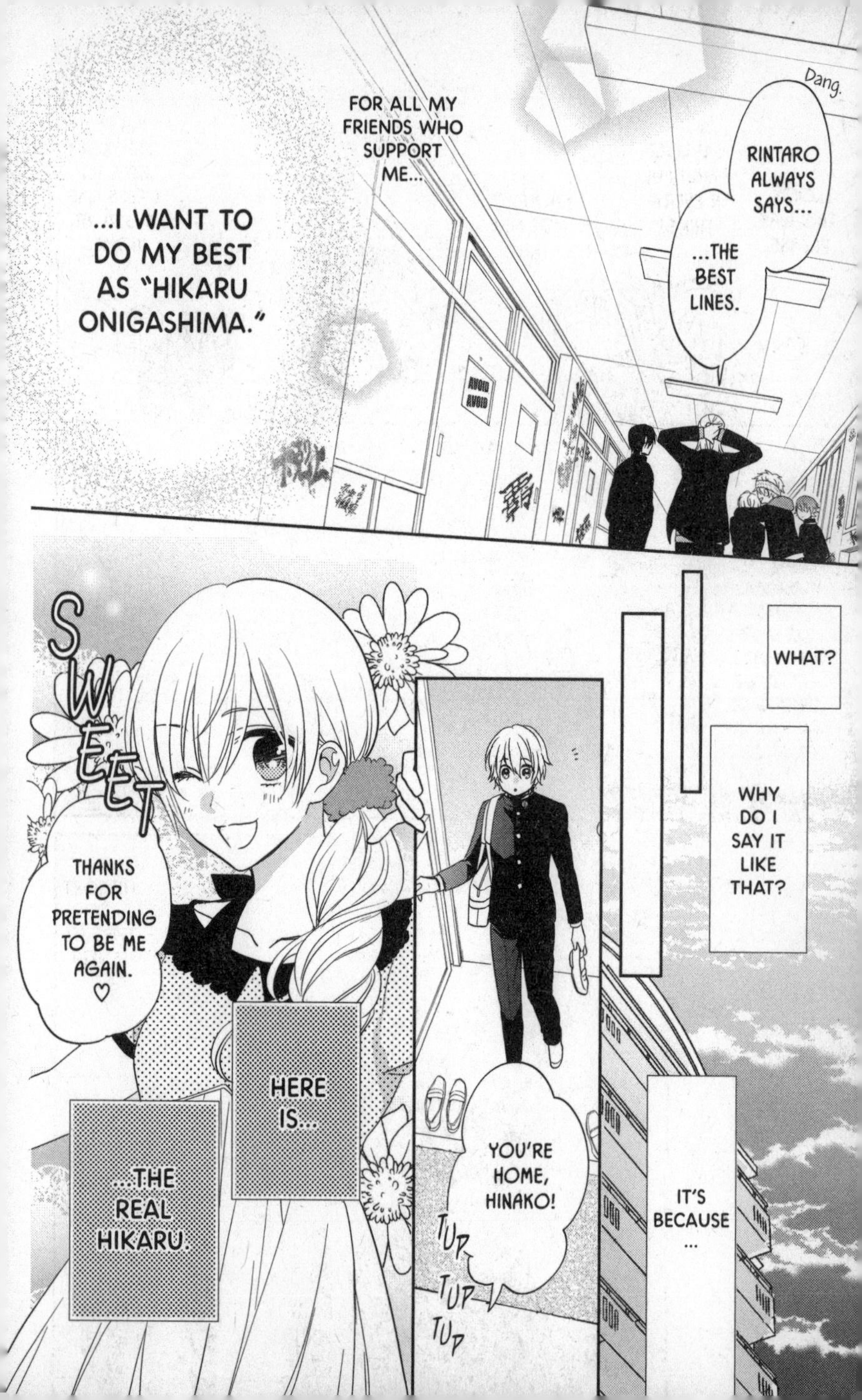
Dang.
RINTARO ALWAYS SAYS...
...THE BEST LINES.
AVOID AVOID
FOR ALL MY FRIENDS WHO SUPPORT ME...
...I WANT TO DO MY BEST AS "HIKARU ONIGASHIMA."
WHAT?
WHY DO I SAY IT LIKE THAT?
IT'S BECAUSE...
YOU'RE HOME, HINAKO!
TUP TUP TUP
SWEET
THANKS FOR PRETENDING TO BE ME AGAIN. ♡
HERE IS...
...THE REAL HIKARU.

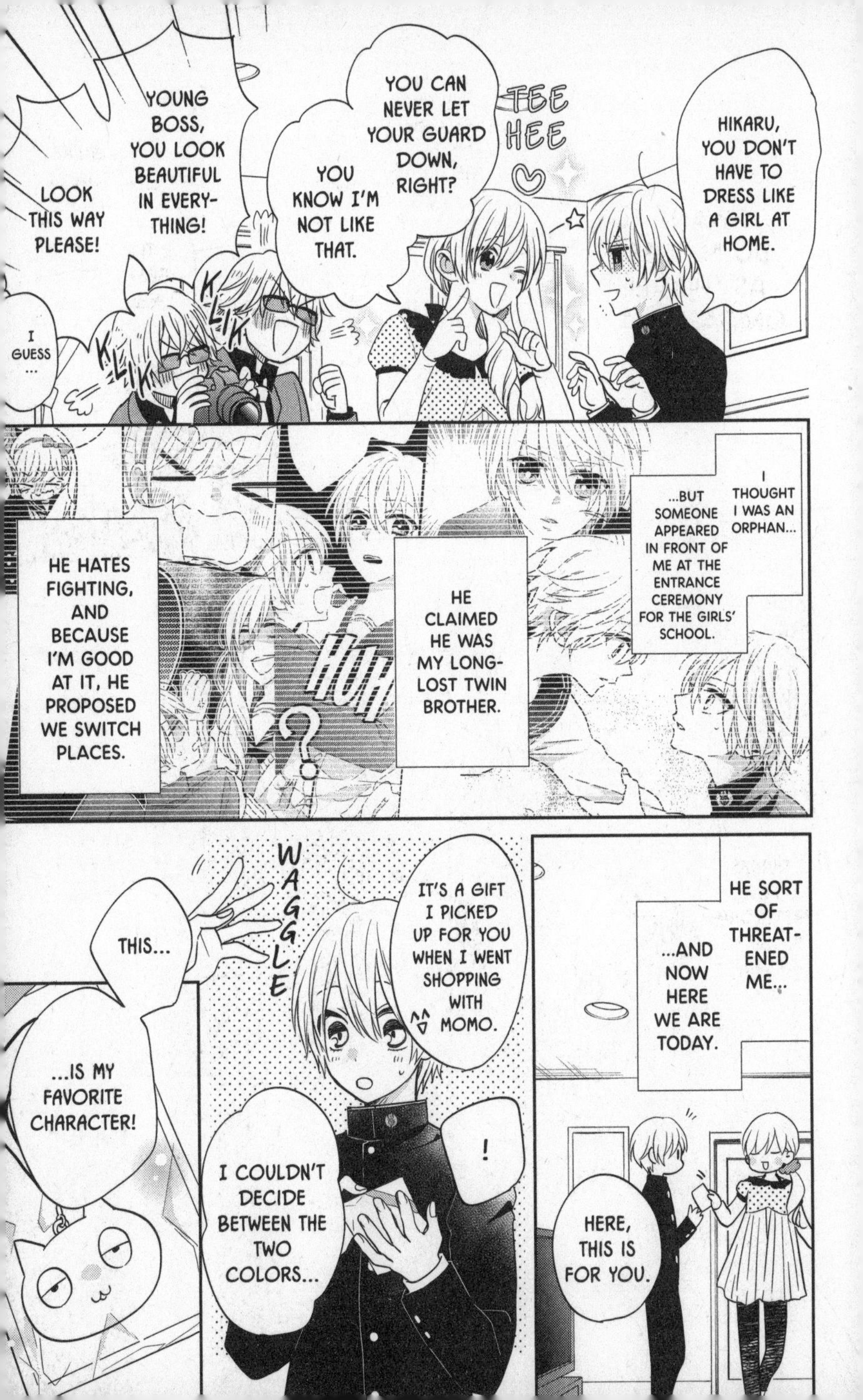
HIKARU, YOU DON'T HAVE TO DRESS LIKE A GIRL AT HOME.
TEE HEE
YOU CAN NEVER LET YOUR GUARD DOWN, RIGHT?
YOU KNOW I'M NOT LIKE THAT.
YOUNG BOSS, YOU LOOK BEAUTIFUL IN EVERY-THING!
KLIK KLIK
LOOK THIS WAY PLEASE!
KLIK KLIK
I GUESS ...
I THOUGHT I WAS AN ORPHAN...
...BUT SOMEONE APPEARED IN FRONT OF ME AT THE ENTRANCE CEREMONY FOR THE GIRLS' SCHOOL.
HE CLAIMED HE WAS MY LONG-LOST TWIN BROTHER.
HUH
?
HE HATES FIGHTING, AND BECAUSE I'M GOOD AT IT, HE PROPOSED WE SWITCH PLACES.
HE SORT OF THREAT-ENED ME...
...AND NOW HERE WE ARE TODAY.
HERE, THIS IS FOR YOU.
IT'S A GIFT I PICKED UP FOR YOU WHEN I WENT SHOPPING WITH MOMO.
WAGGLE
!
I COULDN'T DECIDE BETWEEN THE TWO COLORS...
THIS...
...IS MY FAVORITE CHARACTER!

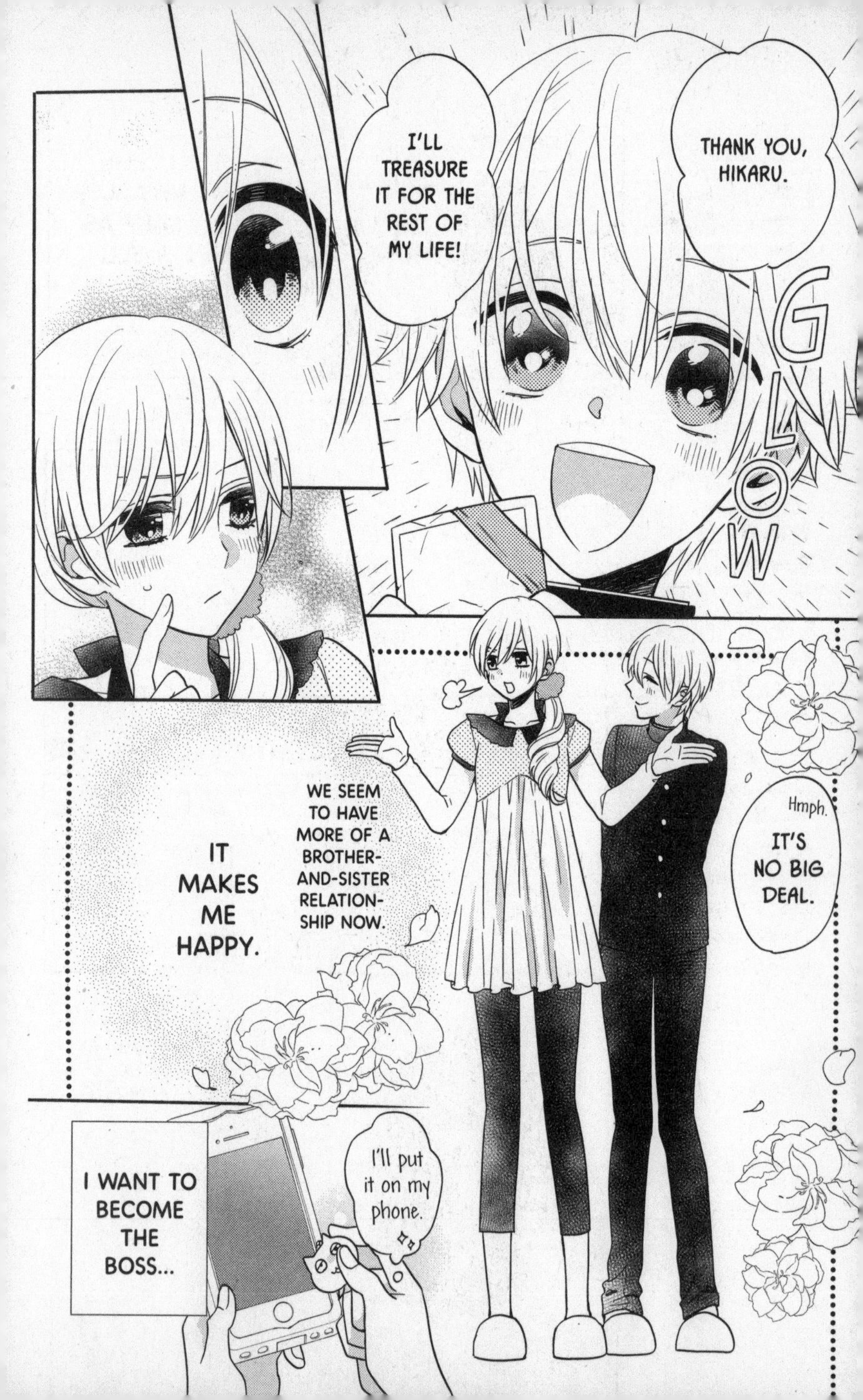
THANK YOU, HIKARU.
GLOW
I'LL TREASURE IT FOR THE REST OF MY LIFE!
Hmph.
IT'S NO BIG DEAL.
WE SEEM TO HAVE MORE OF A BROTHER-AND-SISTER RELATIONSHIP NOW.
IT MAKES ME HAPPY.
I'll put it on my phone.
I WANT TO BECOME THE BOSS...

Volume 2! Yay!

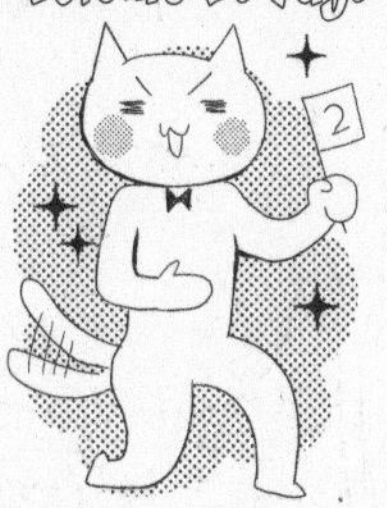
2

Hello, I'm Shimada. Thank you very much for picking up volume 2!! ✧

So much is going on! I got word that *Kenka Bancho Otome* will become an anime. But it'll make me really happy if you continue to enjoy this manga version as well.

The next sidebar will be about my visit to the fifth recording of "Tokoton Totokon Radio" featuring Totomaru (played by KENN) and Konparu (played by Shouta Aoi).

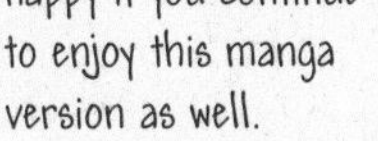
Let's go!!

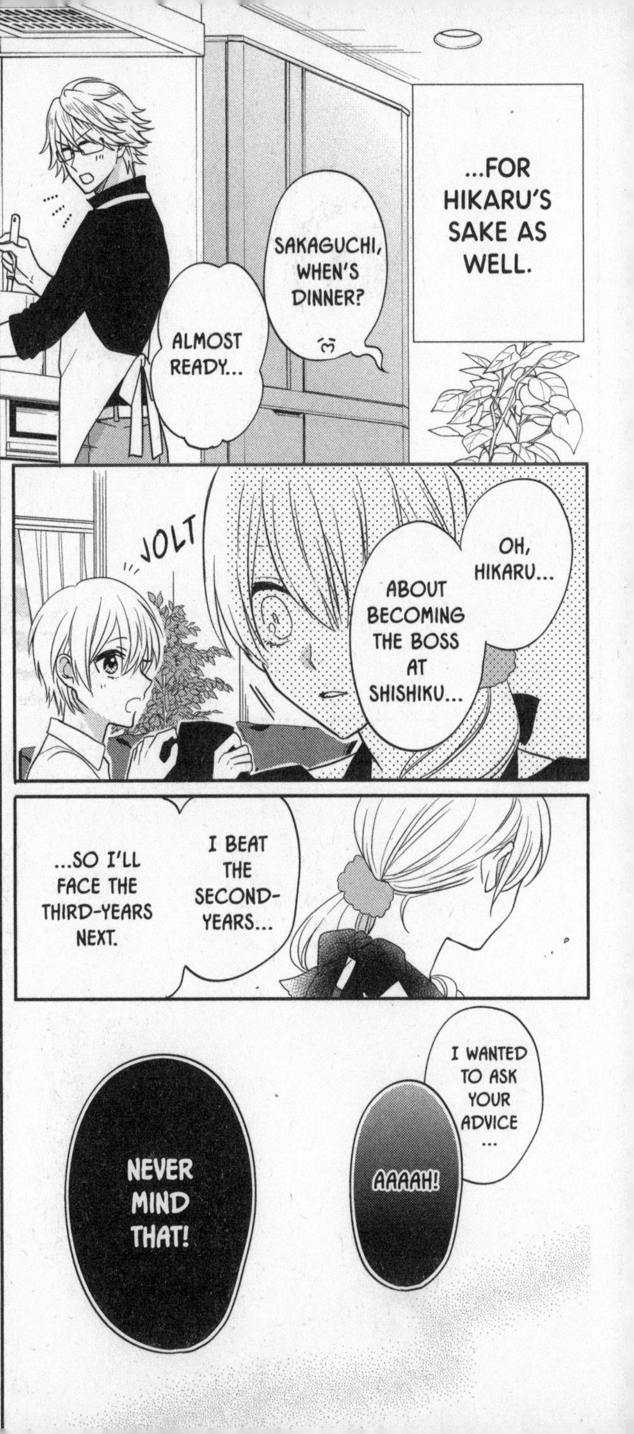
...FOR HIKARU'S SAKE AS WELL.
SAKAGUCHI, WHEN'S DINNER?
ALMOST READY...
OH, HIKARU...
ABOUT BECOMING THE BOSS AT SHISHIKU...
JOLT
I BEAT THE SECOND-YEARS...
...SO I'LL FACE THE THIRD-YEARS NEXT.
I WANTED TO ASK YOUR ADVICE...
AAAAH!
NEVER MIND THAT!

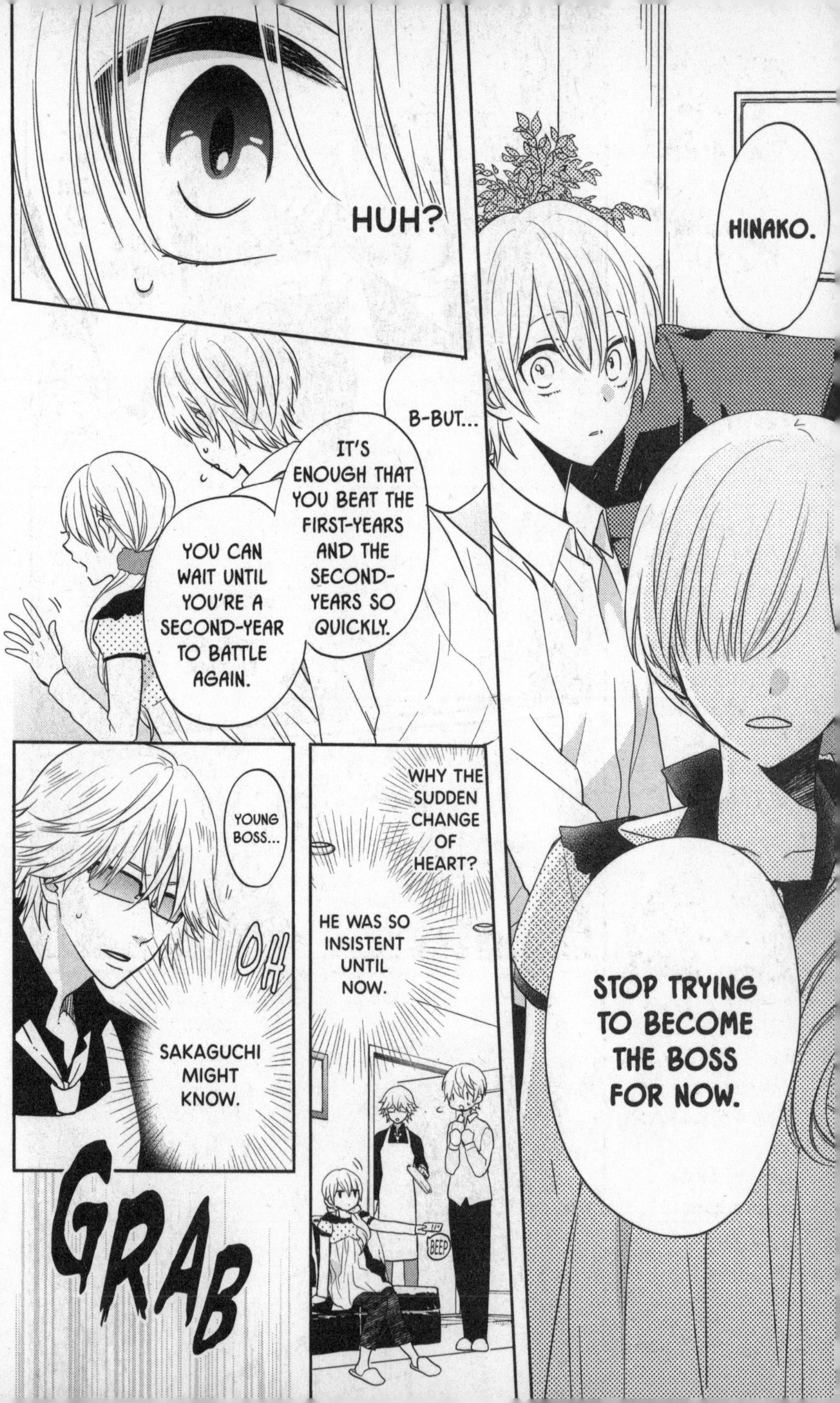
HINAKO.
STOP TRYING TO BECOME THE BOSS FOR NOW.
HUH?
B-BUT...
IT'S ENOUGH THAT YOU BEAT THE FIRST-YEARS AND THE SECOND-YEARS SO QUICKLY.
YOU CAN WAIT UNTIL YOU'RE A SECOND-YEAR TO BATTLE AGAIN.
WHY THE SUDDEN CHANGE OF HEART?
HE WAS SO INSISTENT UNTIL NOW.
BEEP
YOUNG BOSS...
OH
SAKAGUCHI MIGHT KNOW.
GRAB

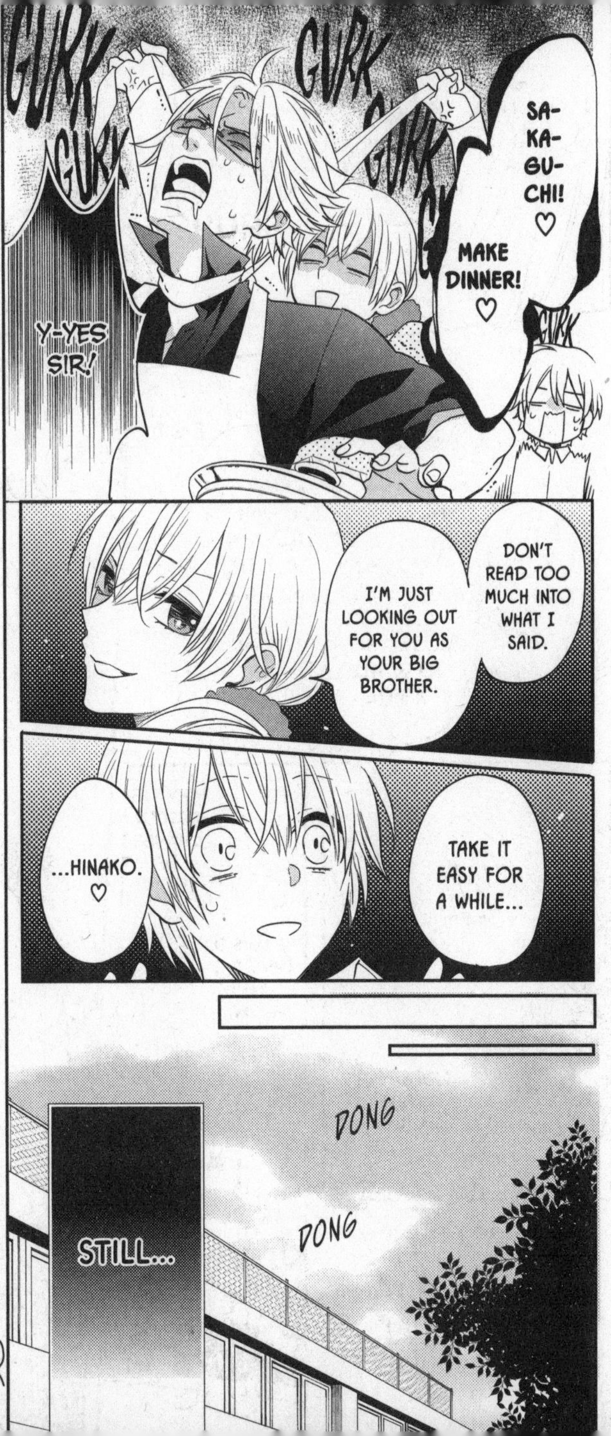
GURK
GURK
GURK
GURK
SA-KA-GU-CHI! ♡
MAKE DINNER! ♡
GURK
GURK
Y-YES SIR!
DON'T READ TOO MUCH INTO WHAT I SAID.
I'M JUST LOOKING OUT FOR YOU AS YOUR BIG BROTHER.
TAKE IT EASY FOR A WHILE...
...HINAKO. ♡
DONG
DONG
STILL...

HERE WE GO! ALL ABOUT TOKO RADIO!!

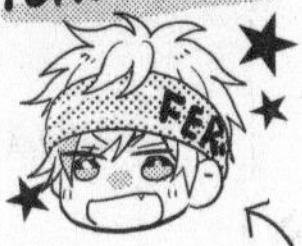
FER

KENN, who plays Totomaru, is easy-going and playful—just like his character.

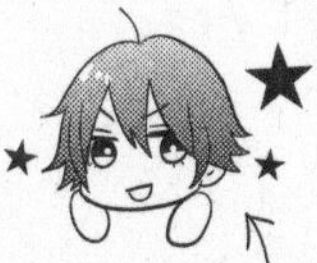

Shouta Aoi is the complete opposite to his cool characterization of Konparu. He's cute and quite feminine. (?!)

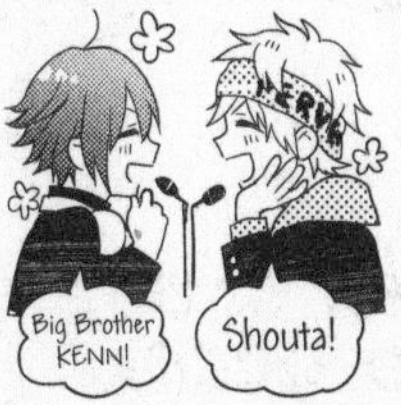
Big Brother KENN!
Shouta!

This is what they call each other, and the conversation was easy, but...
Someone finally makes a guest appearance in the fifth episode.

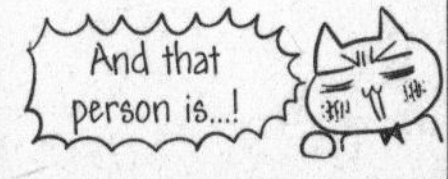
And that person is...!

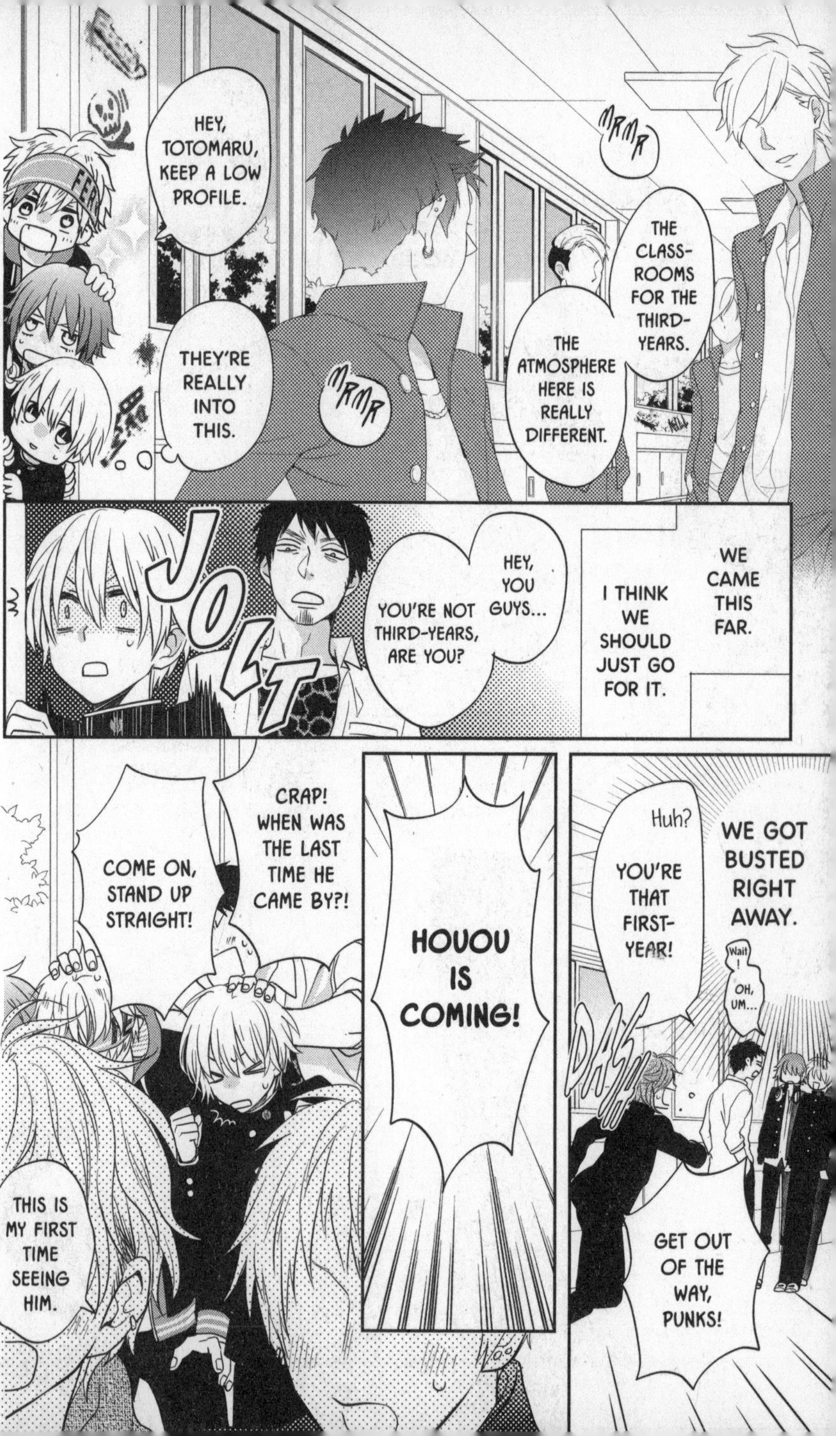
MRMR
THE CLASSROOMS FOR THE THIRD-YEARS.
THE ATMOSPHERE HERE IS REALLY DIFFERENT.
MRMR
HEY, TOTOMARU, KEEP A LOW PROFILE.
THEY'RE REALLY INTO THIS.
WE CAME THIS FAR.
I THINK WE SHOULD JUST GO FOR IT.
HEY, YOU GUYS...
YOU'RE NOT THIRD-YEARS, ARE YOU?
JOLT
WE GOT BUSTED RIGHT AWAY.
Huh?
YOU'RE THAT FIRST-YEAR!
Wait!
OH, UM...
GET OUT OF THE WAY, PUNKS!
HOUOU IS COMING!
CRAP! WHEN WAS THE LAST TIME HE CAME BY?!
COME ON, STAND UP STRAIGHT!
THIS IS MY FIRST TIME SEEING HIM.

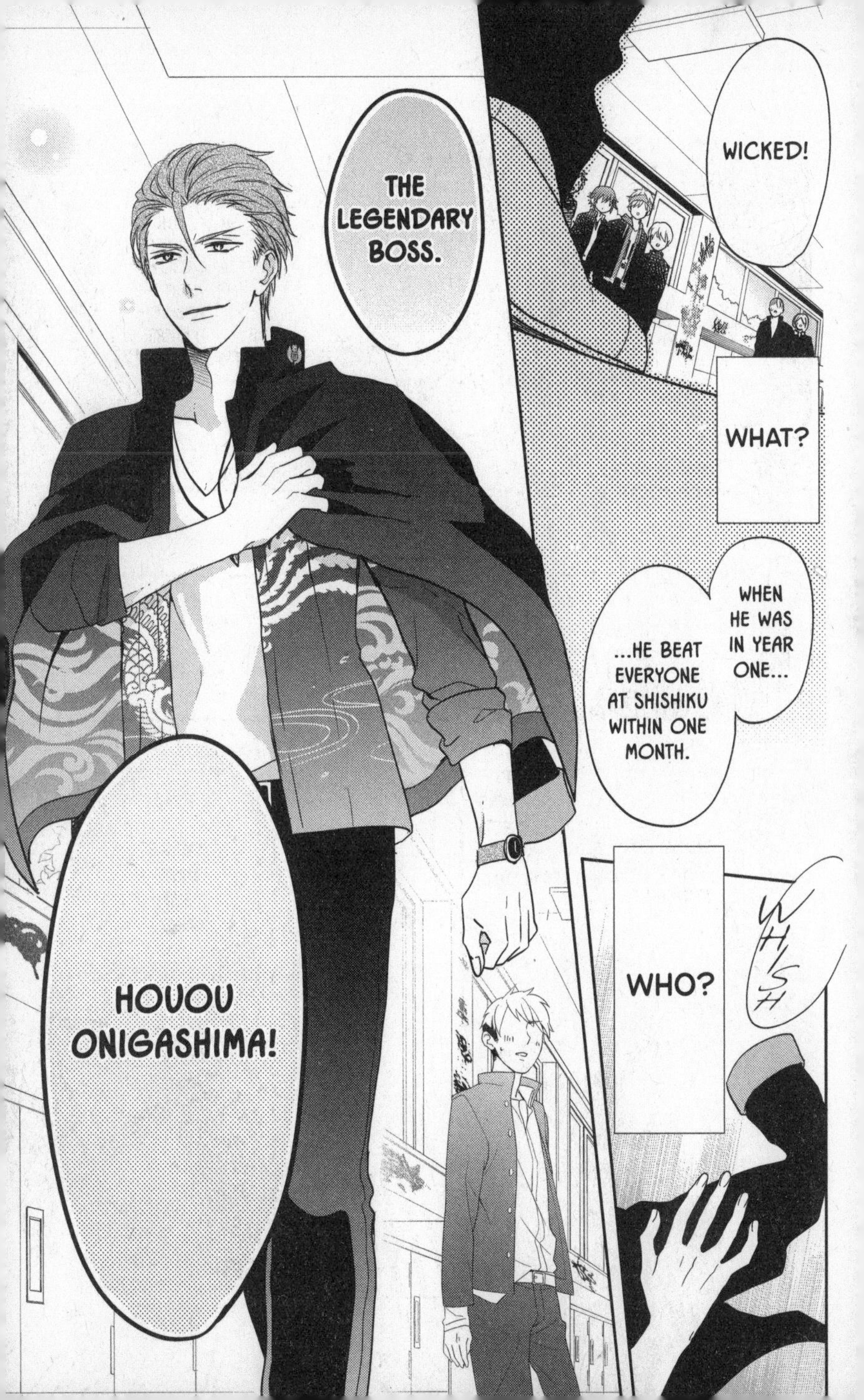
WICKED!
WHAT?
WHEN HE WAS IN YEAR ONE...
...HE BEAT EVERYONE AT SHISHIKU WITHIN ONE MONTH.
WHISH
WHO?
THE LEGENDARY BOSS.
HOUOU ONIGASHIMA!

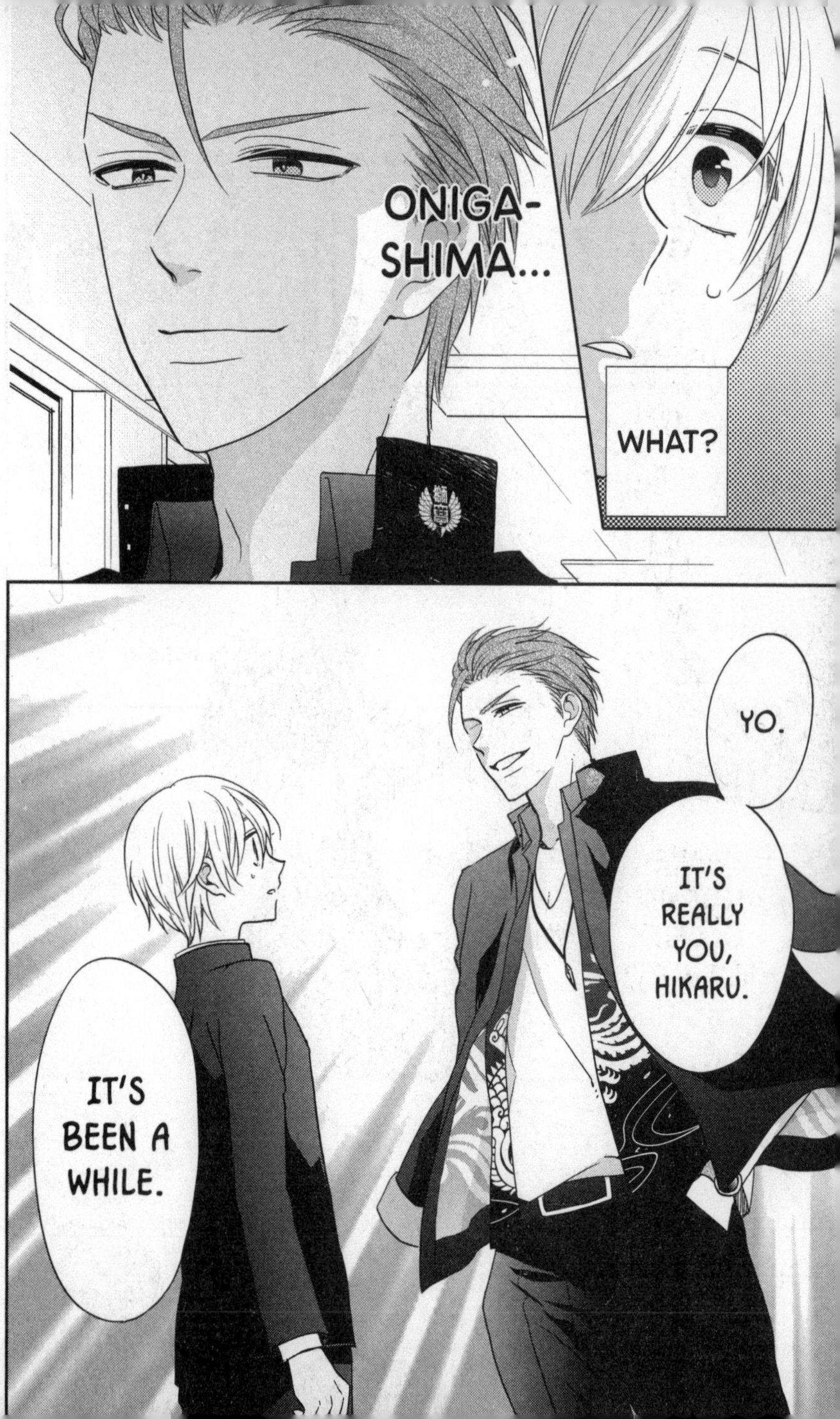
WHAT?
ONIGA-SHIMA...
YO.
IT'S REALLY YOU, HIKARU.
IT'S BEEN A WHILE.

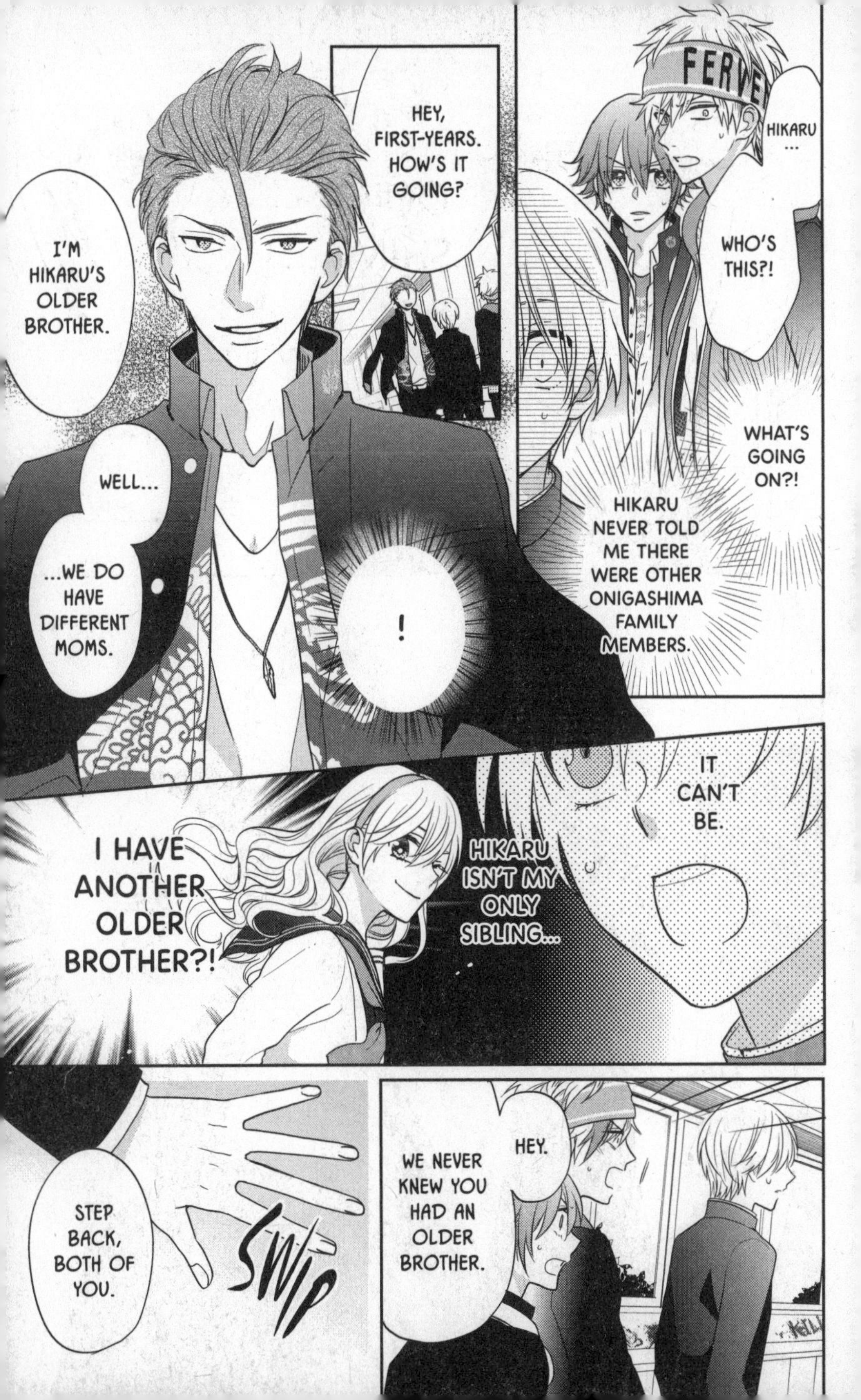

HIKARU...
WHO'S THIS?!
WHAT'S GOING ON?!
HIKARU NEVER TOLD ME THERE WERE OTHER ONIGASHIMA FAMILY MEMBERS.
HEY, FIRST-YEARS. HOW'S IT GOING?
I'M HIKARU'S OLDER BROTHER.
WELL...
...WE DO HAVE DIFFERENT MOMS.
!
IT CAN'T BE.
HIKARU ISN'T MY ONLY SIBLING...
I HAVE ANOTHER OLDER BROTHER?!
HEY.
WE NEVER KNEW YOU HAD AN OLDER BROTHER.
STEP BACK, BOTH OF YOU.
SWIP

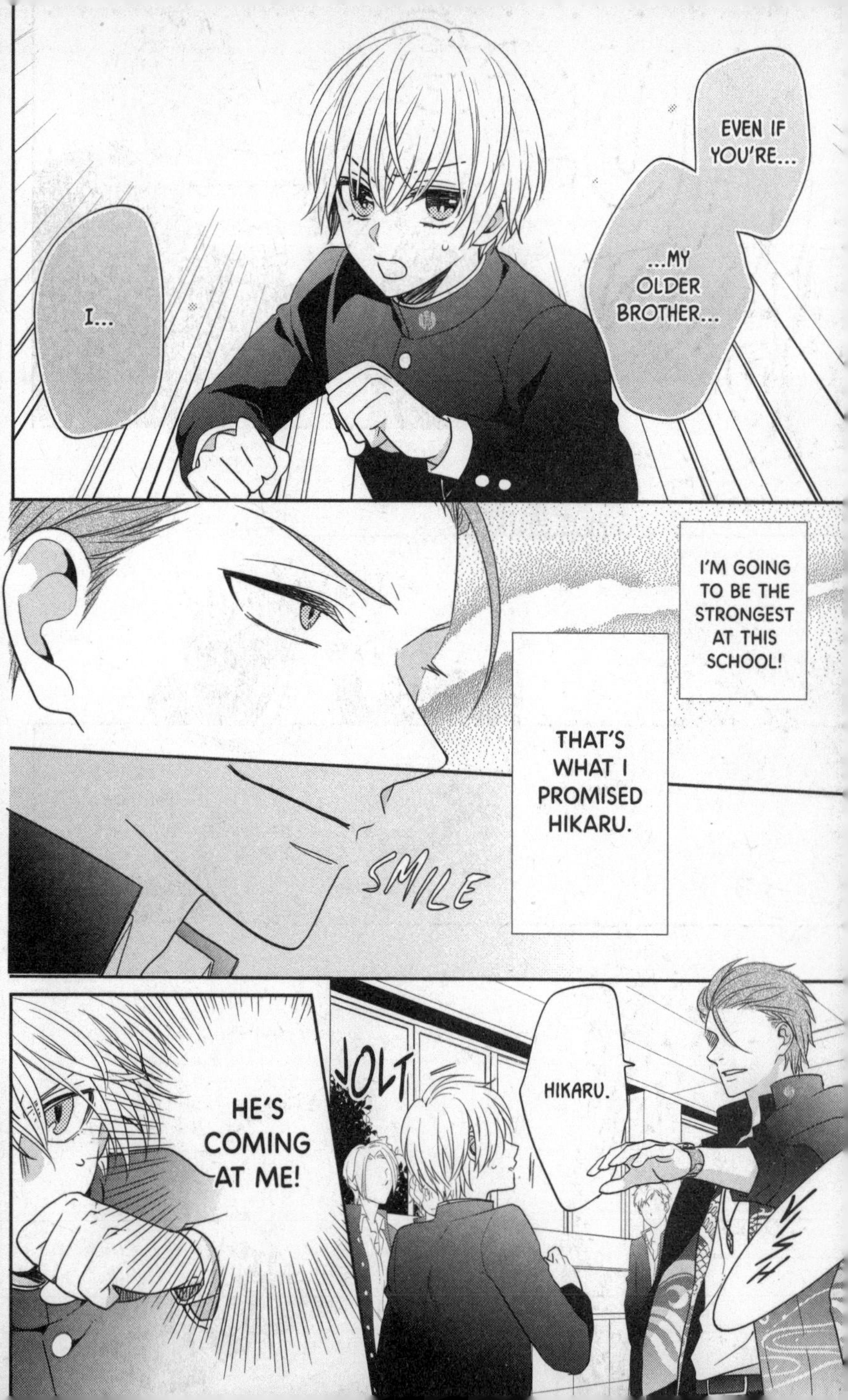
EVEN IF YOU'RE...
...MY OLDER BROTHER...
I...
I'M GOING TO BE THE STRONGEST AT THIS SCHOOL!
THAT'S WHAT I PROMISED HIKARU.
SMILE
HIKARU.
VWSH
JOLT
HE'S COMING AT ME!

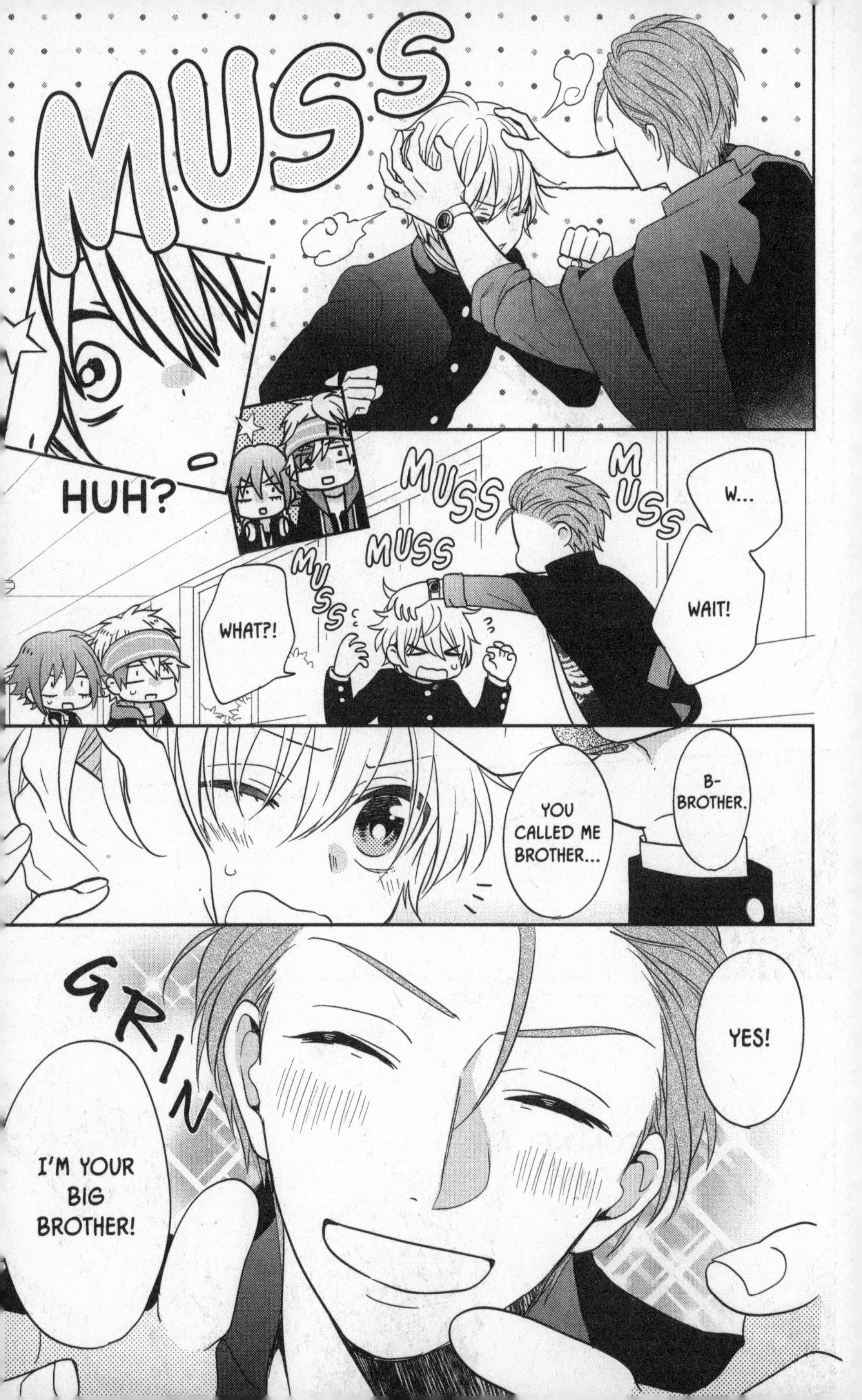
MUSS
HUH?
W... WAIT!
MUSS
MUSS
MUSS
MUSS
WHAT?!
B-BROTHER.
YOU CALLED ME BROTHER...
YES!
GRIN
I'M YOUR BIG BROTHER!

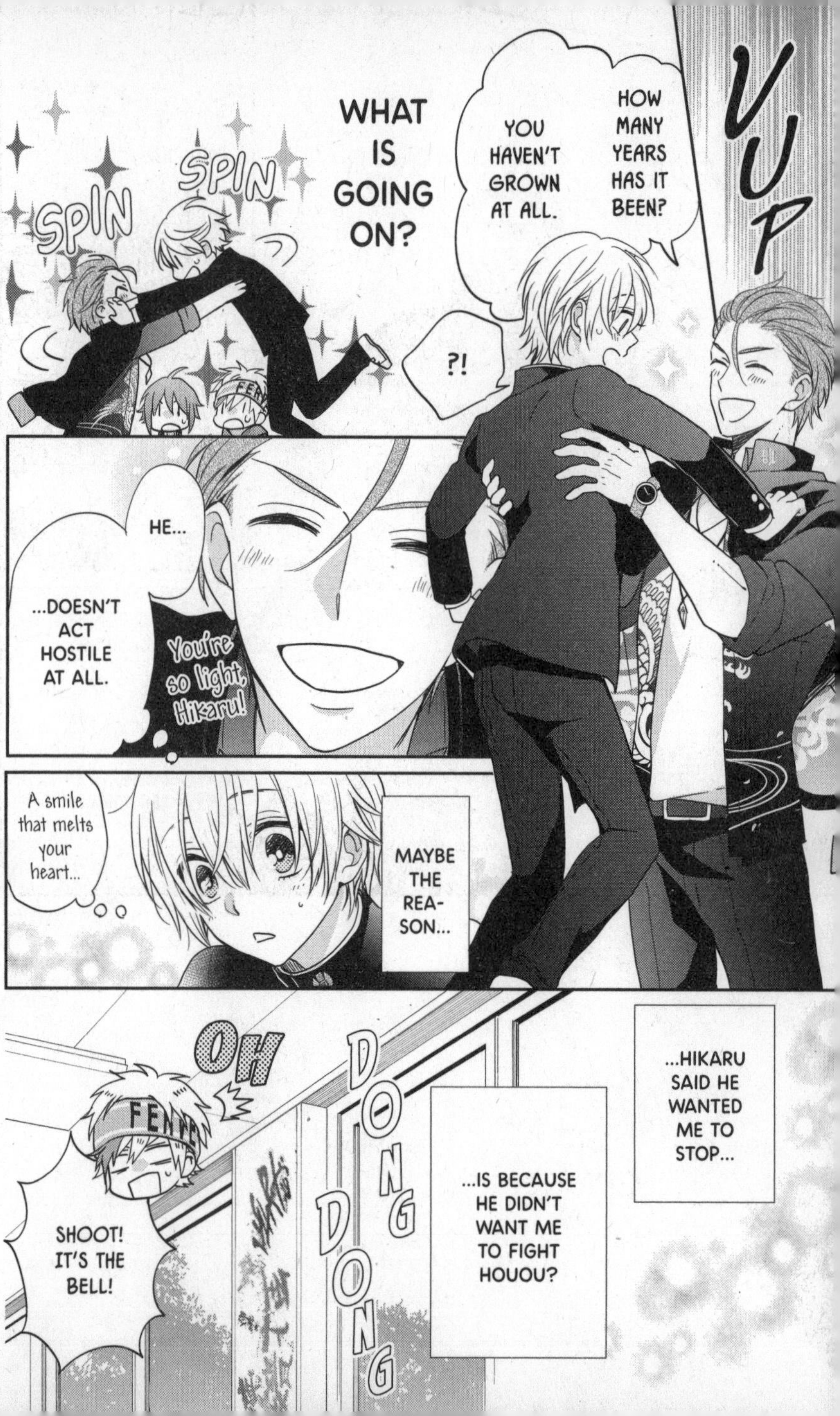
VUP
HOW MANY YEARS HAS IT BEEN?
YOU HAVEN'T GROWN AT ALL.
?!
WHAT IS GOING ON?
SPIN
SPIN
HE...
...DOESN'T ACT HOSTILE AT ALL.
You're so light, Hikaru!
MAYBE THE REA-SON...
A smile that melts your heart...
...HIKARU SAID HE WANTED ME TO STOP...
...IS BECAUSE HE DIDN'T WANT ME TO FIGHT HOUOU?
DONG
DONG
OH
SHOOT! IT'S THE BELL!

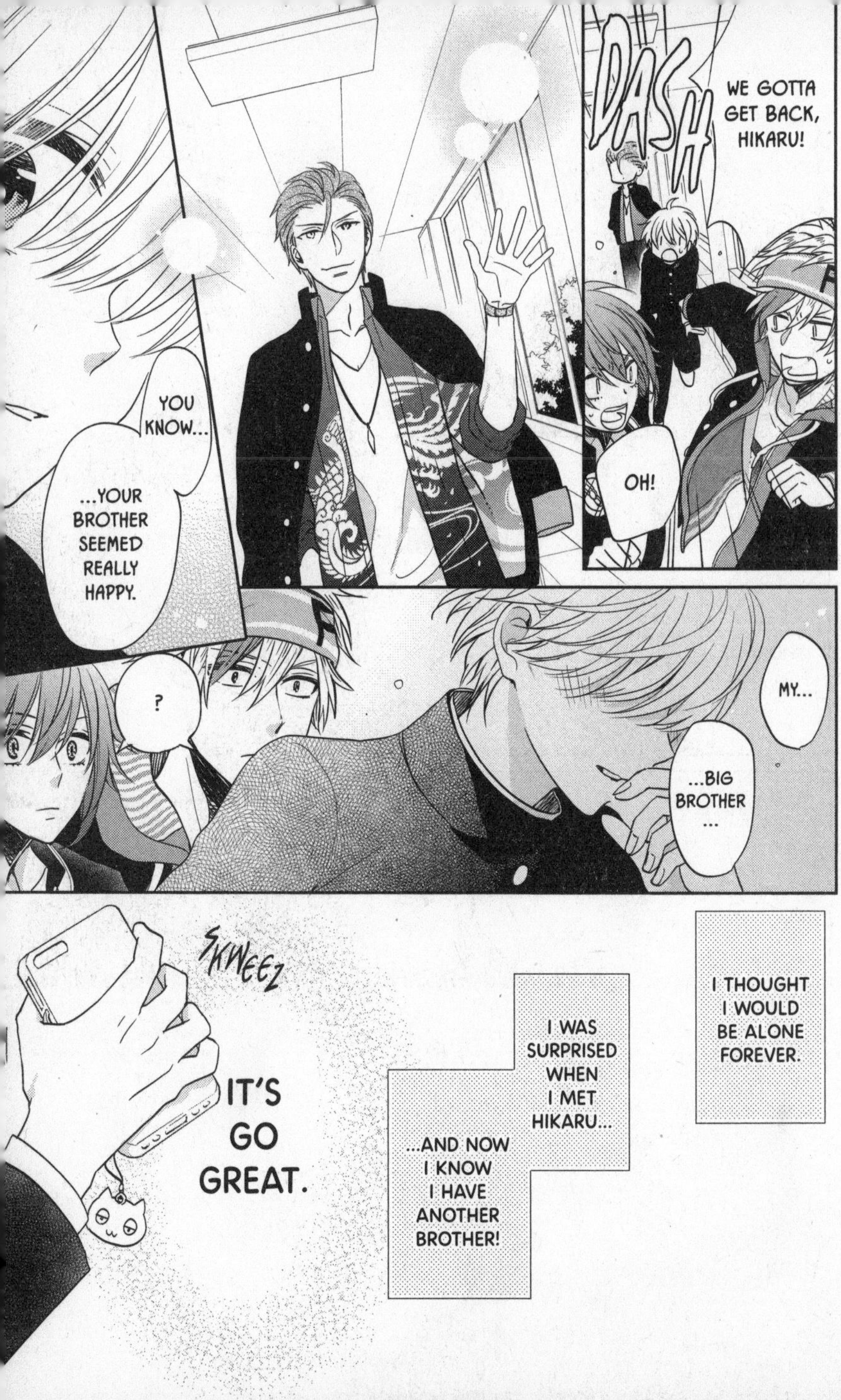
DASH
WE GOTTA GET BACK, HIKARU!
OH!
YOU KNOW...
...YOUR BROTHER SEEMED REALLY HAPPY.
MY...
...BIG BROTHER...
?
I THOUGHT I WOULD BE ALONE FOREVER.
I WAS SURPRISED WHEN I MET HIKARU...
...AND NOW I KNOW I HAVE ANOTHER BROTHER!
SKWEEZ
IT'S GO GREAT.

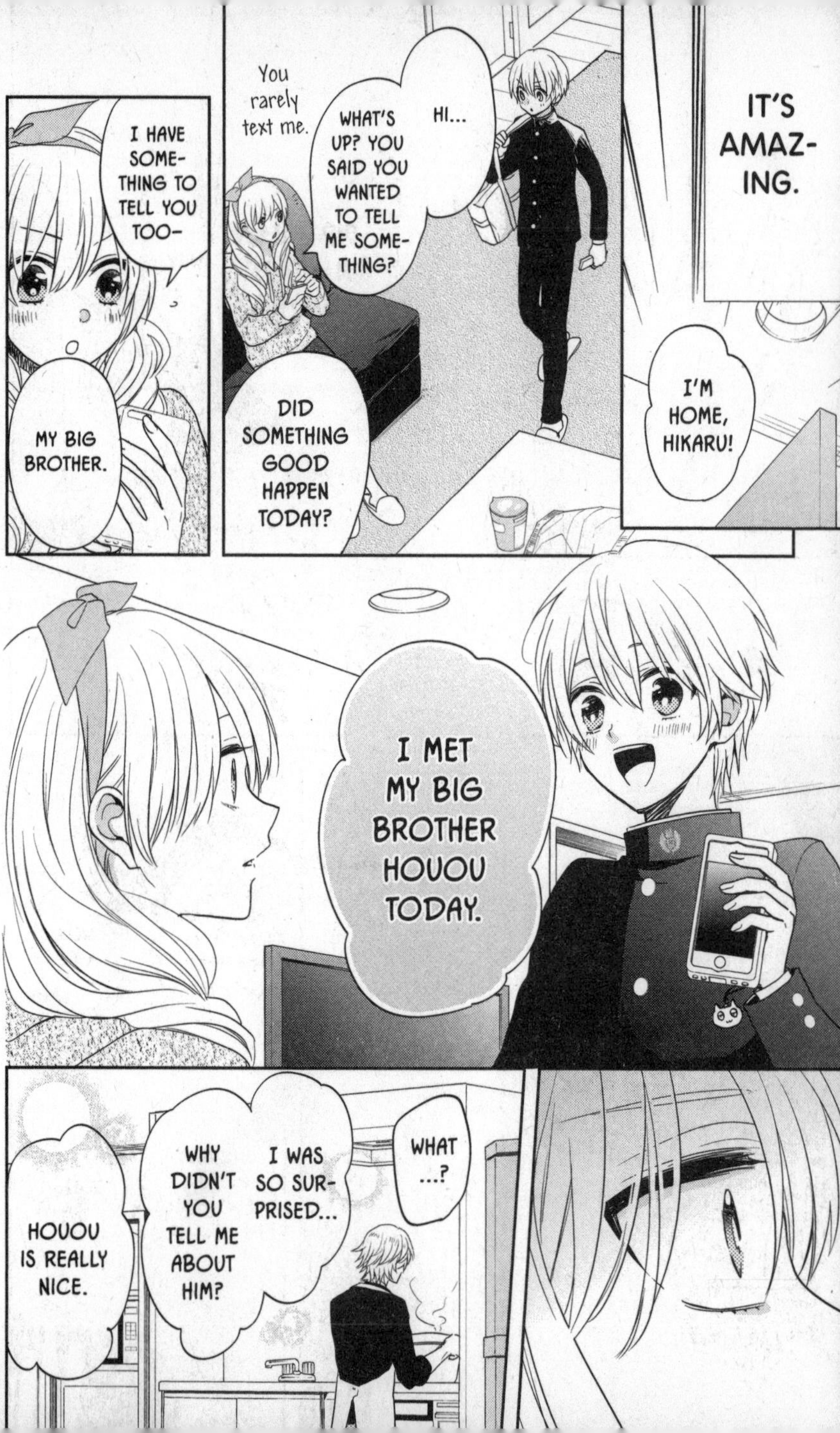
IT'S AMAZ-ING.
I'M HOME, HIKARU!
HI...
WHAT'S UP? YOU SAID YOU WANTED TO TELL ME SOME-THING?
You rarely text me.
DID SOMETHING GOOD HAPPEN TODAY?
I HAVE SOME-THING TO TELL YOU TOO—
MY BIG BROTHER.
I MET MY BIG BROTHER HOUOU TODAY.
WHAT ...?
I WAS SO SUR-PRISED...
WHY DIDN'T YOU TELL ME ABOUT HIM?
HOUOU IS REALLY NICE.

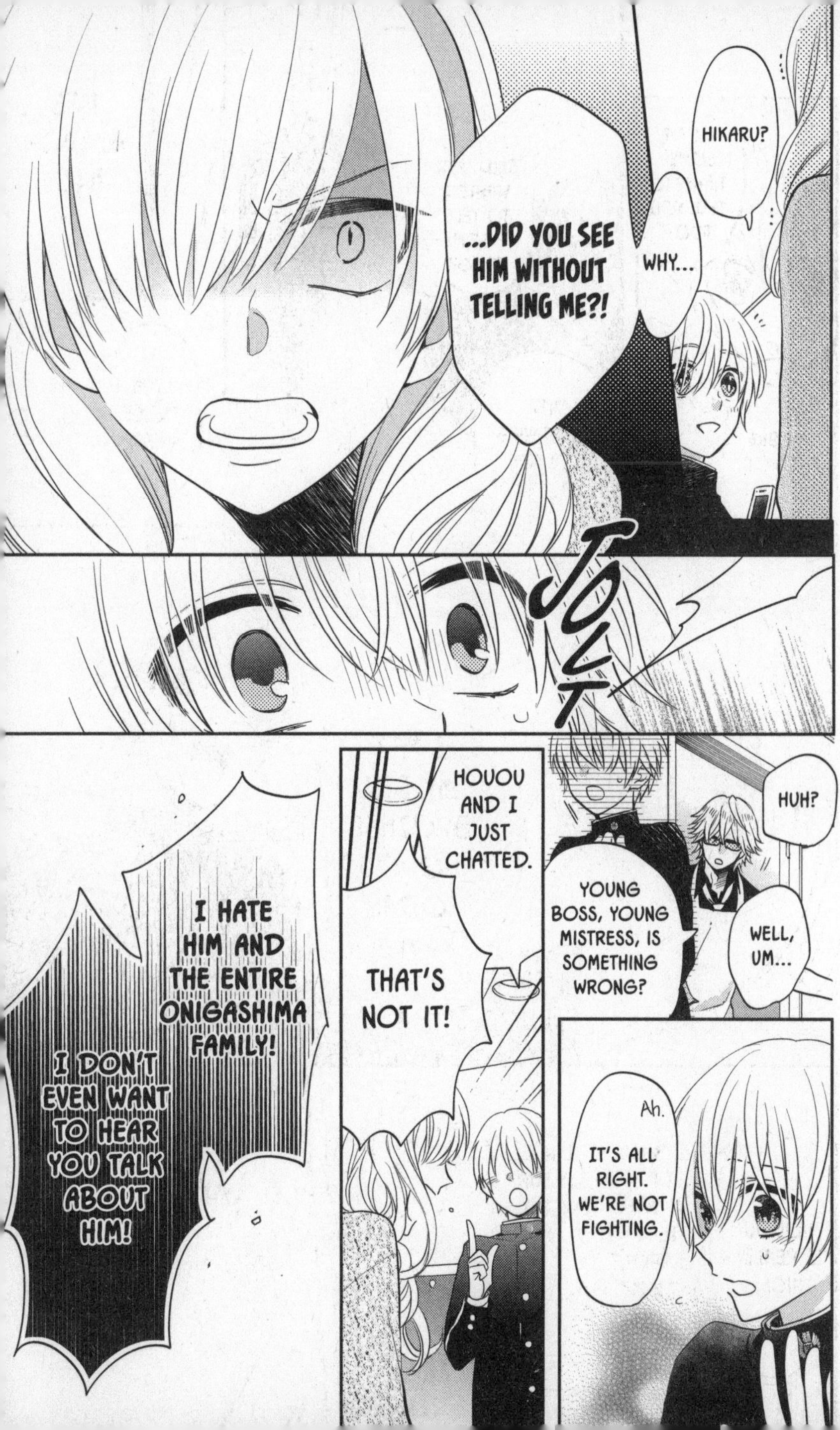
HIKARU?
WHY...
...DID YOU SEE HIM WITHOUT TELLING ME?!
JOLT
HUH?
WELL, UM...
YOUNG BOSS, YOUNG MISTRESS, IS SOMETHING WRONG?
Ah.
IT'S ALL RIGHT. WE'RE NOT FIGHTING.
HOUOU AND I JUST CHATTED.
THAT'S NOT IT!
I HATE HIM AND THE ENTIRE ONIGASHIMA FAMILY!
I DON'T EVEN WANT TO HEAR YOU TALK ABOUT HIM!

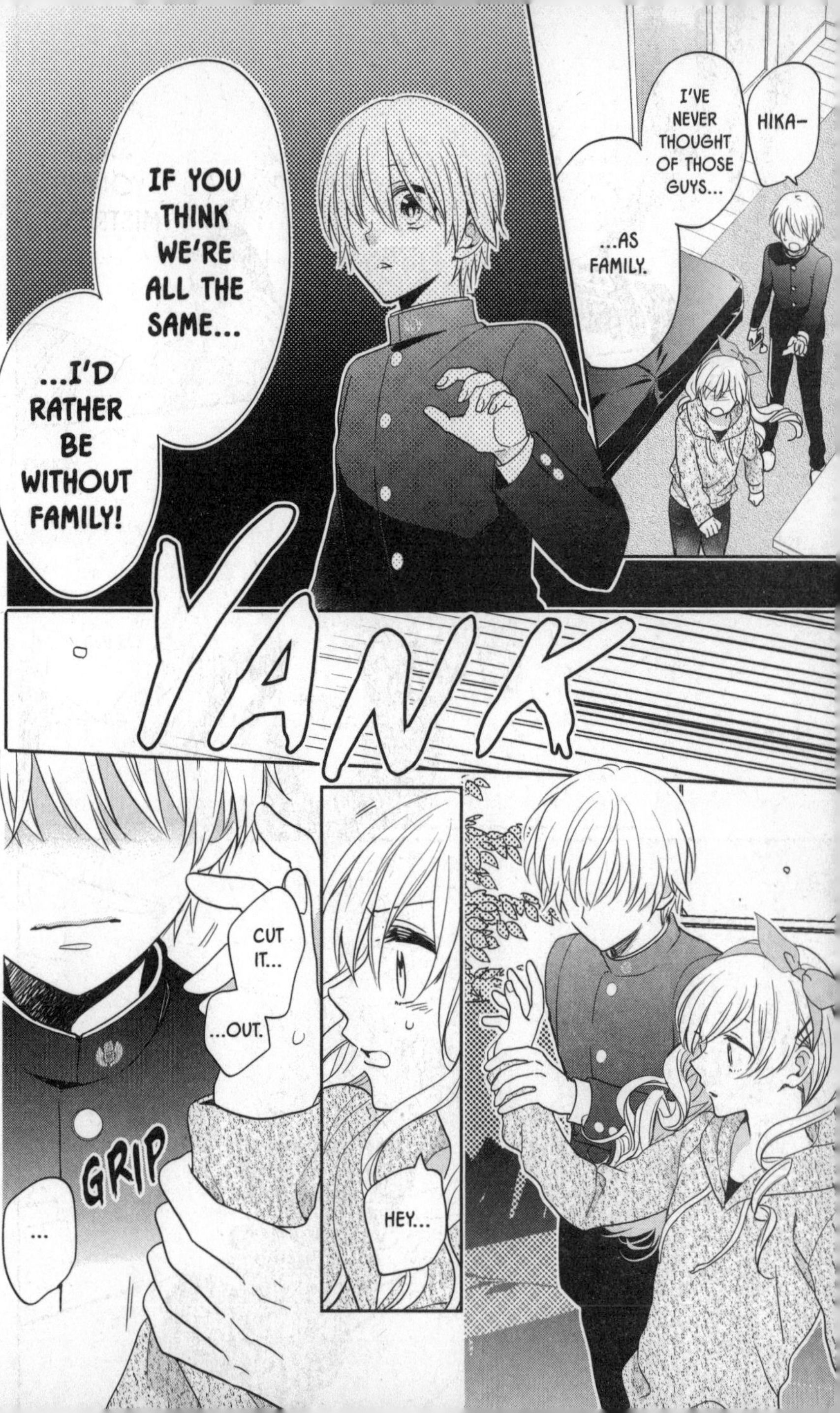
HIKA—
I'VE NEVER THOUGHT OF THOSE GUYS...
...AS FAMILY.
IF YOU THINK WE'RE ALL THE SAME...
...I'D RATHER BE WITHOUT FAMILY!
YANK
HEY...
CUT IT...
...OUT.
GRIP
...

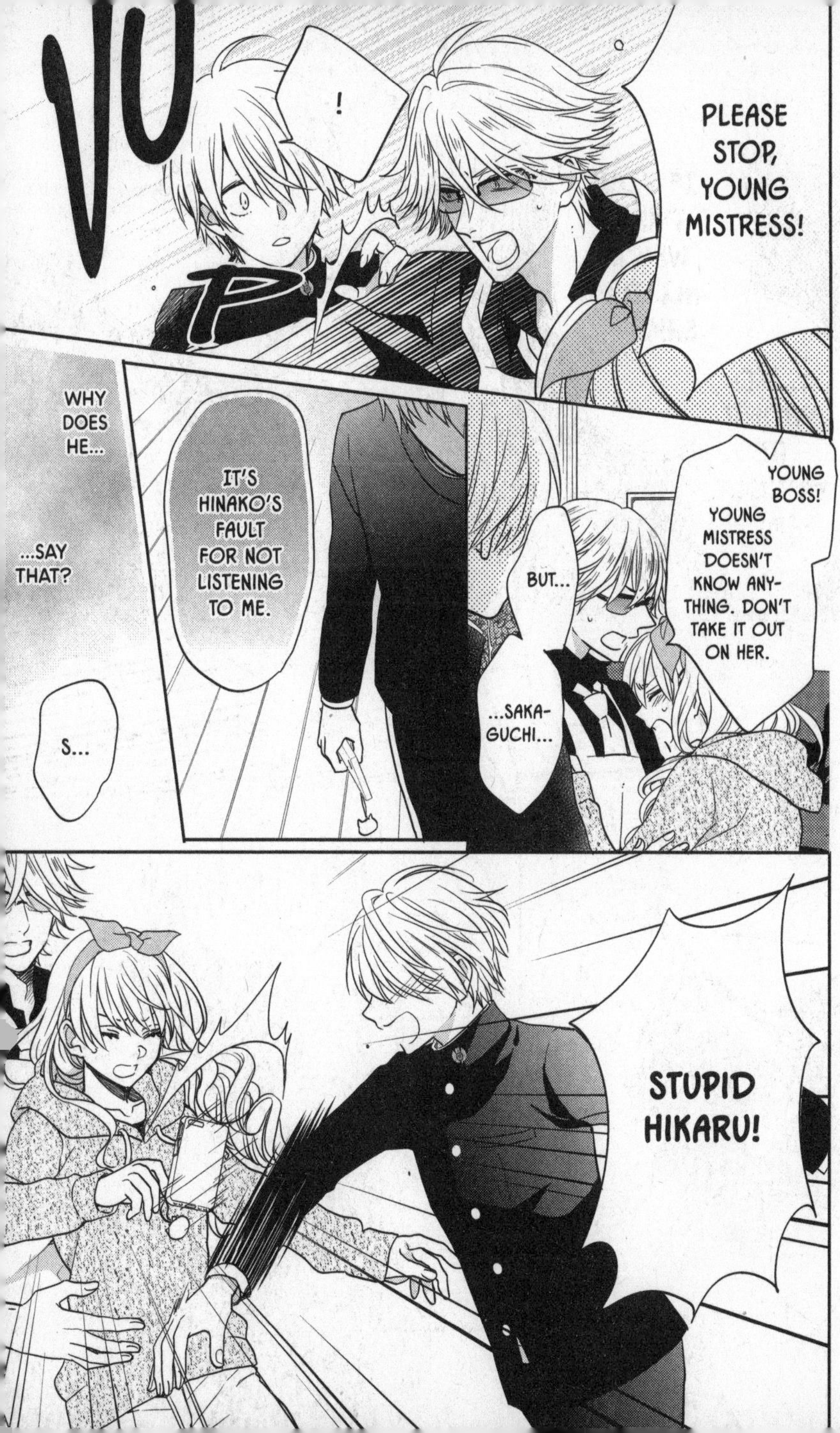
PLEASE STOP, YOUNG MISTRESS!
!
VU
YOUNG BOSS!
YOUNG MISTRESS DOESN'T KNOW ANY-THING. DON'T TAKE IT OUT ON HER.
BUT...
...SAKA-GUCHI...
IT'S HINAKO'S FAULT FOR NOT LISTENING TO ME.
WHY DOES HE...
...SAY THAT?
S...
STUPID HIKARU!

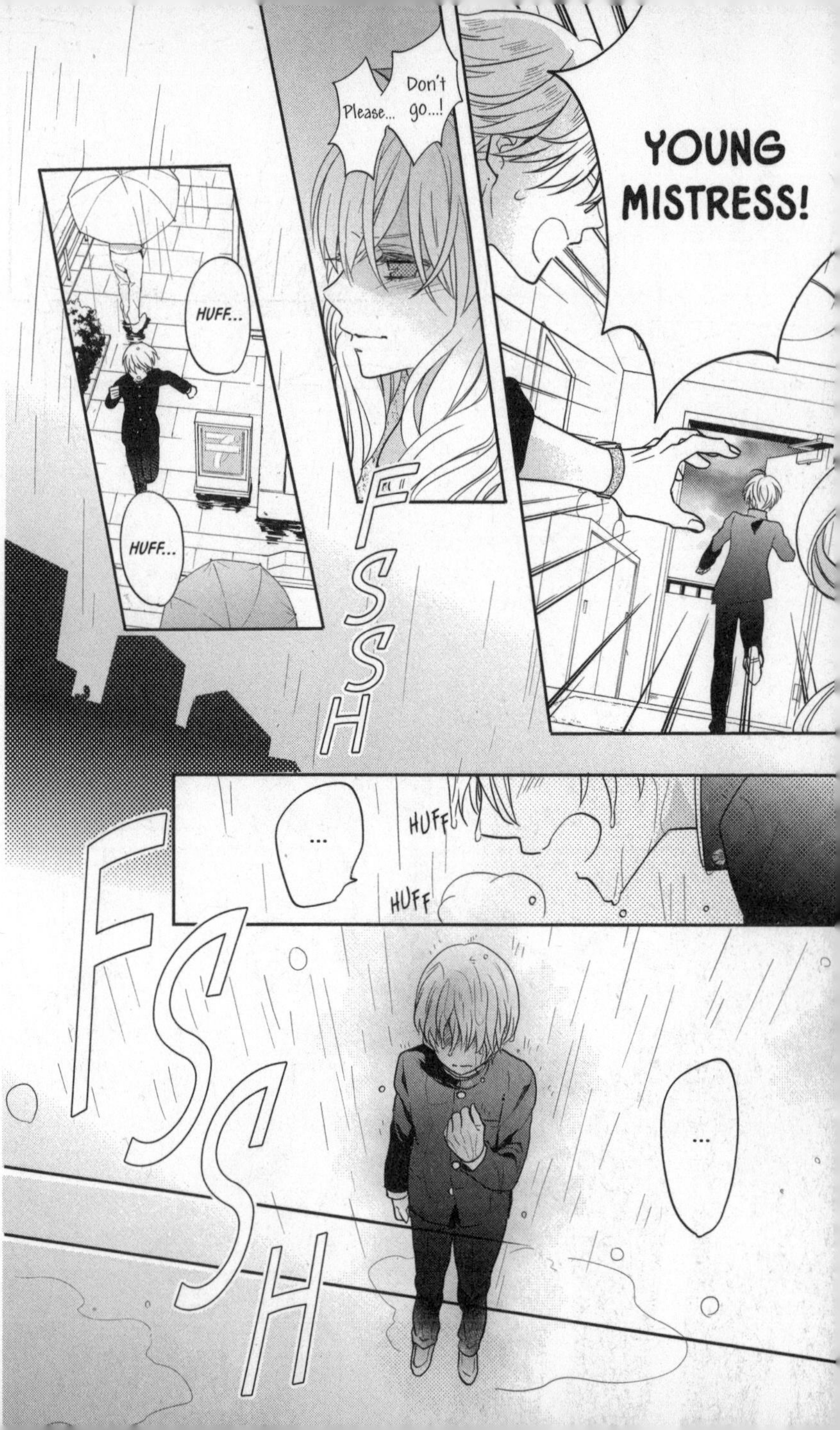
YOUNG MISTRESS!
Please... Don't go...!
FSSH
HUFF...
HUFF...
HUFF
HUFF
...
...
FSSH

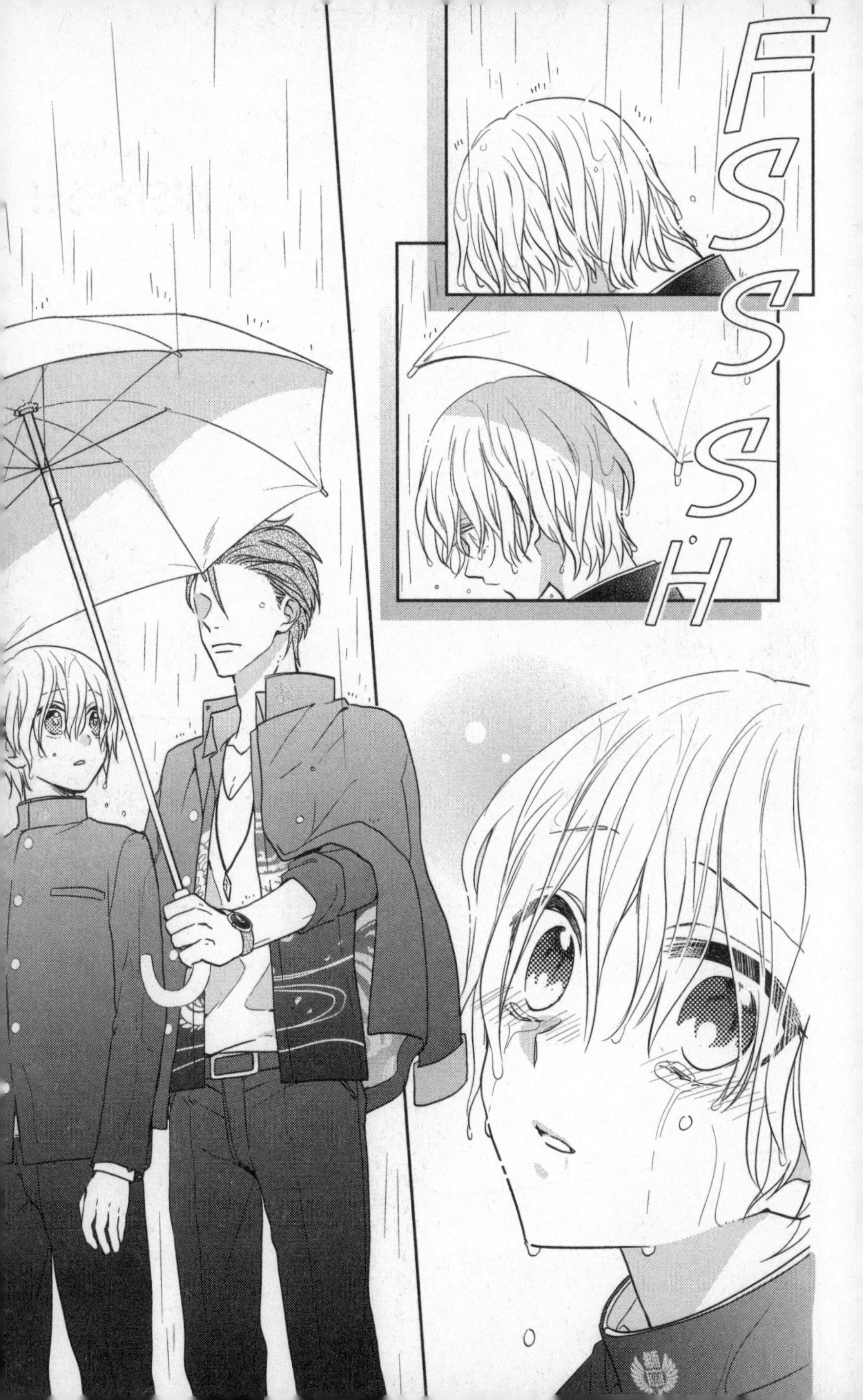
FSSSH

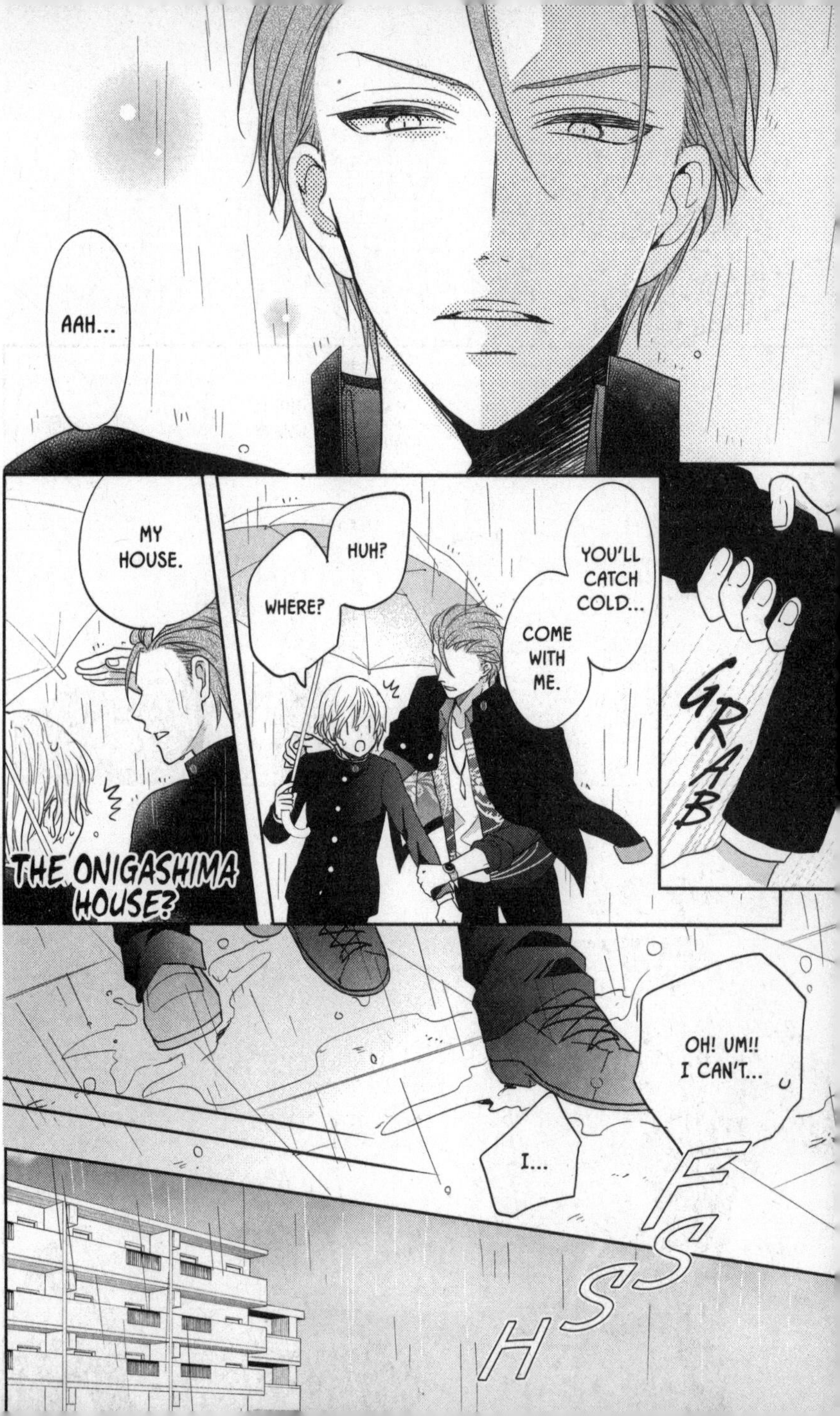
AAH...
GRAB
YOU'LL CATCH COLD...
COME WITH ME.
HUH?
WHERE?
MY HOUSE.
THE ONIGASHIMA HOUSE?
OH! UM!! I CAN'T...
I...
FSSH

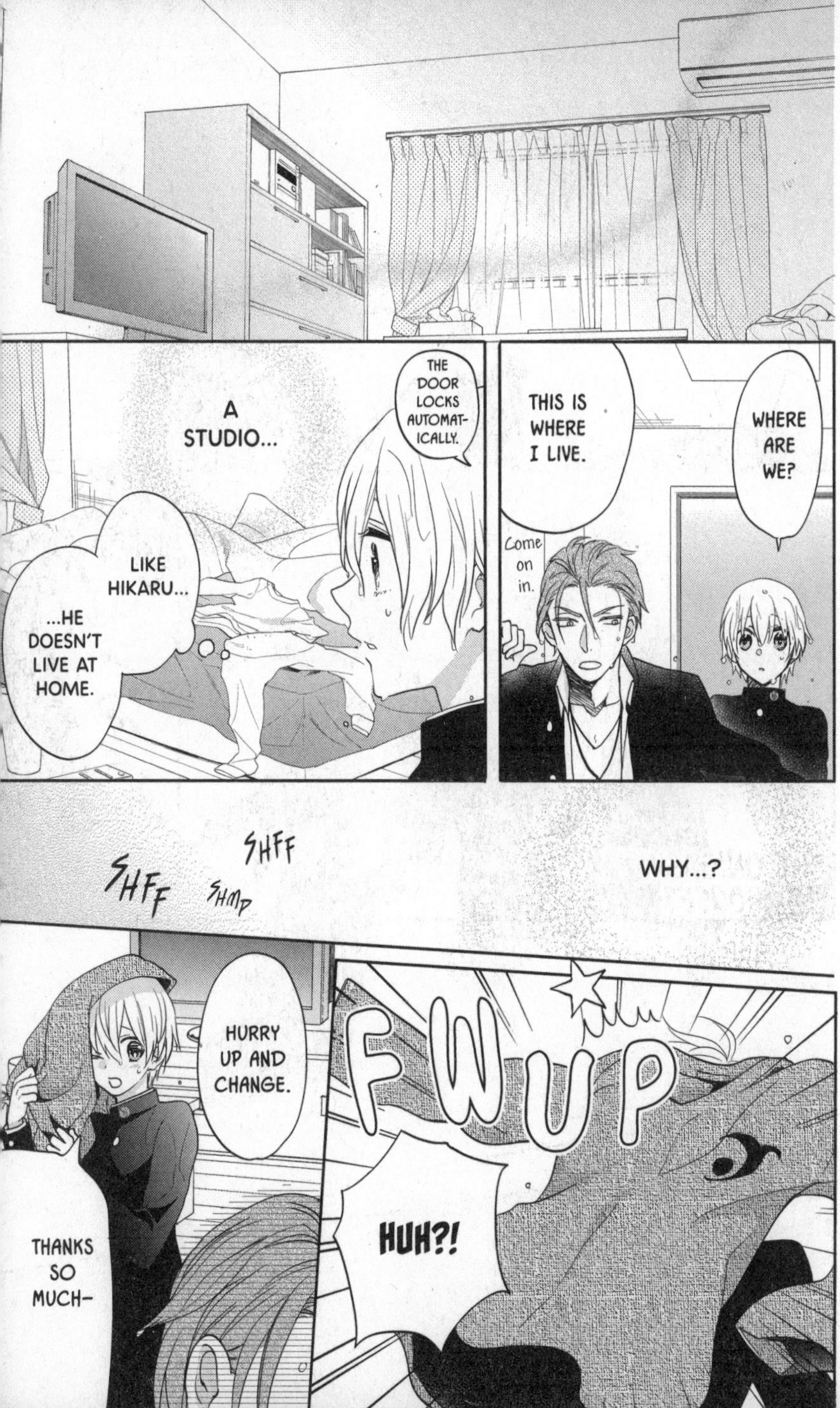
WHERE ARE WE?
THIS IS WHERE I LIVE.
Come on in.
THE DOOR LOCKS AUTOMATICALLY.
A STUDIO...
LIKE HIKARU...
...HE DOESN'T LIVE AT HOME.
WHY...?
SHFF
SHMP
SHFF
FWUP
HUH?!
HURRY UP AND CHANGE.
THANKS SO MUCH—

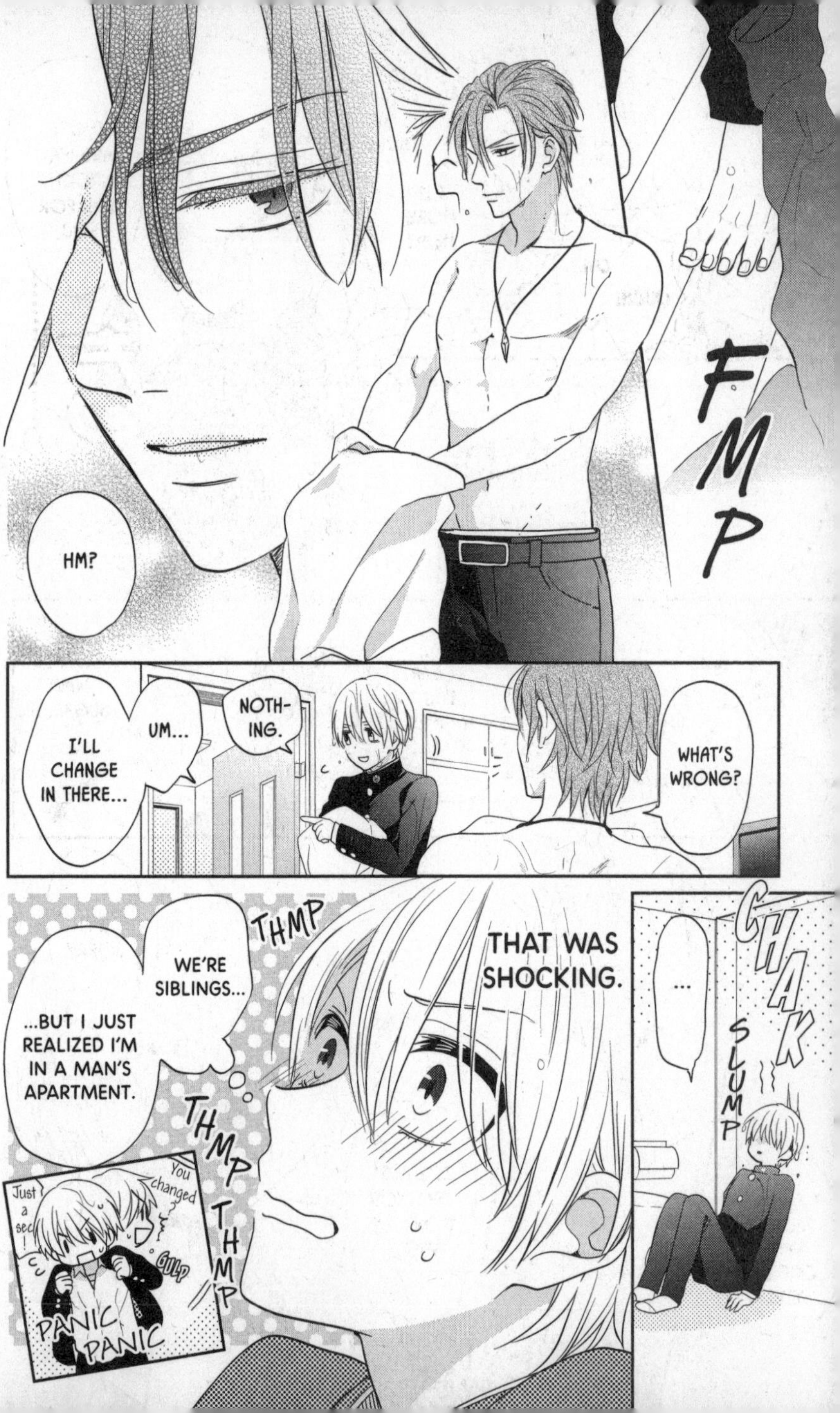
FMP
HM?
WHAT'S WRONG?
NOTH-ING.
UM...
I'LL CHANGE IN THERE...
CHAK
SLUMP
...
THAT WAS SHOCKING.
THMP
WE'RE SIBLINGS...
...BUT I JUST REALIZED I'M IN A MAN'S APARTMENT.
THMP THMP THMP
You changed
Just a sec!
GULP
PANIC PANIC

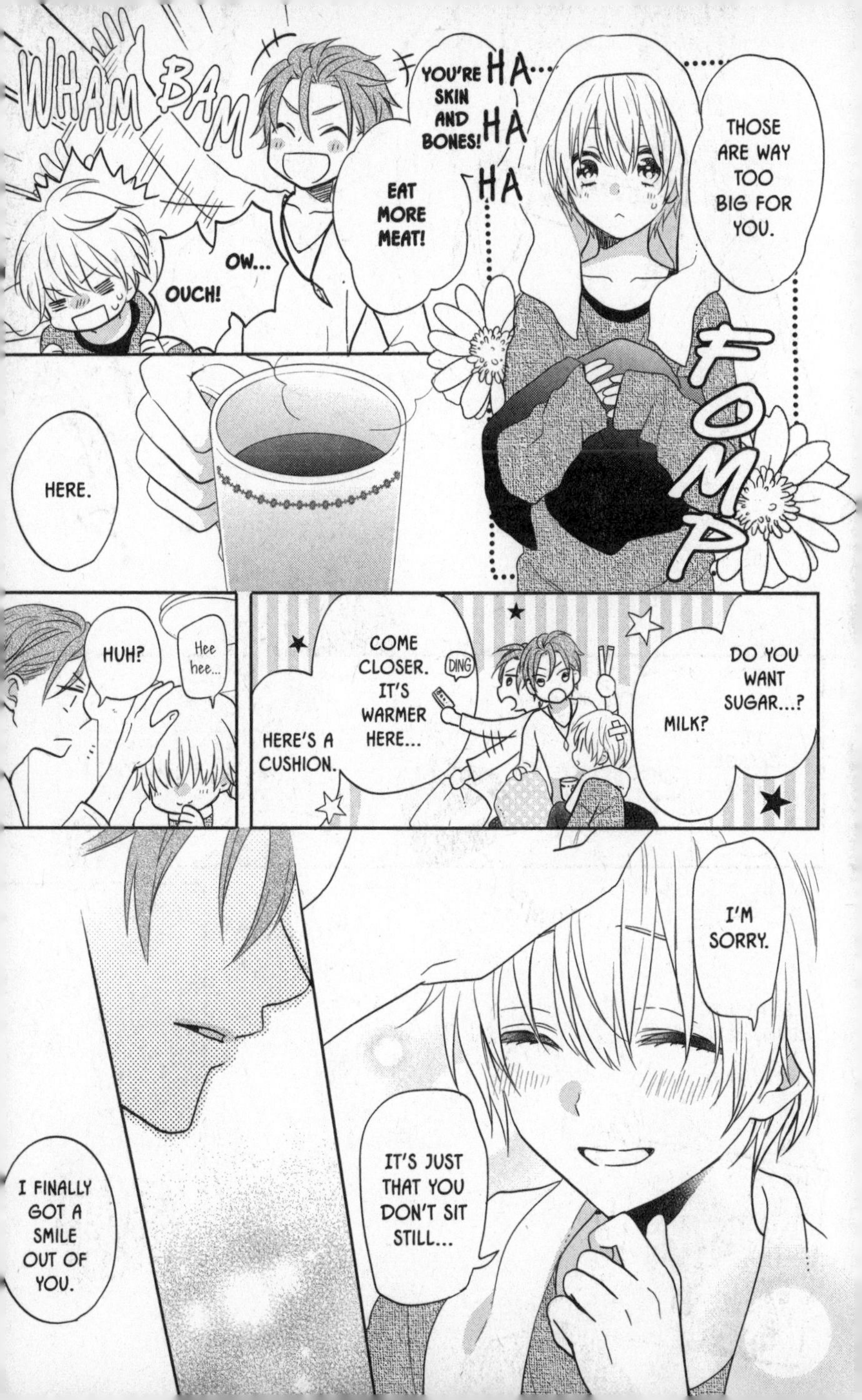
THOSE ARE WAY TOO BIG FOR YOU.
FOMP
YOU'RE SKIN AND BONES!
HA... HA HA
EAT MORE MEAT!
WHAM BAM
OW...
OUCH!
HERE.
DO YOU WANT SUGAR...?
MILK?
COME CLOSER. IT'S WARMER HERE...
DING
HERE'S A CUSHION.
Hee hee...
HUH?
I'M SORRY.
IT'S JUST THAT YOU DON'T SIT STILL...
I FINALLY GOT A SMILE OUT OF YOU.

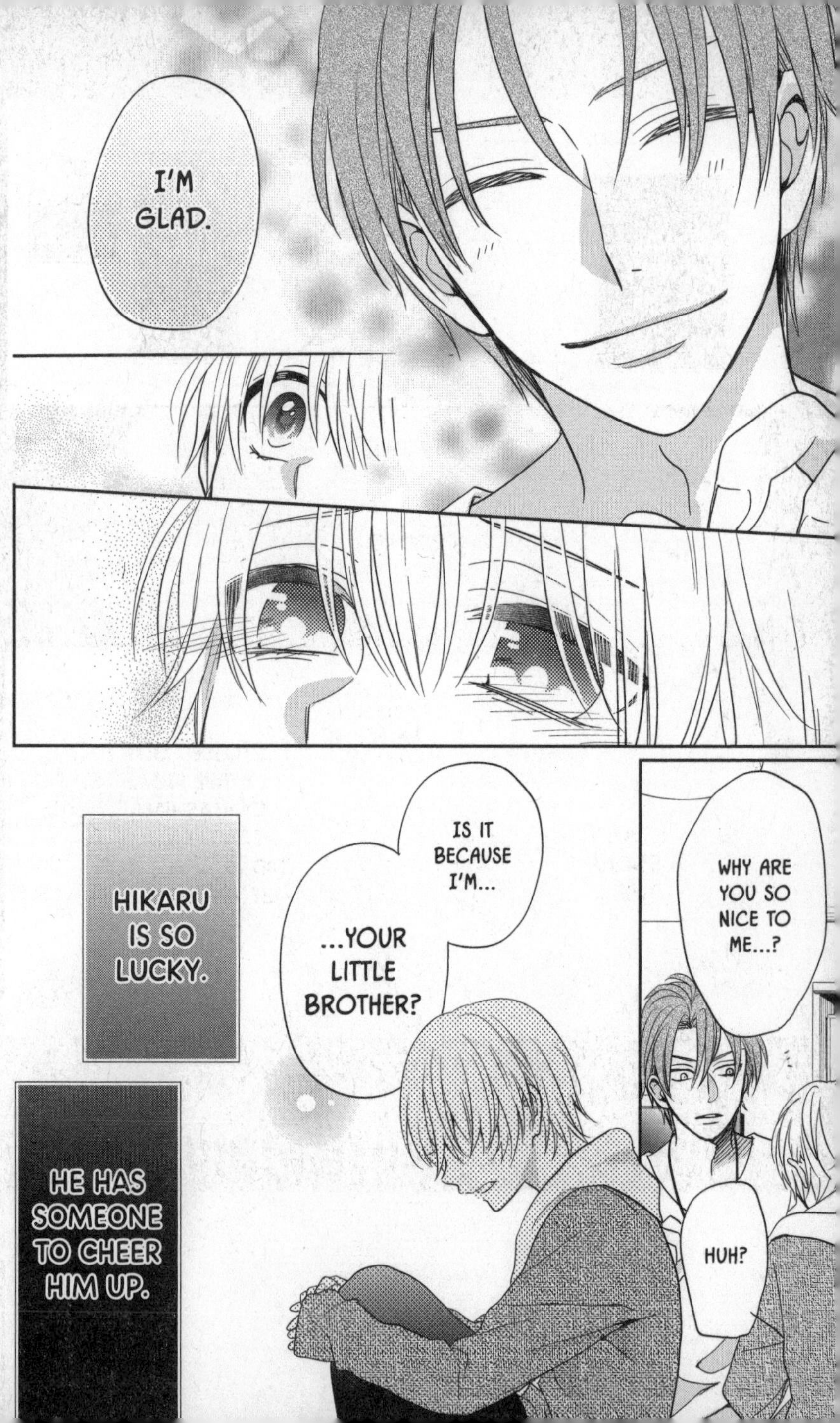
I'M GLAD.
WHY ARE YOU SO NICE TO ME...?
HUH?
IS IT BECAUSE I'M...
...YOUR LITTLE BROTHER?
HIKARU IS SO LUCKY.
HE HAS SOMEONE TO CHEER HIM UP.

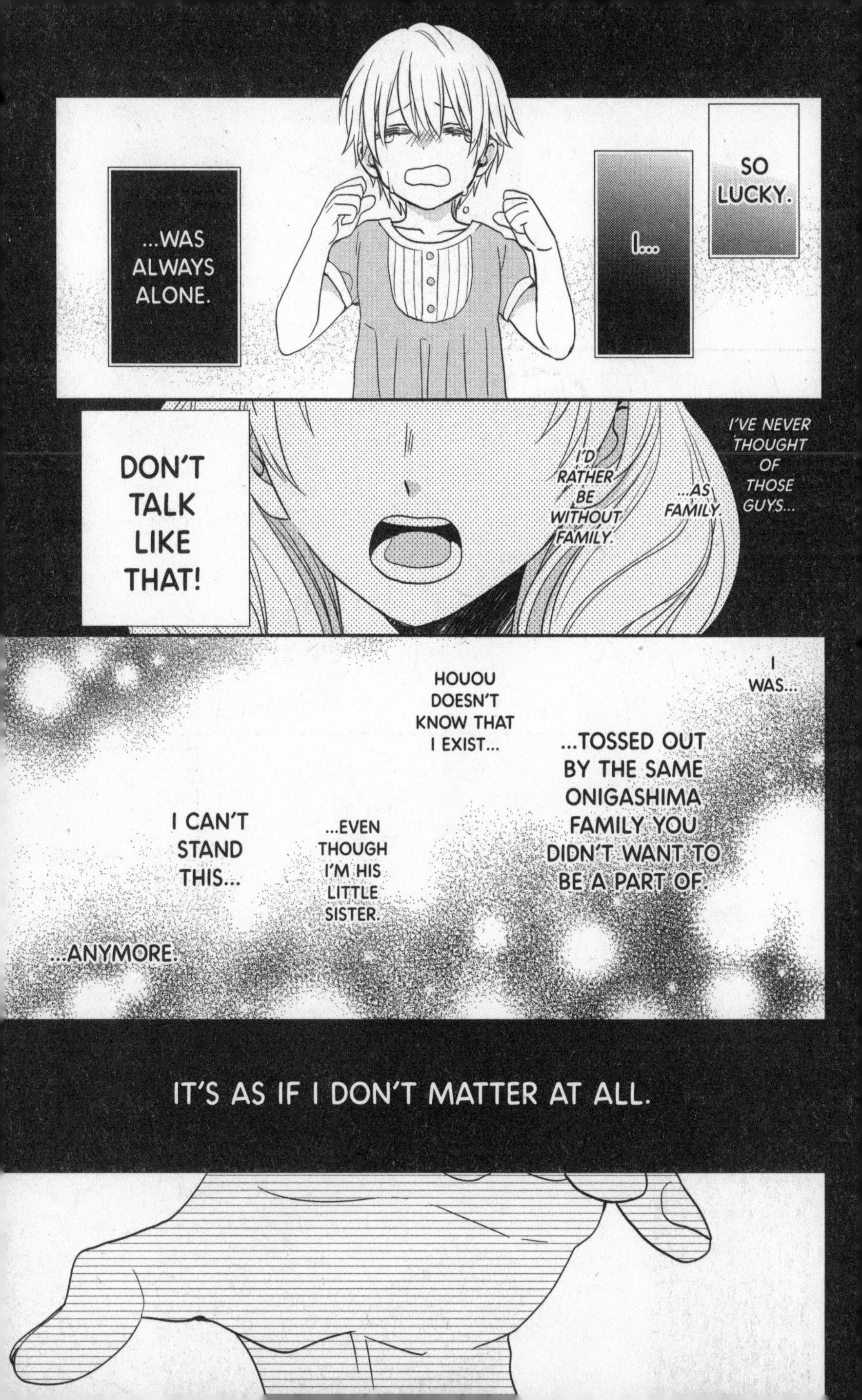

SO LUCKY.
I...
...WAS ALWAYS ALONE.
I'VE NEVER THOUGHT OF THOSE GUYS...
...AS FAMILY.
I'D RATHER BE WITHOUT FAMILY.
DON'T TALK LIKE THAT!
I WAS...
...TOSSED OUT BY THE SAME ONIGASHIMA FAMILY YOU DIDN'T WANT TO BE A PART OF.
HOUOU DOESN'T KNOW THAT I EXIST...
...EVEN THOUGH I'M HIS LITTLE SISTER.
I CAN'T STAND THIS...
...ANYMORE.
IT'S AS IF I DON'T MATTER AT ALL.

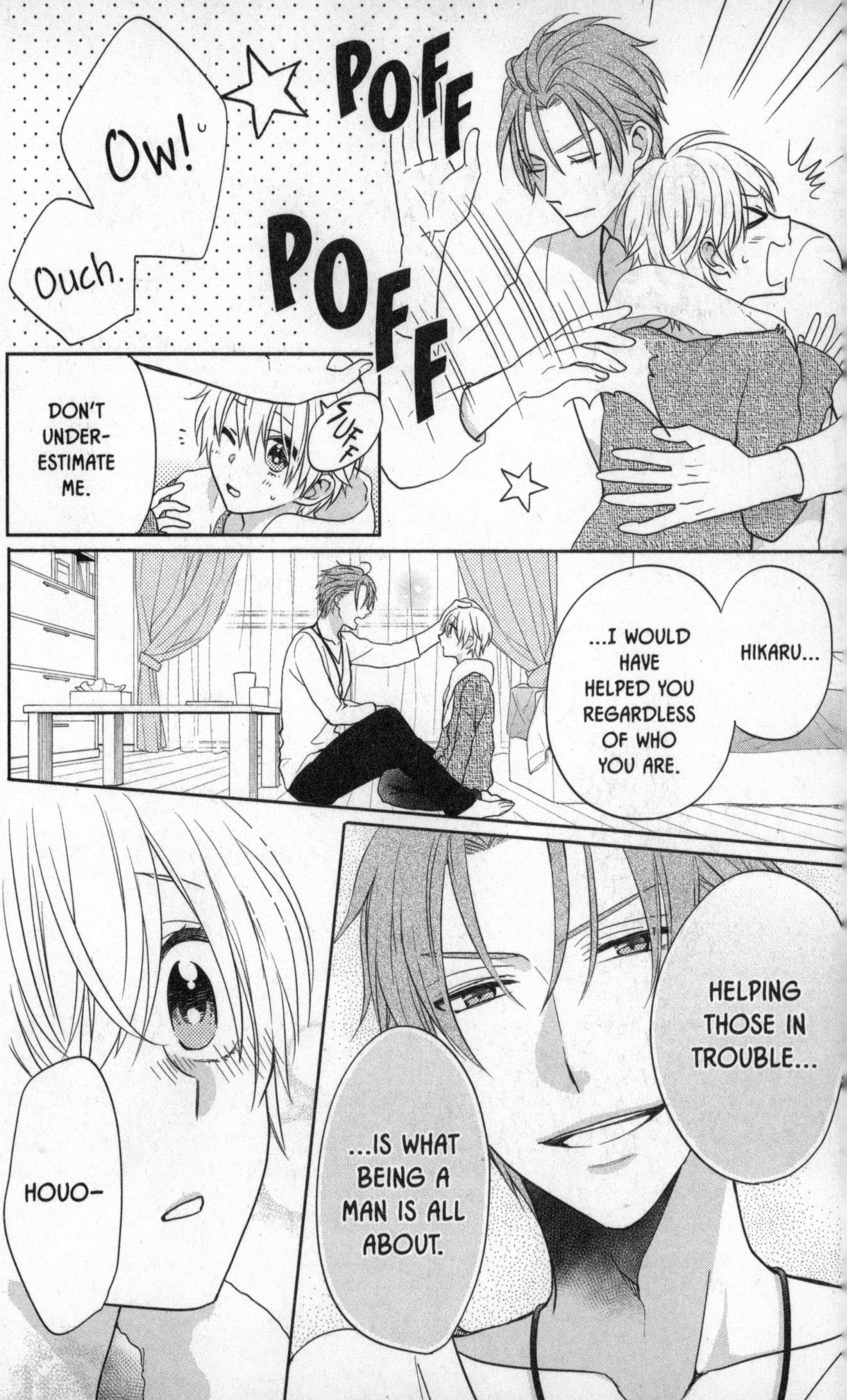
POFF
POFF
Ow!
Ouch.
SUFF
DON'T UNDER-ESTIMATE ME.
HIKARU...
...I WOULD HAVE HELPED YOU REGARDLESS OF WHO YOU ARE.
HELPING THOSE IN TROUBLE...
...IS WHAT BEING A MAN IS ALL ABOUT.
HOUO-

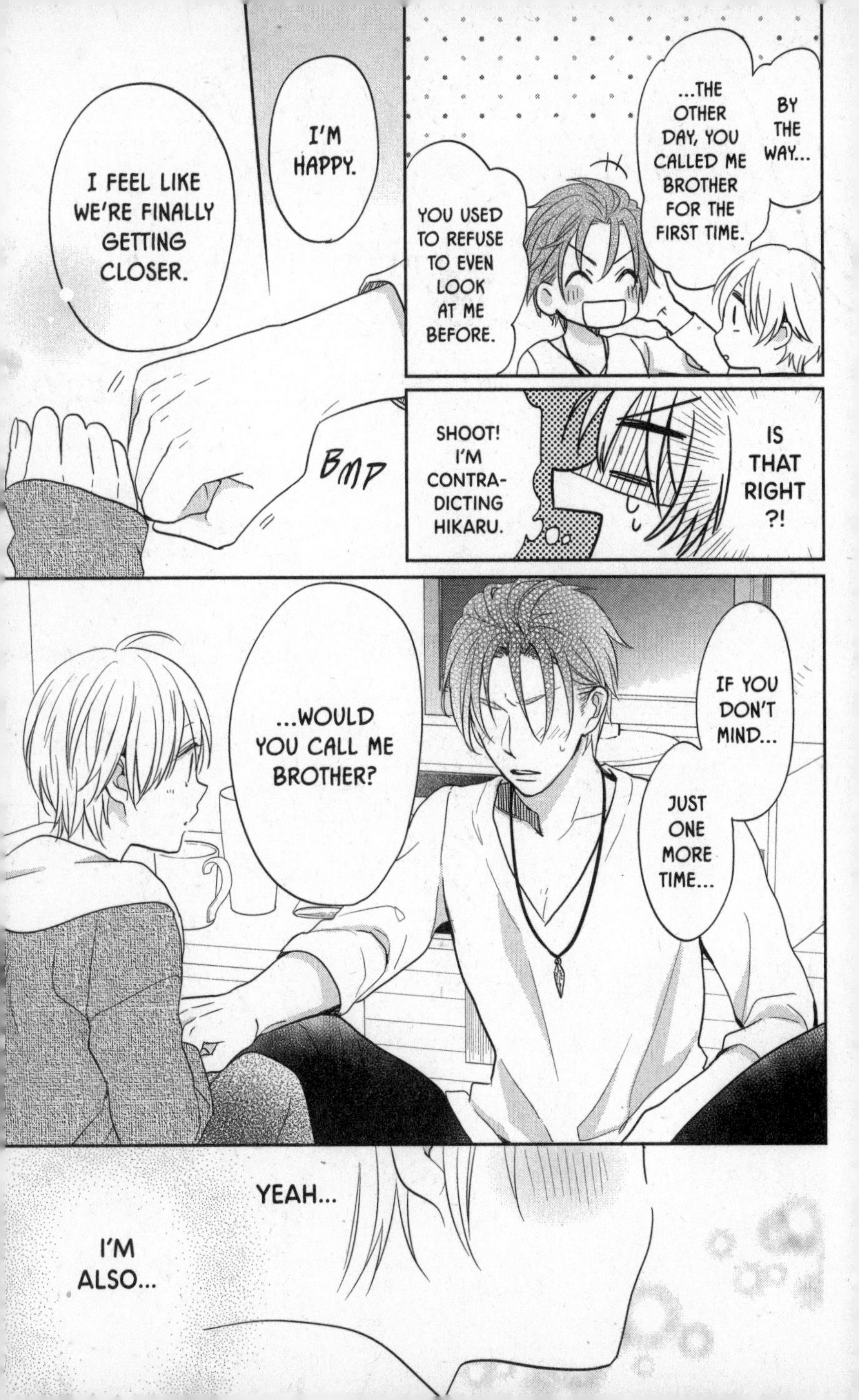
BY THE WAY...
...THE OTHER DAY, YOU CALLED ME BROTHER FOR THE FIRST TIME.
YOU USED TO REFUSE TO EVEN LOOK AT ME BEFORE.
IS THAT RIGHT?!
SHOOT! I'M CONTRA-DICTING HIKARU.
I'M HAPPY.
I FEEL LIKE WE'RE FINALLY GETTING CLOSER.
BMP
IF YOU DON'T MIND...
JUST ONE MORE TIME...
...WOULD YOU CALL ME BROTHER?
YEAH...
I'M ALSO...

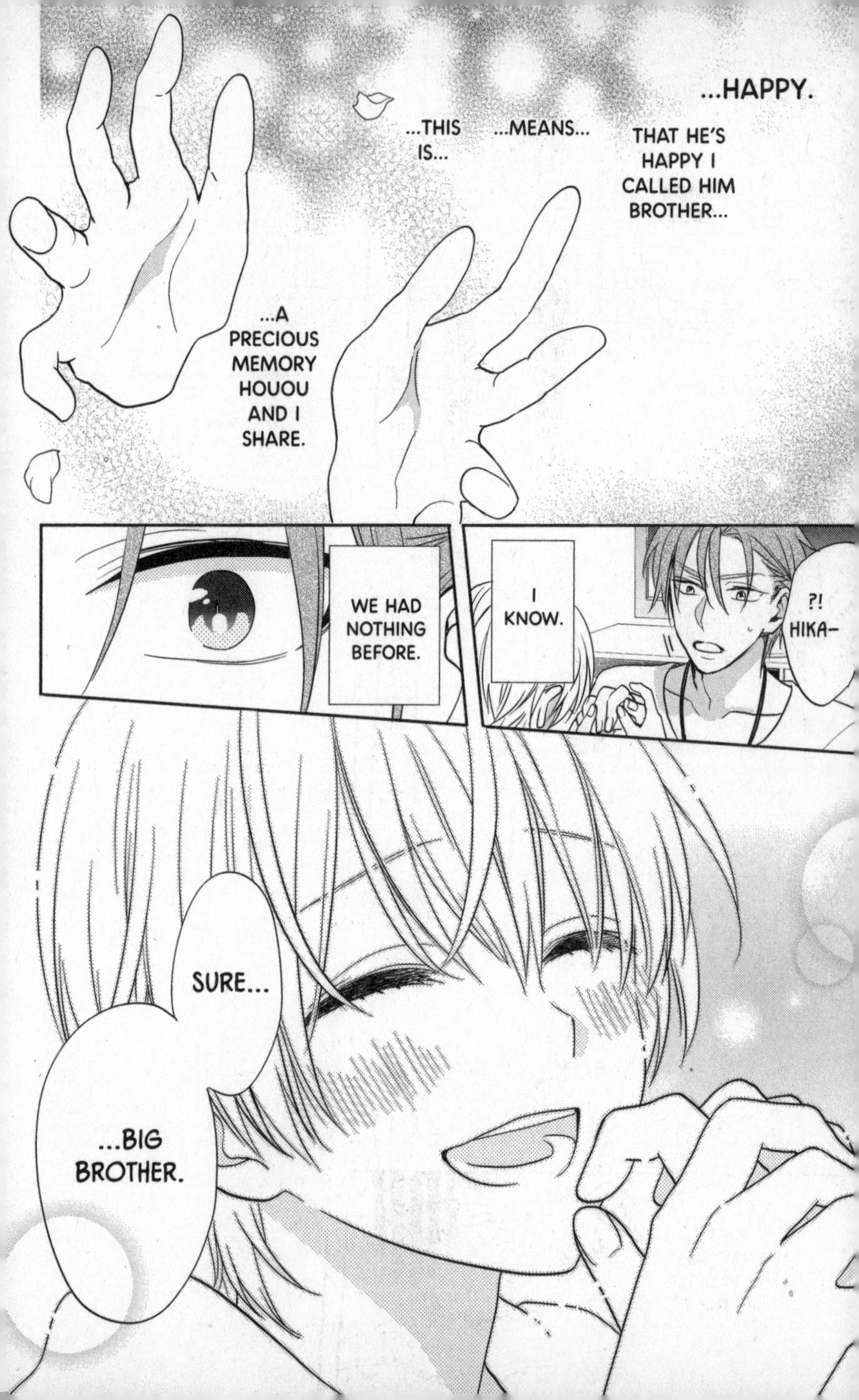
...HAPPY.
THAT HE'S HAPPY I CALLED HIM BROTHER...
...MEANS...
...THIS IS...
...A PRECIOUS MEMORY HOUOU AND I SHARE.
?! HIKA-
I KNOW.
WE HAD NOTHING BEFORE.
SURE...
...BIG BROTHER.

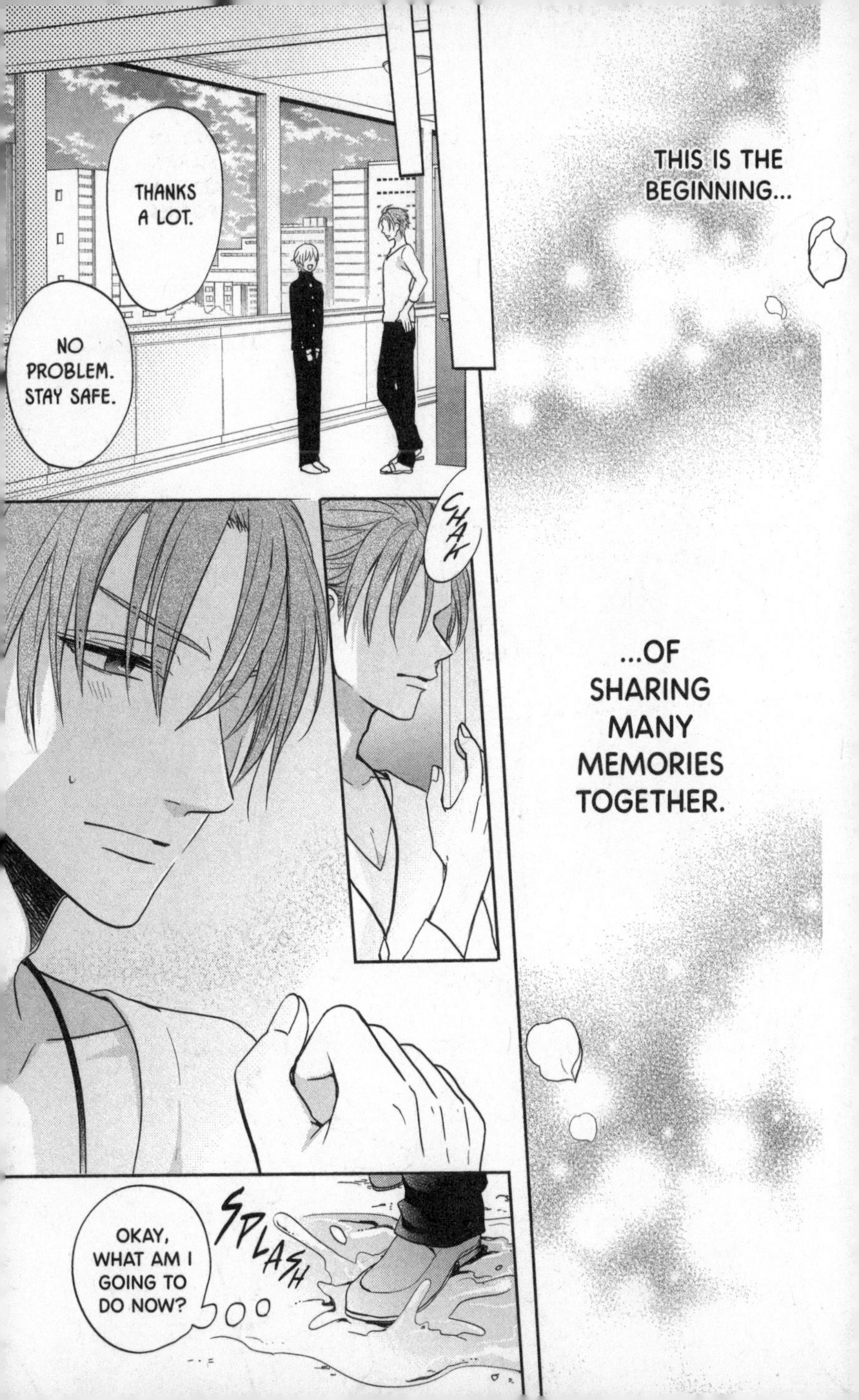
THIS IS THE BEGINNING...
...OF SHARING MANY MEMORIES TOGETHER.
THANKS A LOT.
NO PROBLEM. STAY SAFE.
CHAK
SPLASH
OKAY, WHAT AM I GOING TO DO NOW?

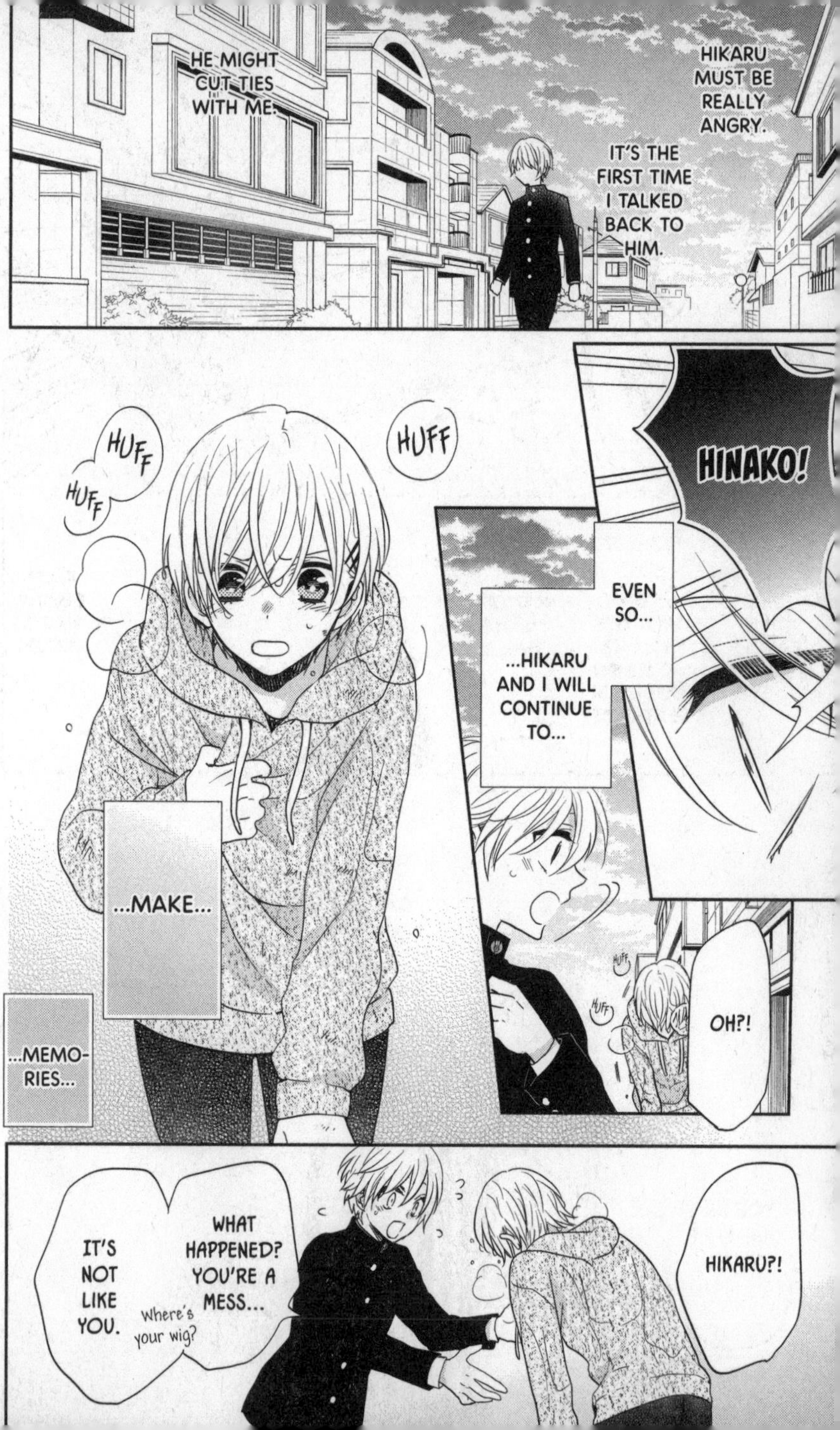

HIKARU MUST BE REALLY ANGRY.
IT'S THE FIRST TIME I TALKED BACK TO HIM.
HE MIGHT CUT TIES WITH ME.
HINAKO!
EVEN SO...
...HIKARU AND I WILL CONTINUE TO...
HUFF
HUFF
OH?!
HUFF
HUFF
HUFF
...MAKE...
...MEMORIES...
HIKARU?!
WHAT HAPPENED? YOU'RE A MESS...
IT'S NOT LIKE YOU.
Where's your wig?

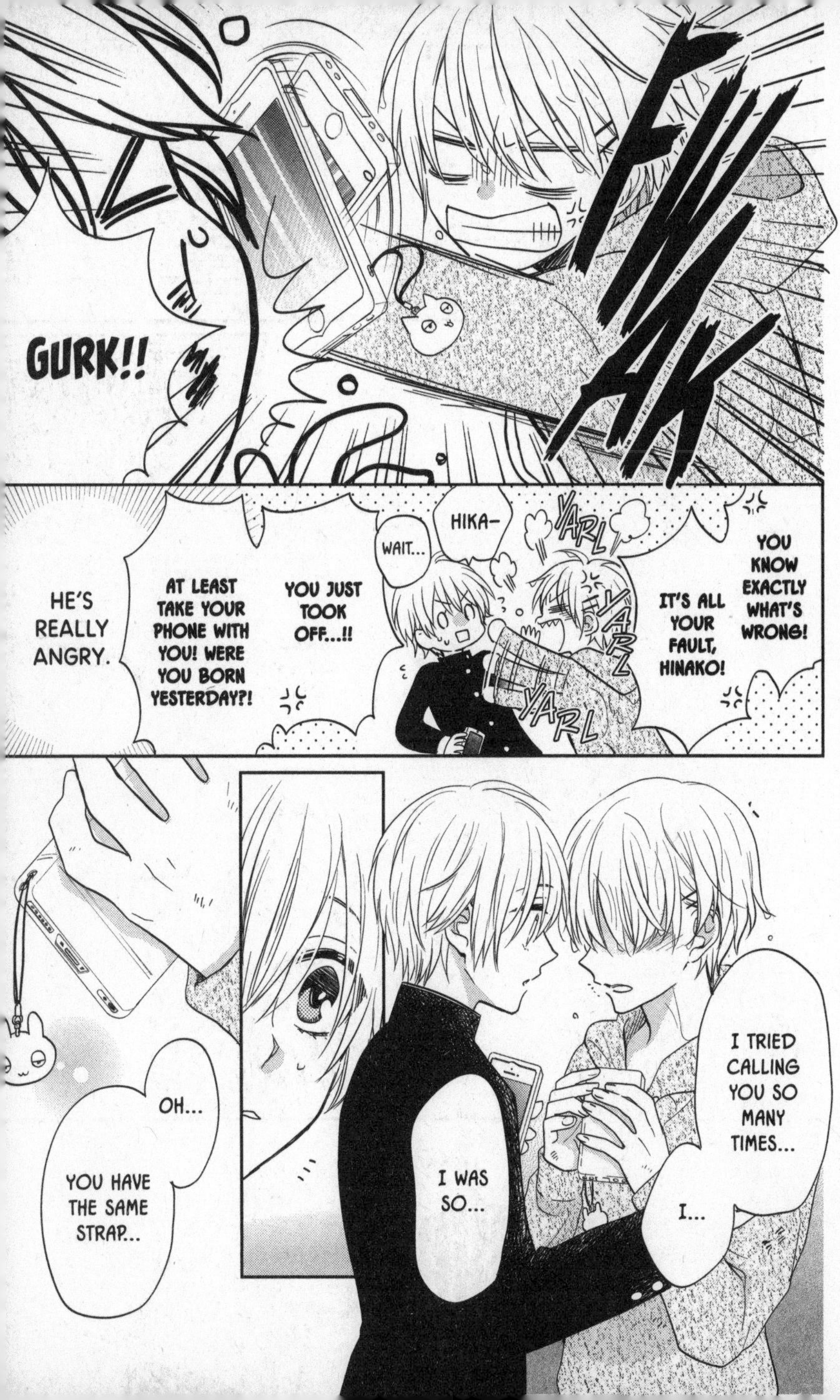
FWAK
GURK!!
YOU KNOW EXACTLY WHAT'S WRONG!
IT'S ALL YOUR FAULT, HINAKO!
YARL
YARL
YARL
HIKA-
WAIT...
YOU JUST TOOK OFF...!!
AT LEAST TAKE YOUR PHONE WITH YOU! WERE YOU BORN YESTERDAY?!
HE'S REALLY ANGRY.
I TRIED CALLING YOU SO MANY TIMES...
I...
I WAS SO...
OH...
YOU HAVE THE SAME STRAP...

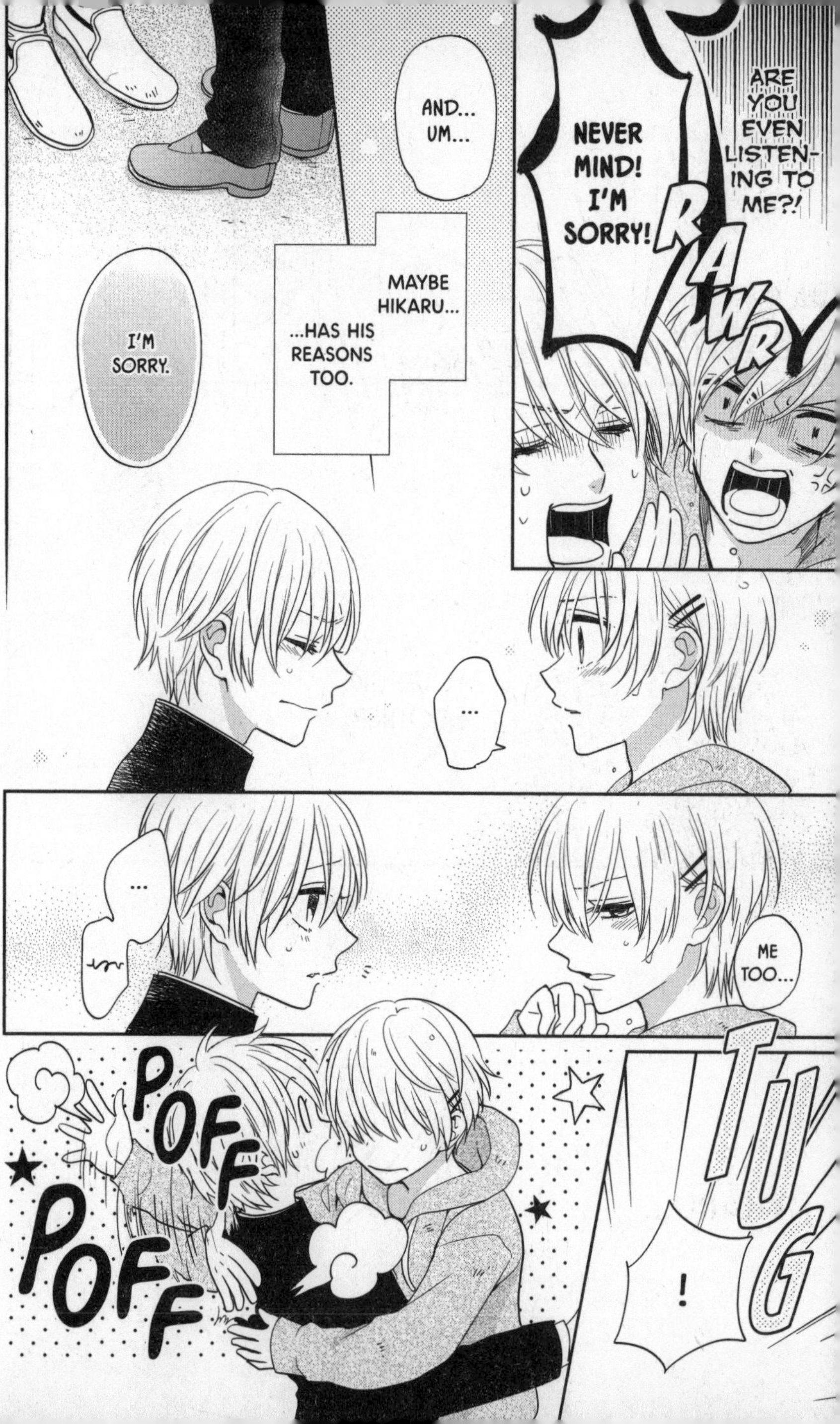
ARE YOU EVEN LISTEN- ING TO ME?!
RAWR
NEVER MIND! I'M SORRY!
AND... UM...
MAYBE HIKARU...
...HAS HIS REASONS TOO.
I'M SORRY.
...
ME TOO...
...
TUG
!
POFF
POFF

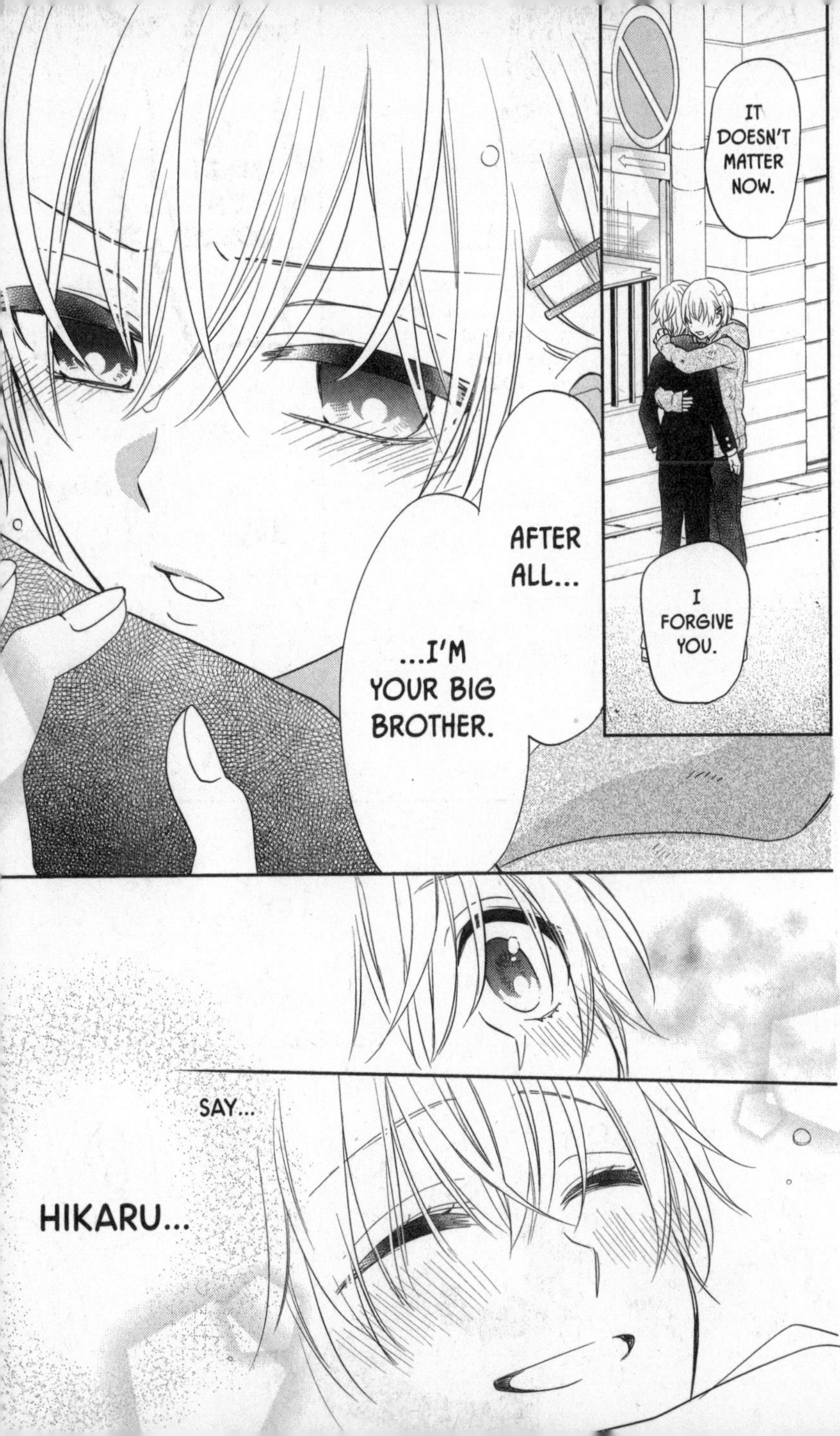
IT DOESN'T MATTER NOW.
I FORGIVE YOU.
AFTER ALL...
...I'M YOUR BIG BROTHER.
SAY...
HIKARU...

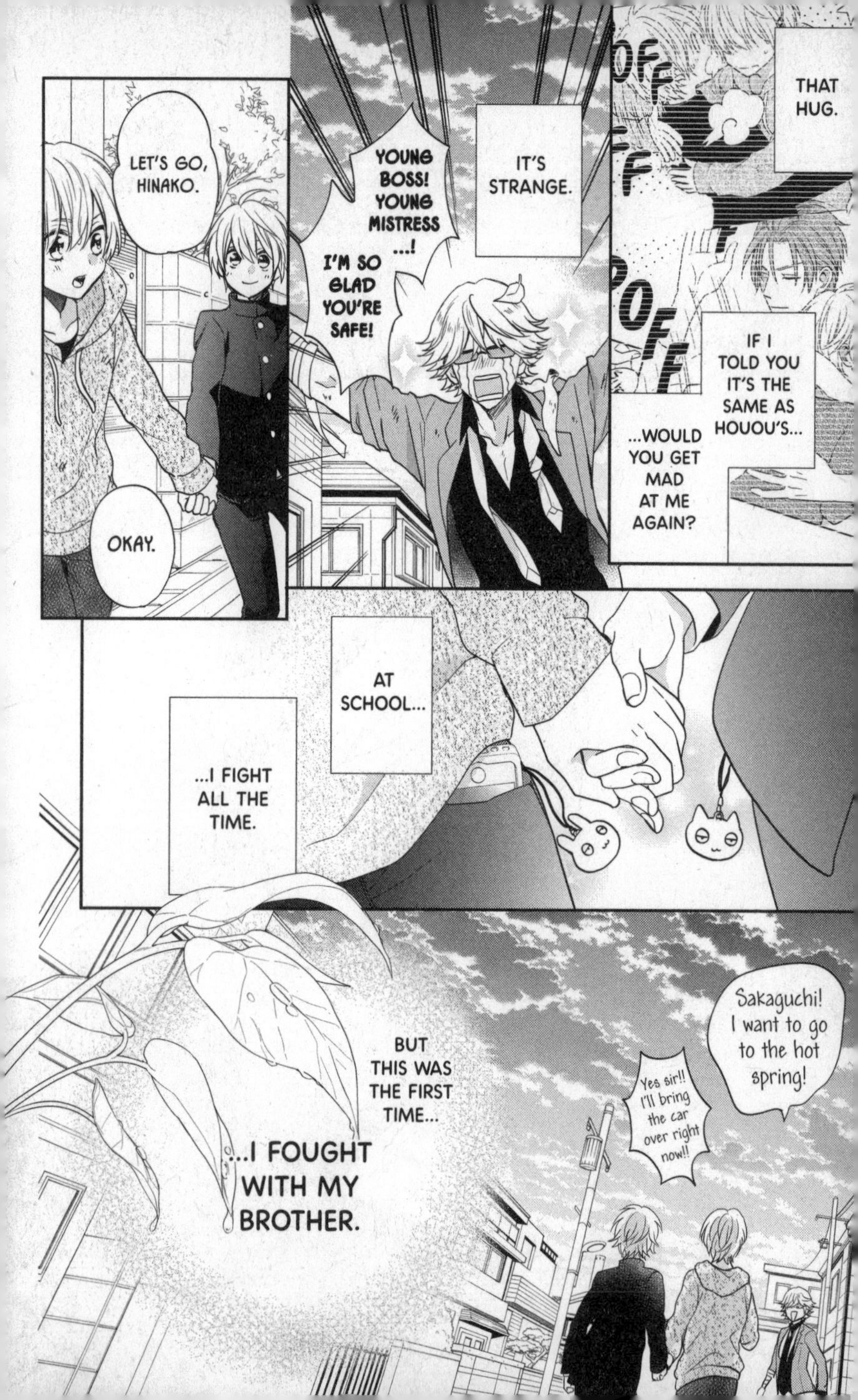
THAT HUG.
POFF
IF I TOLD YOU IT'S THE SAME AS HOUOU'S...
...WOULD YOU GET MAD AT ME AGAIN?
IT'S STRANGE.
YOUNG BOSS! YOUNG MISTRESS ...!
I'M SO GLAD YOU'RE SAFE!
LET'S GO, HINAKO.
OKAY.
AT SCHOOL...
...I FIGHT ALL THE TIME.
Sakaguchi! I want to go to the hot spring!
Yes sir!! I'll bring the car over right now!!
BUT THIS WAS THE FIRST TIME...
...I FOUGHT WITH MY BROTHER.

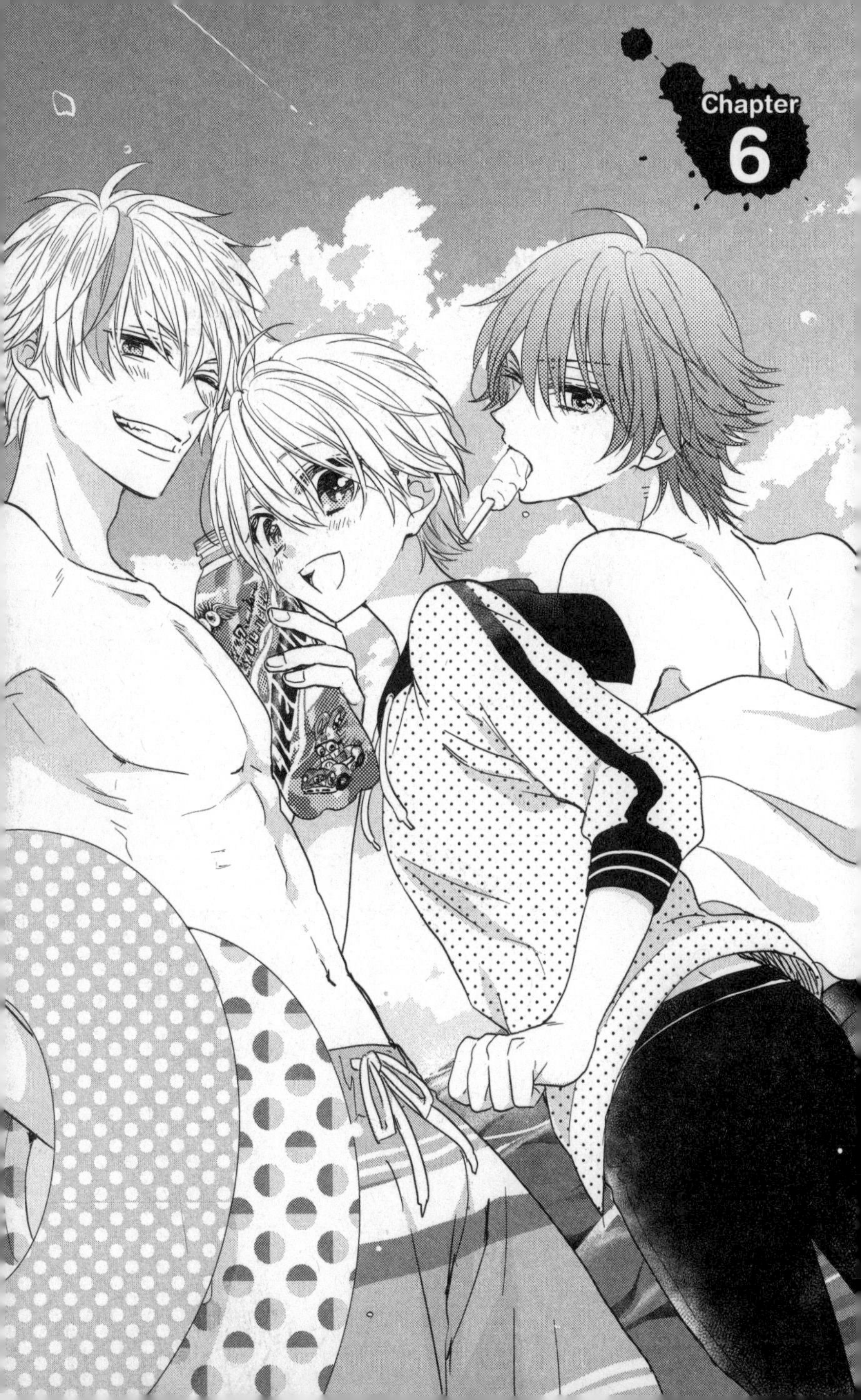
Chapter
6

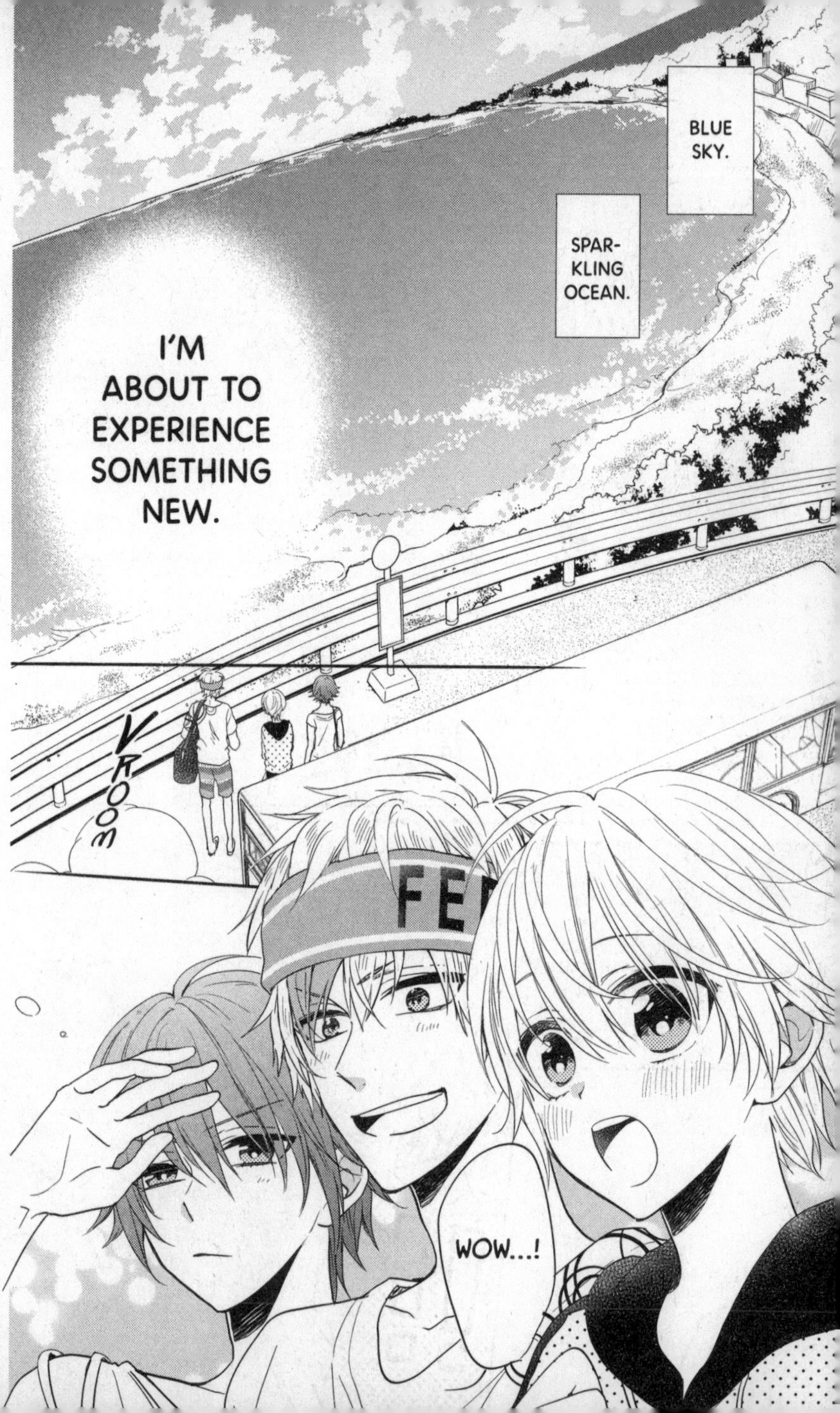
BLUE SKY.
SPAR-KLING OCEAN.
I'M ABOUT TO EXPERIENCE SOMETHING NEW.
VROOOM
FE
WOW...!

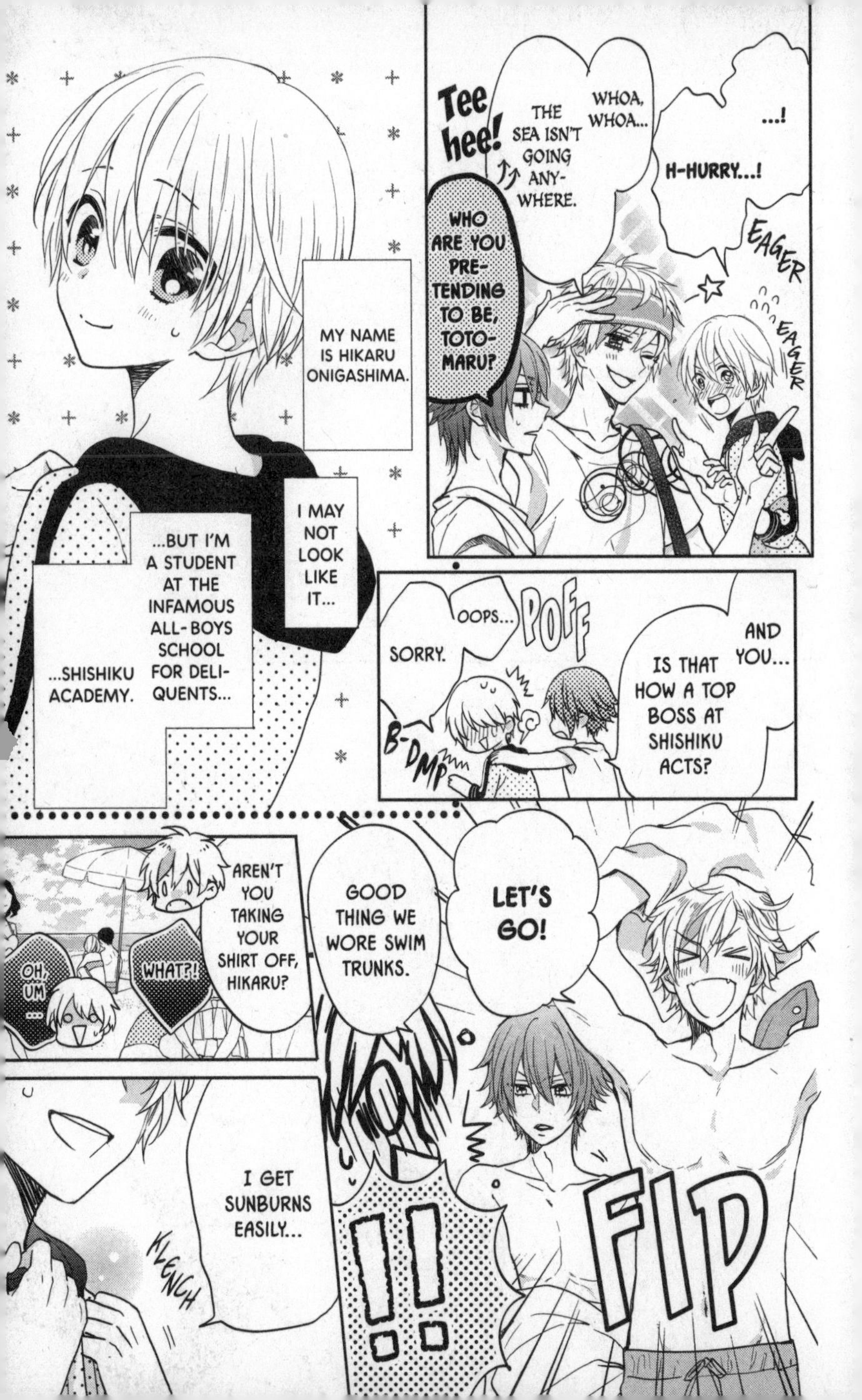
...!
H-HURRY...!
EAGER
EAGER
WHOA, WHOA... THE SEA ISN'T GOING ANYWHERE.
Tee hee!
WHO ARE YOU PRETENDING TO BE, TOTOMARU?
AND YOU... IS THAT HOW A TOP BOSS AT SHISHIKU ACTS?
POFF
OOPS... SORRY.
B-DMP
MY NAME IS HIKARU ONIGASHIMA.
I MAY NOT LOOK LIKE IT...
...BUT I'M A STUDENT AT THE INFAMOUS ALL-BOYS SCHOOL FOR DELI-QUENTS...
...SHISHIKU ACADEMY.
LET'S GO!
GOOD THING WE WORE SWIM TRUNKS.
FIP
WOW
!!
AREN'T YOU TAKING YOUR SHIRT OFF, HIKARU?
WHAT?!
OH, UM...
I GET SUNBURNS EASILY...
KLENCH

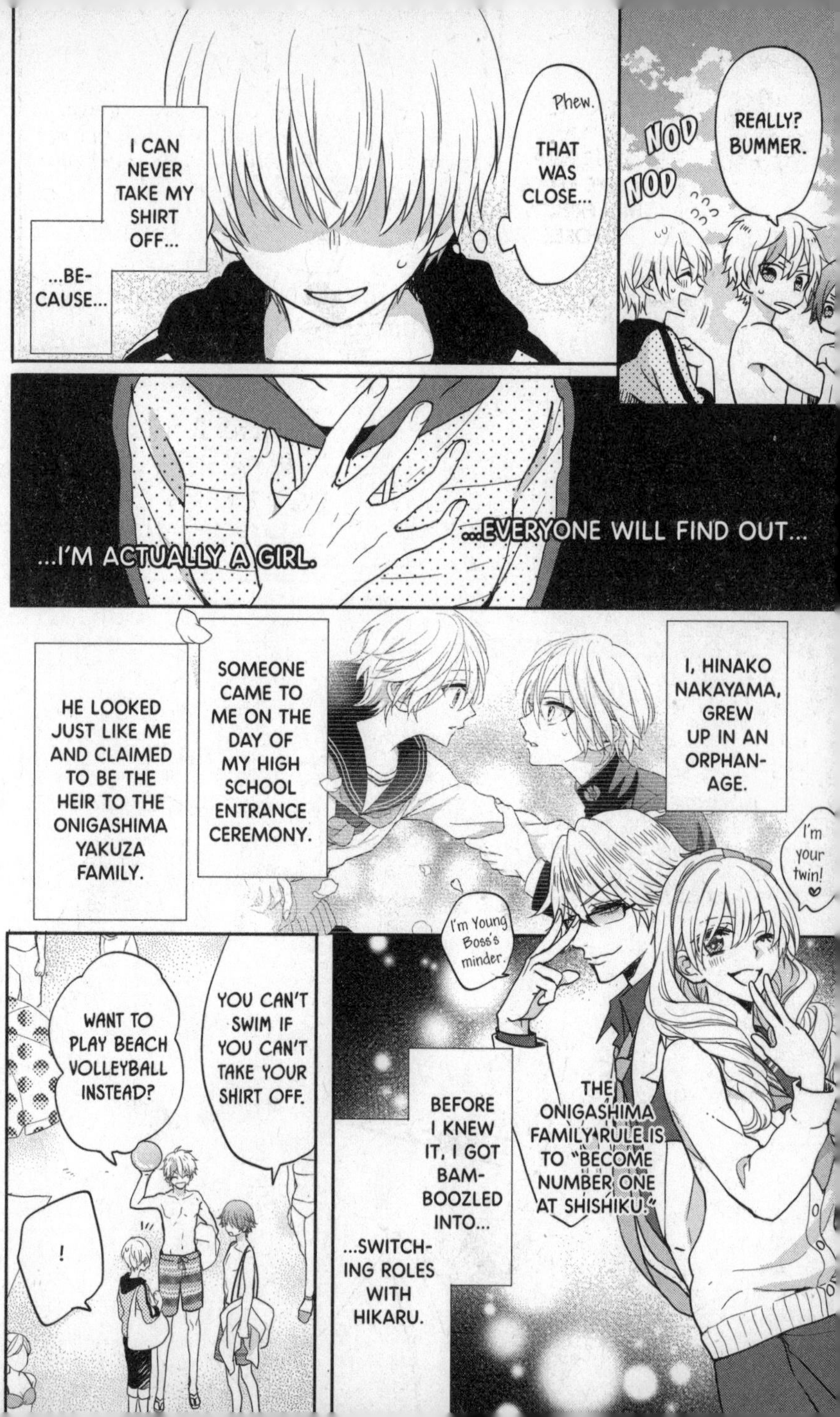
NOD
NOD
REALLY? BUMMER.
Phew.
THAT WAS CLOSE...
I CAN NEVER TAKE MY SHIRT OFF...
...BE-CAUSE...
...EVERYONE WILL FIND OUT...
...I'M ACTUALLY A GIRL.
I, HINAKO NAKAYAMA, GREW UP IN AN ORPHAN-AGE.
I'm your twin!
SOMEONE CAME TO ME ON THE DAY OF MY HIGH SCHOOL ENTRANCE CEREMONY.
HE LOOKED JUST LIKE ME AND CLAIMED TO BE THE HEIR TO THE ONIGASHIMA YAKUZA FAMILY.
I'm Young Boss's minder.
THE ONIGASHIMA FAMILY RULE IS TO "BECOME NUMBER ONE AT SHISHIKU."
BEFORE I KNEW IT, I GOT BAM-BOOZLED INTO...
...SWITCH-ING ROLES WITH HIKARU.
YOU CAN'T SWIM IF YOU CAN'T TAKE YOUR SHIRT OFF.
WANT TO PLAY BEACH VOLLEYBALL INSTEAD?
!

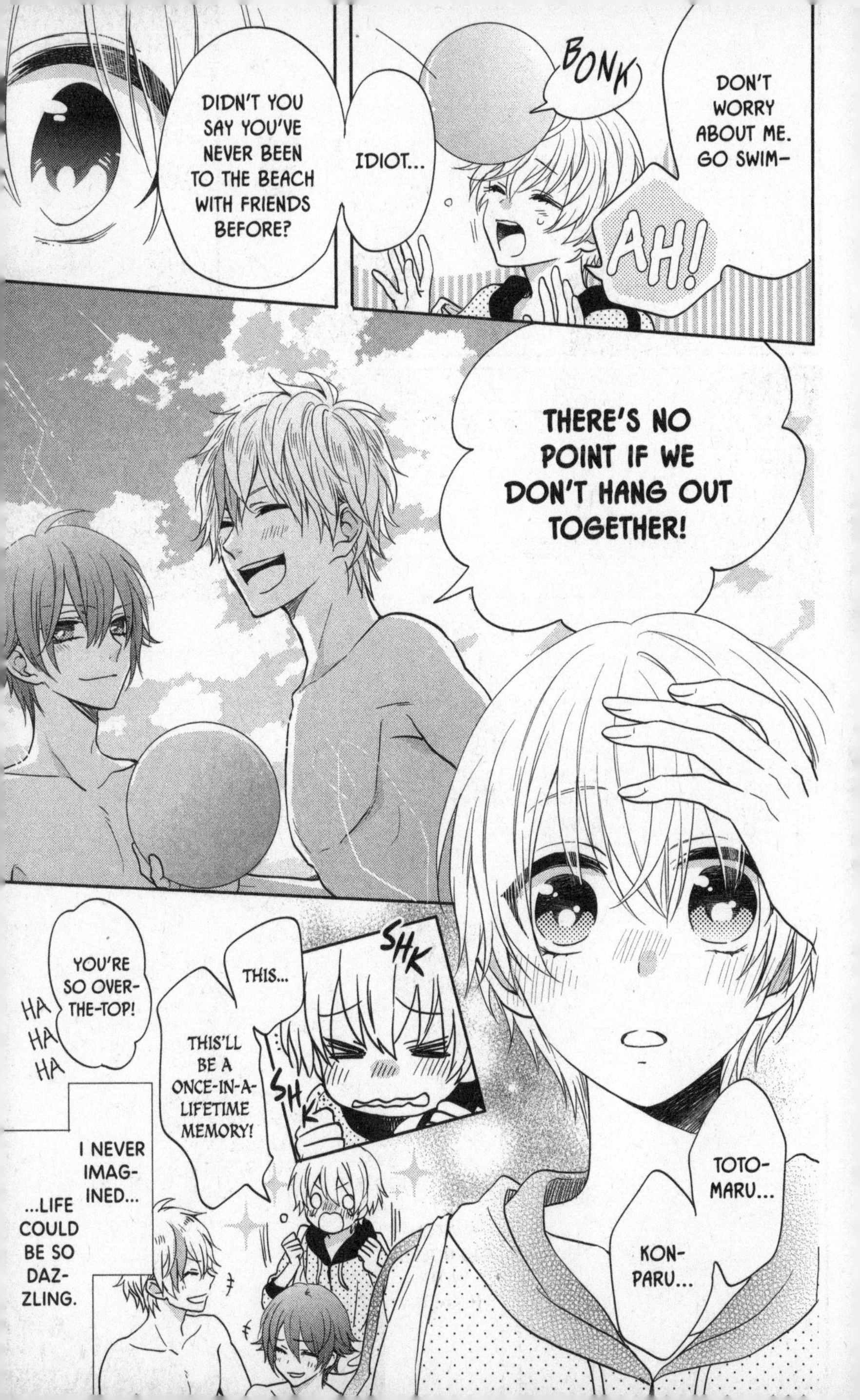
BONK
DON'T WORRY ABOUT ME. GO SWIM–
AH!
IDIOT...
DIDN'T YOU SAY YOU'VE NEVER BEEN TO THE BEACH WITH FRIENDS BEFORE?
THERE'S NO POINT IF WE DON'T HANG OUT TOGETHER!
TOTO-MARU...
KON-PARU...
SHK
THIS...
THIS'LL BE A ONCE-IN-A-LIFETIME MEMORY!
SHK
YOU'RE SO OVER-THE-TOP!
HA HA HA
I NEVER IMAG-INED...
...LIFE COULD BE SO DAZ-ZLING.

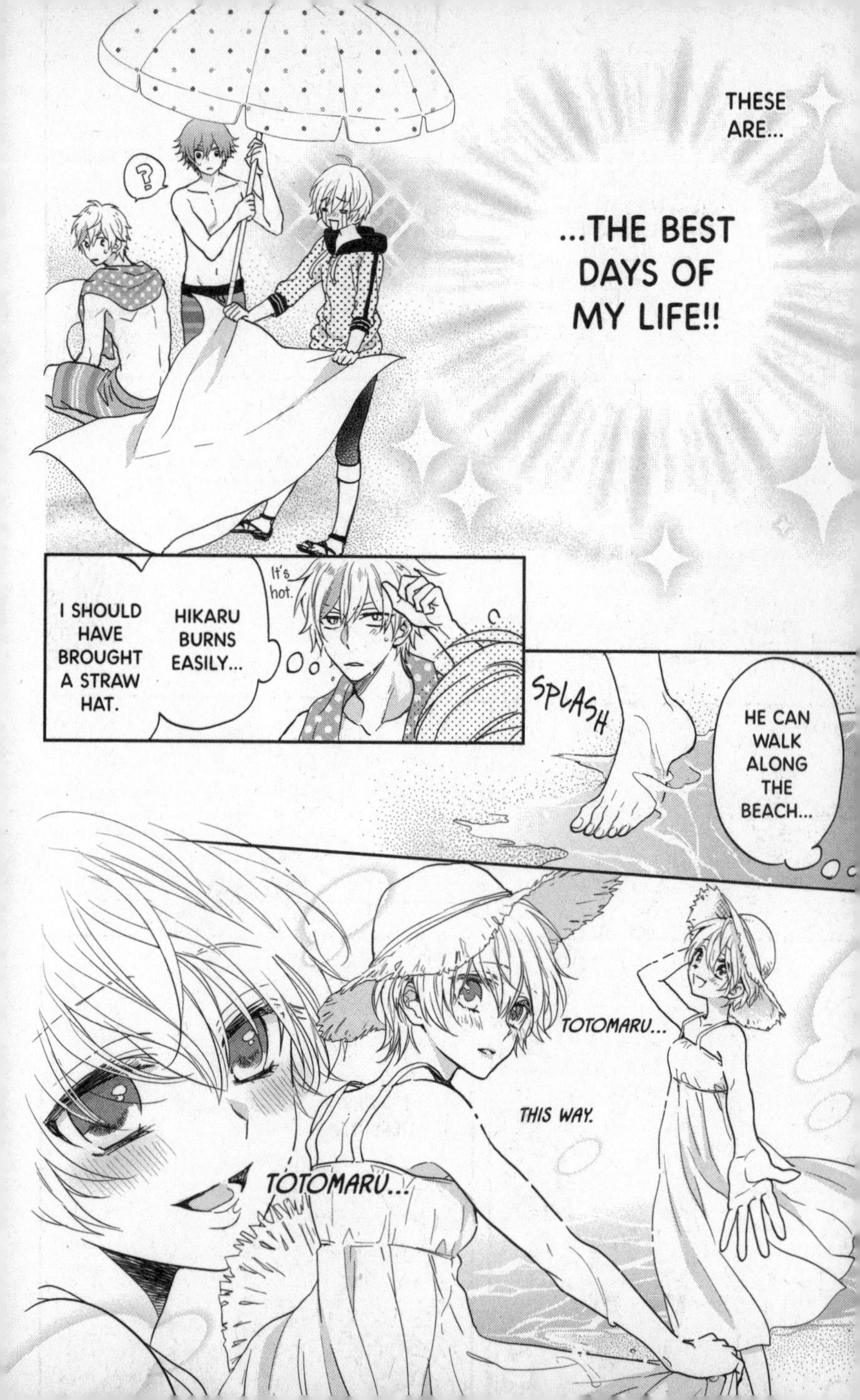
THESE ARE...
...THE BEST DAYS OF MY LIFE!!
?
It's hot.
HIKARU BURNS EASILY...
I SHOULD HAVE BROUGHT A STRAW HAT.
SPLASH
HE CAN WALK ALONG THE BEACH...
TOTOMARU...
THIS WAY.
TOTOMARU...

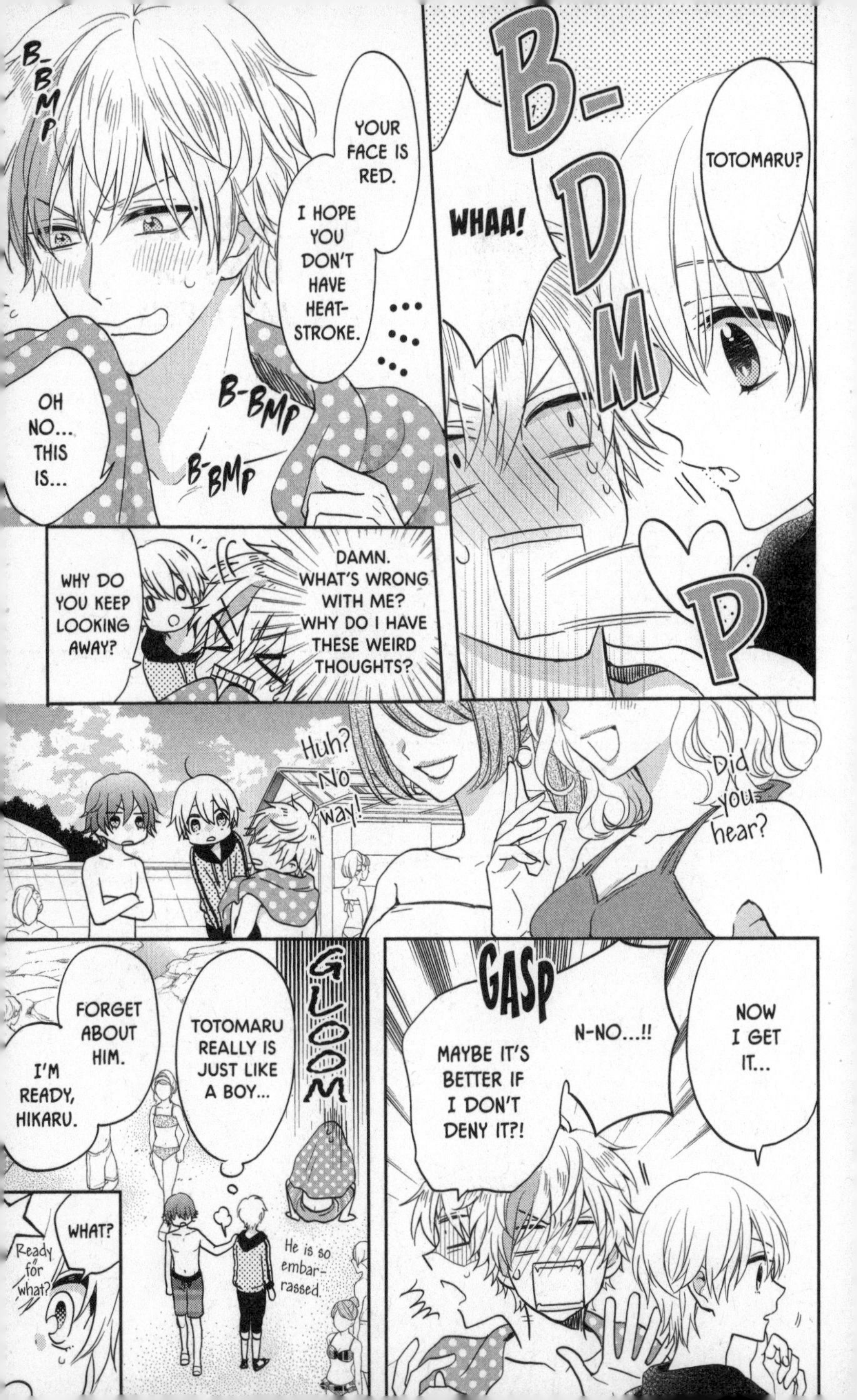
TOTOMARU?
WHAA!
B-DMP
B-BMP
YOUR FACE IS RED.
I HOPE YOU DON'T HAVE HEAT-STROKE.
...
...
OH NO... THIS IS...
B-BMP
B-BMP
DAMN. WHAT'S WRONG WITH ME? WHY DO I HAVE THESE WEIRD THOUGHTS?
WHY DO YOU KEEP LOOKING AWAY?
Did you hear?
Huh? No way!
NOW I GET IT...
GASP
N-NO...!!
MAYBE IT'S BETTER IF I DON'T DENY IT?!
GLOOM
TOTOMARU REALLY IS JUST LIKE A BOY...
FORGET ABOUT HIM.
I'M READY, HIKARU.
He is so embar-rassed.
WHAT?
Ready for what?

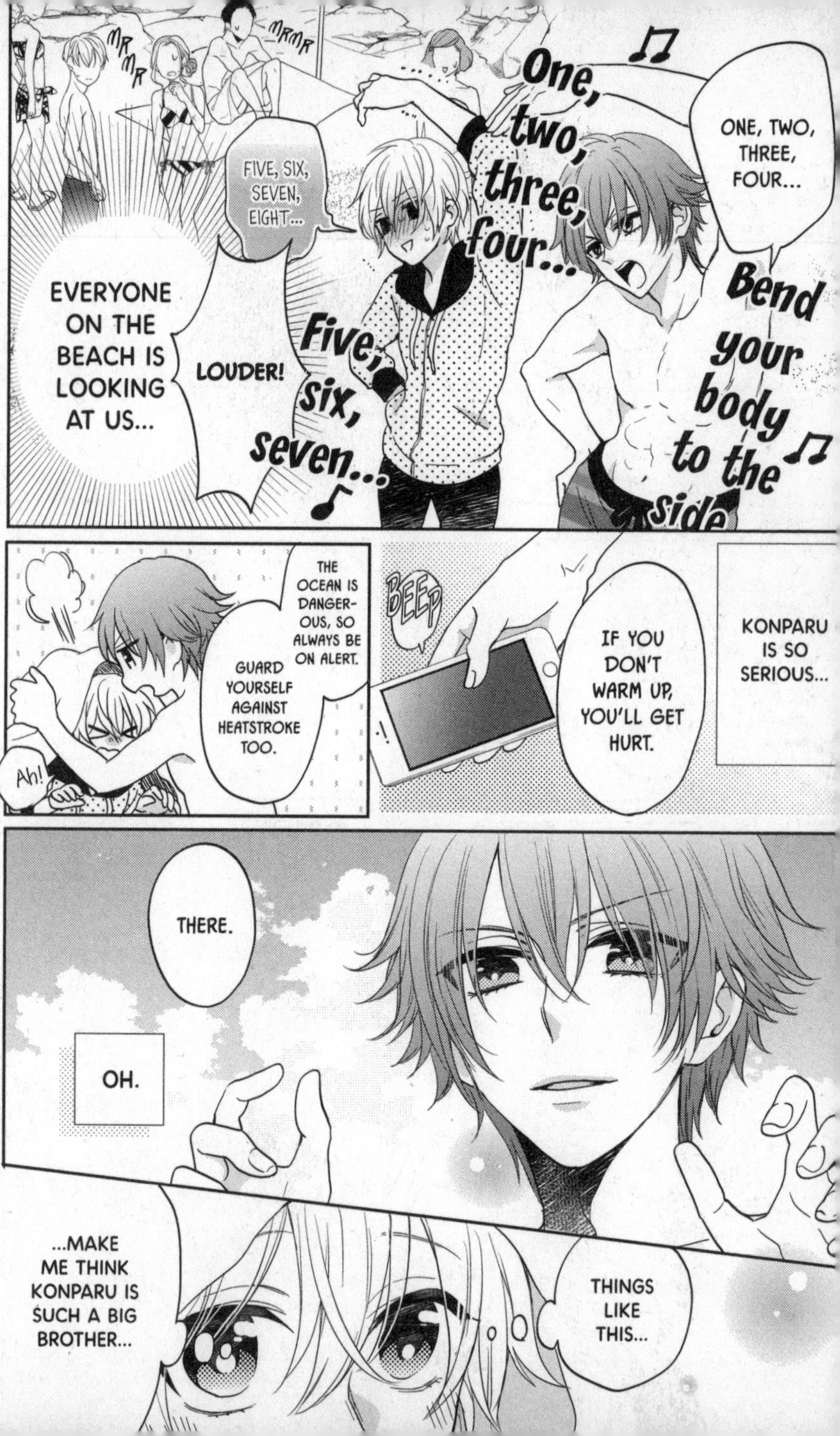
ONE, TWO, THREE, FOUR...
One, two, three, four...
Bend your body to the side
FIVE, SIX, SEVEN, EIGHT...
Five, six, seven...
LOUDER!
MRMRMR
MRMR
EVERYONE ON THE BEACH IS LOOKING AT US...
KONPARU IS SO SERIOUS...
IF YOU DON'T WARM UP, YOU'LL GET HURT.
BEEP
THE OCEAN IS DANGER-OUS, SO ALWAYS BE ON ALERT.
GUARD YOURSELF AGAINST HEATSTROKE TOO.
Ah!
THERE.
OH.
THINGS LIKE THIS...
...MAKE ME THINK KONPARU IS SUCH A BIG BROTHER...

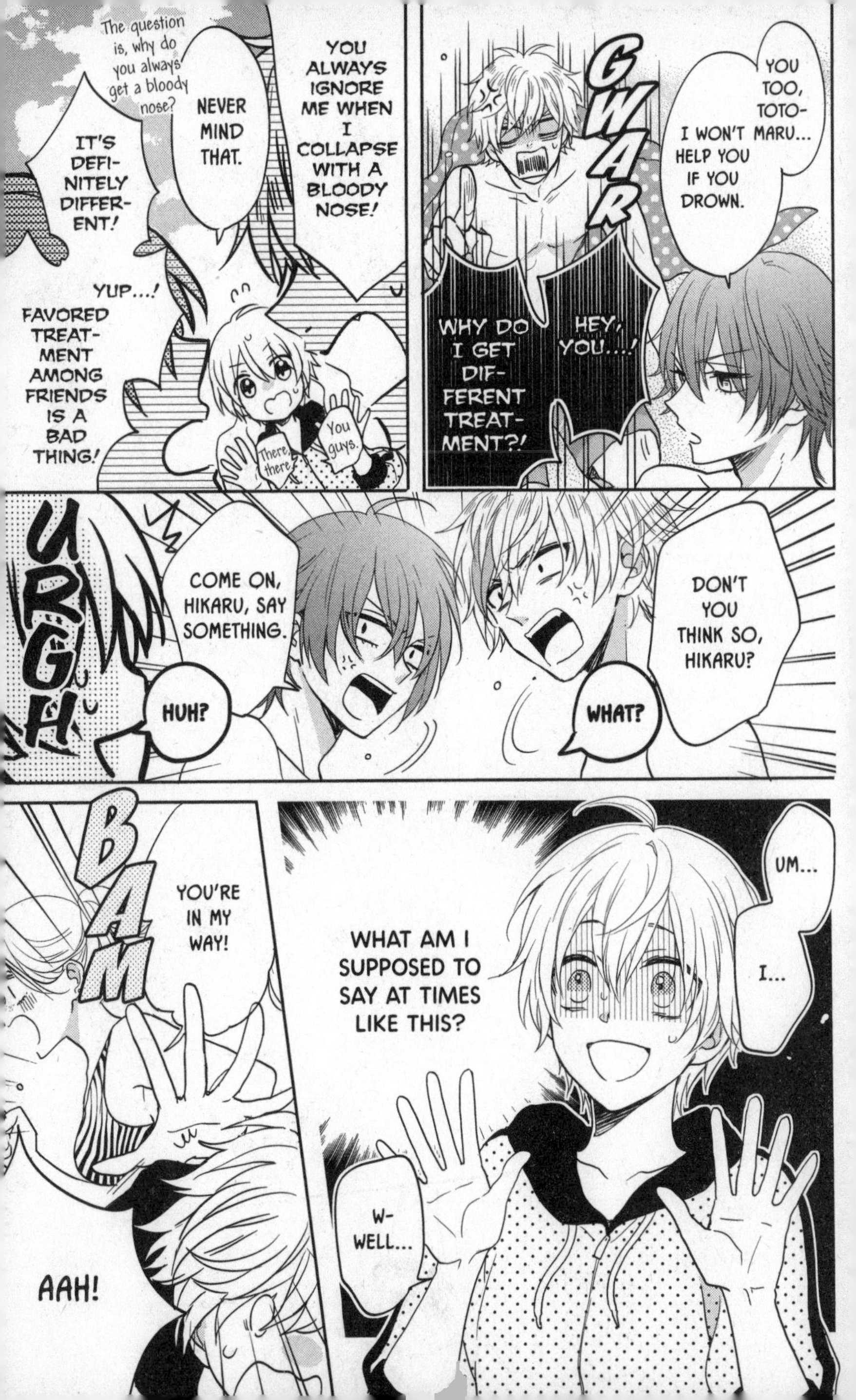
YOU TOO, TOTOMARU... I WON'T HELP YOU IF YOU DROWN.
GWAR
HEY, YOU...!
WHY DO I GET DIFFERENT TREATMENT?!
YOU ALWAYS IGNORE ME WHEN I COLLAPSE WITH A BLOODY NOSE!
NEVER MIND THAT.
The question is, why do you always get a bloody nose?
IT'S DEFINITELY DIFFERENT!
YUP...!
FAVORED TREATMENT AMONG FRIENDS IS A BAD THING!
You guys.
There, there.
DON'T YOU THINK SO, HIKARU?
WHAT?
COME ON, HIKARU, SAY SOMETHING.
HUH?
URGH
UM...
I...
WHAT AM I SUPPOSED TO SAY AT TIMES LIKE THIS?
W-WELL...
BAM
YOU'RE IN MY WAY!
AAH!

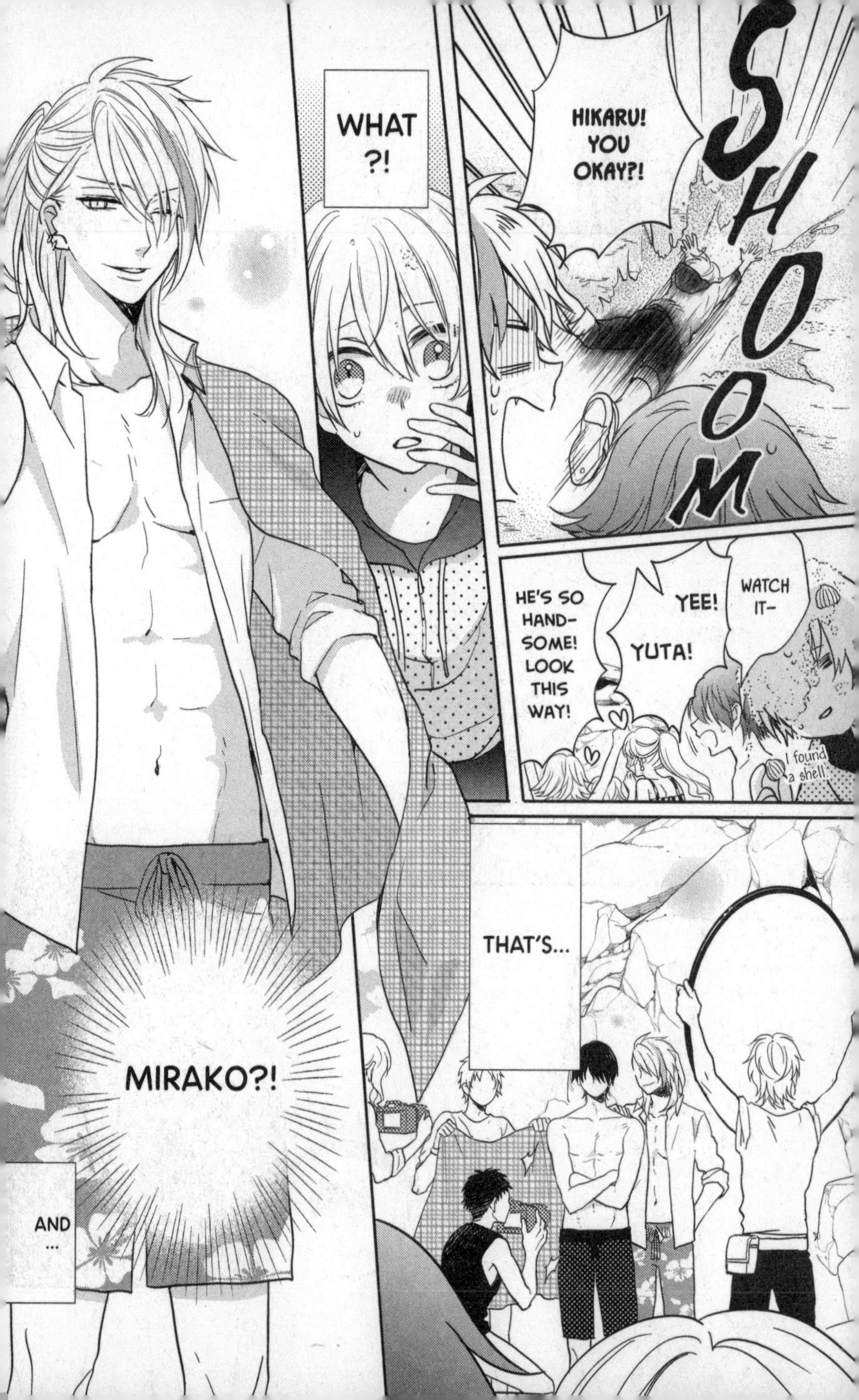
HIKARU! YOU OKAY?!
SHOOM
WATCH IT–
YUTA!
YEE!
HE'S SO HANDSOME! LOOK THIS WAY!
I found a shell!
WHAT ?!
THAT'S...
AND ...
MIRAKO?!

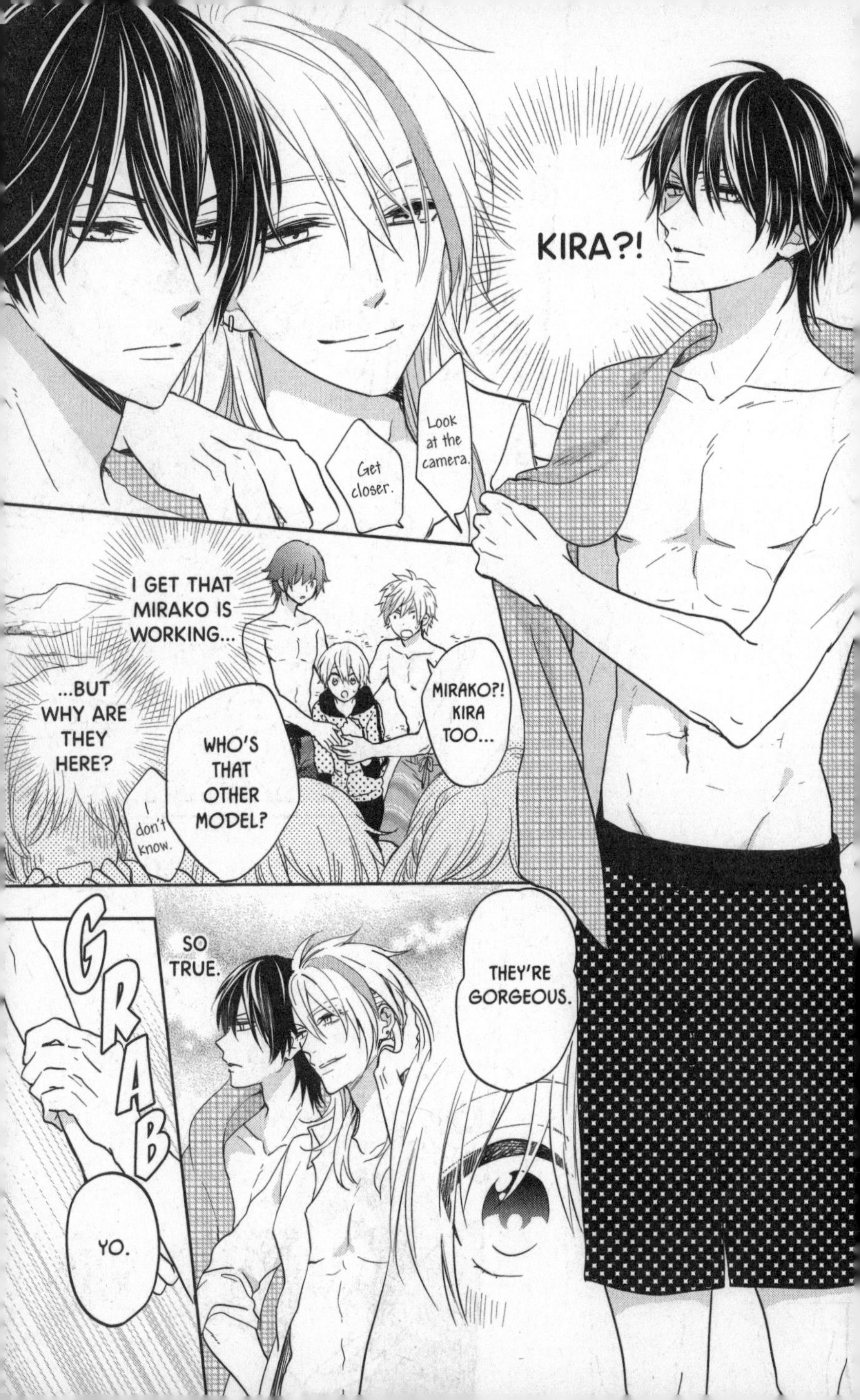
KIRA?!
Look at the camera.
Get closer.
MIRAKO?! KIRA TOO...
I GET THAT MIRAKO IS WORKING...
...BUT WHY ARE THEY HERE?
WHO'S THAT OTHER MODEL?
I don't know.
THEY'RE GORGEOUS.
SO TRUE.
GRAB
YO.

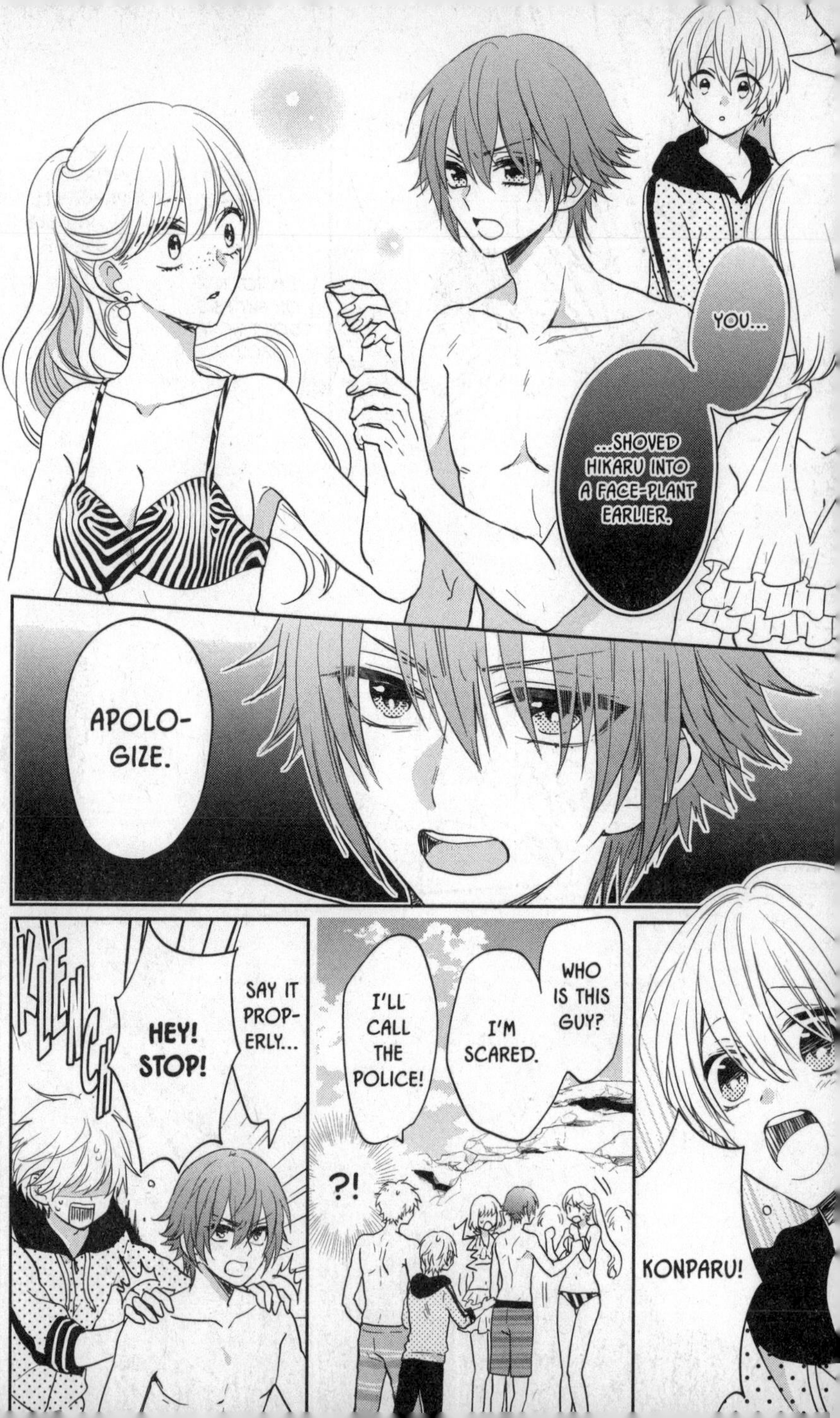
YOU...
...SHOVED HIKARU INTO A FACE-PLANT EARLIER.
APOLO-GIZE.
KONPARU!
WHO IS THIS GUY?
I'M SCARED.
I'LL CALL THE POLICE!
?!
SAY IT PROP-ERLY...
HEY! STOP!
KLENCH

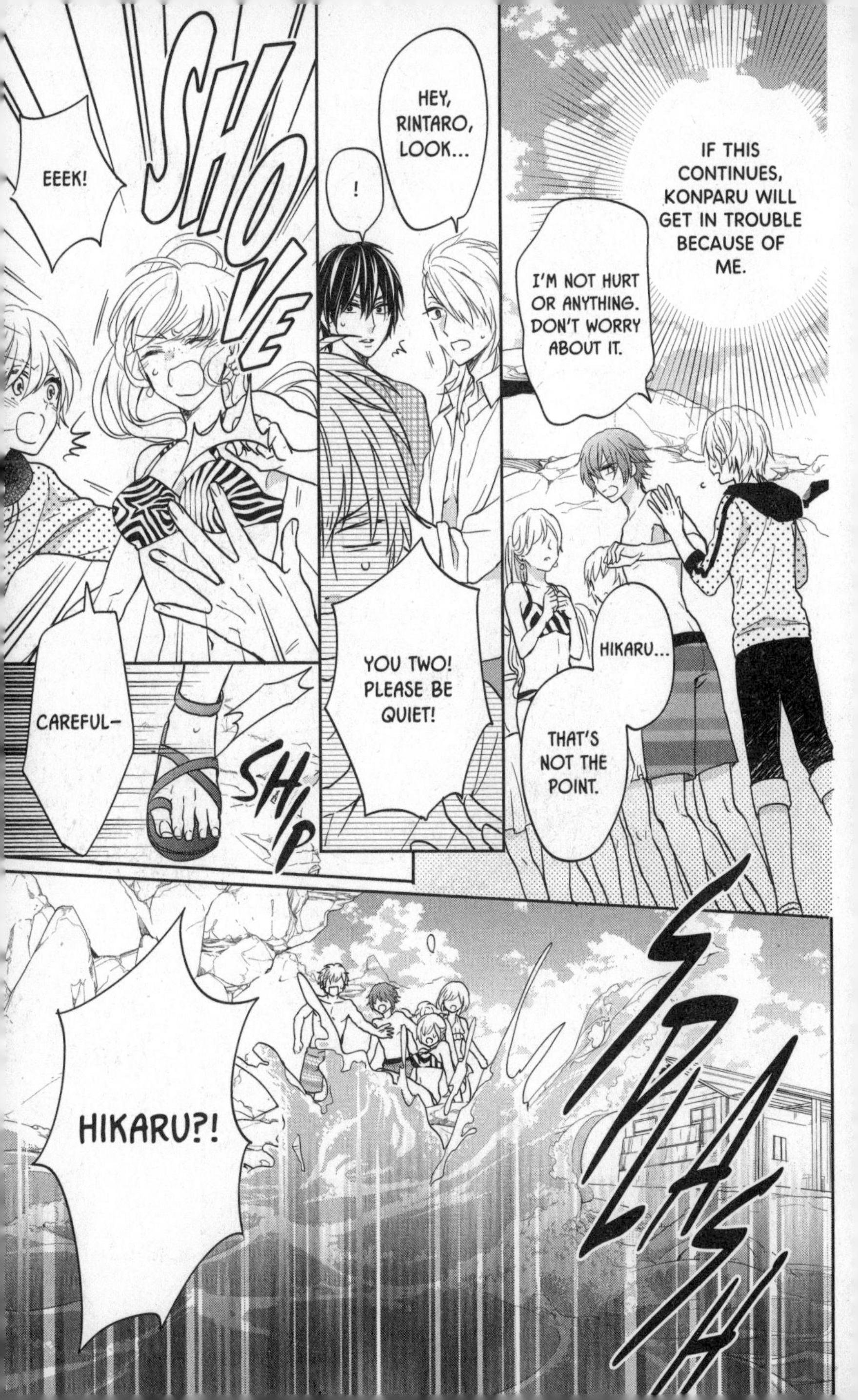
IF THIS CONTINUES, KONPARU WILL GET IN TROUBLE BECAUSE OF ME.
I'M NOT HURT OR ANYTHING. DON'T WORRY ABOUT IT.
HIKARU...
THAT'S NOT THE POINT.
HEY, RINTARO, LOOK...
!
YOU TWO! PLEASE BE QUIET!
SHOVE
EEEK!
CAREFUL-
SLIP
SPLASH
HIKARU?!

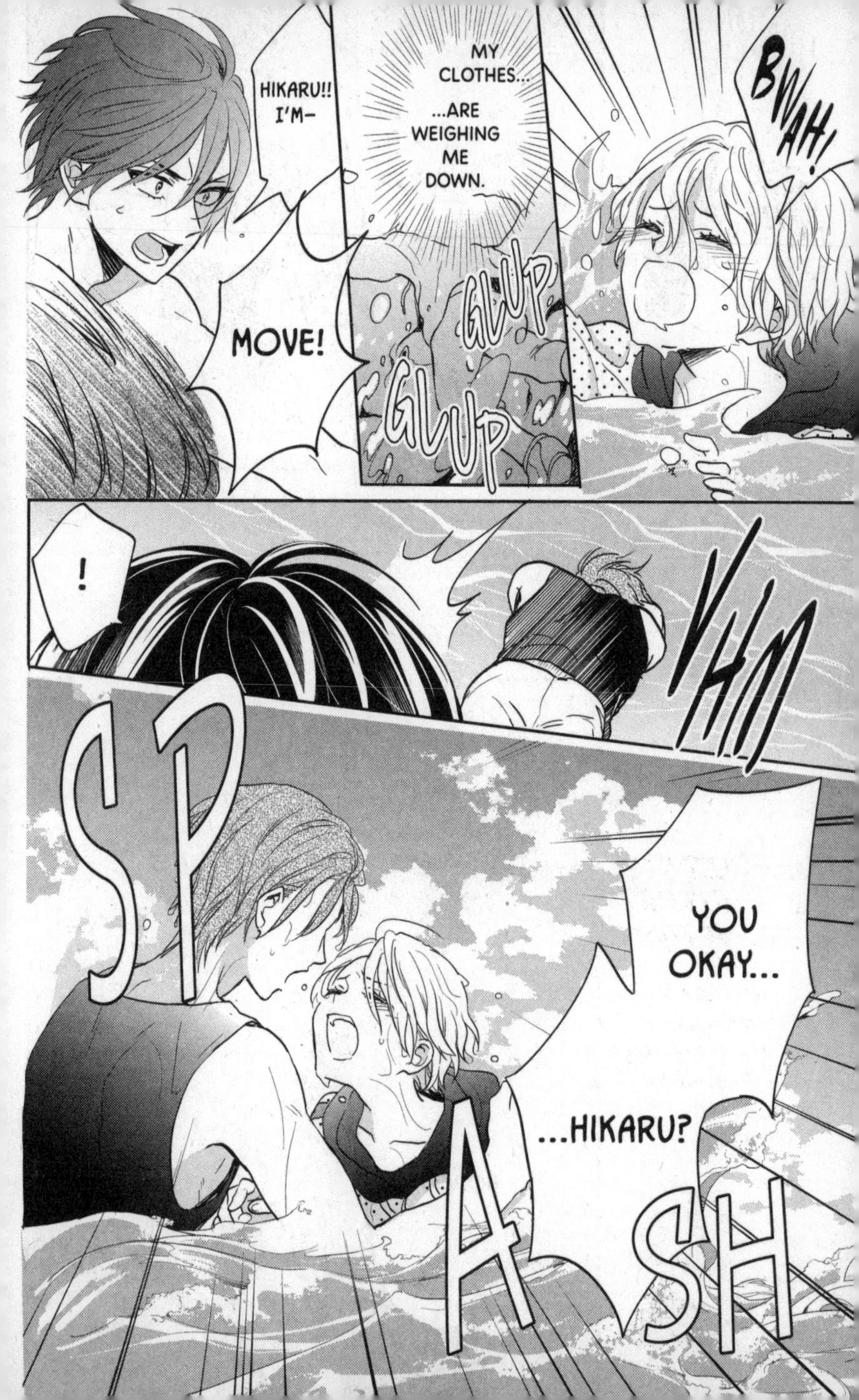
BWAH!
MY CLOTHES...
...ARE WEIGHING ME DOWN.
GLUP GLUP
HIKARU!! I'M—
MOVE!
VHM
!
SPLASH
YOU OKAY...
...HIKARU?

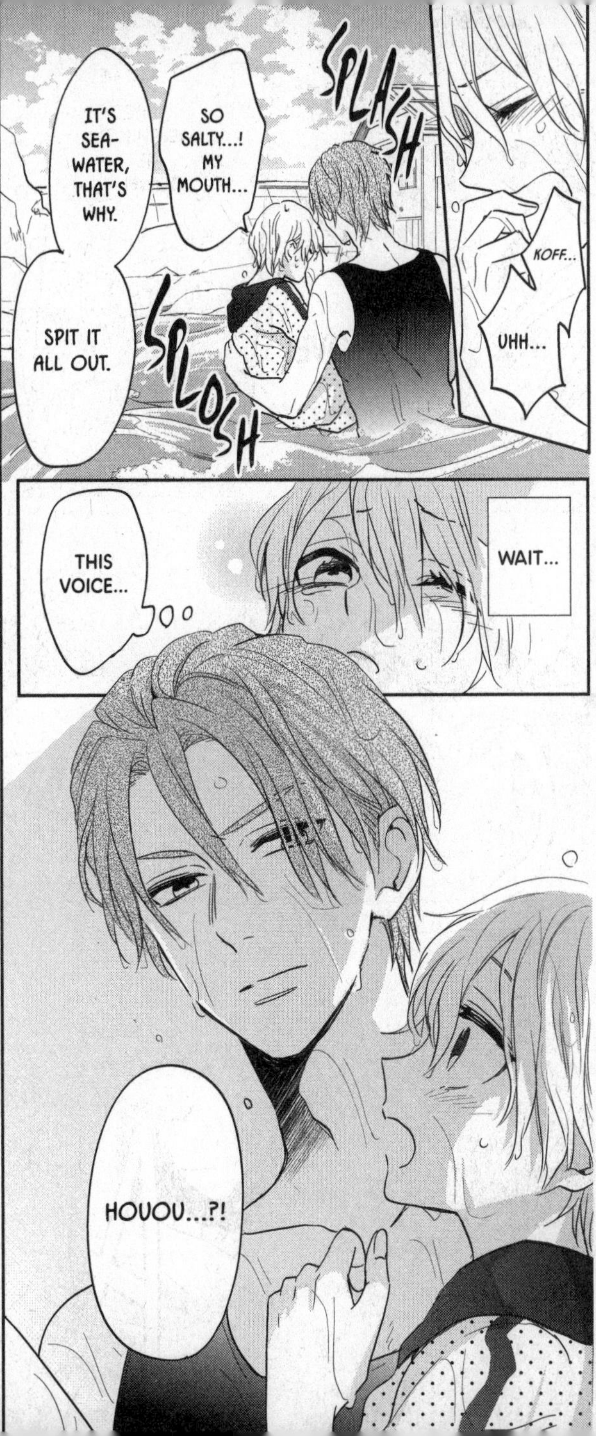
KOFF...
UHH...
SPLASH
SO SALTY...! MY MOUTH...
IT'S SEA-WATER, THAT'S WHY.
SPIT IT ALL OUT.
SPLOSH
WAIT...
THIS VOICE...
HOUOU...?!

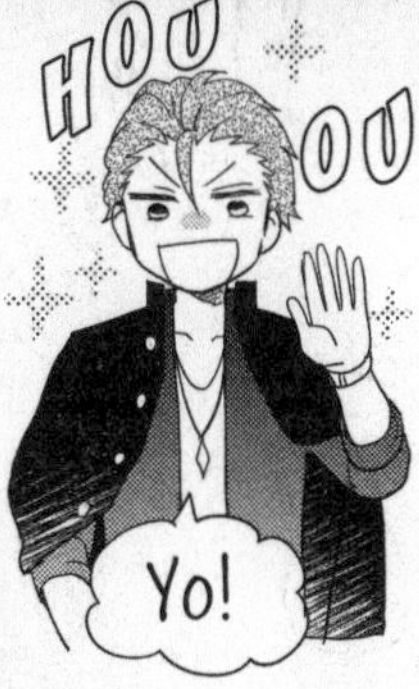
HOU OU
Yo!

Tomoaki Maeno plays Houou Onigashima! Right off the bat...

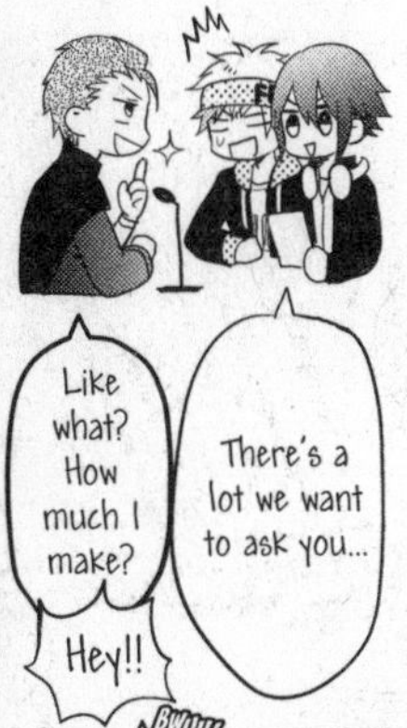
There's a lot we want to ask you...
Like what? How much I make?
Hey!!

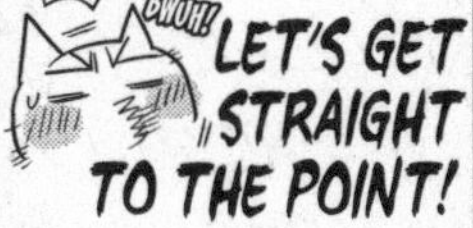
BWUH!
LET'S GET STRAIGHT TO THE POINT!

The studio came to life with Houou's great lines and wicked conversation skills. It's no wonder he's known as a legendary delinquent...

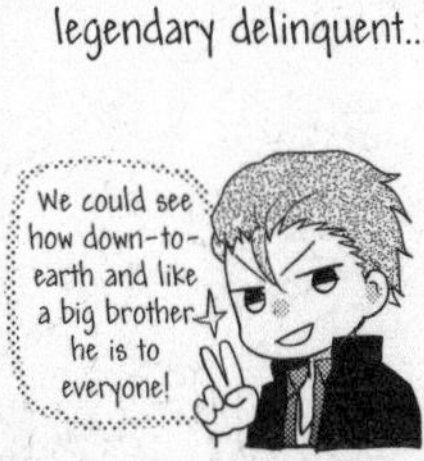
We could see how down-to-earth and like a big brother he is to everyone!

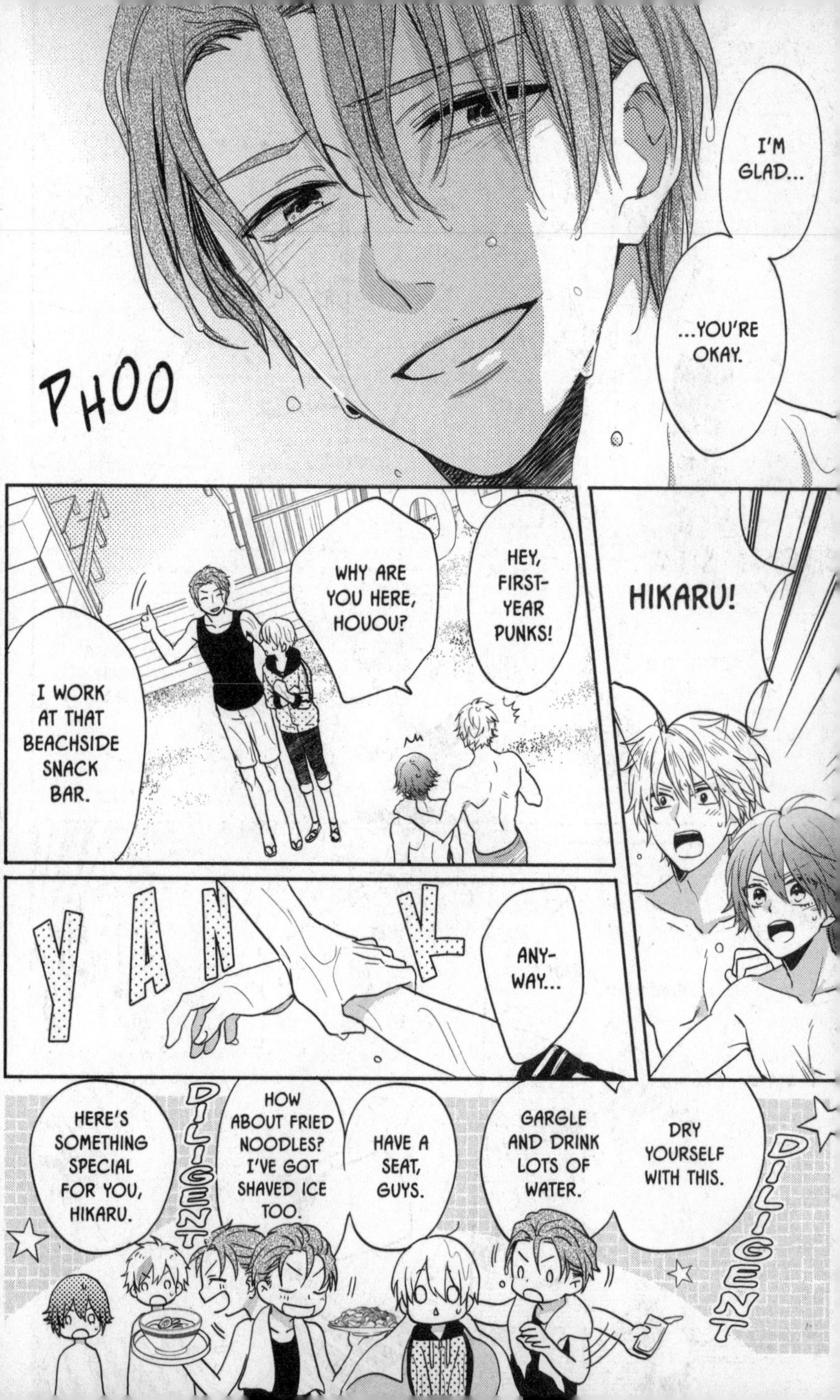
I'M GLAD...
...YOU'RE OKAY.
PHOO
HIKARU!
HEY, FIRST-YEAR PUNKS!
WHY ARE YOU HERE, HOUOU?
I WORK AT THAT BEACHSIDE SNACK BAR.
ANY-WAY...
YANK
DILIGENT
DRY YOURSELF WITH THIS.
GARGLE AND DRINK LOTS OF WATER.
HAVE A SEAT, GUYS.
HOW ABOUT FRIED NOODLES? I'VE GOT SHAVED ICE TOO.
DILIGENT
HERE'S SOMETHING SPECIAL FOR YOU, HIKARU.

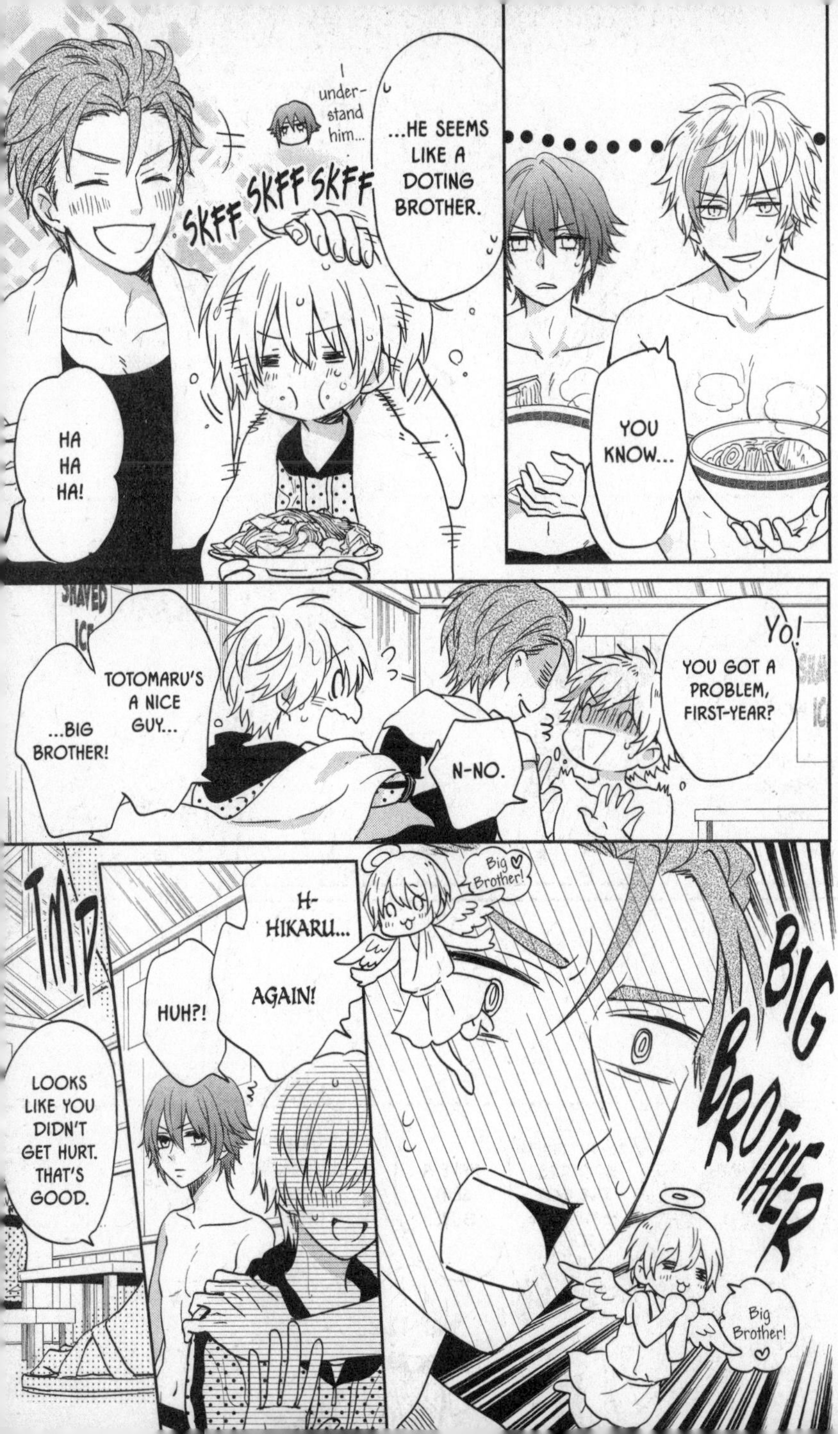
YOU KNOW...
...HE SEEMS LIKE A DOTING BROTHER.
I under-stand him...
SKFF SKFF SKFF
HA HA HA!
Yo!
YOU GOT A PROBLEM, FIRST-YEAR?
N-NO.
TOTOMARU'S A NICE GUY...
...BIG BROTHER!
SHAVED ICE
BIG BROTHER
Big Brother!
Big Brother!
H-HIKARU...
AGAIN!
HUH?!
TMP
LOOKS LIKE YOU DIDN'T GET HURT. THAT'S GOOD.

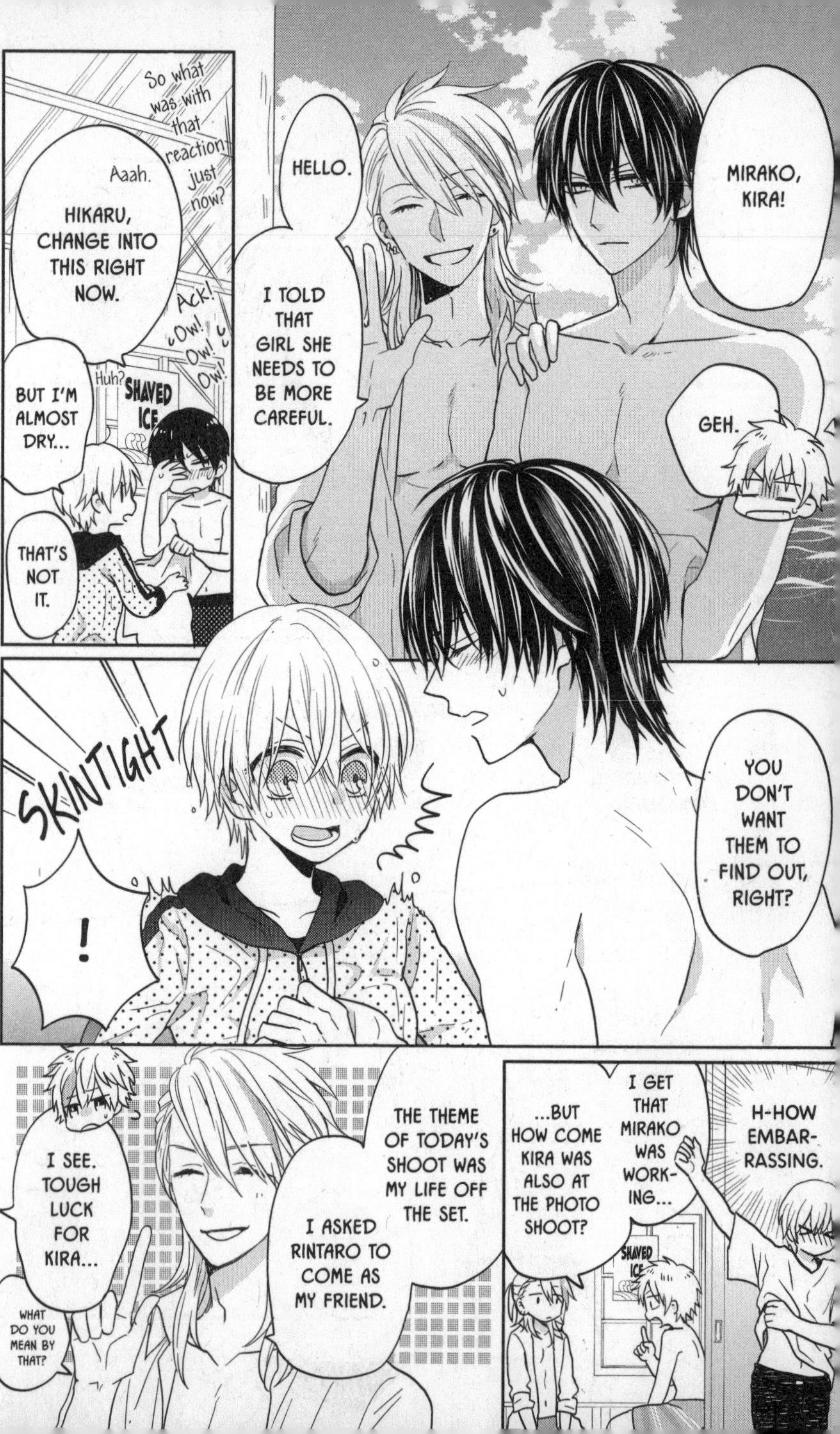
MIRAKO, KIRA!
HELLO.
I TOLD THAT GIRL SHE NEEDS TO BE MORE CAREFUL.
GEH.
So what was with that reaction just now?
Aaah.
HIKARU, CHANGE INTO THIS RIGHT NOW.
Ack! Ow! Ow! Ow!
Huh?
SHAVED ICE
BUT I'M ALMOST DRY...
THAT'S NOT IT.
YOU DON'T WANT THEM TO FIND OUT, RIGHT?
SKINTIGHT
!
H-HOW EMBAR-RASSING.
I GET THAT MIRAKO WAS WORK-ING...
...BUT HOW COME KIRA WAS ALSO AT THE PHOTO SHOOT?
SHAVED ICE
THE THEME OF TODAY'S SHOOT WAS MY LIFE OFF THE SET.
I ASKED RINTARO TO COME AS MY FRIEND.
I SEE. TOUGH LUCK FOR KIRA...
WHAT DO YOU MEAN BY THAT?

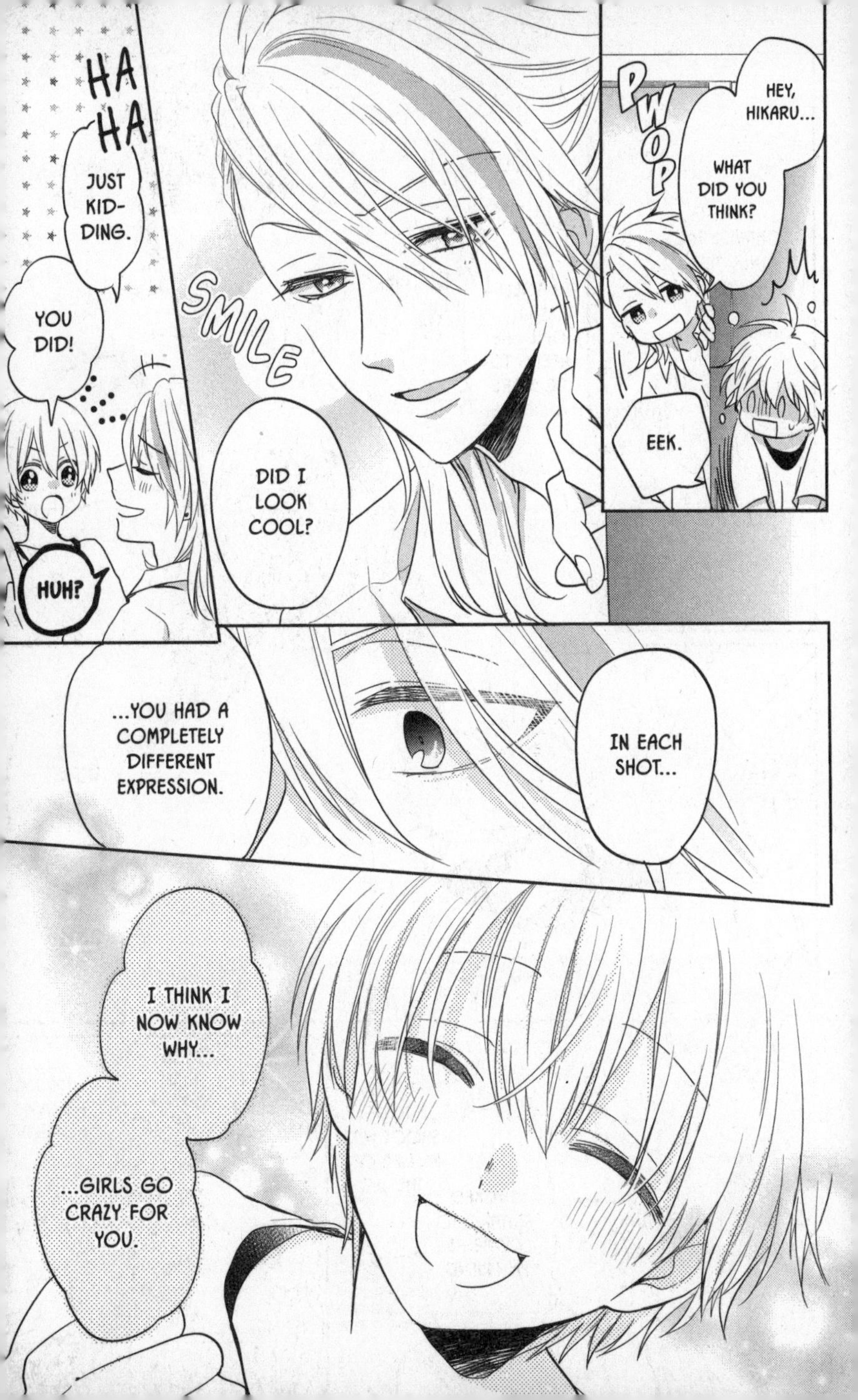
PWOP
HEY, HIKARU... WHAT DID YOU THINK?
EEK.
SMILE
DID I LOOK COOL?
HA HA
JUST KID-DING.
YOU DID!
HUH?
IN EACH SHOT...
...YOU HAD A COMPLETELY DIFFERENT EXPRESSION.
I THINK I NOW KNOW WHY...
...GIRLS GO CRAZY FOR YOU.

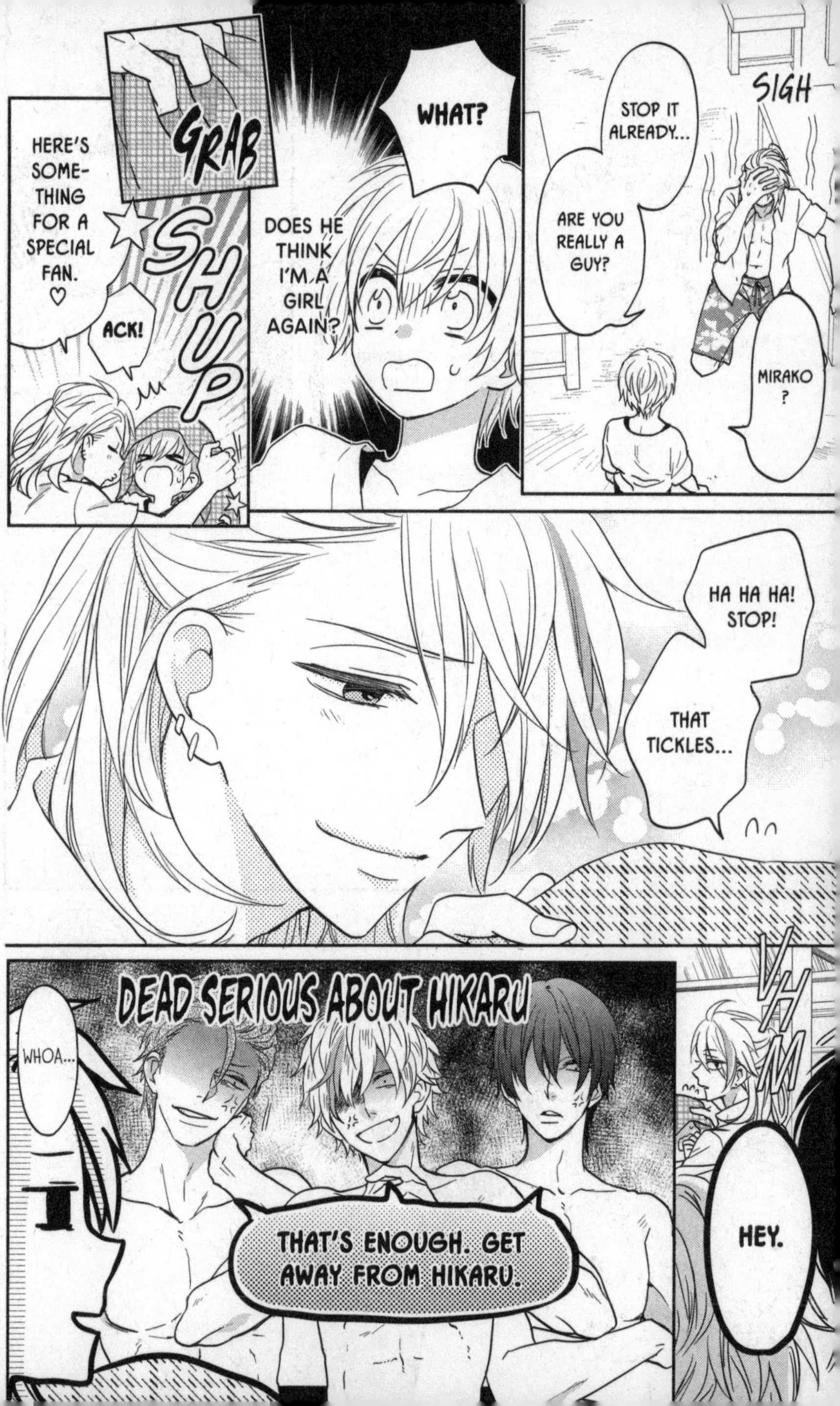

SIGH
STOP IT ALREADY...
ARE YOU REALLY A GUY?
MIRAKO ?
WHAT?
DOES HE THINK I'M A GIRL AGAIN?
GRAB
SHUP
HERE'S SOME-THING FOR A SPECIAL FAN. ♡
ACK!
HA HA HA! STOP!
THAT TICKLES...
VHM
HEY.
DEAD SERIOUS ABOUT HIKARU
WHOA...
THAT'S ENOUGH. GET AWAY FROM HIKARU.

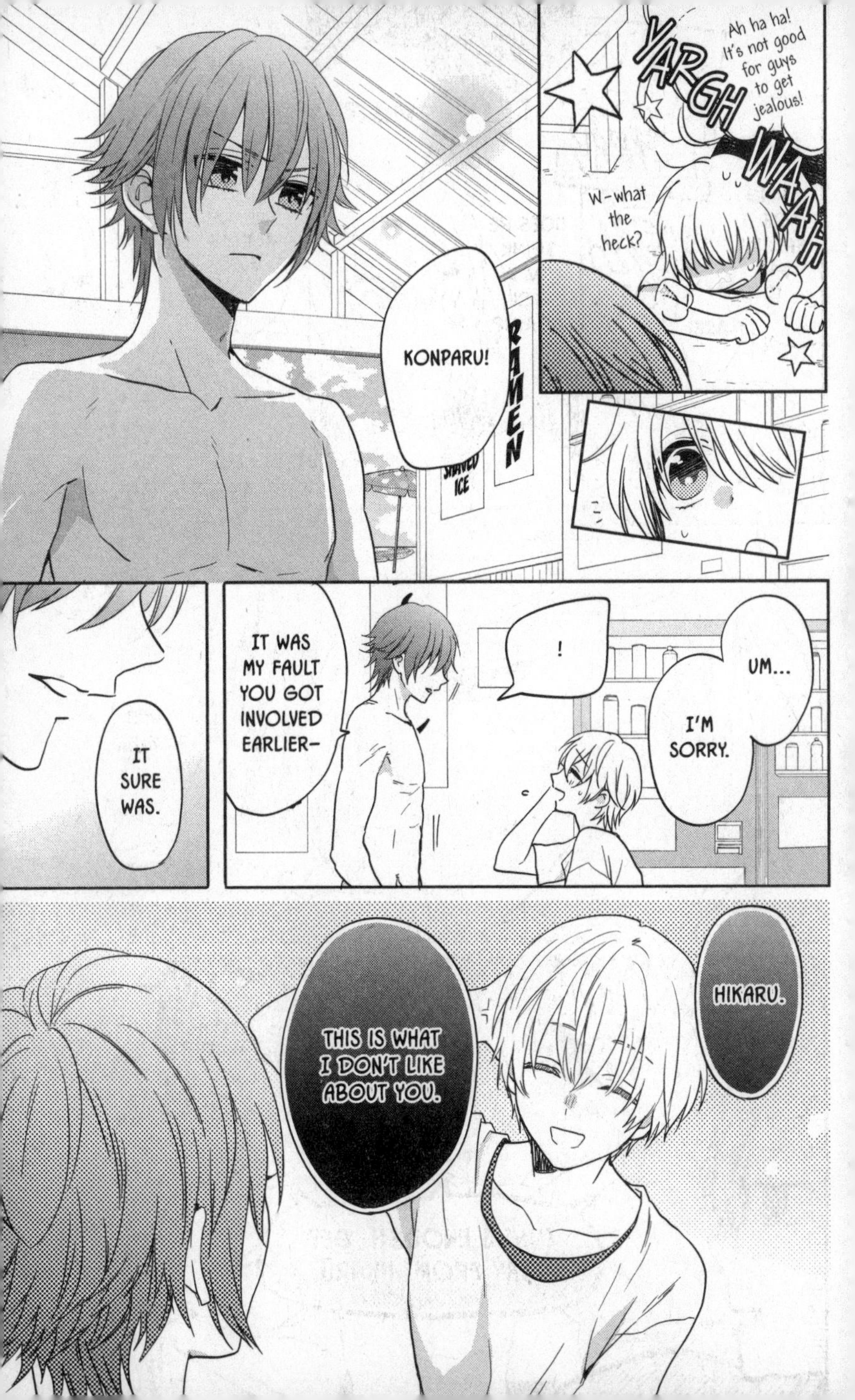
Ah ha ha! It's not good for guys to get jealous!
YARGH
WAAAH
W-what the heck?
KONPARU!
RAMEN
SHAVED ICE
UM... I'M SORRY.
!
IT WAS MY FAULT YOU GOT INVOLVED EARLIER–
IT SURE WAS.
HIKARU.
THIS IS WHAT I DON'T LIKE ABOUT YOU.

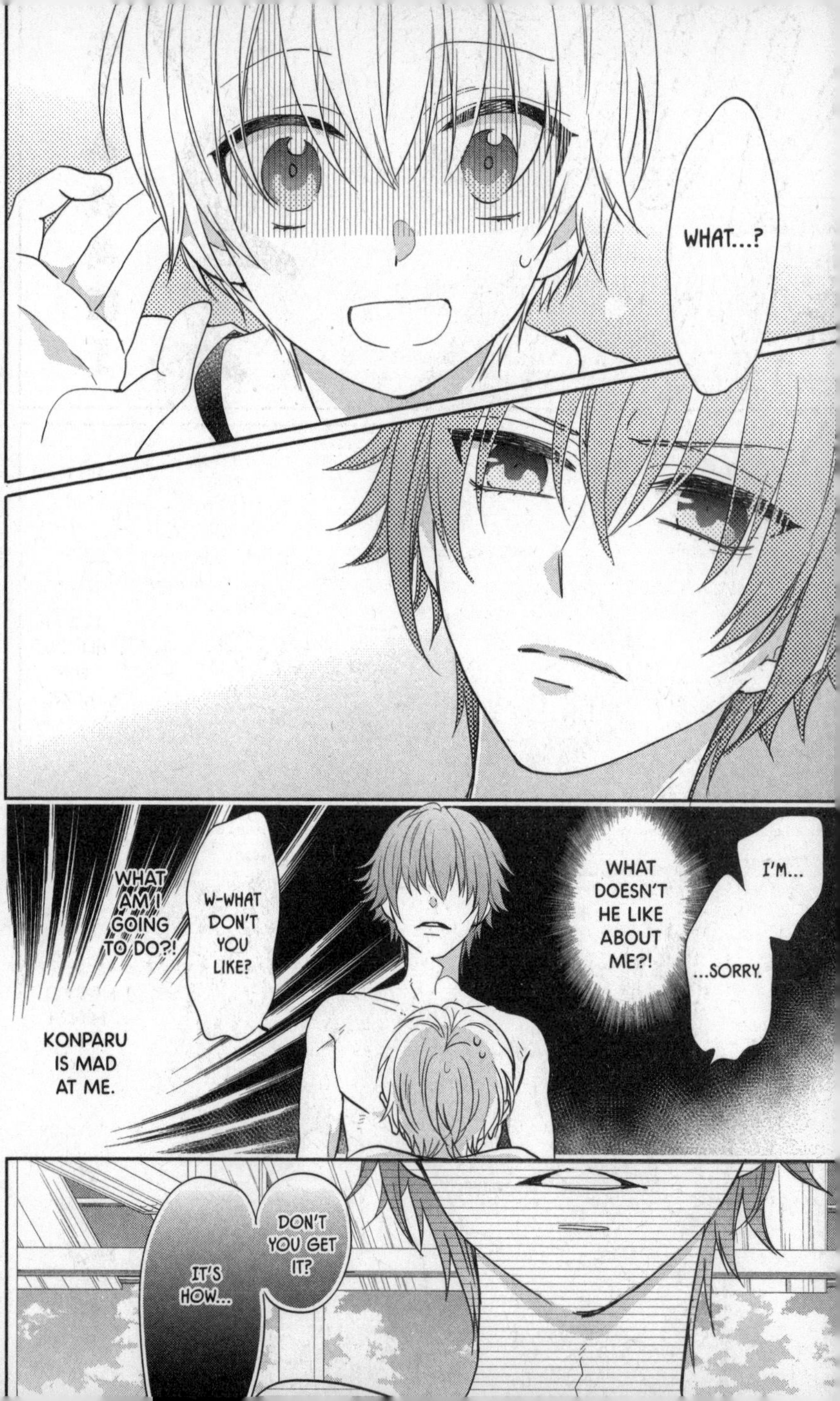
WHAT...?
I'M...
...SORRY.
WHAT DOESN'T HE LIKE ABOUT ME?!
W-WHAT DON'T YOU LIKE?
WHAT AM I GOING TO DO?!
KONPARU IS MAD AT ME.
DON'T YOU GET IT?
IT'S HOW...

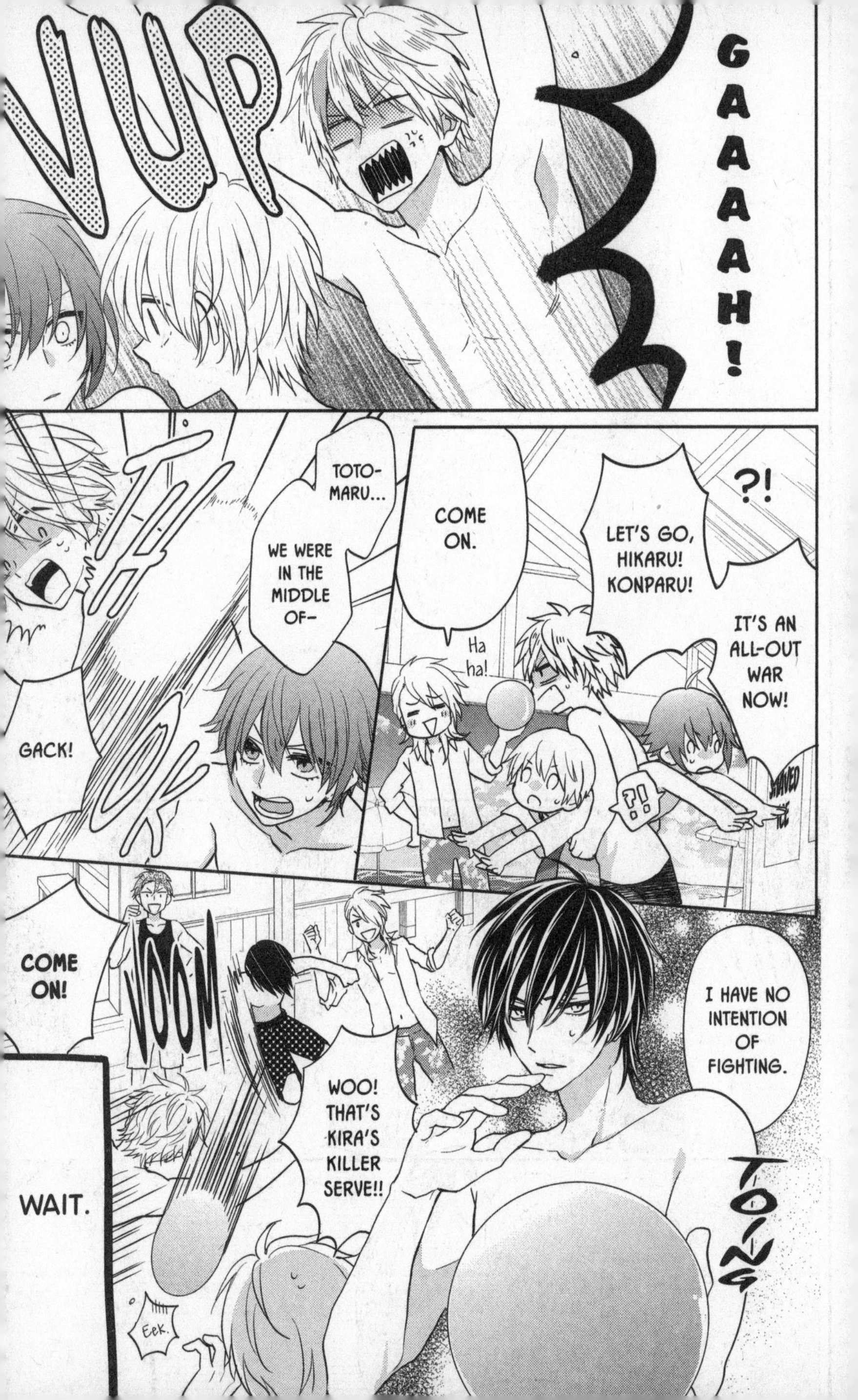
VUP
GAAAAH!
?!
LET'S GO, HIKARU! KONPARU!
IT'S AN ALL-OUT WAR NOW!
COME ON.
Ha ha!
?!!
TOTO-MARU...
WE WERE IN THE MIDDLE OF-
THUK
GACK!
I HAVE NO INTENTION OF FIGHTING.
TOING
WOO! THAT'S KIRA'S KILLER SERVE!!
VOOM
COME ON!
WAIT.
Eek.

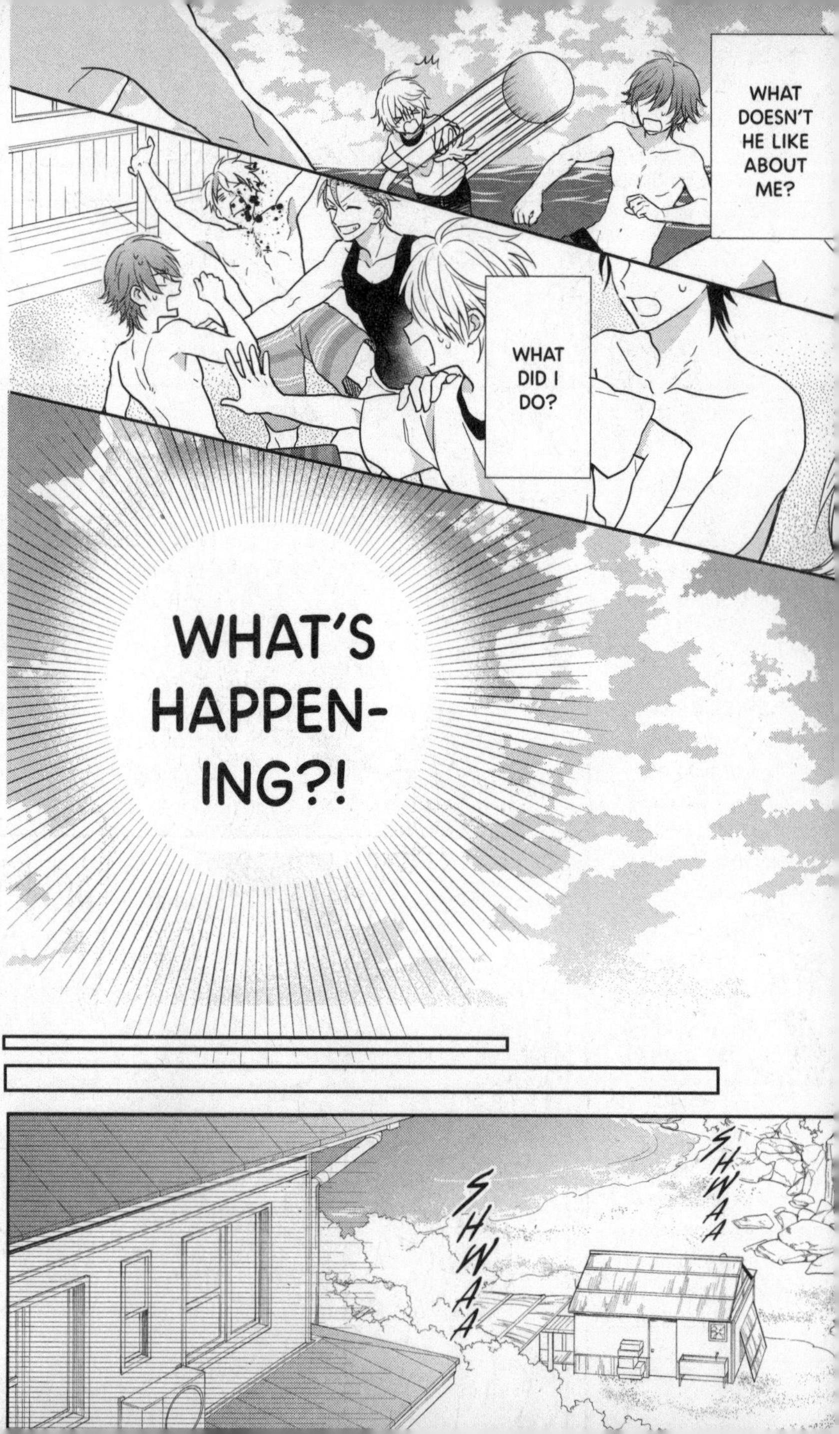
WHAT DOESN'T HE LIKE ABOUT ME?
WHAT DID I DO?
WHAT'S HAPPEN-ING?!
SHWAA
SHWAA

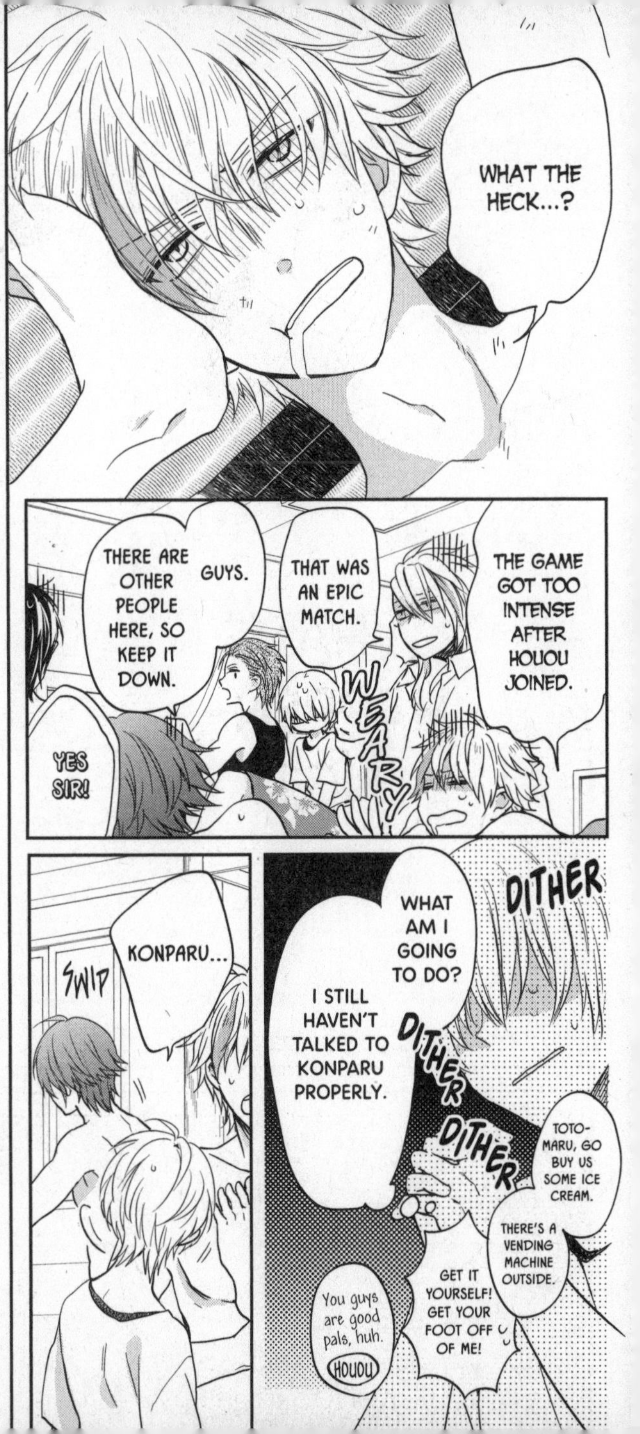
WHAT THE HECK...?
THE GAME GOT TOO INTENSE AFTER HOUOU JOINED.
WEARY
THAT WAS AN EPIC MATCH.
GUYS.
THERE ARE OTHER PEOPLE HERE, SO KEEP IT DOWN.
YES SIR!
DITHER
WHAT AM I GOING TO DO?
I STILL HAVEN'T TALKED TO KONPARU PROPERLY.
DITHER
DITHER
TOTO-MARU, GO BUY US SOME ICE CREAM.
THERE'S A VENDING MACHINE OUTSIDE.
GET IT YOURSELF! GET YOUR FOOT OFF OF ME!
You guys are good pals, huh.
HOUOU
KONPARU...
SWIP

In the radio show, the two call each other "Big Brother KENN" and "Shouta," so we wondered what Maeno would want to be called.

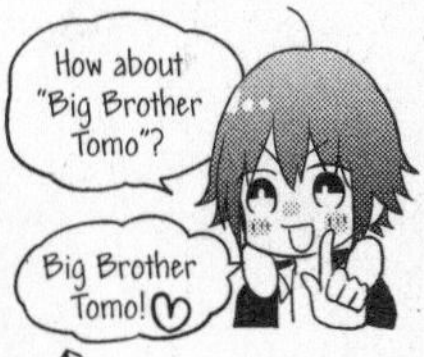
How about "Big Brother Tomo"?
Big Brother Tomo! ♡

You can see the heart symbol after the word!

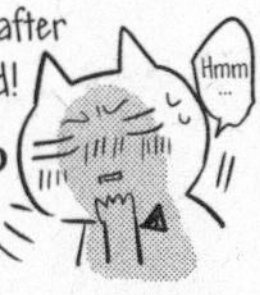
Hmm ...

Is it too cute?

"But we call KENN 'Big Brother,' so will this make him jealous?" asks Aoi, acting like a little devil...!!

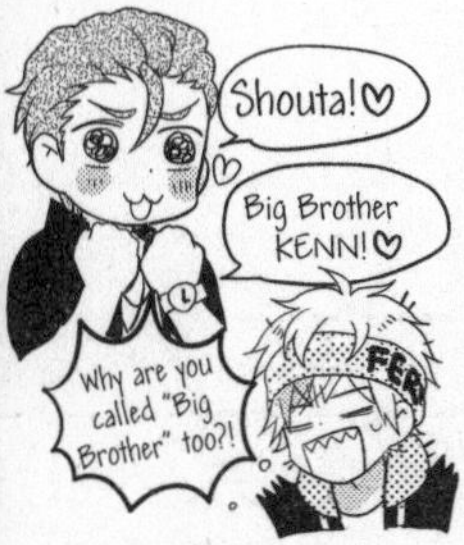
Shouta! ♡
Big Brother KENN! ♡
Why are you called "Big Brother" too?!
FER

KENN and Maeno are the same age, so it's more natural for them to refer to each other without titles.

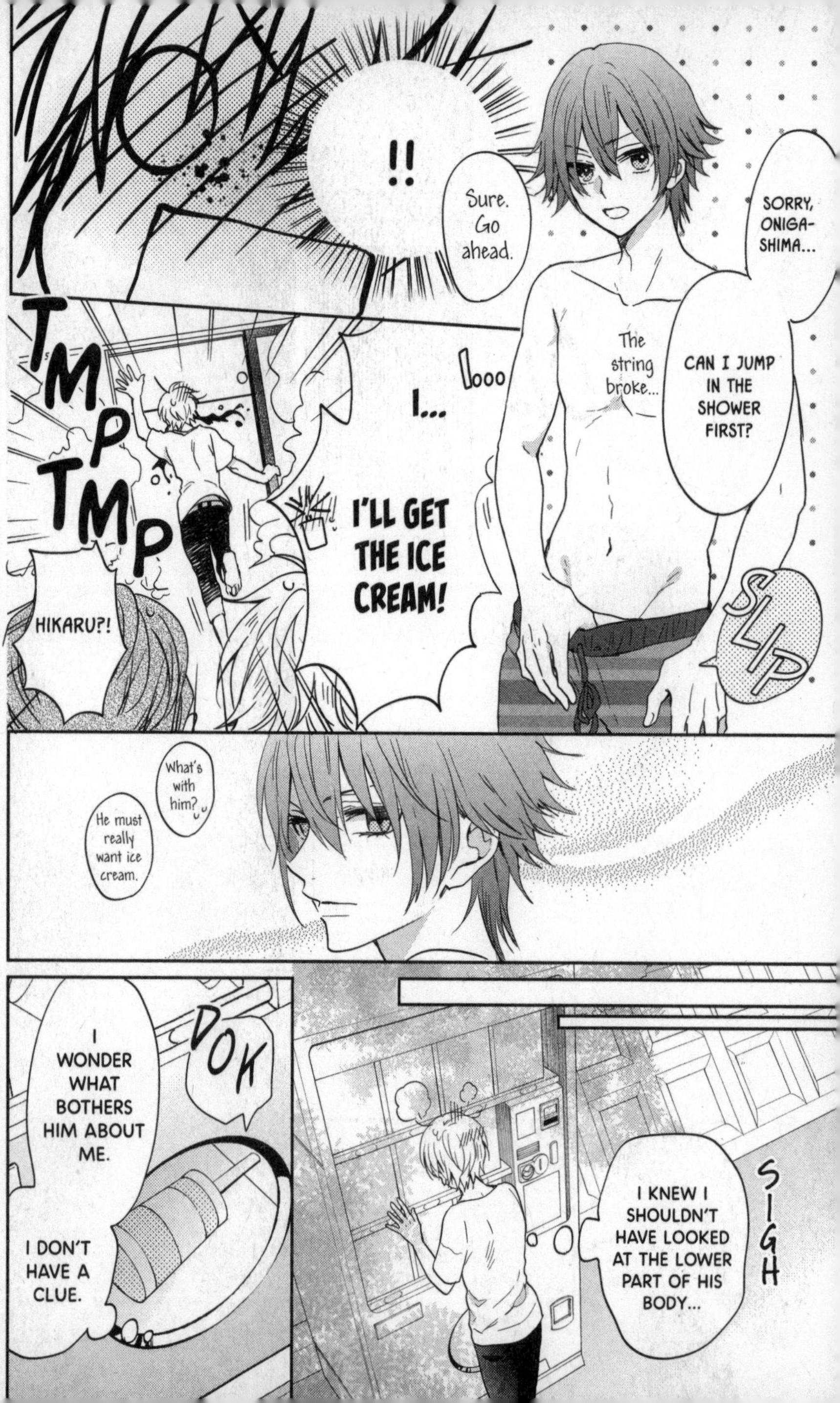
SORRY, ONIGA-SHIMA...
CAN I JUMP IN THE SHOWER FIRST?
Sure. Go ahead.
SLIP
The string broke...
!!
Iooo
I...
I'LL GET THE ICE CREAM!
TMP TMP
HIKARU?!
What's with him?
He must really want ice cream.
SIGH
I KNEW I SHOULDN'T HAVE LOOKED AT THE LOWER PART OF HIS BODY...
DOK
I WONDER WHAT BOTHERS HIM ABOUT ME.
I DON'T HAVE A CLUE.

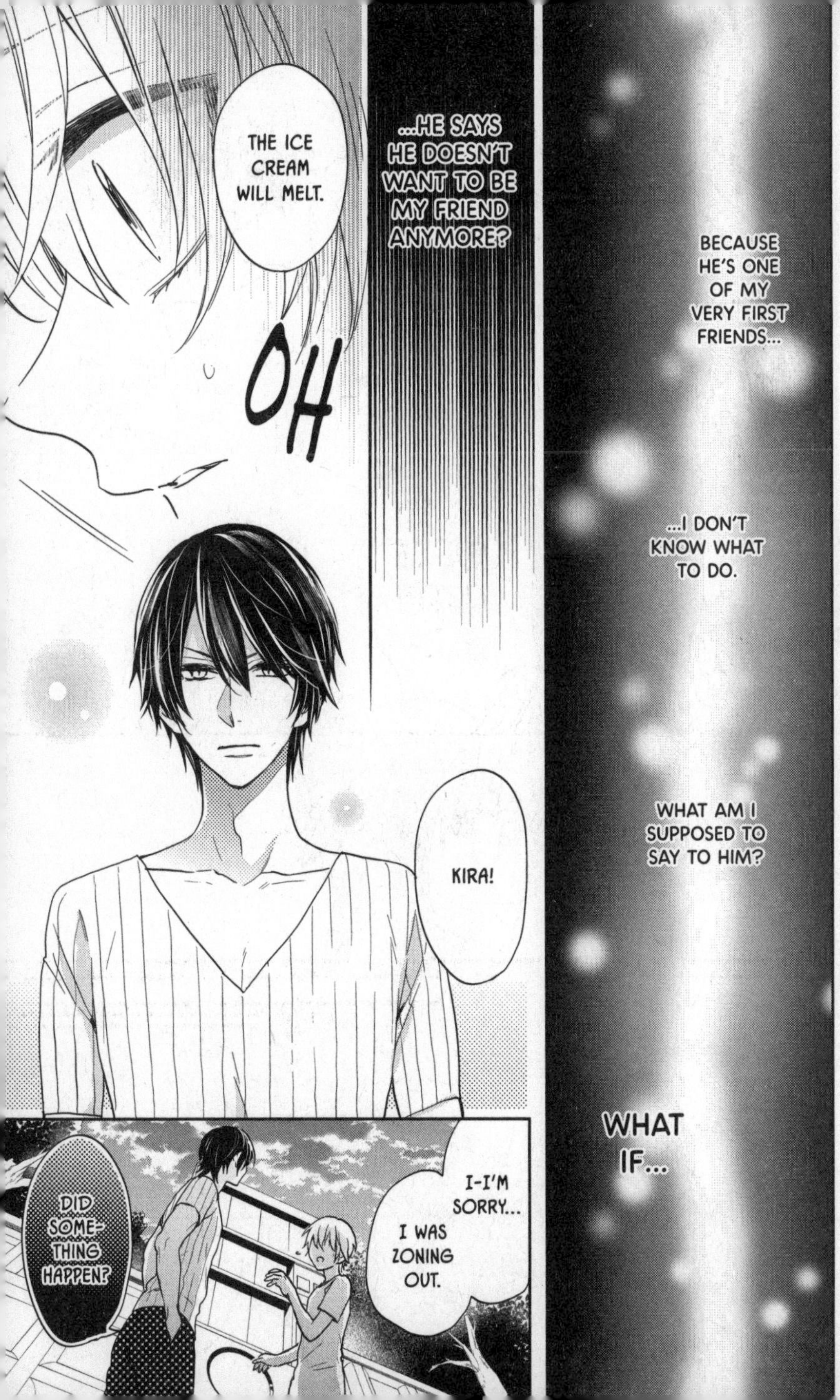
BECAUSE HE'S ONE OF MY VERY FIRST FRIENDS...
...I DON'T KNOW WHAT TO DO.
WHAT AM I SUPPOSED TO SAY TO HIM?
WHAT IF...
...HE SAYS HE DOESN'T WANT TO BE MY FRIEND ANYMORE?
THE ICE CREAM WILL MELT.
OH
KIRA!
I-I'M SORRY... I WAS ZONING OUT.
DID SOME-THING HAPPEN?

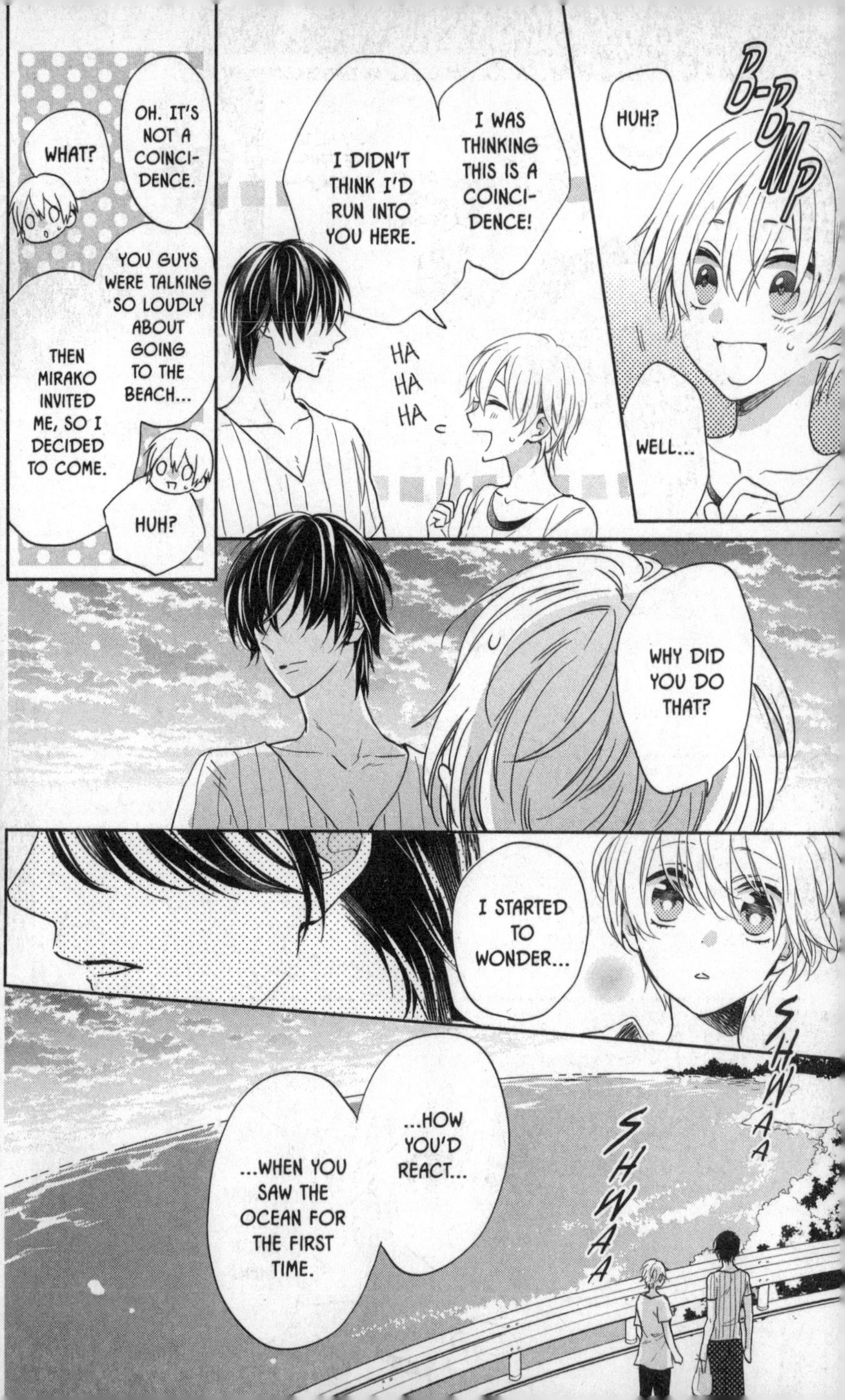
B-BMP
HUH?
WELL...
I WAS THINKING THIS IS A COINCIDENCE!
I DIDN'T THINK I'D RUN INTO YOU HERE.
HA HA HA
OH. IT'S NOT A COINCIDENCE.
WHAT?
YOU GUYS WERE TALKING SO LOUDLY ABOUT GOING TO THE BEACH...
THEN MIRAKO INVITED ME, SO I DECIDED TO COME.
HUH?
WHY DID YOU DO THAT?
I STARTED TO WONDER...
SHWAA
SHWAA
...HOW YOU'D REACT...
...WHEN YOU SAW THE OCEAN FOR THE FIRST TIME.

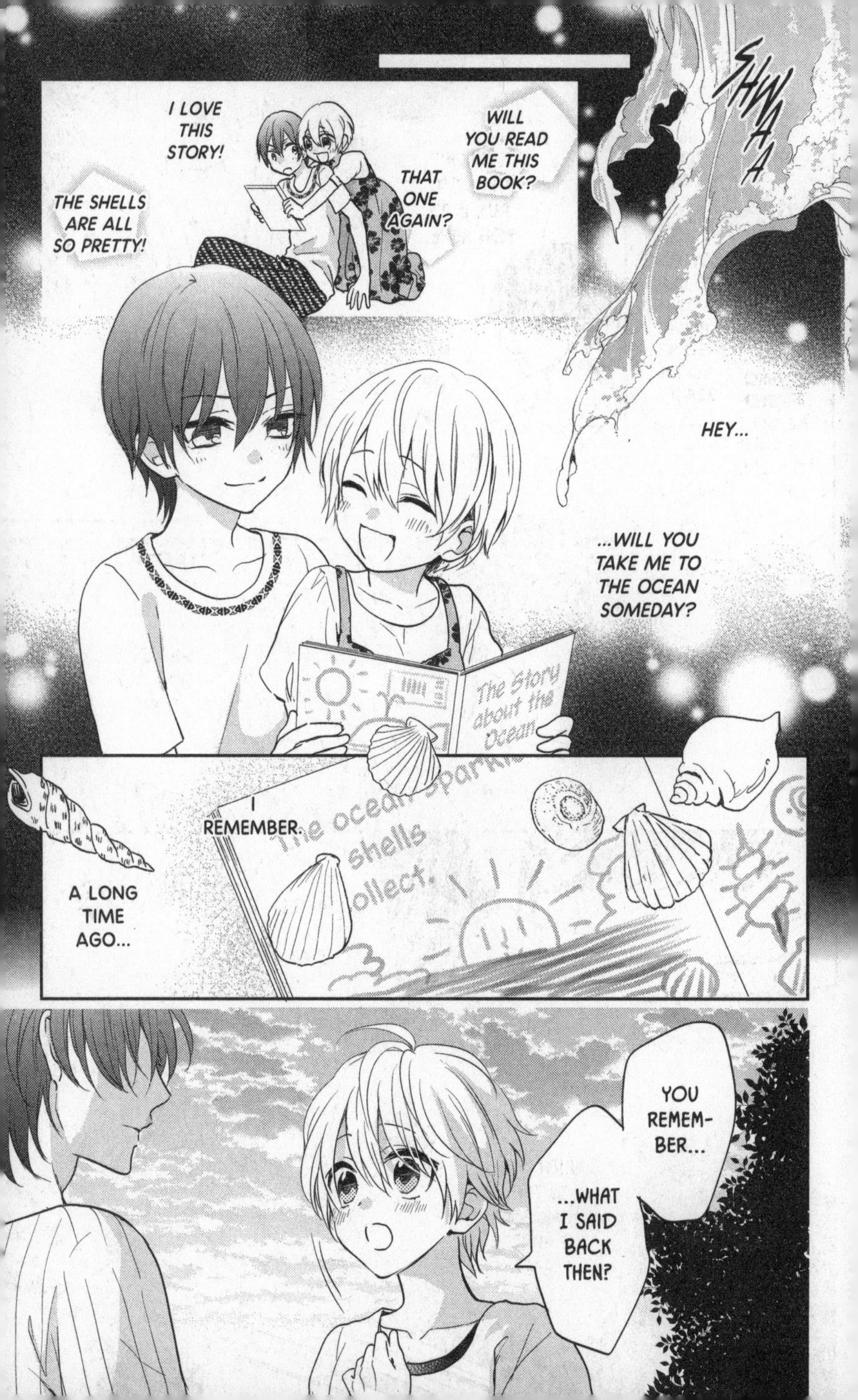
SHWAAA
WILL YOU READ ME THIS BOOK?
THAT ONE AGAIN?
I LOVE THIS STORY!
THE SHELLS ARE ALL SO PRETTY!
HEY...
...WILL YOU TAKE ME TO THE OCEAN SOMEDAY?
The Story about the Ocean
I REMEMBER.
A LONG TIME AGO...
YOU REMEMBER...
...WHAT I SAID BACK THEN?

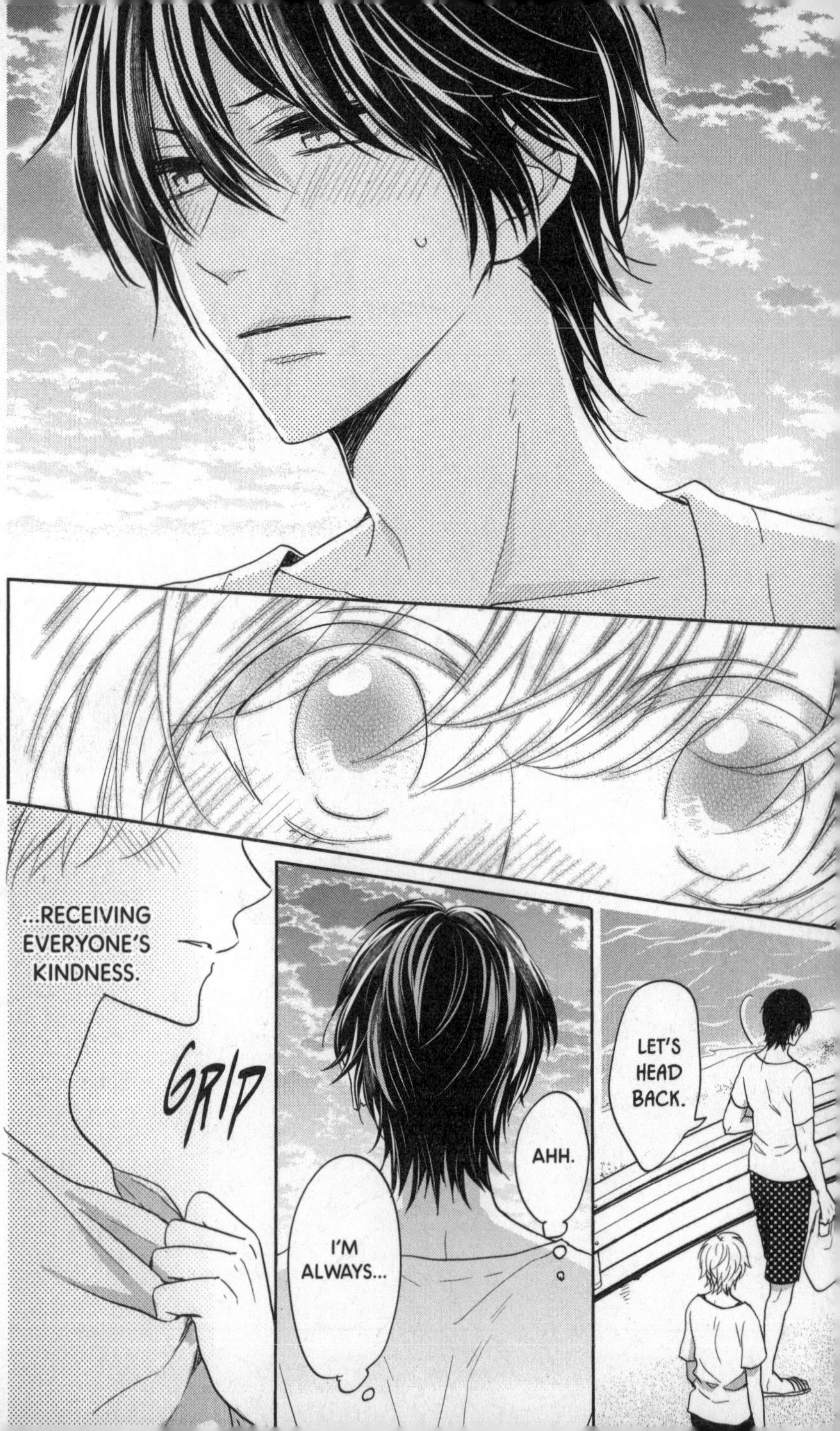
LET'S HEAD BACK.
AHH.
I'M ALWAYS...
...RECEIVING EVERYONE'S KINDNESS.
GRIP

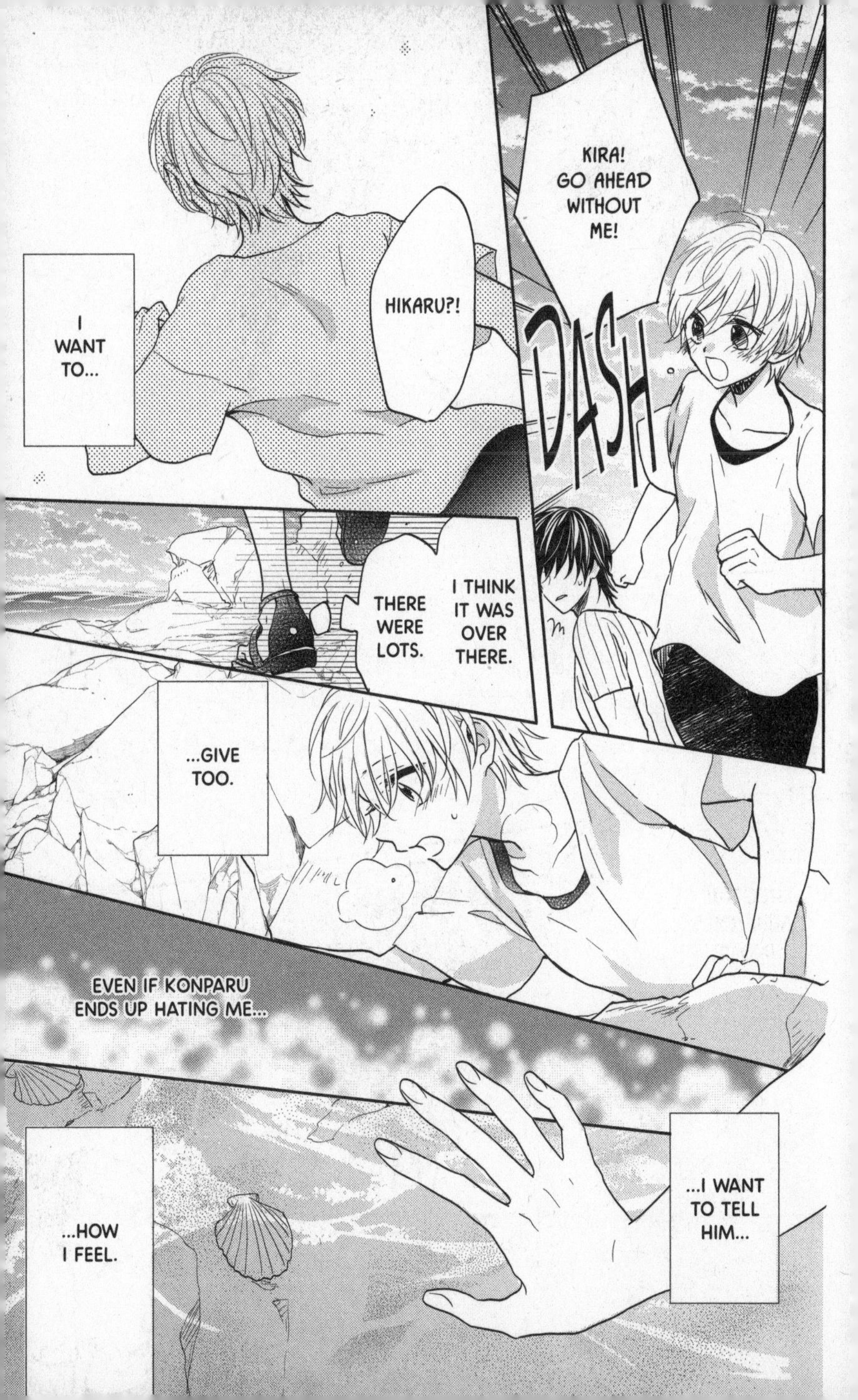
KIRA! GO AHEAD WITHOUT ME!
DASH
HIKARU?!
I WANT TO...
I THINK IT WAS OVER THERE.
THERE WERE LOTS.
...GIVE TOO.
EVEN IF KONPARU ENDS UP HATING ME...
...I WANT TO TELL HIM...
...HOW I FEEL.

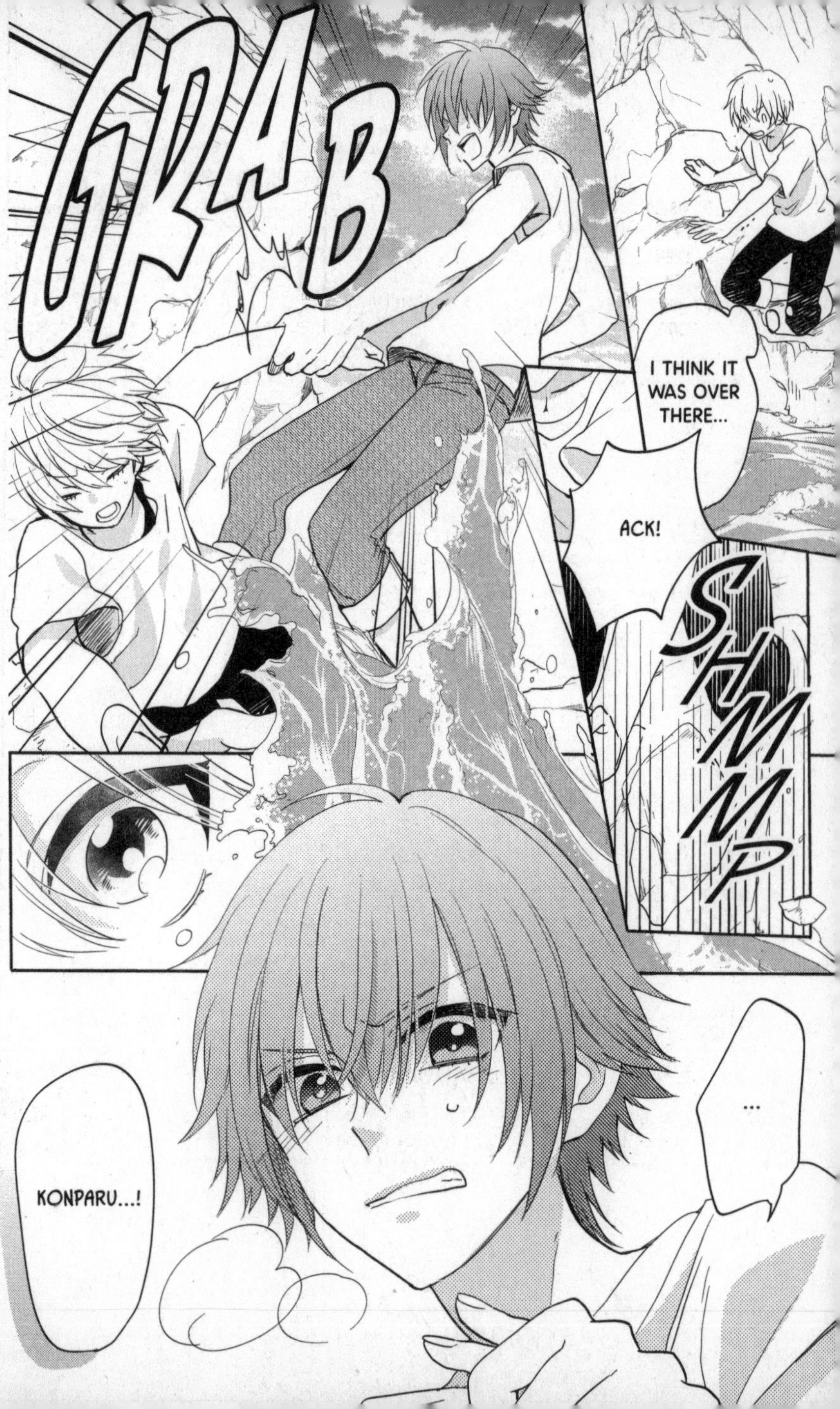
I THINK IT WAS OVER THERE...
ACK!
SHMMP
GRAB
...
KONPARU...!

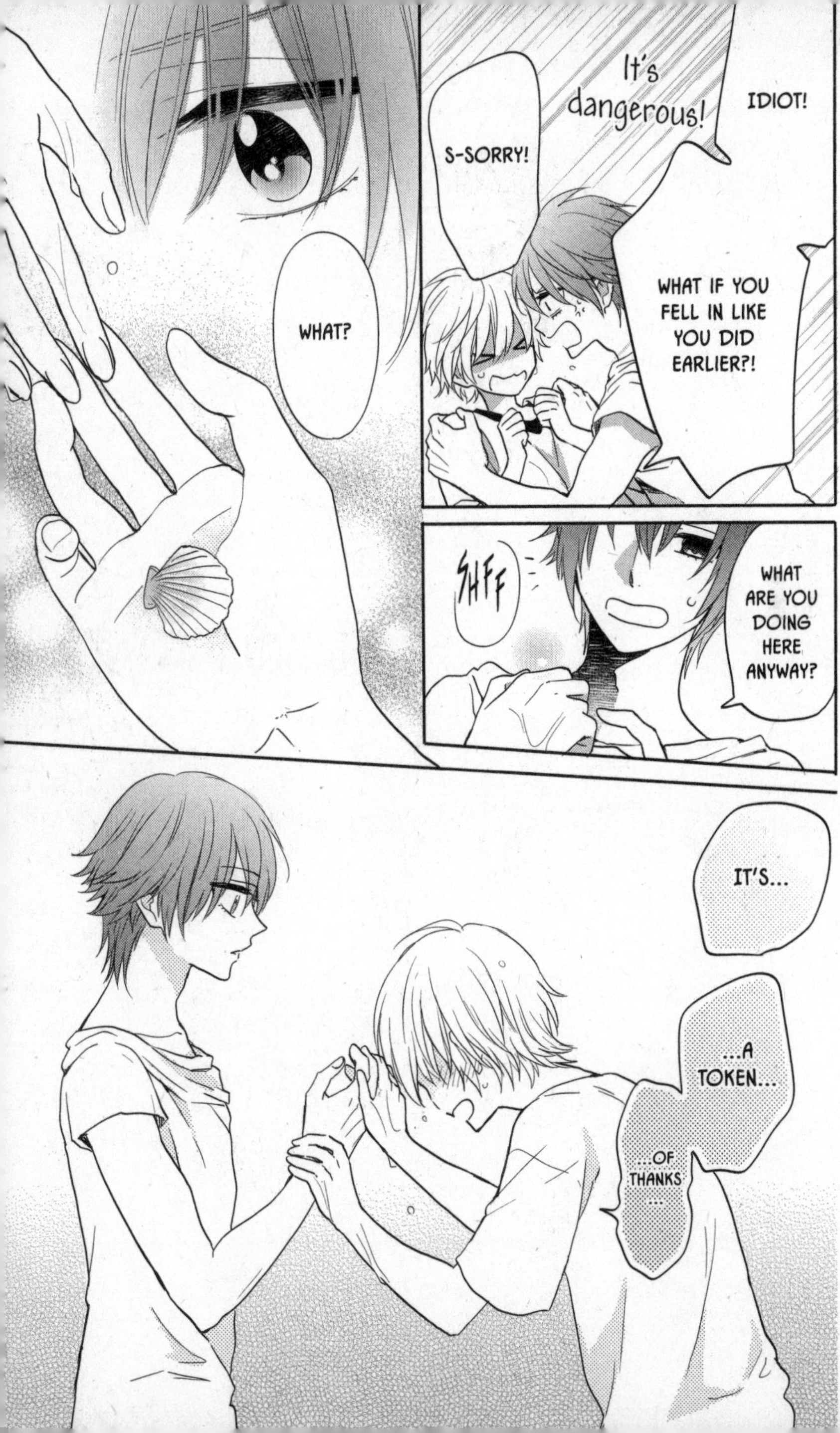
IDIOT!
It's dangerous!
WHAT IF YOU FELL IN LIKE YOU DID EARLIER?!
S-SORRY!
SHFF
WHAT ARE YOU DOING HERE ANYWAY?
WHAT?
IT'S...
...A TOKEN...
...OF THANKS...

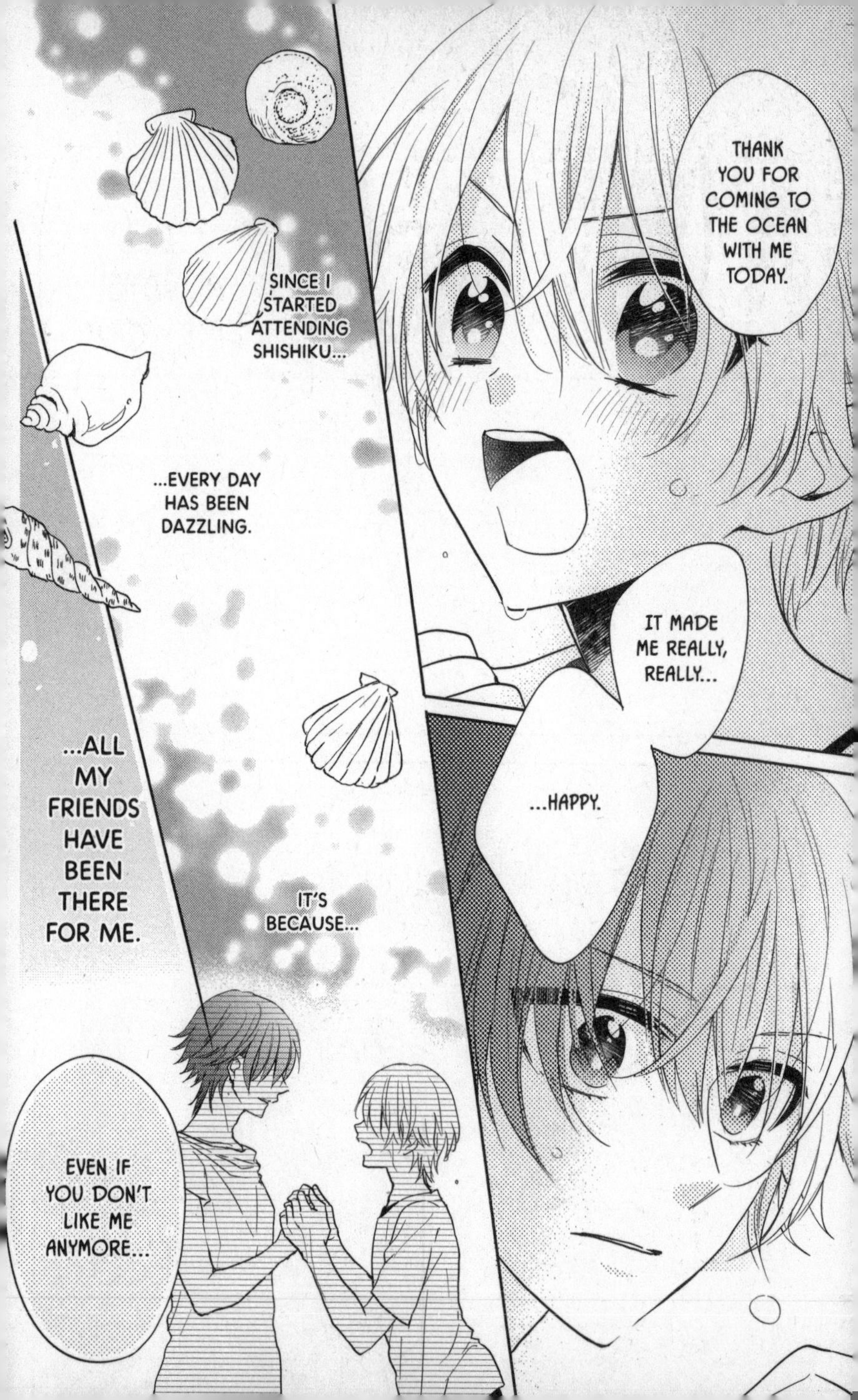
THANK YOU FOR COMING TO THE OCEAN WITH ME TODAY.
IT MADE ME REALLY, REALLY...
...HAPPY.
SINCE I STARTED ATTENDING SHISHIKU...
...EVERY DAY HAS BEEN DAZZLING.
IT'S BECAUSE...
...ALL MY FRIENDS HAVE BEEN THERE FOR ME.
EVEN IF YOU DON'T LIKE ME ANYMORE...

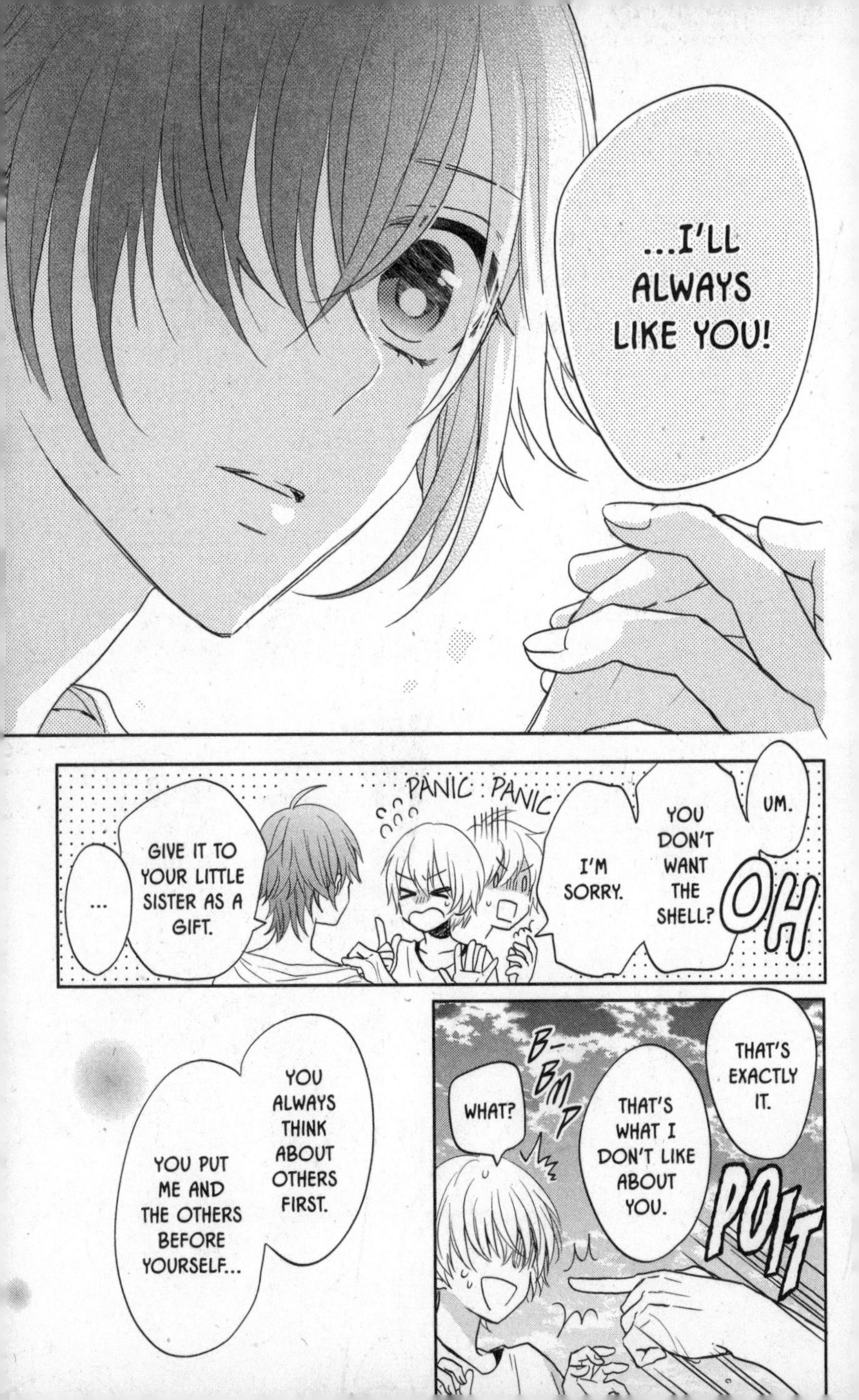
...I'LL ALWAYS LIKE YOU!
UM.
OH
YOU DON'T WANT THE SHELL?
I'M SORRY.
PANIC PANIC
GIVE IT TO YOUR LITTLE SISTER AS A GIFT.
...
THAT'S EXACTLY IT.
POIT
THAT'S WHAT I DON'T LIKE ABOUT YOU.
B-BMP
WHAT?
YOU ALWAYS THINK ABOUT OTHERS FIRST.
YOU PUT ME AND THE OTHERS BEFORE YOURSELF...

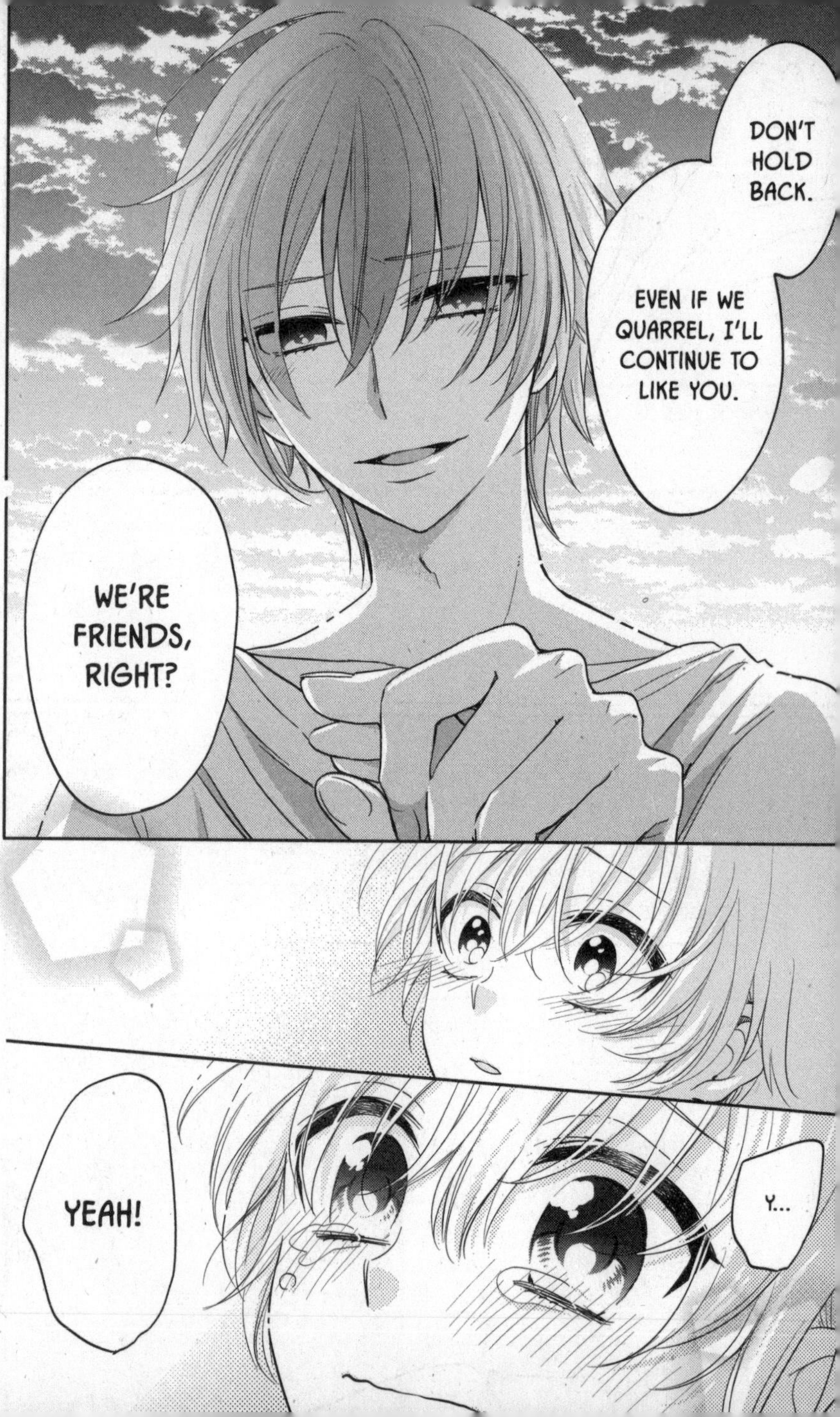
DON'T HOLD BACK.
EVEN IF WE QUARREL, I'LL CONTINUE TO LIKE YOU.
WE'RE FRIENDS, RIGHT?
Y...
YEAH!

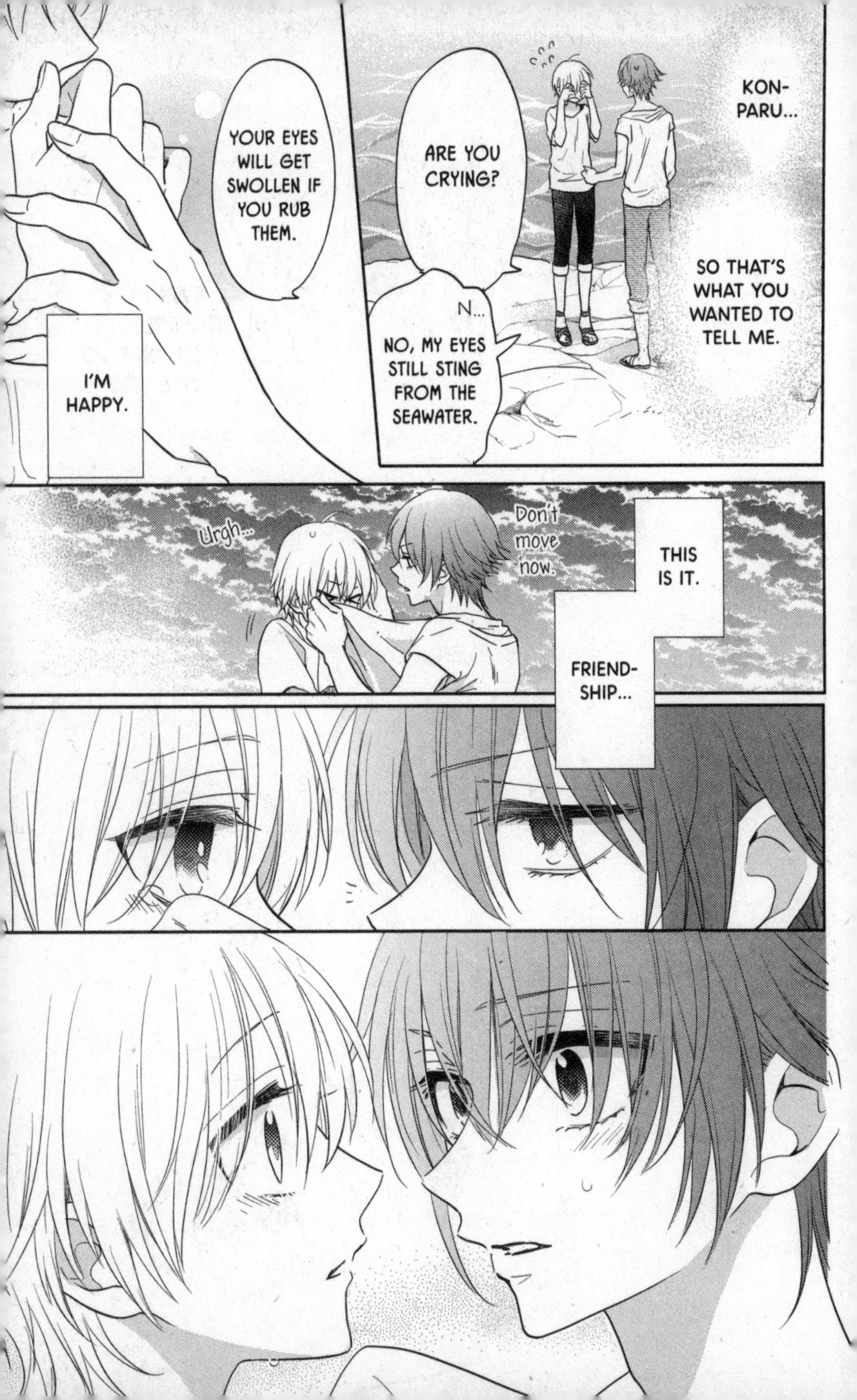
KON-PARU...
SO THAT'S WHAT YOU WANTED TO TELL ME.
ARE YOU CRYING?
N...
NO, MY EYES STILL STING FROM THE SEAWATER.
YOUR EYES WILL GET SWOLLEN IF YOU RUB THEM.
I'M HAPPY.
THIS IS IT.
Don't move now.
Urgh...
FRIENDSHIP...

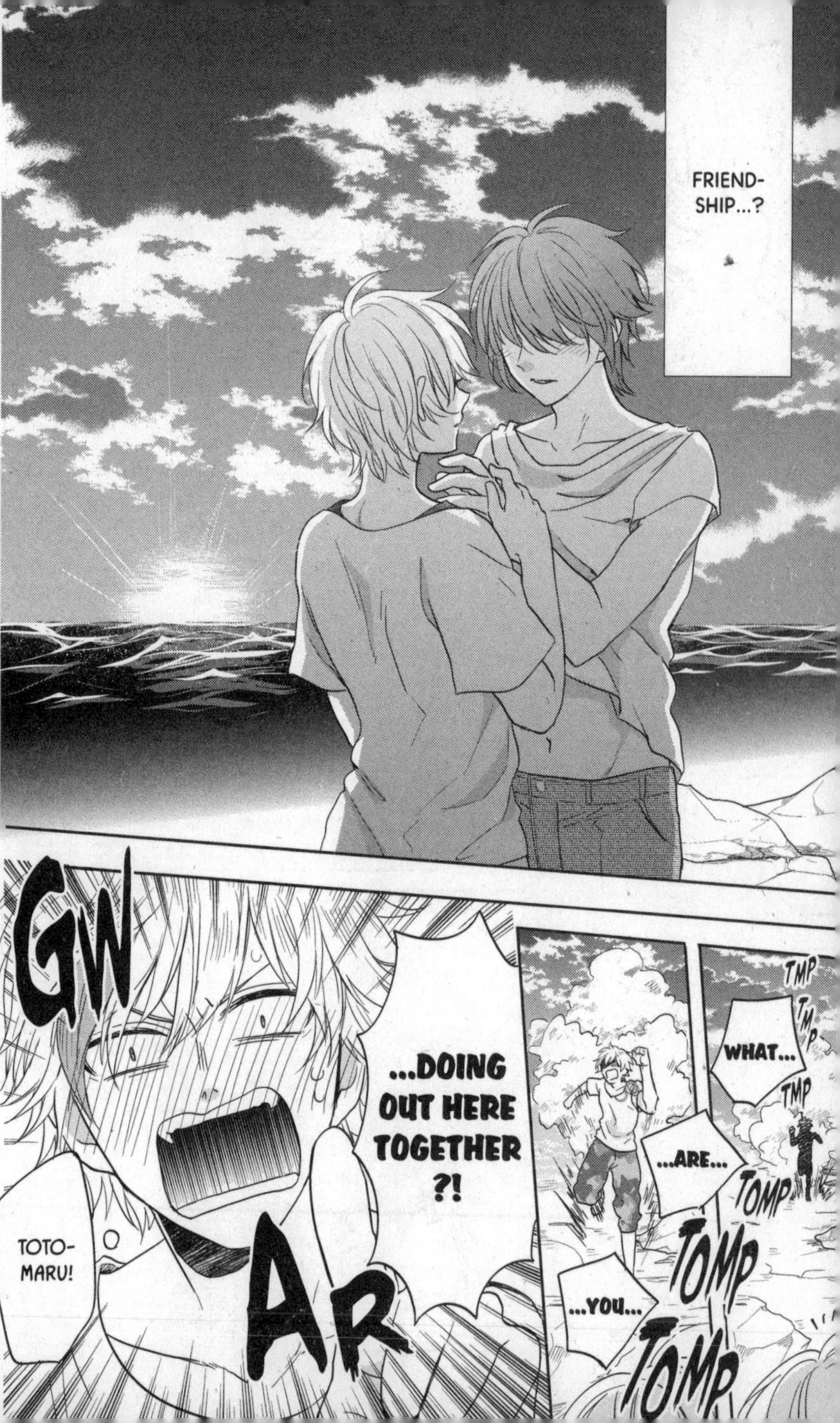
FRIEND-SHIP...?
TMP
TMP
WHAT...
TMP
TOMP
...ARE...
...YOU...
TOMP
TOMP
GW
AR
...DOING OUT HERE TOGETHER?!
TOTO-MARU!

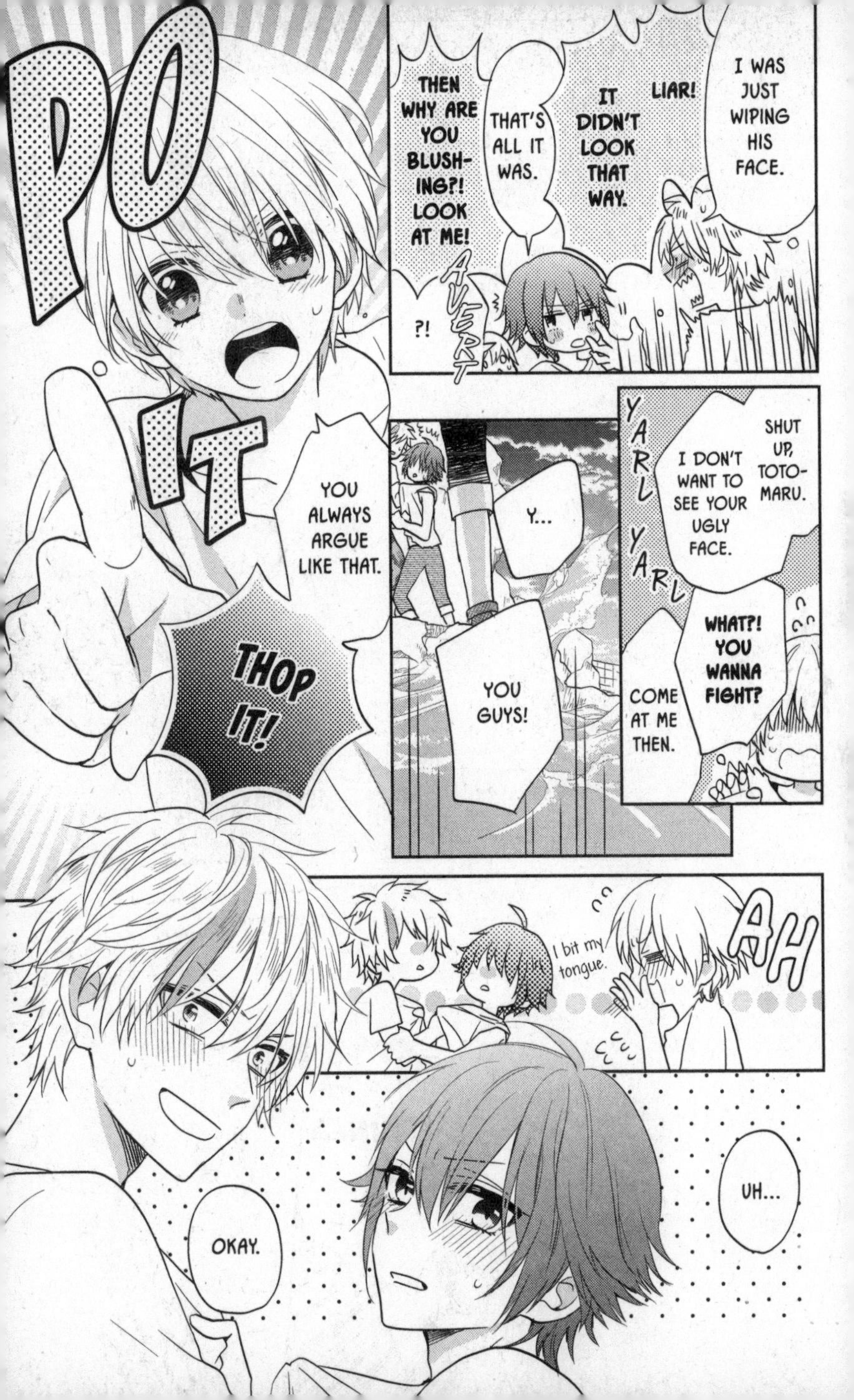
I WAS JUST WIPING HIS FACE.
LIAR!
IT DIDN'T LOOK THAT WAY.
THAT'S ALL IT WAS.
THEN WHY ARE YOU BLUSH-ING?! LOOK AT ME!
AVERT
?!
SHUT UP, TOTO-MARU.
I DON'T WANT TO SEE YOUR UGLY FACE.
YARL YARL
WHAT?! YOU WANNA FIGHT?
COME AT ME THEN.
Y...
YOU GUYS!
PO IT
YOU ALWAYS ARGUE LIKE THAT.
THOP IT!
AH
I bit my tongue.
UH...
OKAY.

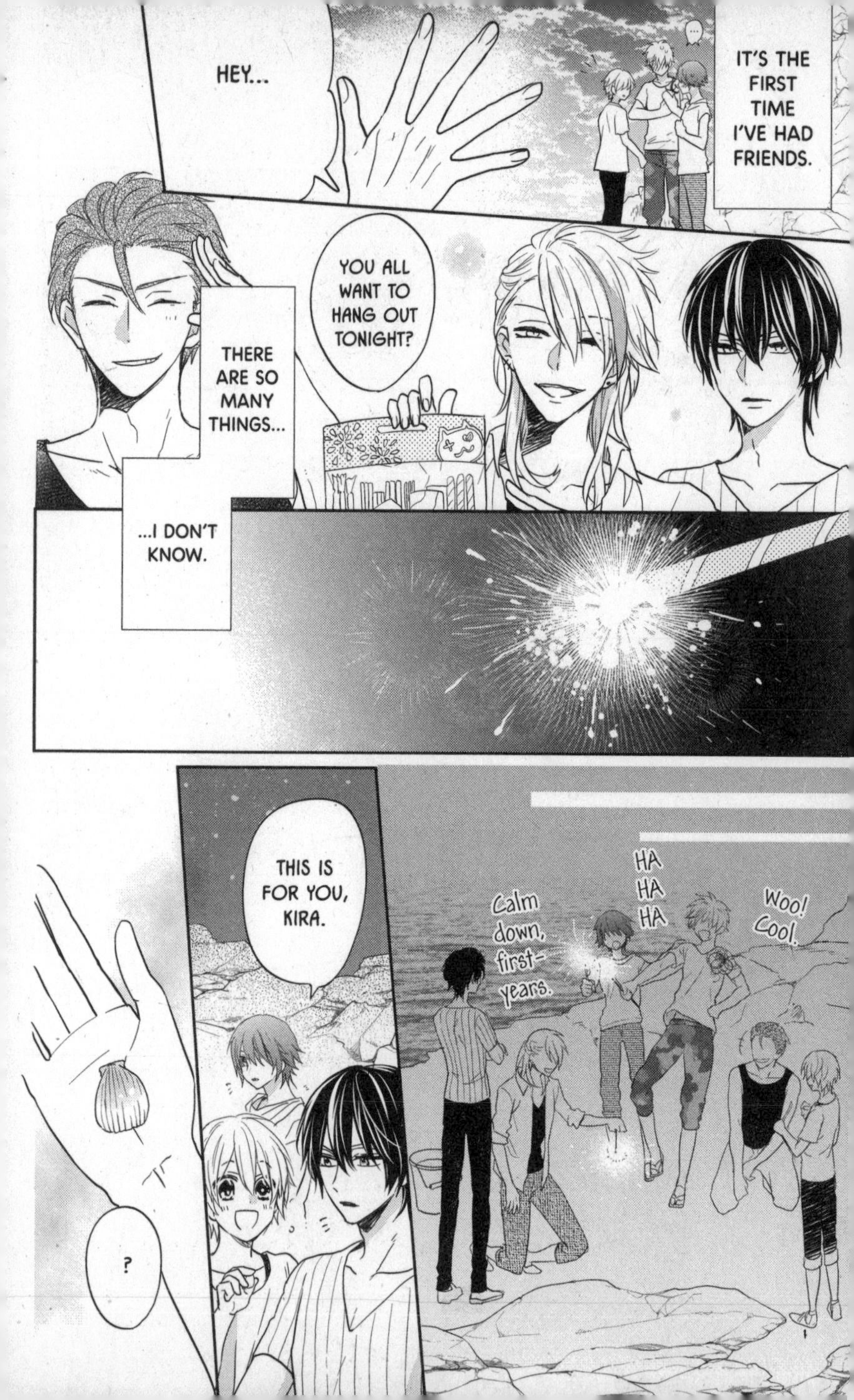
IT'S THE FIRST TIME I'VE HAD FRIENDS.
...
HEY...
YOU ALL WANT TO HANG OUT TONIGHT?
THERE ARE SO MANY THINGS...
...I DON'T KNOW.
Woo! Cool.
HA HA HA
Calm down, first-years.
THIS IS FOR YOU, KIRA.
?

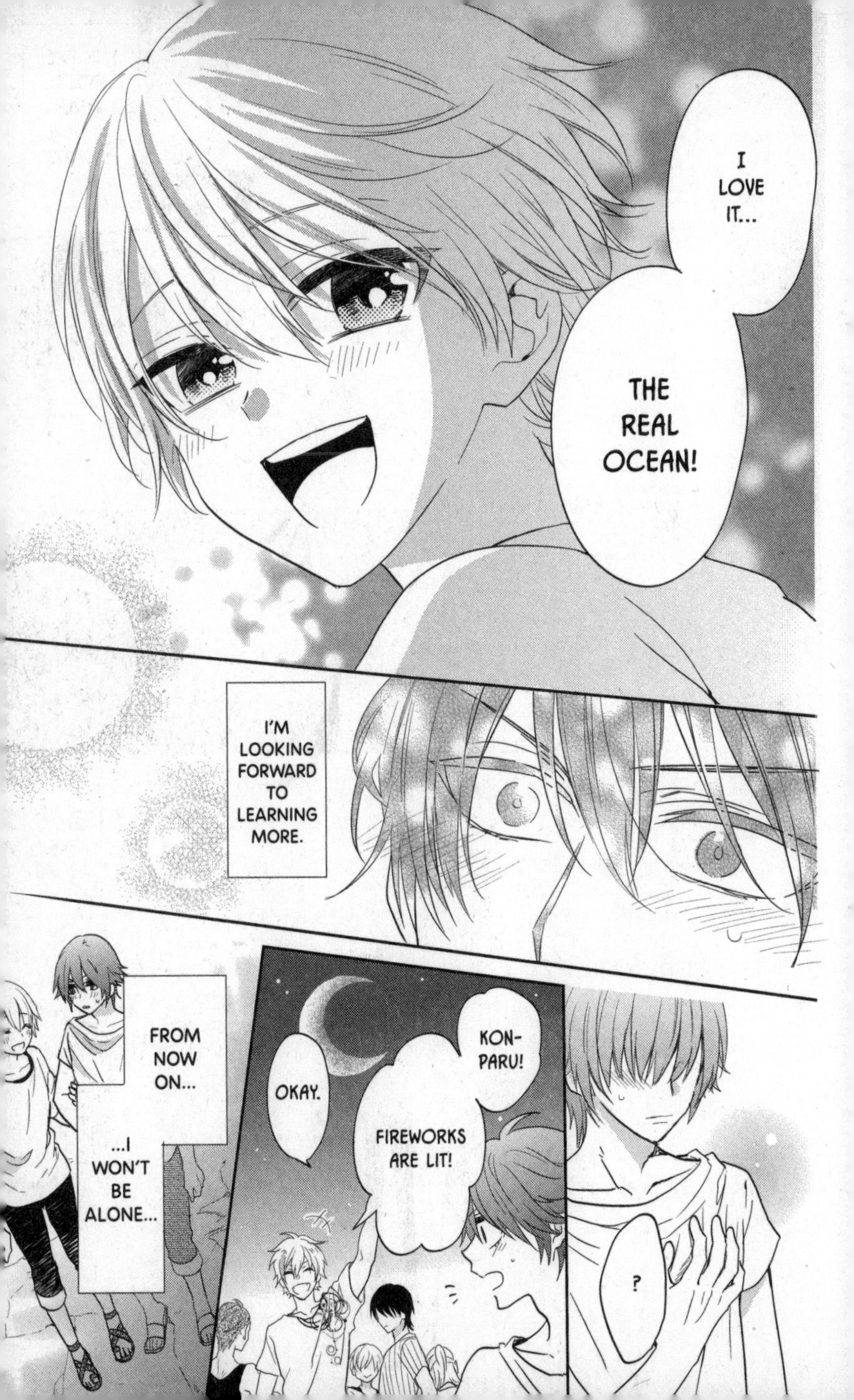
I LOVE IT...
THE REAL OCEAN!
I'M LOOKING FORWARD TO LEARNING MORE.
?
KON-PARU!
FIREWORKS ARE LIT!
OKAY.
FROM NOW ON...
...I WON'T BE ALONE...

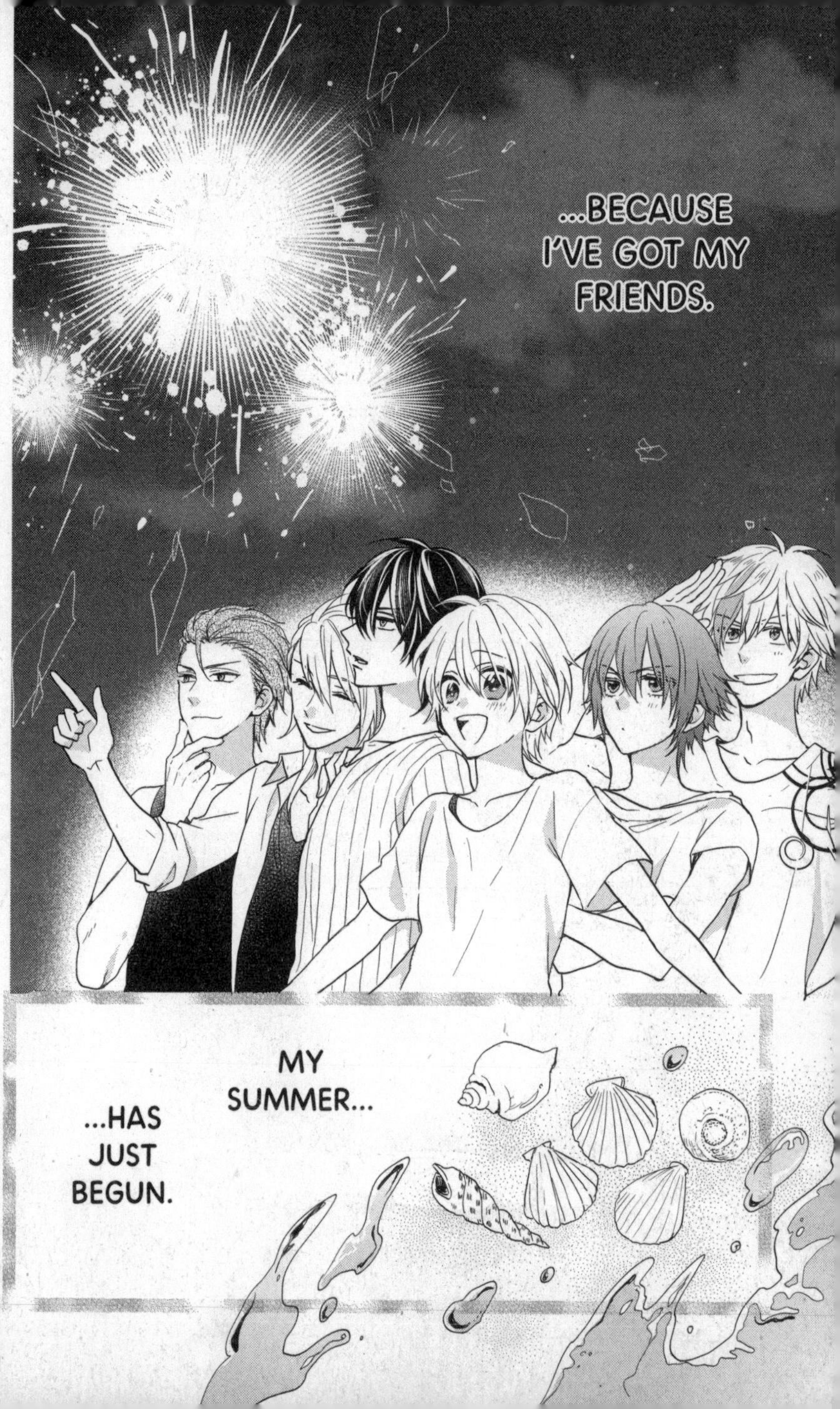
...BECAUSE I'VE GOT MY FRIENDS.
MY SUMMER...
...HAS JUST BEGUN.

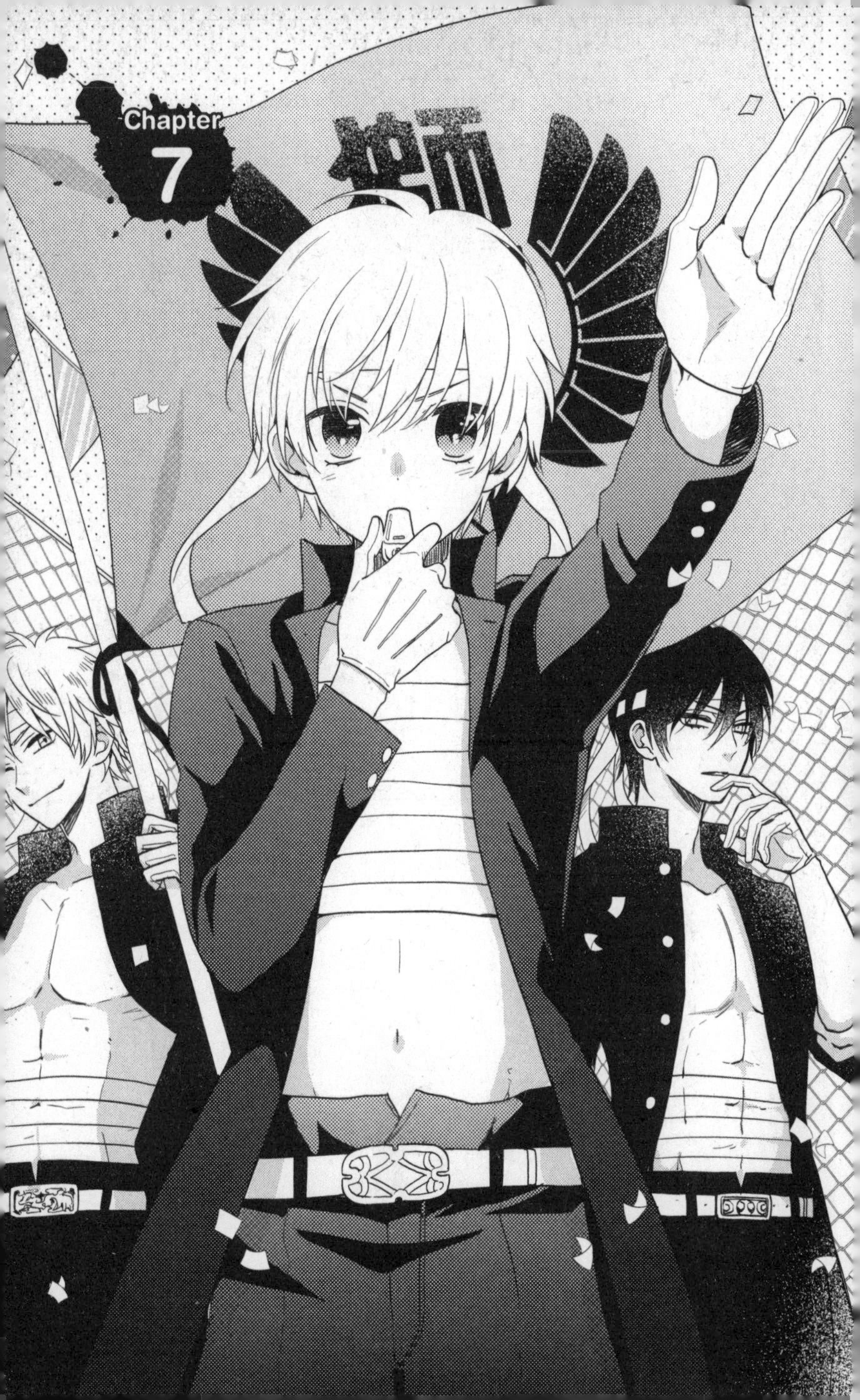
Chapter
7

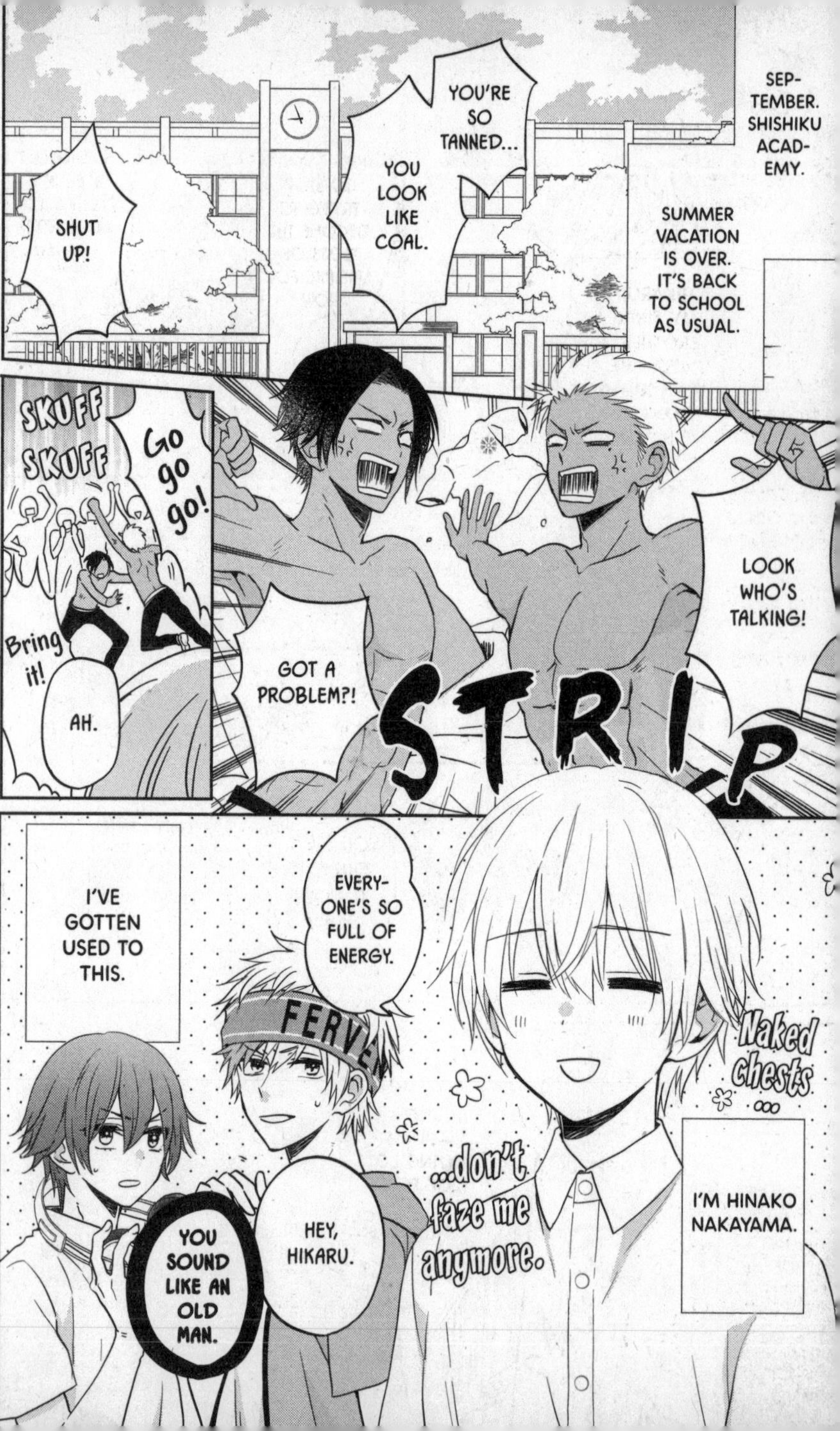
SEPTEMBER. SHISHIKU ACADEMY.
SUMMER VACATION IS OVER. IT'S BACK TO SCHOOL AS USUAL.
YOU'RE SO TANNED...
YOU LOOK LIKE COAL.
SHUT UP!
LOOK WHO'S TALKING!
STRIP
GOT A PROBLEM?!
Go go go!
SKUFF SKUFF
Bring it!
AH.
Naked chests...
...don't faze me anymore.
I'M HINAKO NAKAYAMA.
EVERYONE'S SO FULL OF ENERGY.
I'VE GOTTEN USED TO THIS.
HEY, HIKARU.
YOU SOUND LIKE AN OLD MAN.

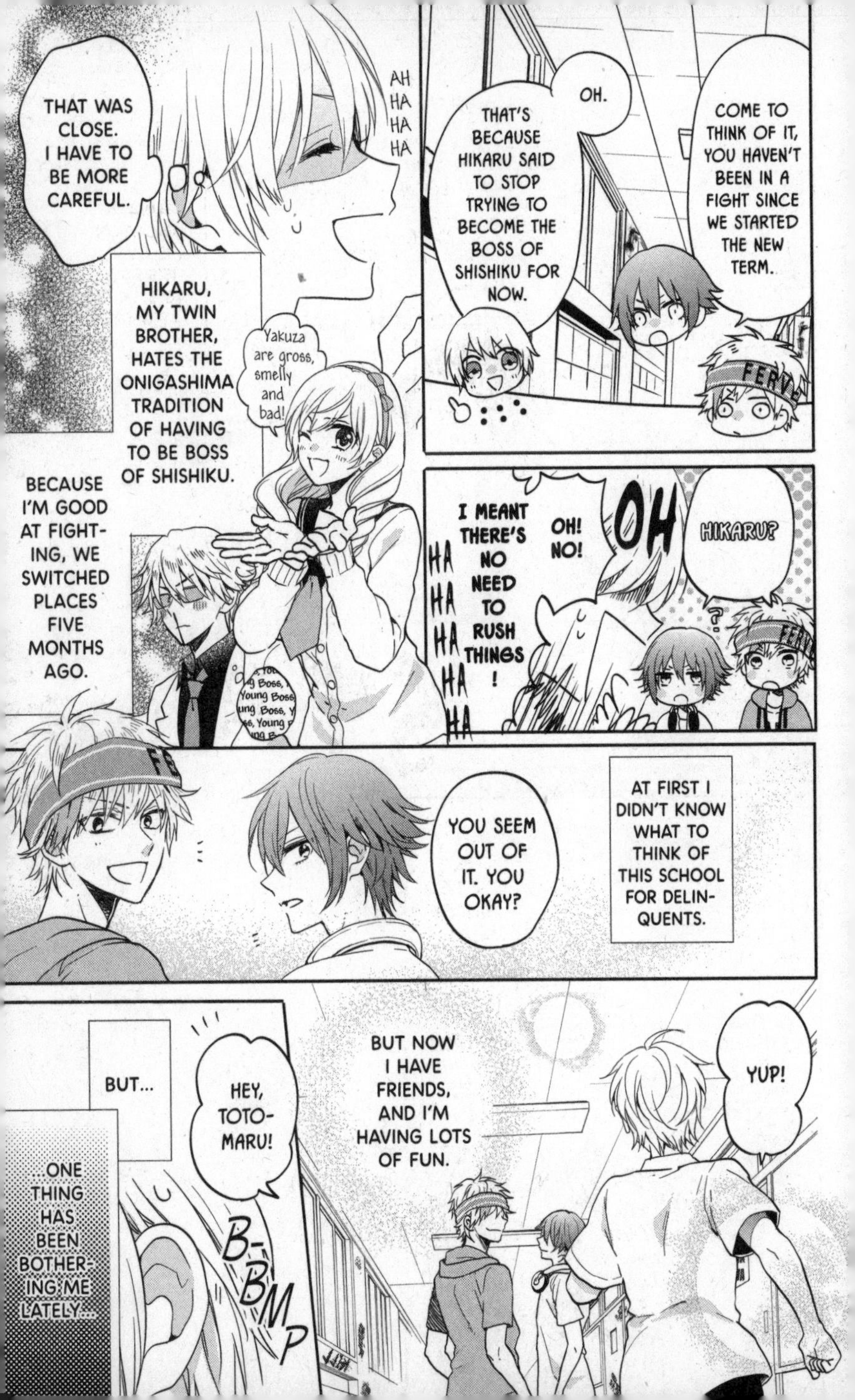

COME TO THINK OF IT, YOU HAVEN'T BEEN IN A FIGHT SINCE WE STARTED THE NEW TERM.
OH.
THAT'S BECAUSE HIKARU SAID TO STOP TRYING TO BECOME THE BOSS OF SHISHIKU FOR NOW.
HIKARU?
OH
OH! NO!
I MEANT THERE'S NO NEED TO RUSH THINGS!
HA HA HA HA HA HA
AH HA HA HA
THAT WAS CLOSE. I HAVE TO BE MORE CAREFUL.
HIKARU, MY TWIN BROTHER, HATES THE ONIGASHIMA TRADITION OF HAVING TO BE BOSS OF SHISHIKU.
Yakuza are gross, smelly and bad!
BECAUSE I'M GOOD AT FIGHTING, WE SWITCHED PLACES FIVE MONTHS AGO.
AT FIRST I DIDN'T KNOW WHAT TO THINK OF THIS SCHOOL FOR DELINQUENTS.
YOU SEEM OUT OF IT. YOU OKAY?
YUP!
BUT NOW I HAVE FRIENDS, AND I'M HAVING LOTS OF FUN.
HEY, TOTOMARU!
BUT...
...ONE THING HAS BEEN BOTHERING ME LATELY...
B-BMP

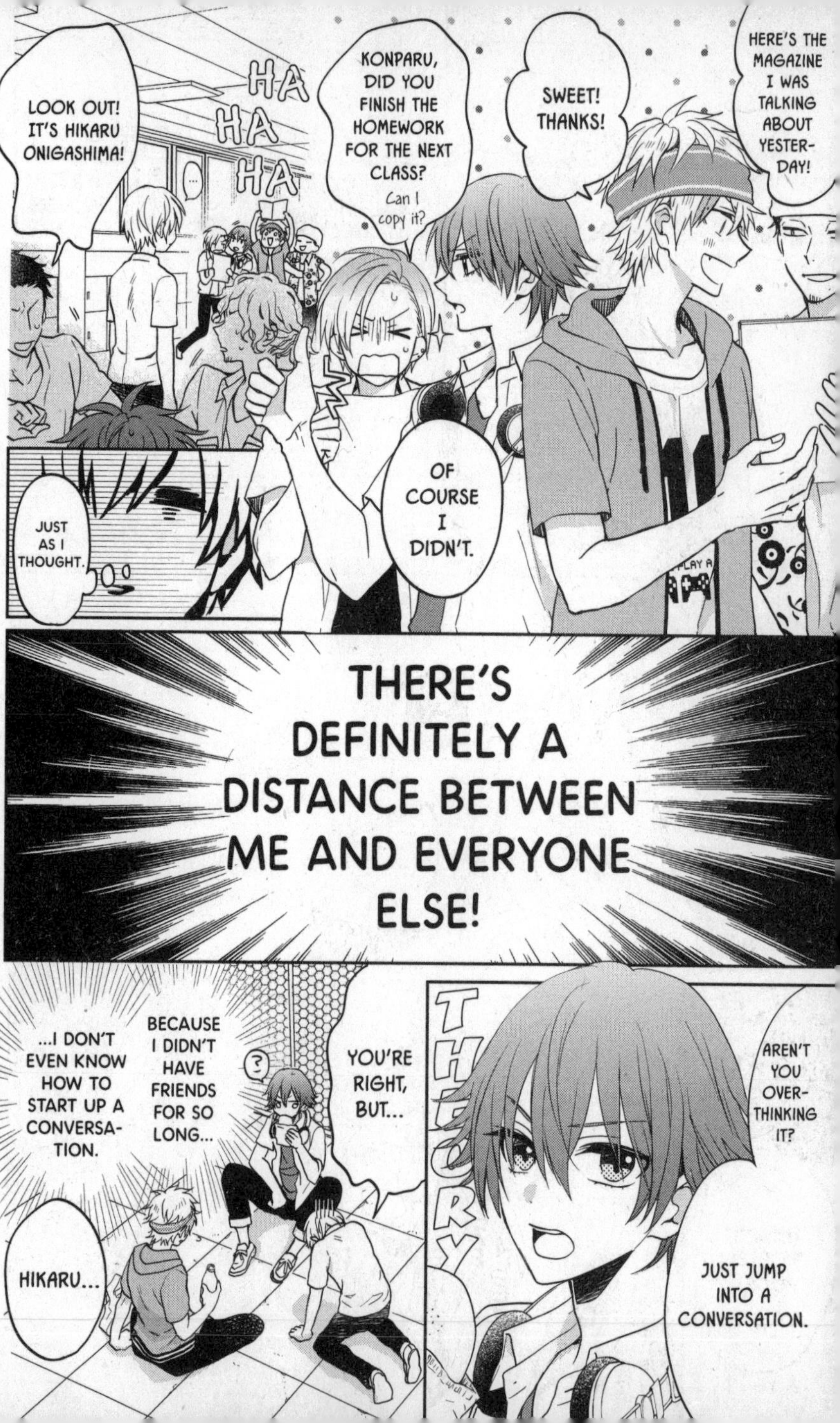
HERE'S THE MAGAZINE I WAS TALKING ABOUT YESTER-DAY!
SWEET! THANKS!
KONPARU, DID YOU FINISH THE HOMEWORK FOR THE NEXT CLASS?
Can I copy it?
HA HA HA
...
LOOK OUT! IT'S HIKARU ONIGASHIMA!
OF COURSE I DIDN'T.
JUST AS I THOUGHT.
THERE'S DEFINITELY A DISTANCE BETWEEN ME AND EVERYONE ELSE!
AREN'T YOU OVER-THINKING IT?
THEORY
JUST JUMP INTO A CONVERSATION.
YOU'RE RIGHT, BUT...
?
BECAUSE I DIDN'T HAVE FRIENDS FOR SO LONG...
...I DON'T EVEN KNOW HOW TO START UP A CONVERSA-TION.
HIKARU...

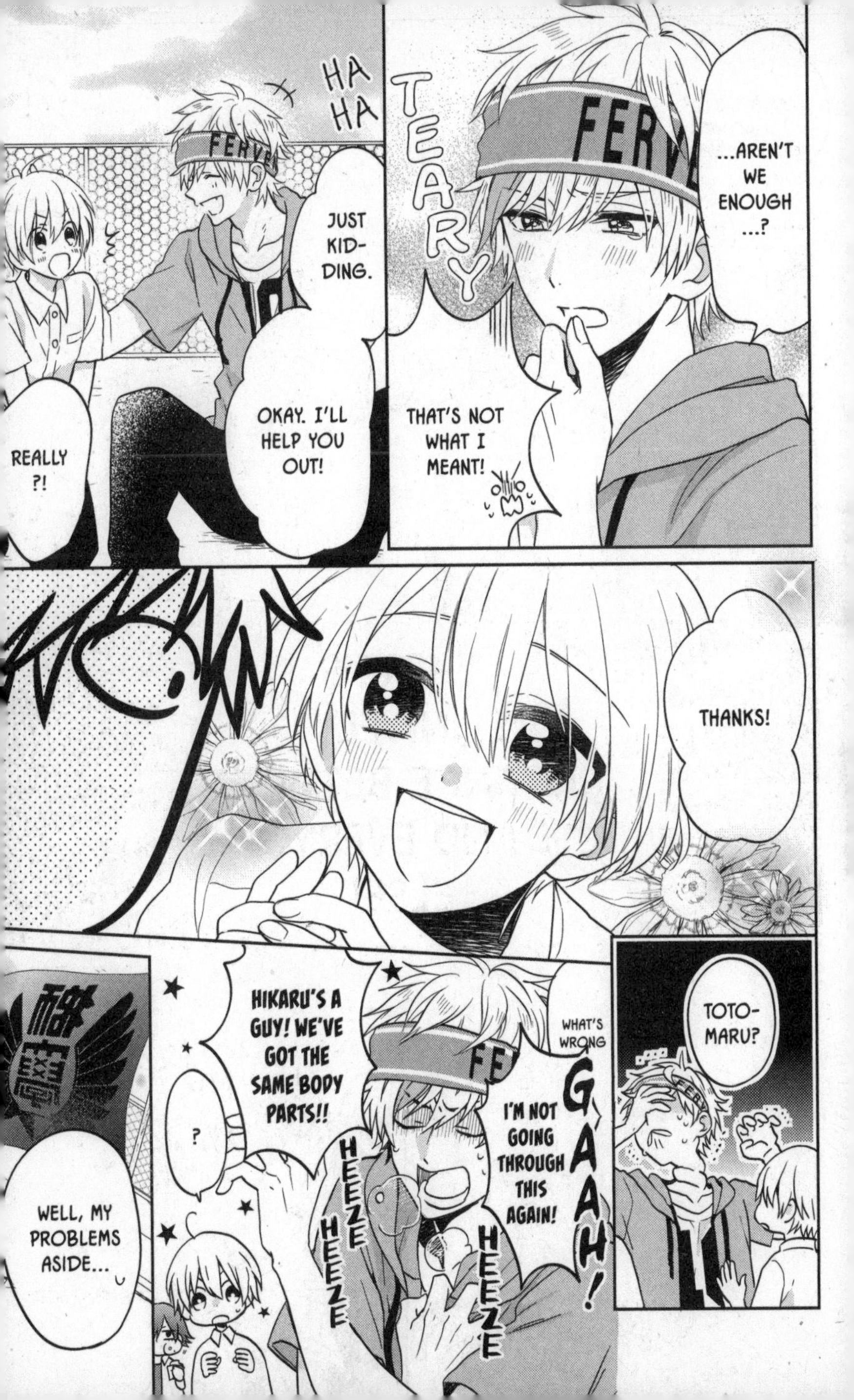
TEARY
...AREN'T WE ENOUGH ...?
THAT'S NOT WHAT I MEANT!
HA HA
JUST KID-DING.
OKAY. I'LL HELP YOU OUT!
REALLY ?!
THANKS!
TOTO-MARU?
WHAT'S WRONG
GAAH!
I'M NOT GOING THROUGH THIS AGAIN!
HIKARU'S A GUY! WE'VE GOT THE SAME BODY PARTS!!
HEEZE HEEZE HEEZE
?
WELL, MY PROBLEMS ASIDE...

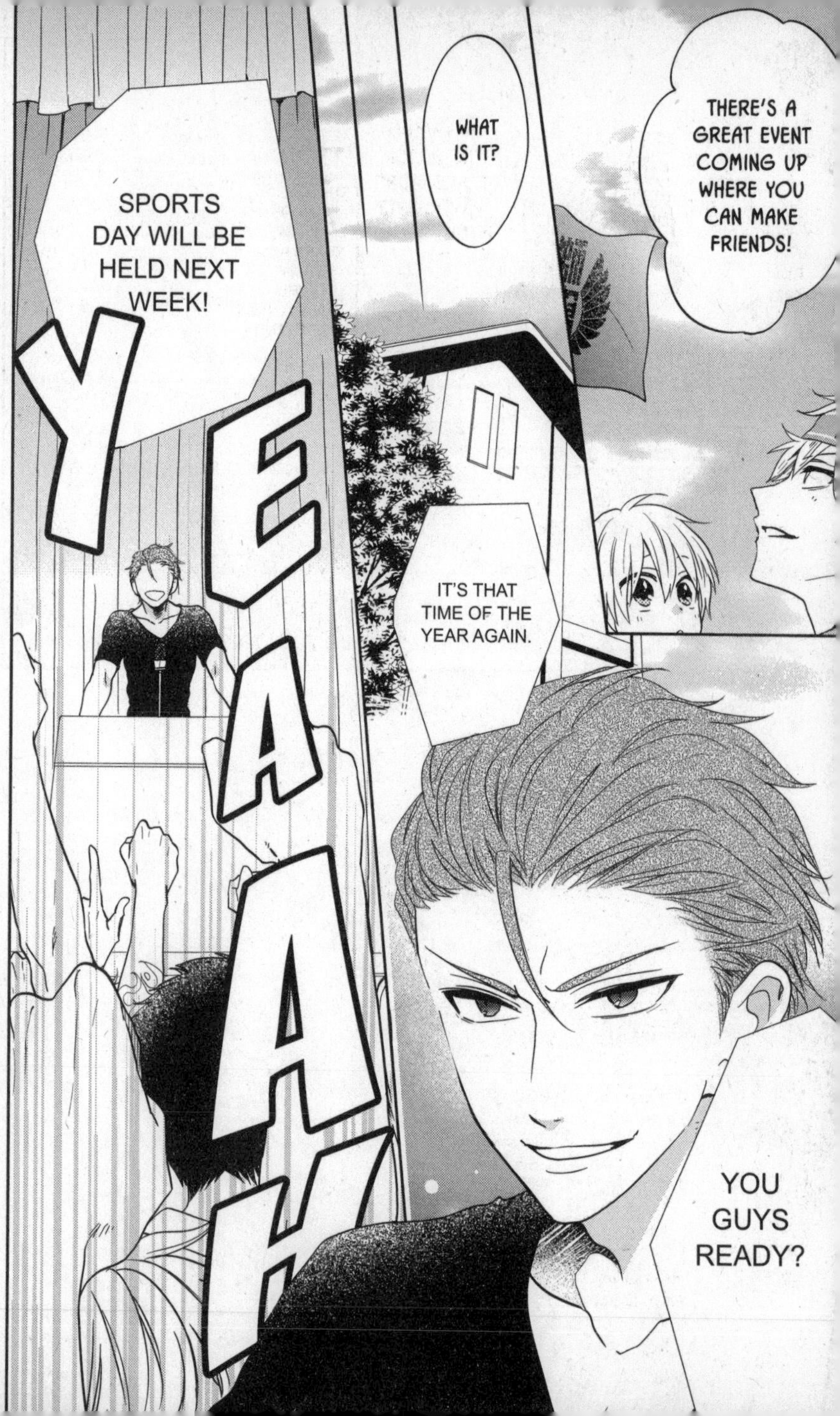
THERE'S A GREAT EVENT COMING UP WHERE YOU CAN MAKE FRIENDS!
WHAT IS IT?
IT'S THAT TIME OF THE YEAR AGAIN.
YOU GUYS READY?
SPORTS DAY WILL BE HELD NEXT WEEK!
YEAAAH

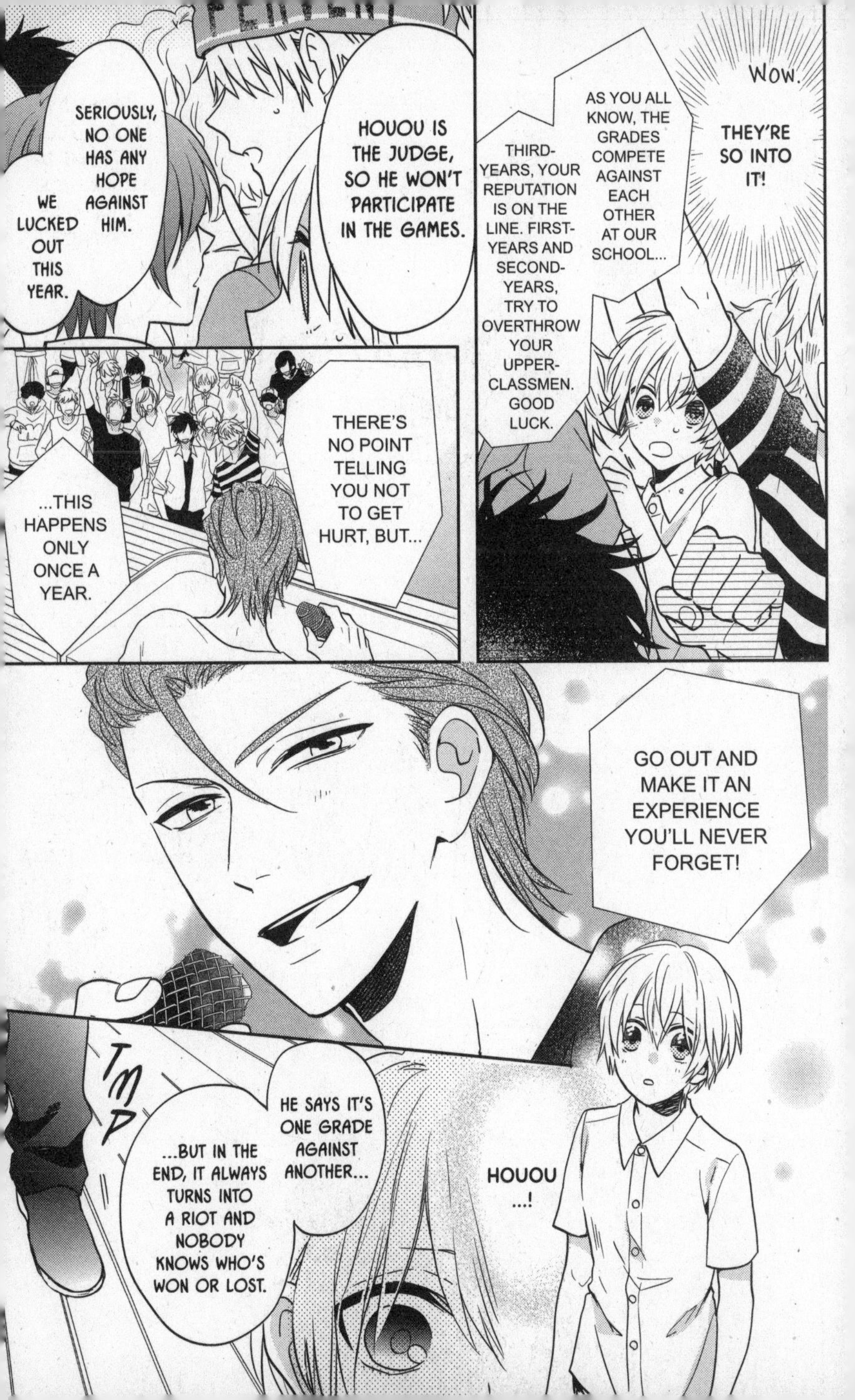
WOW.
THEY'RE SO INTO IT!
AS YOU ALL KNOW, THE GRADES COMPETE AGAINST EACH OTHER AT OUR SCHOOL...
THIRD-YEARS, YOUR REPUTATION IS ON THE LINE. FIRST-YEARS AND SECOND-YEARS, TRY TO OVERTHROW YOUR UPPERCLASSMEN. GOOD LUCK.
HOUOU IS THE JUDGE, SO HE WON'T PARTICIPATE IN THE GAMES.
SERIOUSLY, NO ONE HAS ANY HOPE AGAINST HIM.
WE LUCKED OUT THIS YEAR.
THERE'S NO POINT TELLING YOU NOT TO GET HURT, BUT...
...THIS HAPPENS ONLY ONCE A YEAR.
GO OUT AND MAKE IT AN EXPERIENCE YOU'LL NEVER FORGET!
HOUOU ...!
HE SAYS IT'S ONE GRADE AGAINST ANOTHER...
...BUT IN THE END, IT ALWAYS TURNS INTO A RIOT AND NOBODY KNOWS WHO'S WON OR LOST.
TMP

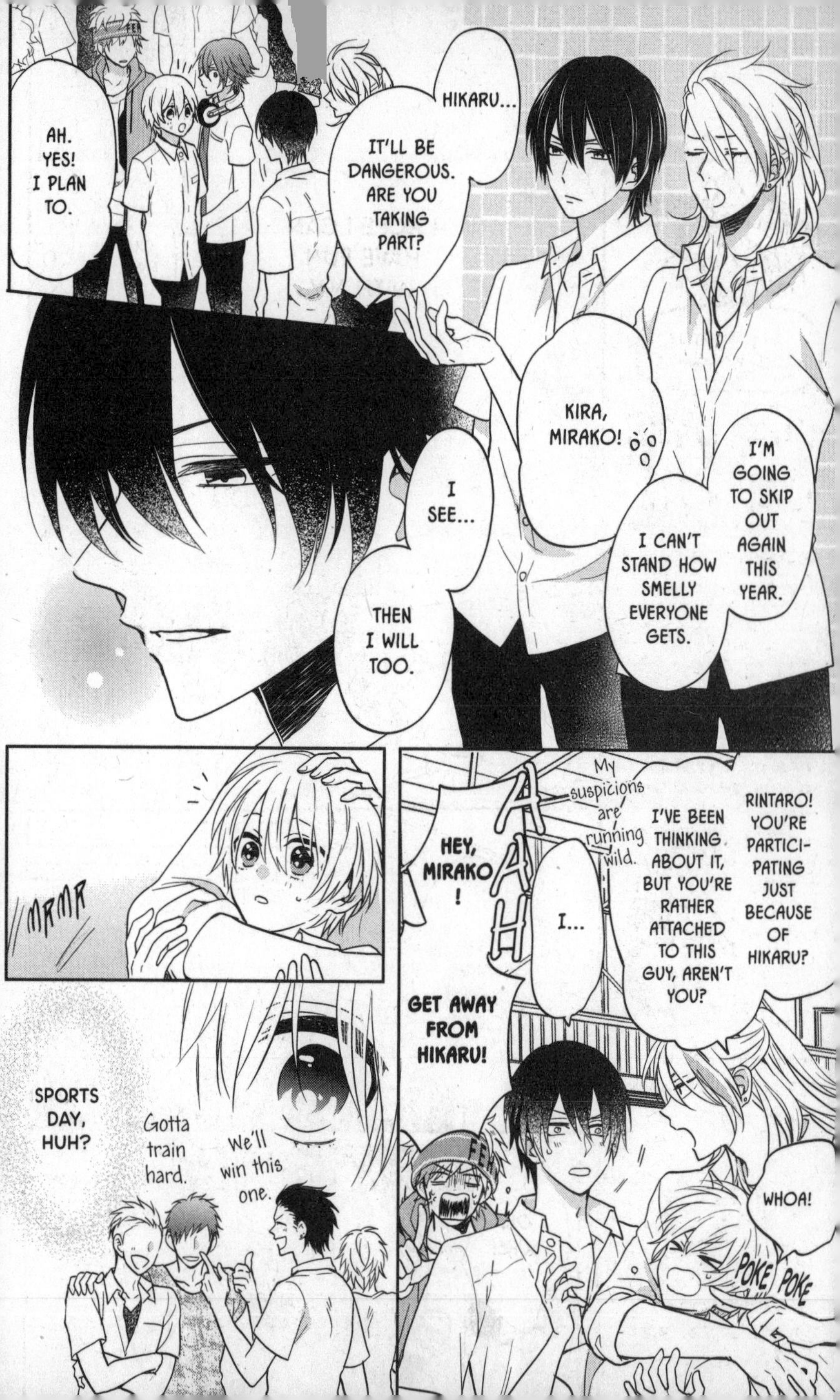
HIKARU...
IT'LL BE DANGEROUS. ARE YOU TAKING PART?
AH. YES! I PLAN TO.
KIRA, MIRAKO!
I'M GOING TO SKIP OUT AGAIN THIS YEAR.
I CAN'T STAND HOW SMELLY EVERYONE GETS.
I SEE...
THEN I WILL TOO.
RINTARO! YOU'RE PARTICI-PATING JUST BECAUSE OF HIKARU?
I'VE BEEN THINKING ABOUT IT, BUT YOU'RE RATHER ATTACHED TO THIS GUY, AREN'T YOU?
My suspicions are running wild.
I...
AAH
HEY, MIRAKO!
GET AWAY FROM HIKARU!
WHOA!
POKE POKE
MRMR
SPORTS DAY, HUH?
Gotta train hard.
We'll win this one.

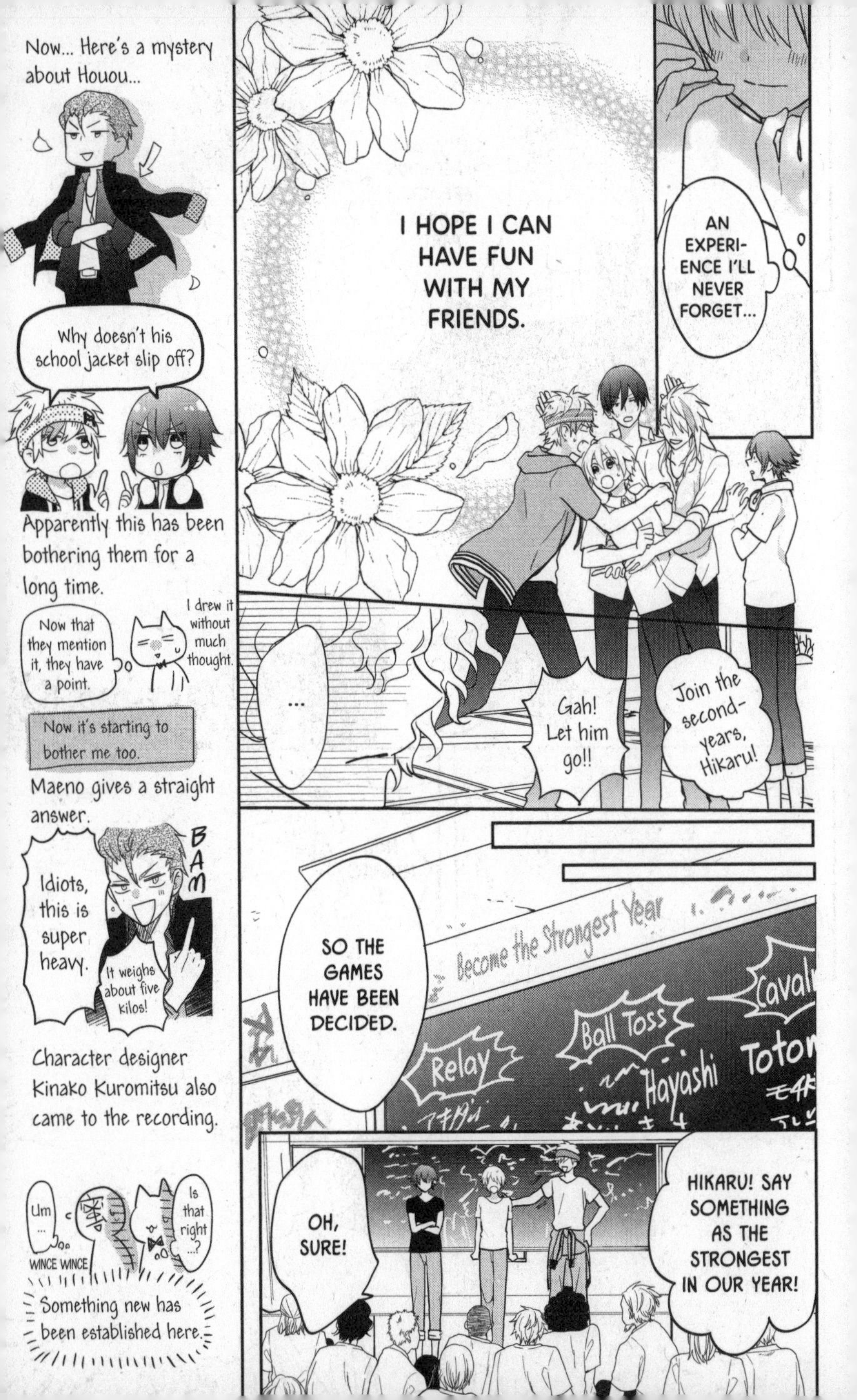
AN EXPERIENCE I'LL NEVER FORGET...
I HOPE I CAN HAVE FUN WITH MY FRIENDS.
Join the second-years, Hikaru!
Gah! Let him go!!
...
SO THE GAMES HAVE BEEN DECIDED.
Become the Strongest Year
Relay
Ball Toss
Hayashi
Toto
HIKARU! SAY SOMETHING AS THE STRONGEST IN OUR YEAR!
OH, SURE!

Now... Here's a mystery about Houou...

Why doesn't his school jacket slip off?

Apparently this has been bothering them for a long time.

Now that they mention it, they have a point.

I drew it without much thought.

Now it's starting to bother me too.

Maeno gives a straight answer.

Idiots, this is super heavy.

BAM

It weighs about five kilos!

Character designer Kinako Kuromitsu also came to the recording.

Um...

WINCE WINCE

Is that right...?

Something new has been established here.

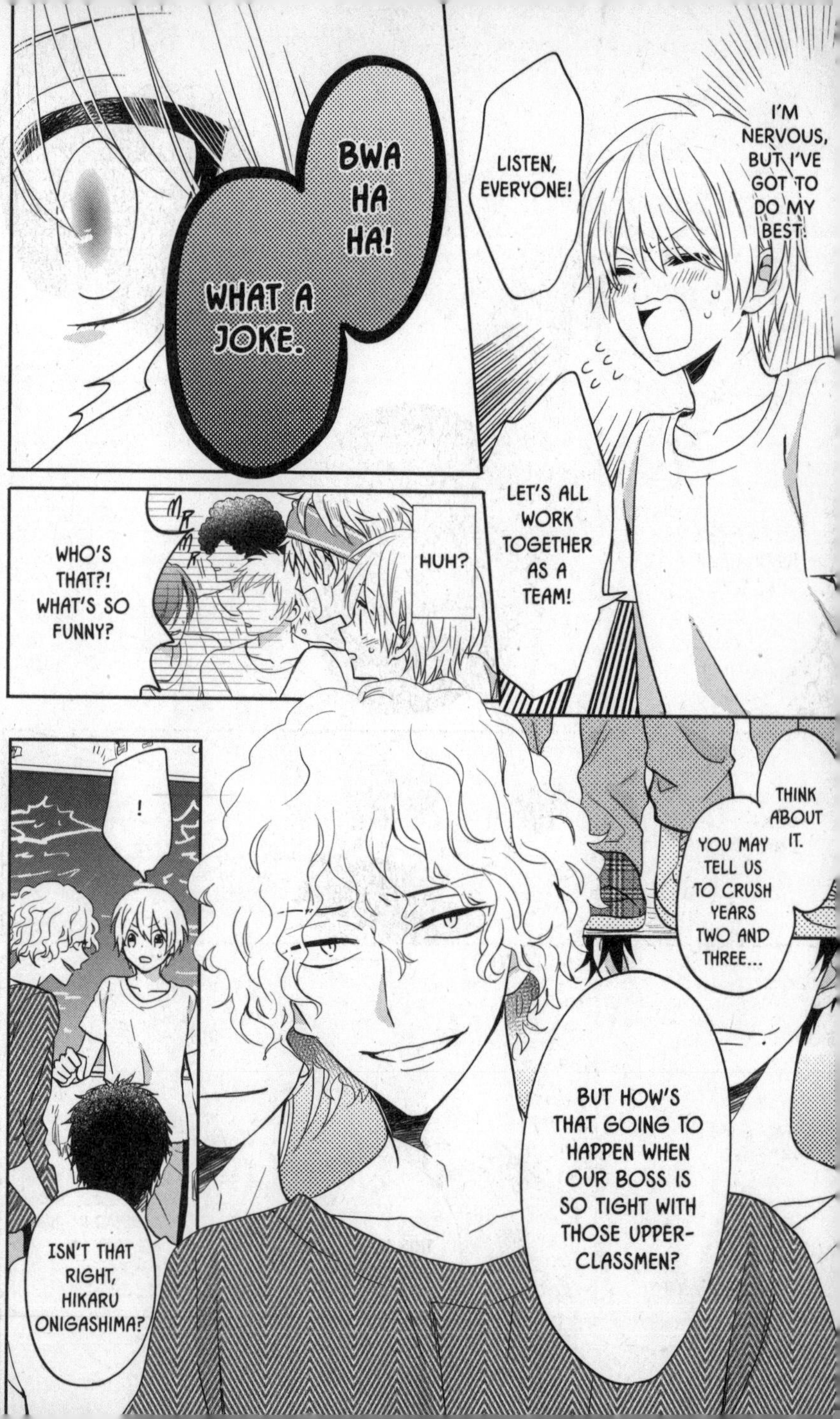
I'M NERVOUS, BUT I'VE GOT TO DO MY BEST.
LISTEN, EVERYONE!
LET'S ALL WORK TOGETHER AS A TEAM!
BWA HA HA!
WHAT A JOKE.
HUH?
WHO'S THAT?! WHAT'S SO FUNNY?
THINK ABOUT IT.
YOU MAY TELL US TO CRUSH YEARS TWO AND THREE...
BUT HOW'S THAT GOING TO HAPPEN WHEN OUR BOSS IS SO TIGHT WITH THOSE UPPER-CLASSMEN?
ISN'T THAT RIGHT, HIKARU ONIGASHIMA?
!

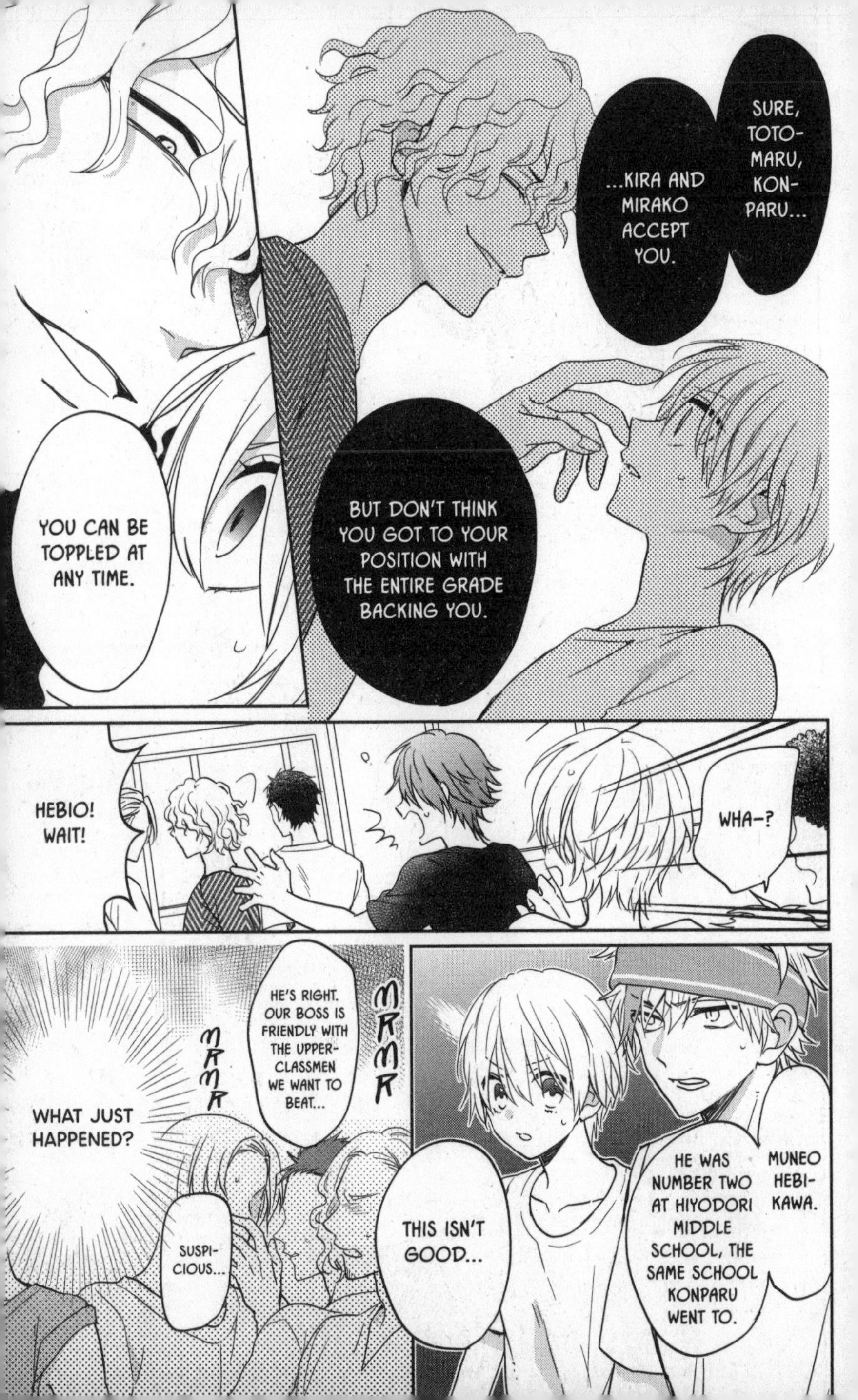
SURE, TOTO-MARU, KON-PARU...
...KIRA AND MIRAKO ACCEPT YOU.
BUT DON'T THINK YOU GOT TO YOUR POSITION WITH THE ENTIRE GRADE BACKING YOU.
YOU CAN BE TOPPLED AT ANY TIME.
WHA-?
HEBIO! WAIT!
MUNEO HEBI-KAWA.
HE WAS NUMBER TWO AT HIYODORI MIDDLE SCHOOL, THE SAME SCHOOL KONPARU WENT TO.
THIS ISN'T GOOD...
MRMR
HE'S RIGHT. OUR BOSS IS FRIENDLY WITH THE UPPER-CLASSMEN WE WANT TO BEAT...
MRMR
WHAT JUST HAPPENED?
SUSPI-CIOUS...

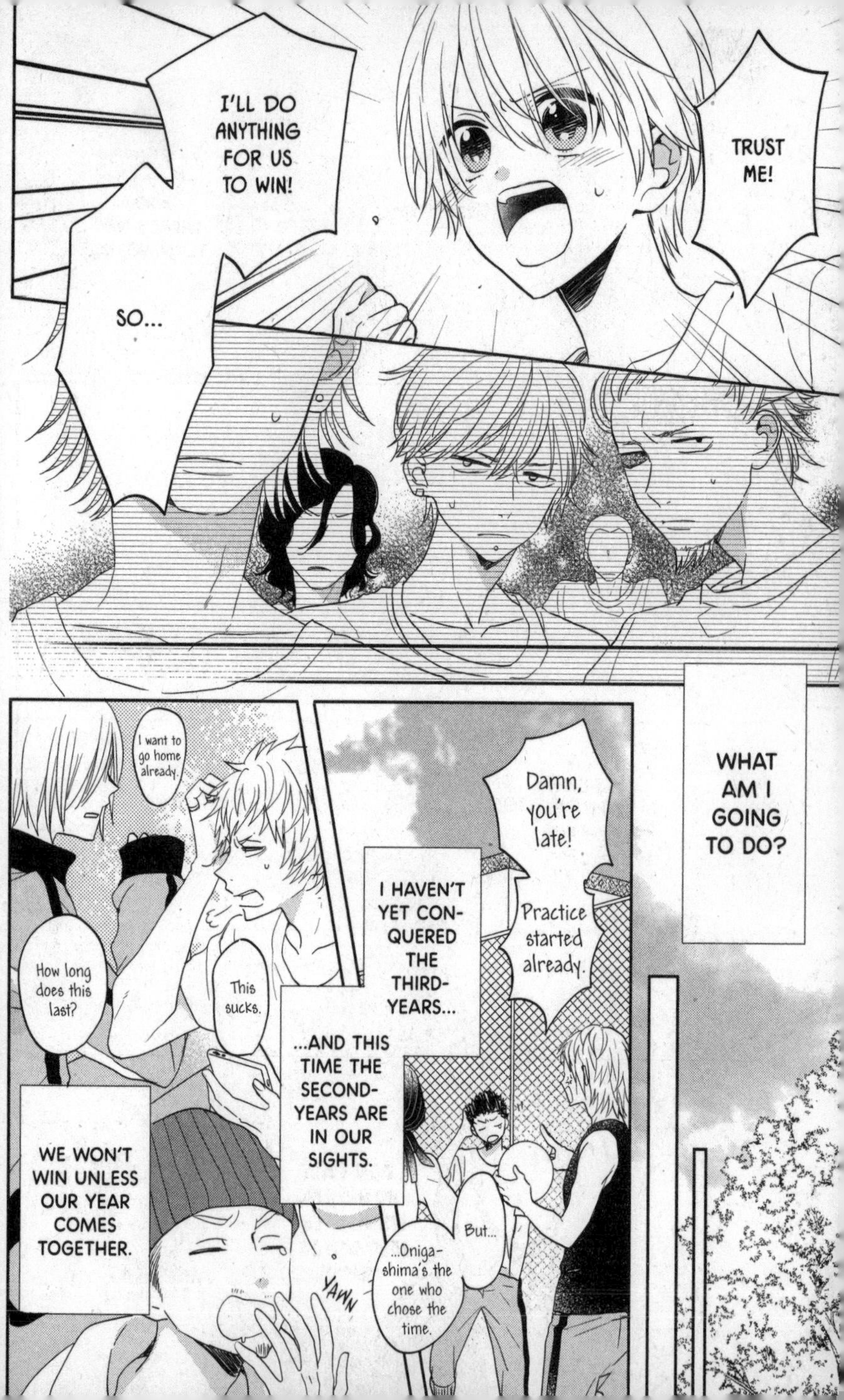
TRUST ME!
I'LL DO ANYTHING FOR US TO WIN!
SO...
WHAT AM I GOING TO DO?
Damn, you're late!
Practice started already.
I HAVEN'T YET CON-QUERED THE THIRD-YEARS...
...AND THIS TIME THE SECOND-YEARS ARE IN OUR SIGHTS.
But...
...Oniga-shima's the one who chose the time.
I want to go home already.
This sucks.
How long does this last?
WE WON'T WIN UNLESS OUR YEAR COMES TOGETHER.
YAWN

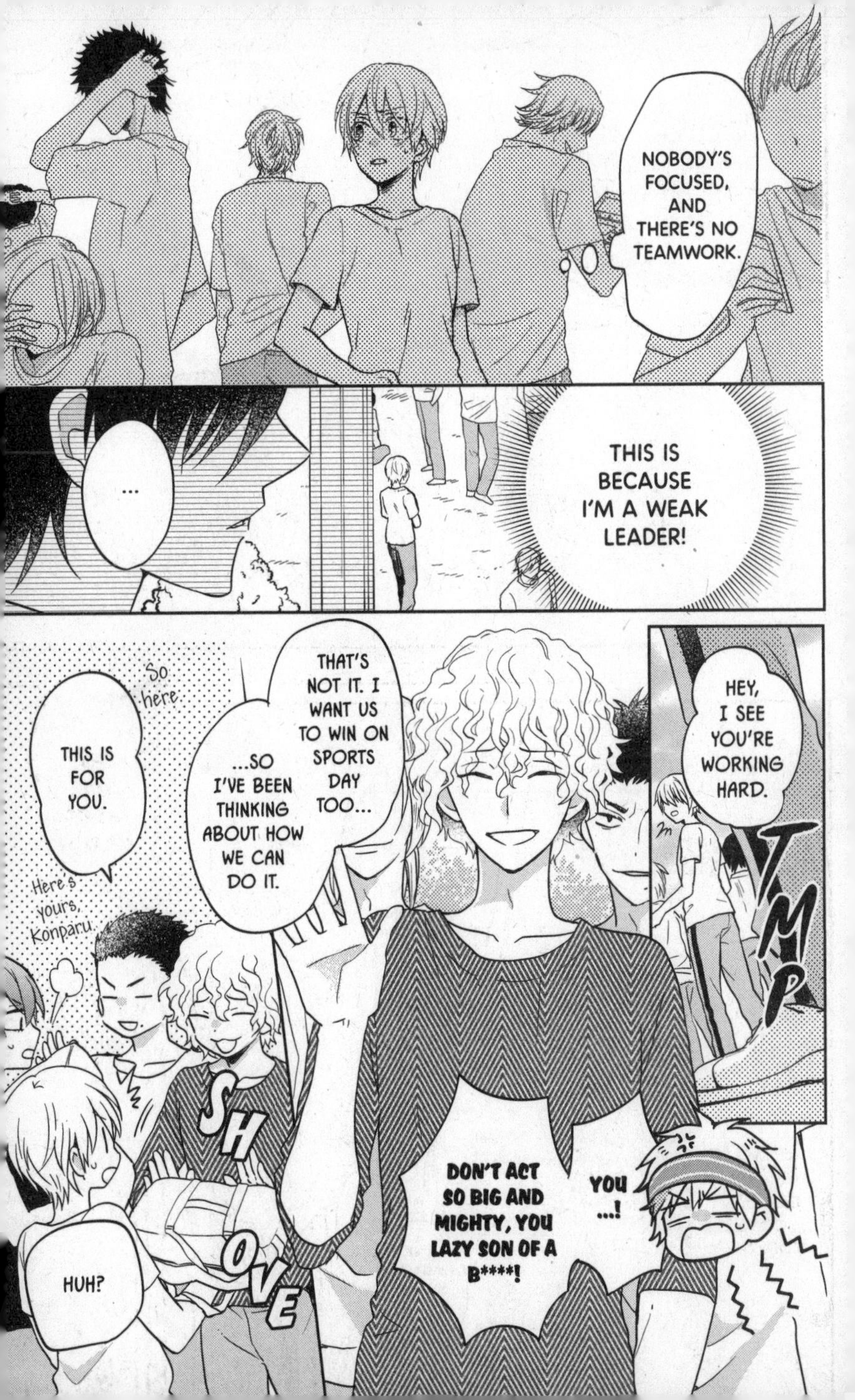
NOBODY'S FOCUSED, AND THERE'S NO TEAMWORK.
THIS IS BECAUSE I'M A WEAK LEADER!
...
HEY, I SEE YOU'RE WORKING HARD.
TMP
THAT'S NOT IT. I WANT US TO WIN ON SPORTS DAY TOO...
...SO I'VE BEEN THINKING ABOUT HOW WE CAN DO IT.
So here
THIS IS FOR YOU.
Here's yours, Konparu.
SHOVE
YOU ...!
DON'T ACT SO BIG AND MIGHTY, YOU LAZY SON OF A B****!
HUH?

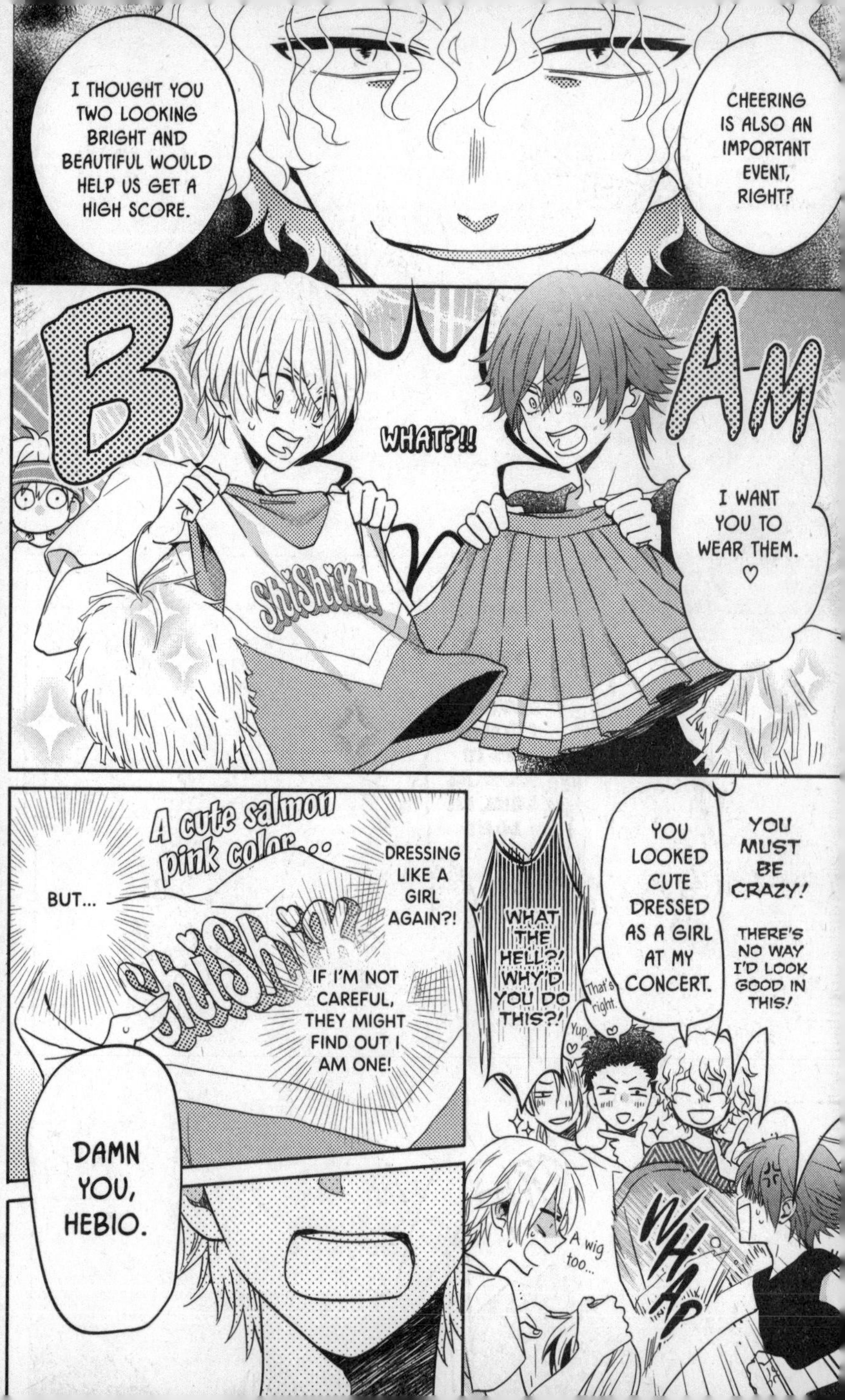
CHEERING IS ALSO AN IMPORTANT EVENT, RIGHT?
I THOUGHT YOU TWO LOOKING BRIGHT AND BEAUTIFUL WOULD HELP US GET A HIGH SCORE.
BAM
I WANT YOU TO WEAR THEM. ♡
WHAT?!!
ShiShiKu
YOU MUST BE CRAZY!
THERE'S NO WAY I'D LOOK GOOD IN THIS!
YOU LOOKED CUTE DRESSED AS A GIRL AT MY CONCERT.
WHAT THE HELL?! WHY'D YOU DO THIS?!
That's right.
Yup.
A wig too...
WHAP
DRESSING LIKE A GIRL AGAIN?!
A cute salmon pink color...
BUT...
IF I'M NOT CAREFUL, THEY MIGHT FIND OUT I AM ONE!
DAMN YOU, HEBIO.

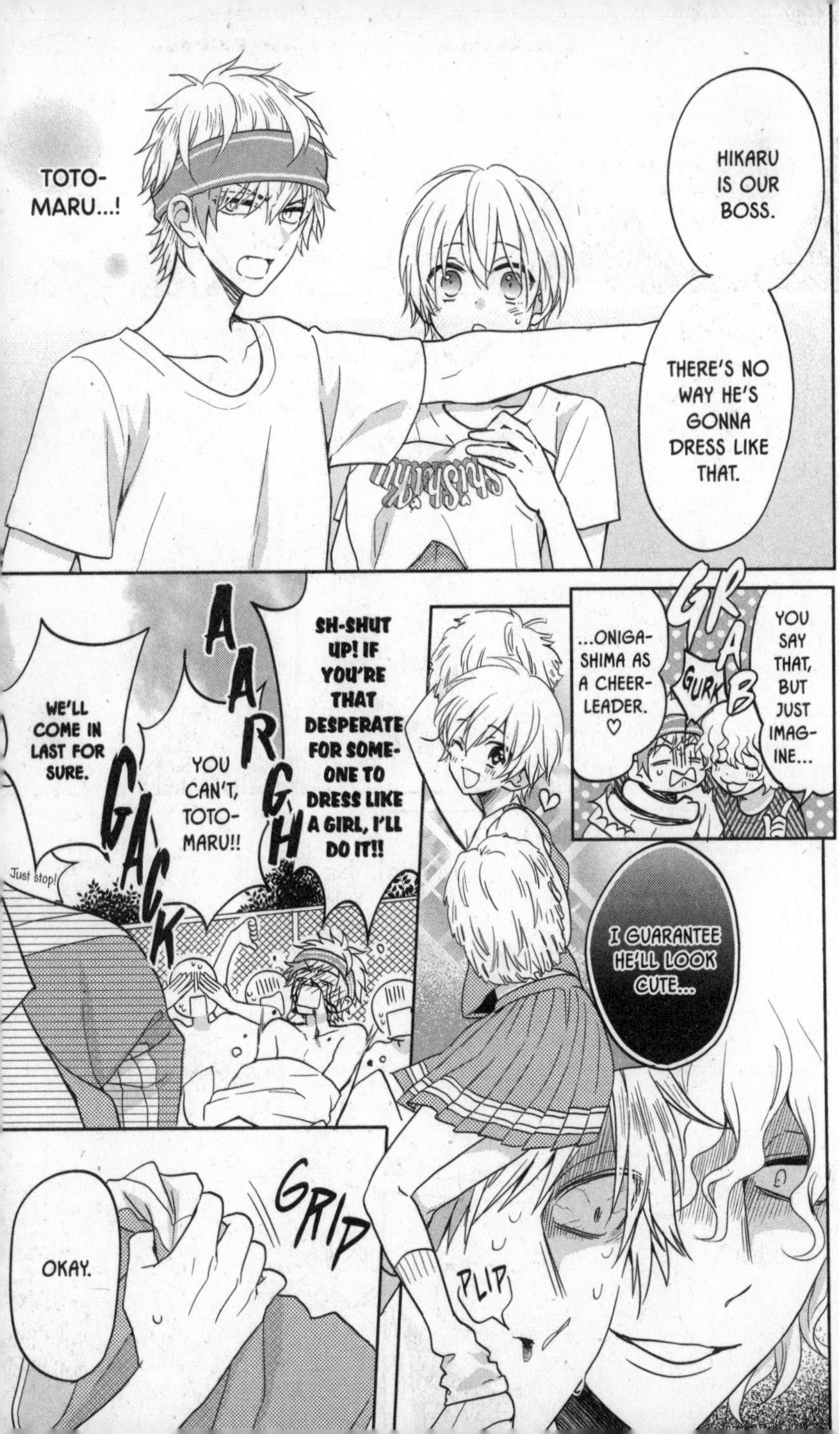
HIKARU IS OUR BOSS.
THERE'S NO WAY HE'S GONNA DRESS LIKE THAT.
TOTO-MARU...!
YOU SAY THAT, BUT JUST IMAG-INE...
GRAB
GURK
...ONIGA-SHIMA AS A CHEER-LEADER. ♡
I GUARANTEE HE'LL LOOK CUTE...
SH-SHUT UP! IF YOU'RE THAT DESPERATE FOR SOME-ONE TO DRESS LIKE A GIRL, I'LL DO IT!!
AARGH
YOU CAN'T, TOTO-MARU!!
GACK
WE'LL COME IN LAST FOR SURE.
Just stop!
PLIP
GRIP
OKAY.

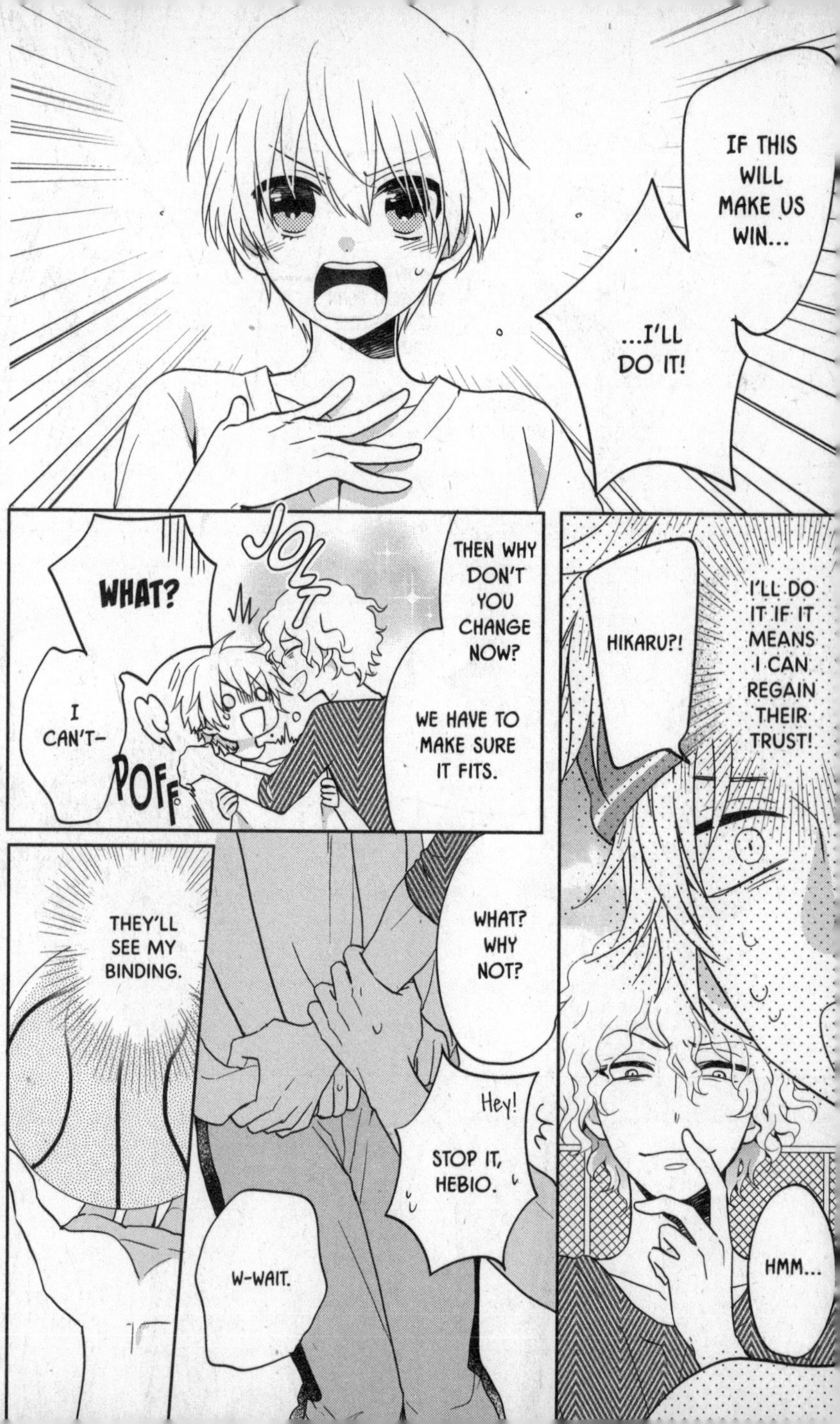
IF THIS WILL MAKE US WIN...
...I'LL DO IT!
I'LL DO IT IF IT MEANS I CAN REGAIN THEIR TRUST!
HIKARU?!
HMM...
THEN WHY DON'T YOU CHANGE NOW?
WE HAVE TO MAKE SURE IT FITS.
JOLT
WHAT?
I CAN'T-
POFF
WHAT? WHY NOT?
Hey!
STOP IT, HEBIO.
W-WAIT.
THEY'LL SEE MY BINDING.

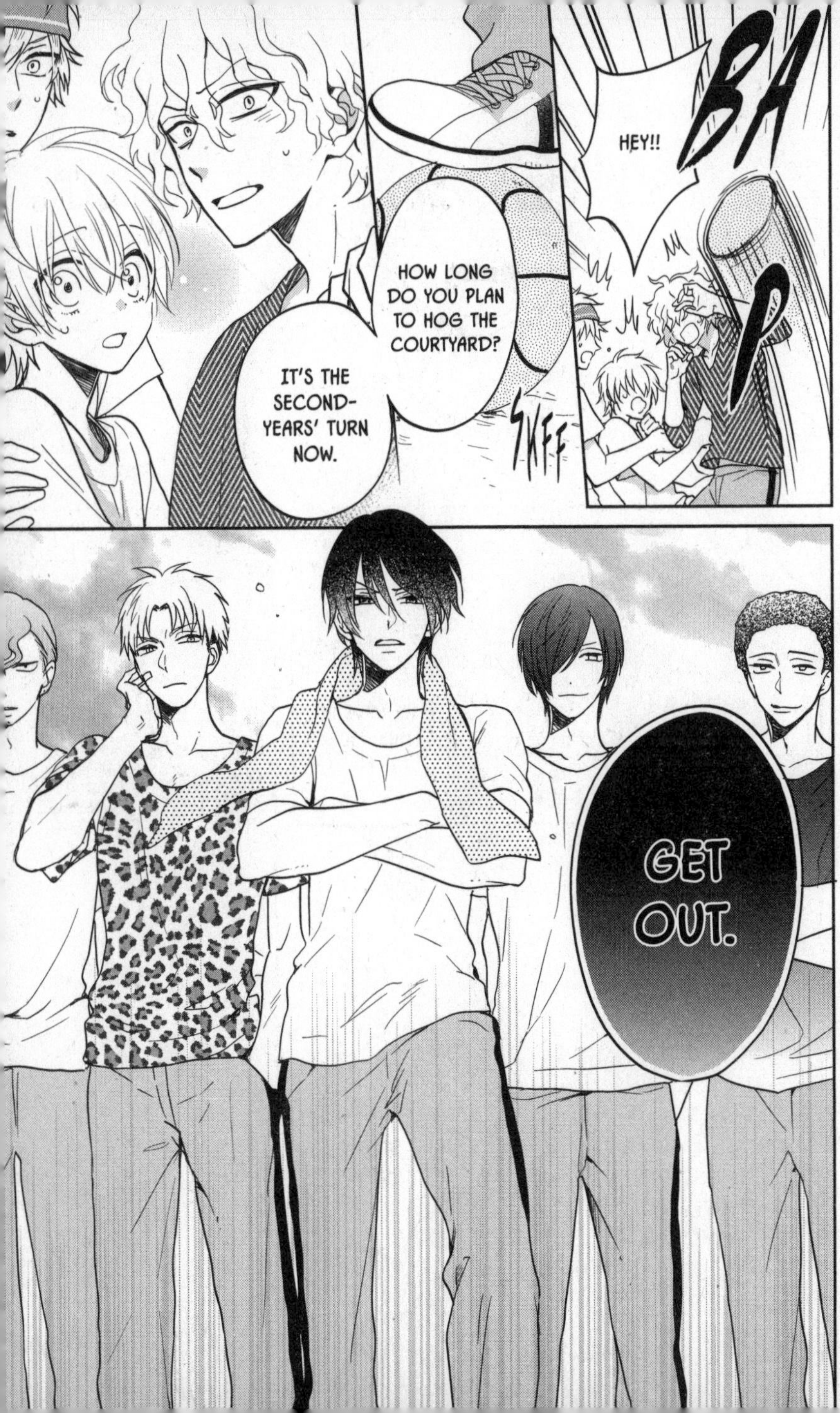

HEY!!
BAP
SKFF
HOW LONG DO YOU PLAN TO HOG THE COURTYARD?
IT'S THE SECOND-YEARS' TURN NOW.
GET OUT.

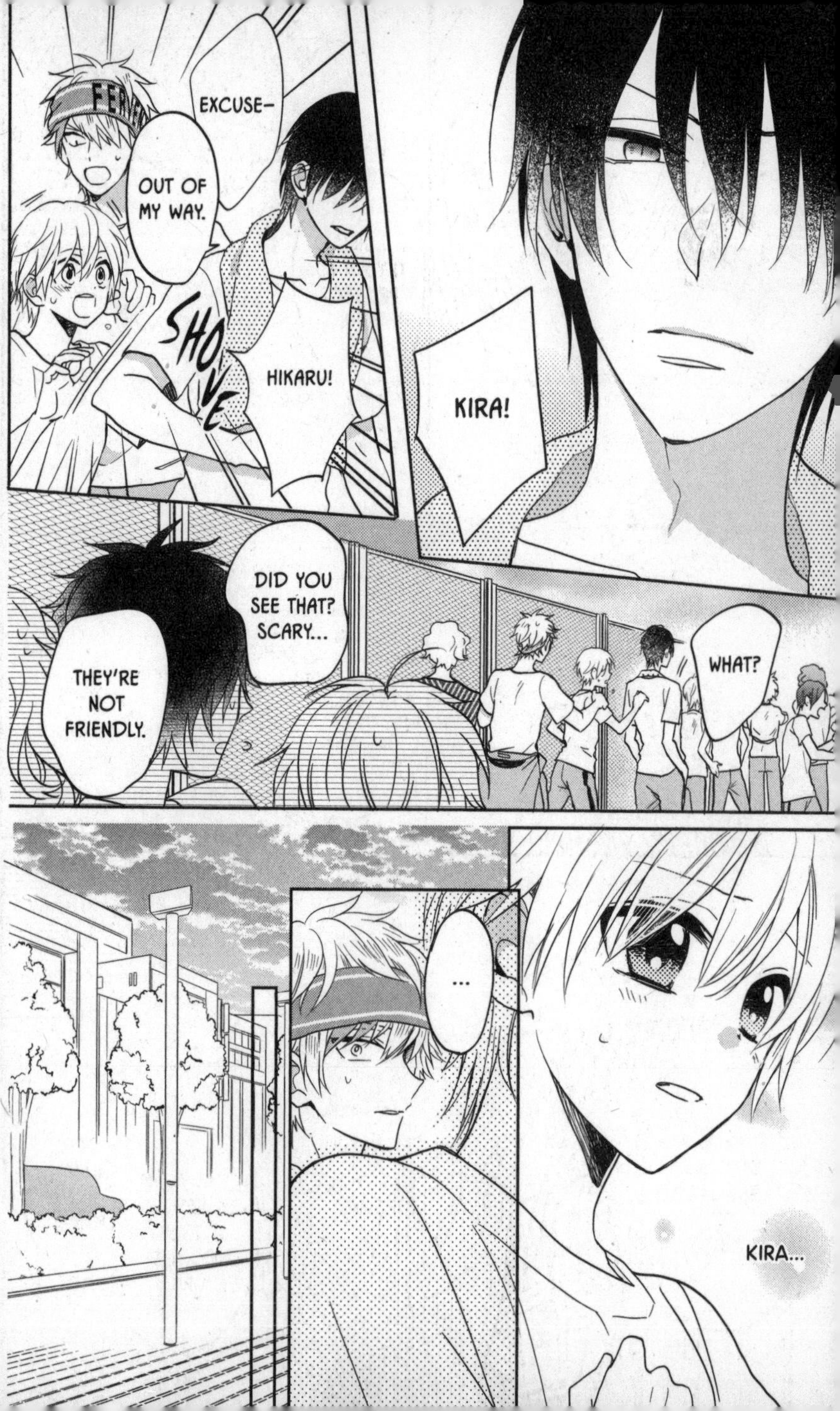
KIRA!
EXCUSE—
OUT OF MY WAY.
HIKARU!
SHOVE
WHAT?
DID YOU SEE THAT? SCARY...
THEY'RE NOT FRIENDLY.
KIRA...
...

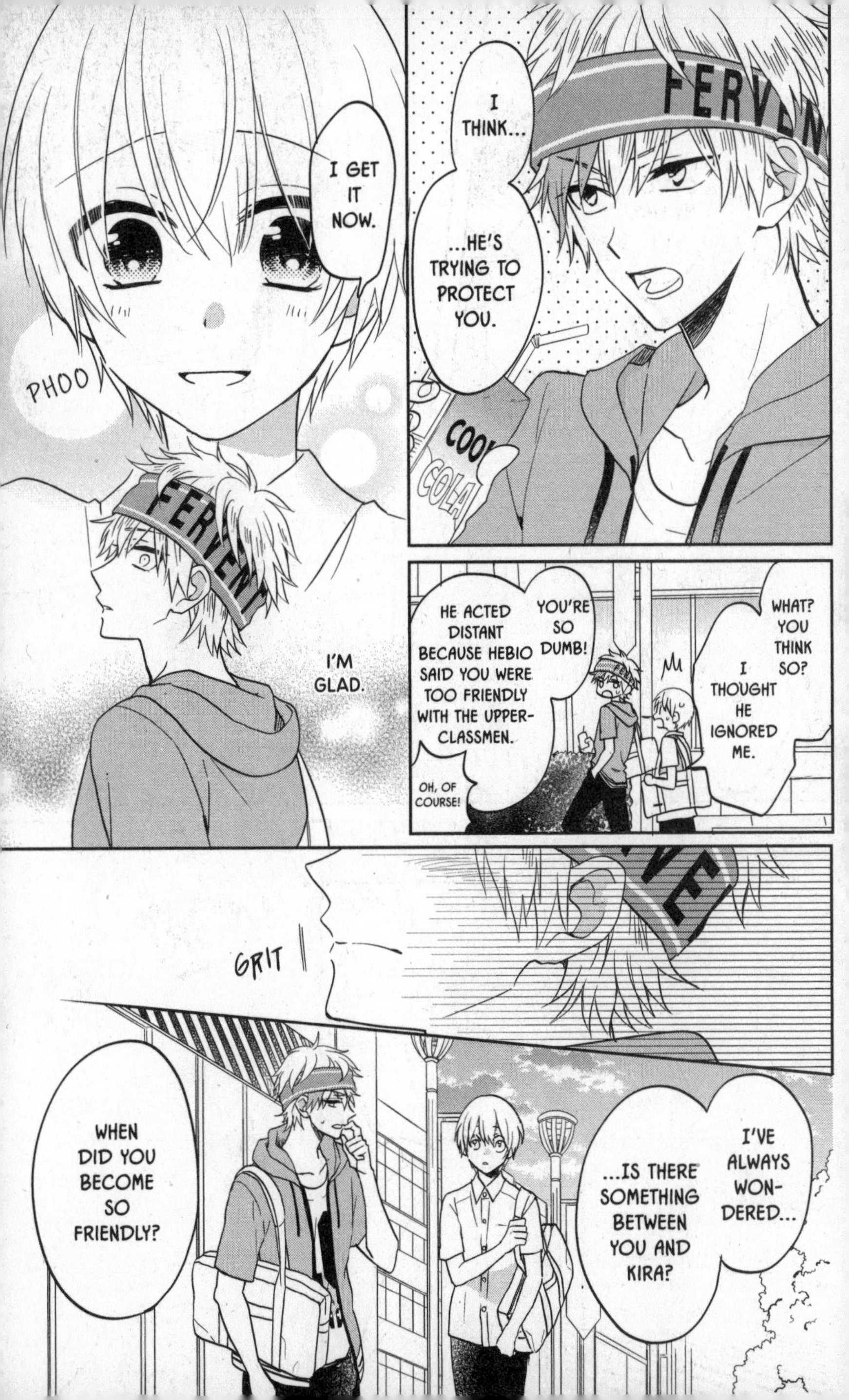
I THINK...
...HE'S TRYING TO PROTECT YOU.
COO
COLA
WHAT? YOU THINK SO?
I THOUGHT HE IGNORED ME.
YOU'RE SO DUMB!
HE ACTED DISTANT BECAUSE HEBIO SAID YOU WERE TOO FRIENDLY WITH THE UPPER-CLASSMEN.
OH, OF COURSE!
I GET IT NOW.
PHOO
I'M GLAD.
GRIT
I'VE ALWAYS WON-DERED...
...IS THERE SOMETHING BETWEEN YOU AND KIRA?
WHEN DID YOU BECOME SO FRIENDLY?

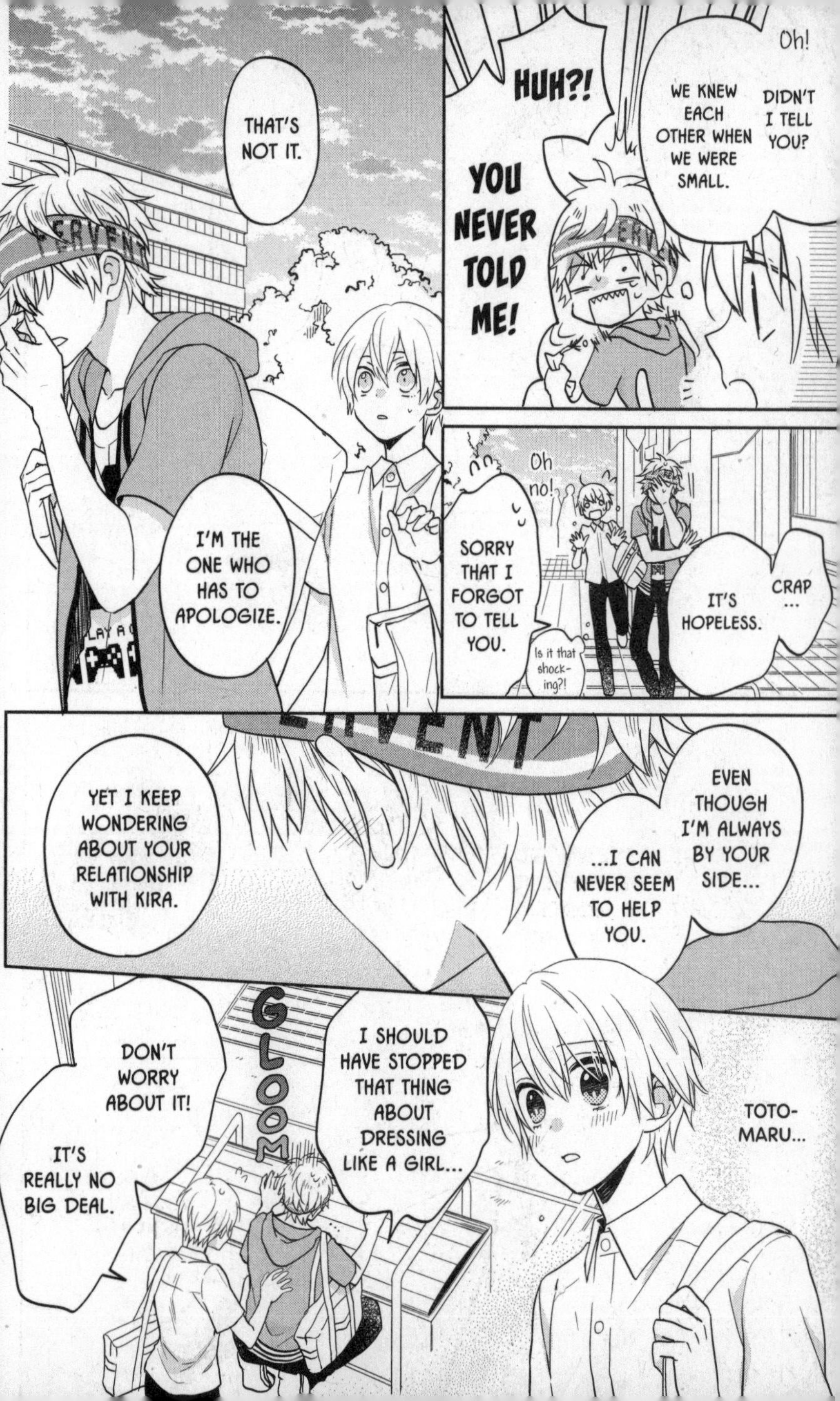
Oh!
WE KNEW EACH OTHER WHEN WE WERE SMALL.
DIDN'T I TELL YOU?
HUH?!
YOU NEVER TOLD ME!
CRAP...
IT'S HOPELESS.
Oh no!
SORRY THAT I FORGOT TO TELL YOU.
Is it that shocking?!
THAT'S NOT IT.
I'M THE ONE WHO HAS TO APOLOGIZE.
EVEN THOUGH I'M ALWAYS BY YOUR SIDE...
...I CAN NEVER SEEM TO HELP YOU.
YET I KEEP WONDERING ABOUT YOUR RELATIONSHIP WITH KIRA.
TOTO-MARU...
I SHOULD HAVE STOPPED THAT THING ABOUT DRESSING LIKE A GIRL...
GLOOM
DON'T WORRY ABOUT IT!
IT'S REALLY NO BIG DEAL.

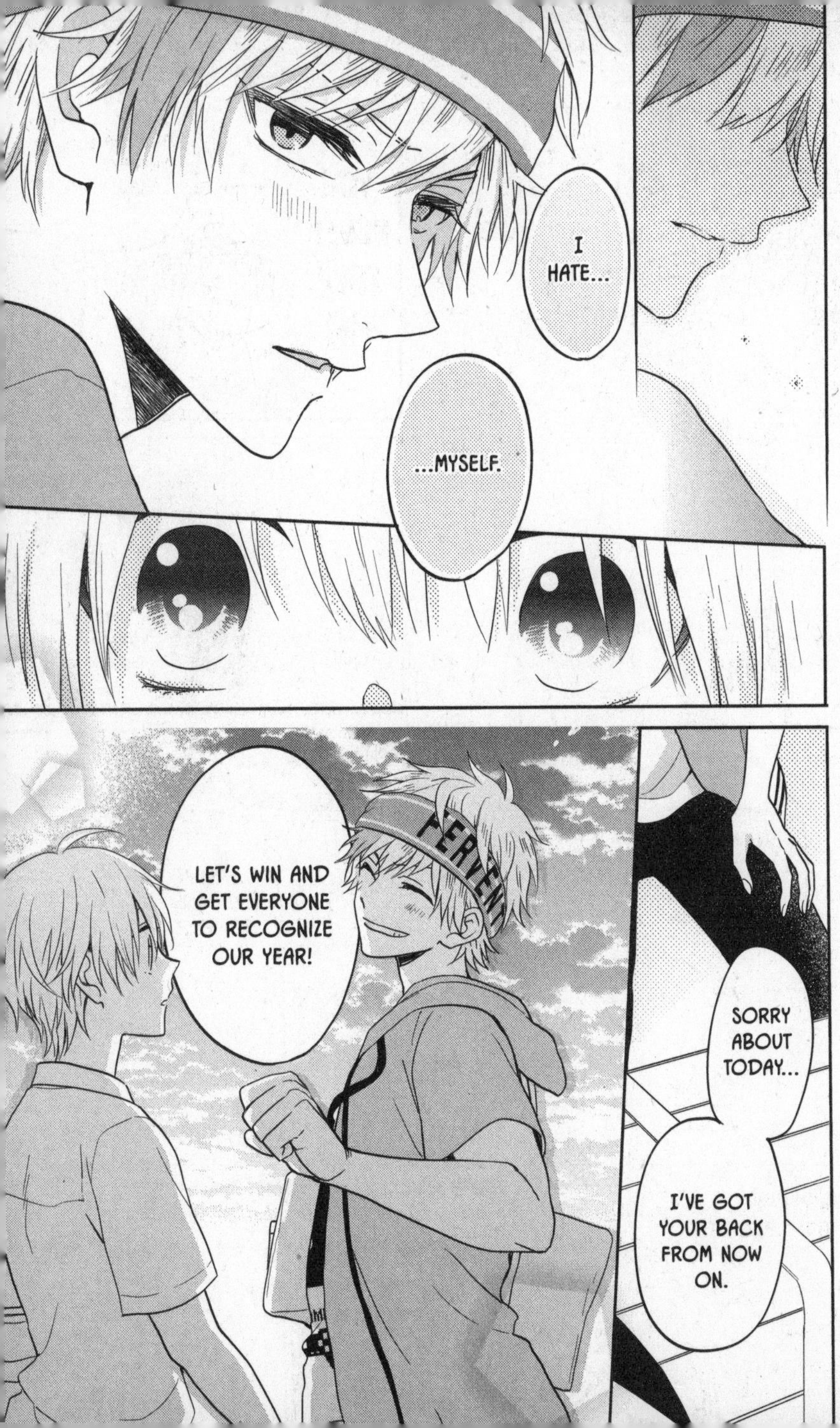
I HATE...
...MYSELF.
SORRY ABOUT TODAY...
I'VE GOT YOUR BACK FROM NOW ON.
LET'S WIN AND GET EVERYONE TO RECOGNIZE OUR YEAR!
FERVENT

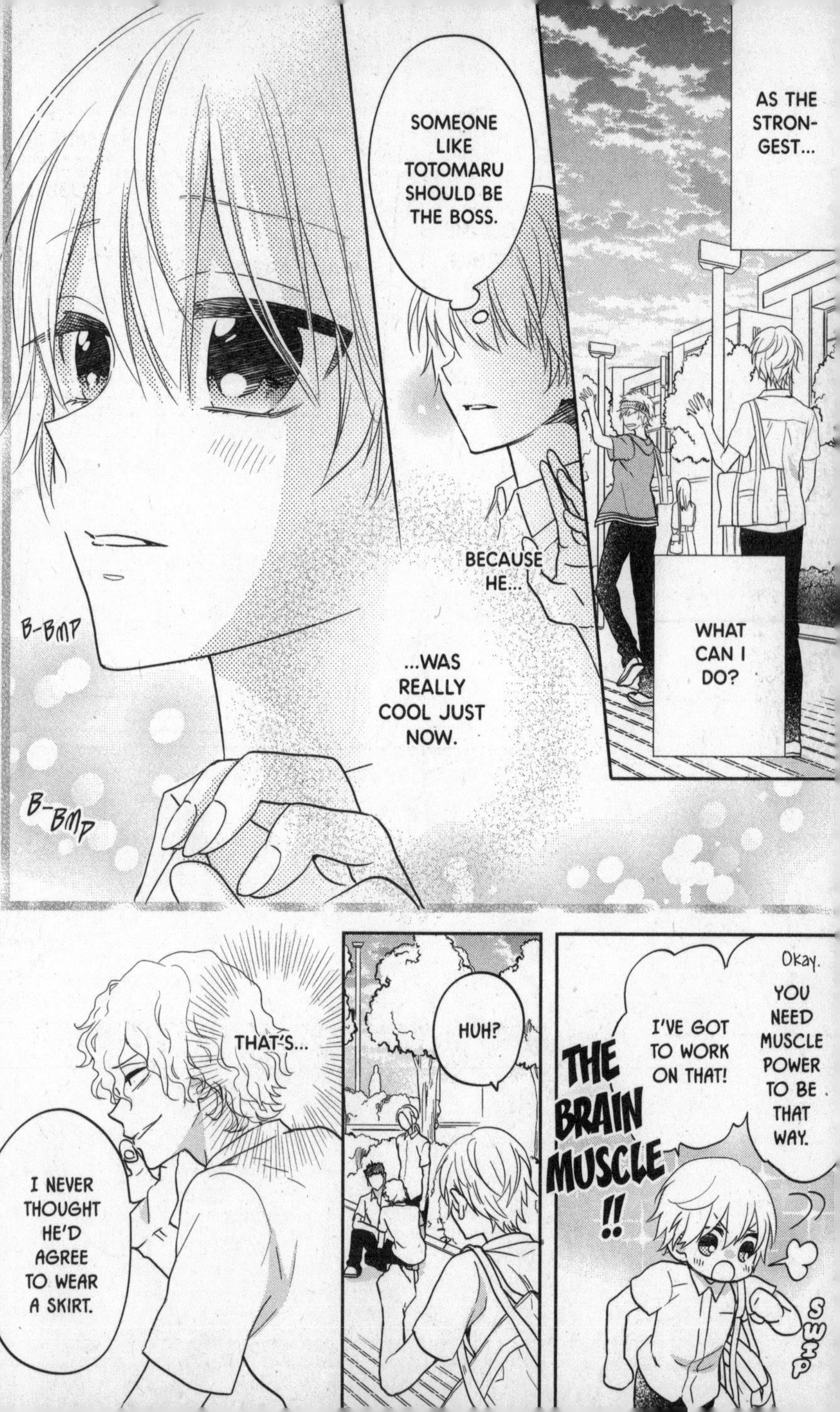
AS THE STRONGEST...
WHAT CAN I DO?
SOMEONE LIKE TOTOMARU SHOULD BE THE BOSS.
BECAUSE HE...
...WAS REALLY COOL JUST NOW.
B-BMP
B-BMP
Okay.
YOU NEED MUSCLE POWER TO BE THAT WAY.
I'VE GOT TO WORK ON THAT!
THE BRAIN MUSCLE!!
HUH?
THAT'S...
I NEVER THOUGHT HE'D AGREE TO WEAR A SKIRT.

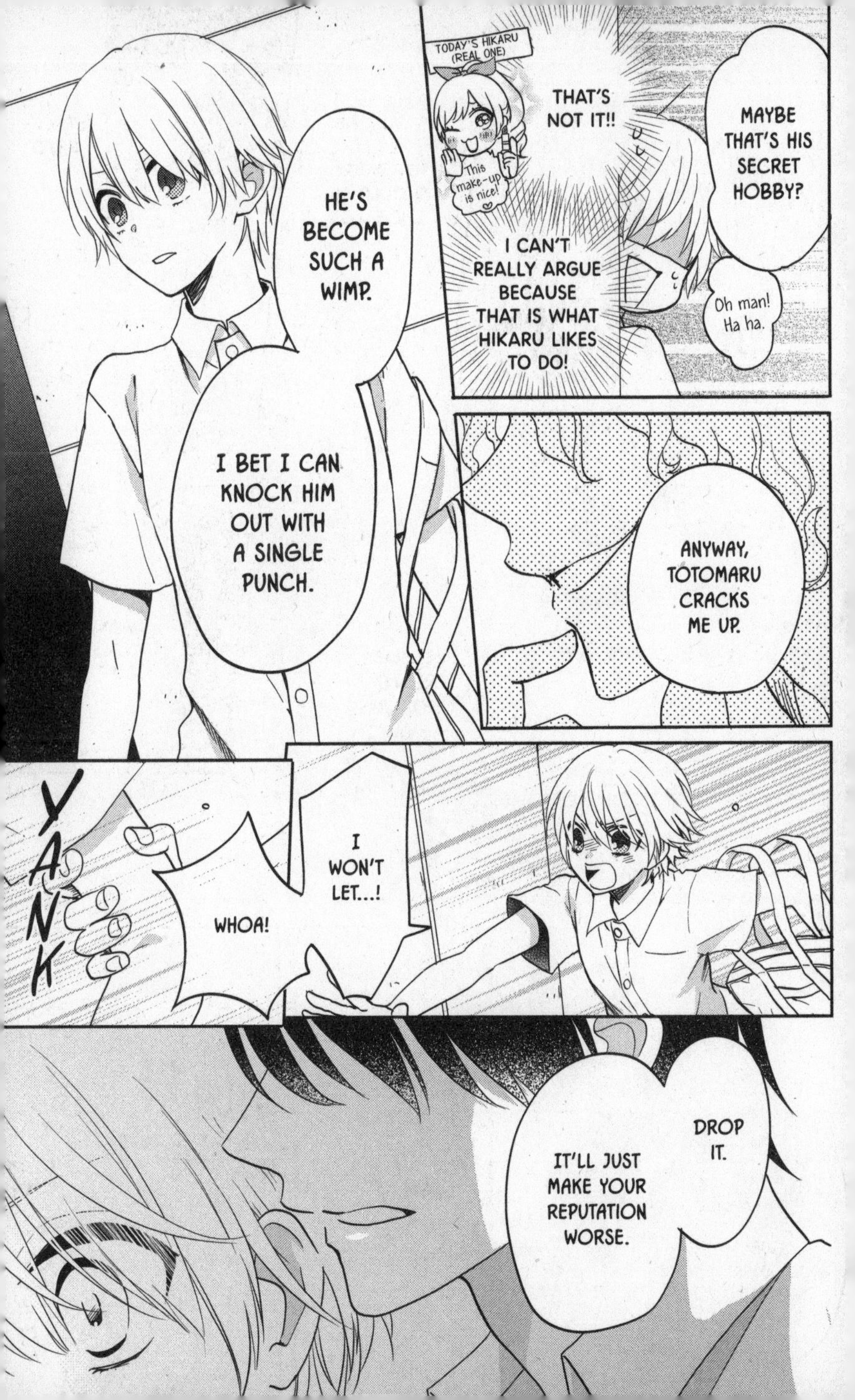
MAYBE THAT'S HIS SECRET HOBBY?
Oh man! Ha ha.
THAT'S NOT IT!!
TODAY'S HIKARU (REAL ONE)
This make-up is nice!
I CAN'T REALLY ARGUE BECAUSE THAT IS WHAT HIKARU LIKES TO DO!
ANYWAY, TOTOMARU CRACKS ME UP.
HE'S BECOME SUCH A WIMP.
I BET I CAN KNOCK HIM OUT WITH A SINGLE PUNCH.
I WON'T LET...!
WHOA!
YANK
DROP IT.
IT'LL JUST MAKE YOUR REPUTATION WORSE.

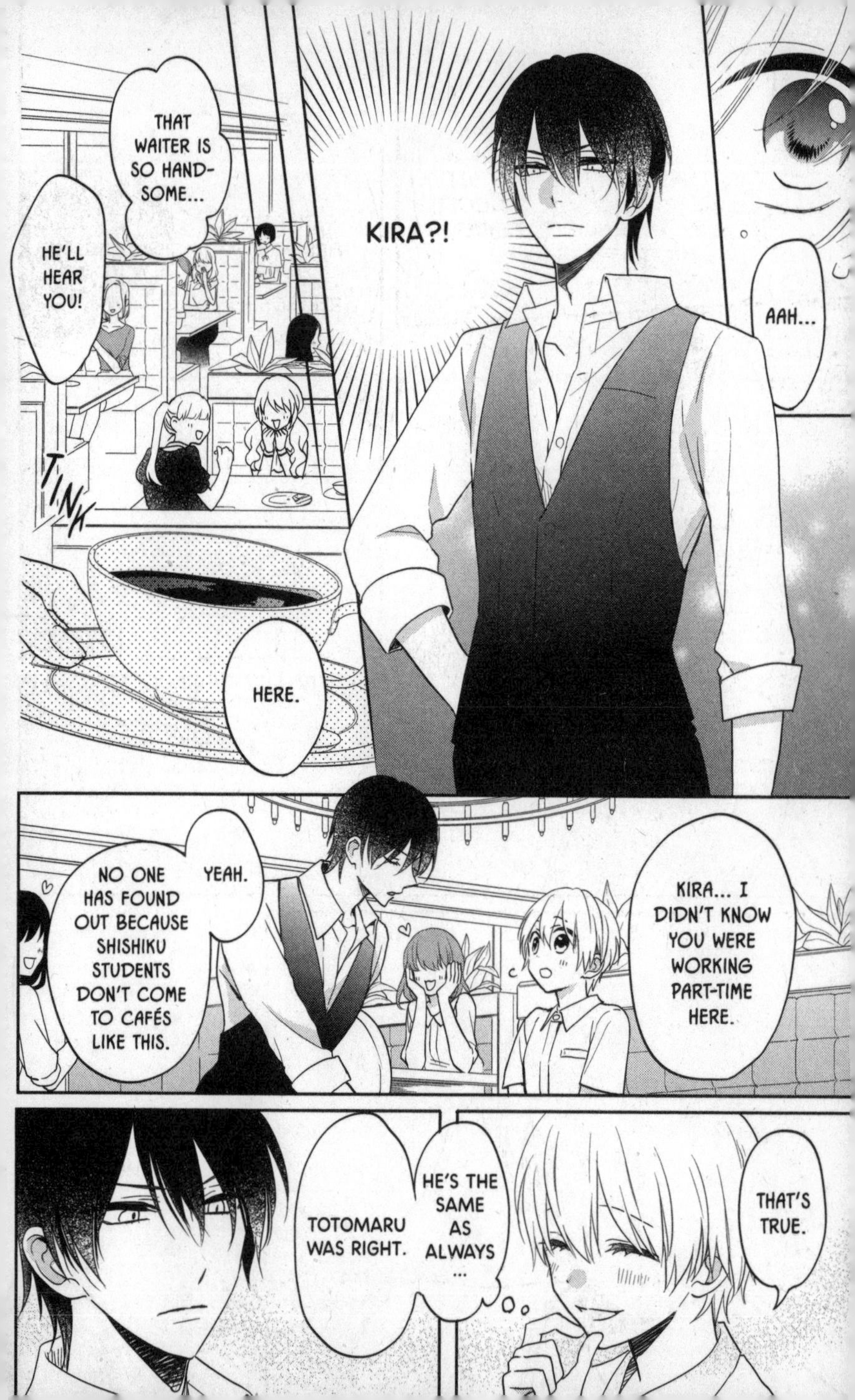
AAH...
KIRA?!
THAT WAITER IS SO HAND-SOME...
HE'LL HEAR YOU!
TINK
HERE.
KIRA... I DIDN'T KNOW YOU WERE WORKING PART-TIME HERE.
YEAH.
NO ONE HAS FOUND OUT BECAUSE SHISHIKU STUDENTS DON'T COME TO CAFÉS LIKE THIS.
THAT'S TRUE.
HE'S THE SAME AS ALWAYS ...
TOTOMARU WAS RIGHT.

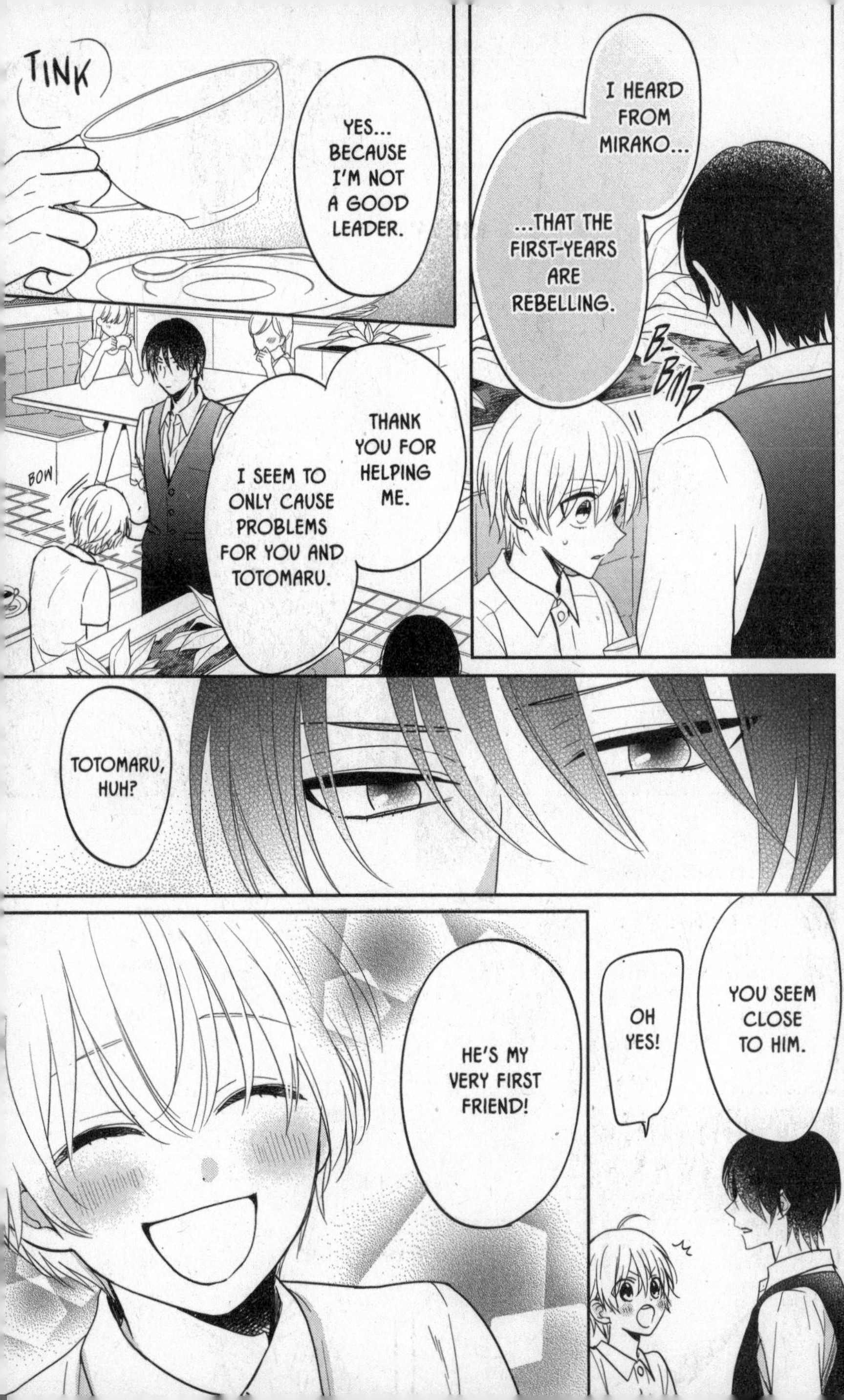
I HEARD FROM MIRAKO...
...THAT THE FIRST-YEARS ARE REBELLING.
B-BMP
TINK
YES... BECAUSE I'M NOT A GOOD LEADER.
THANK YOU FOR HELPING ME.
I SEEM TO ONLY CAUSE PROBLEMS FOR YOU AND TOTOMARU.
BOW
TOTOMARU, HUH?
YOU SEEM CLOSE TO HIM.
OH YES!
HE'S MY VERY FIRST FRIEND!

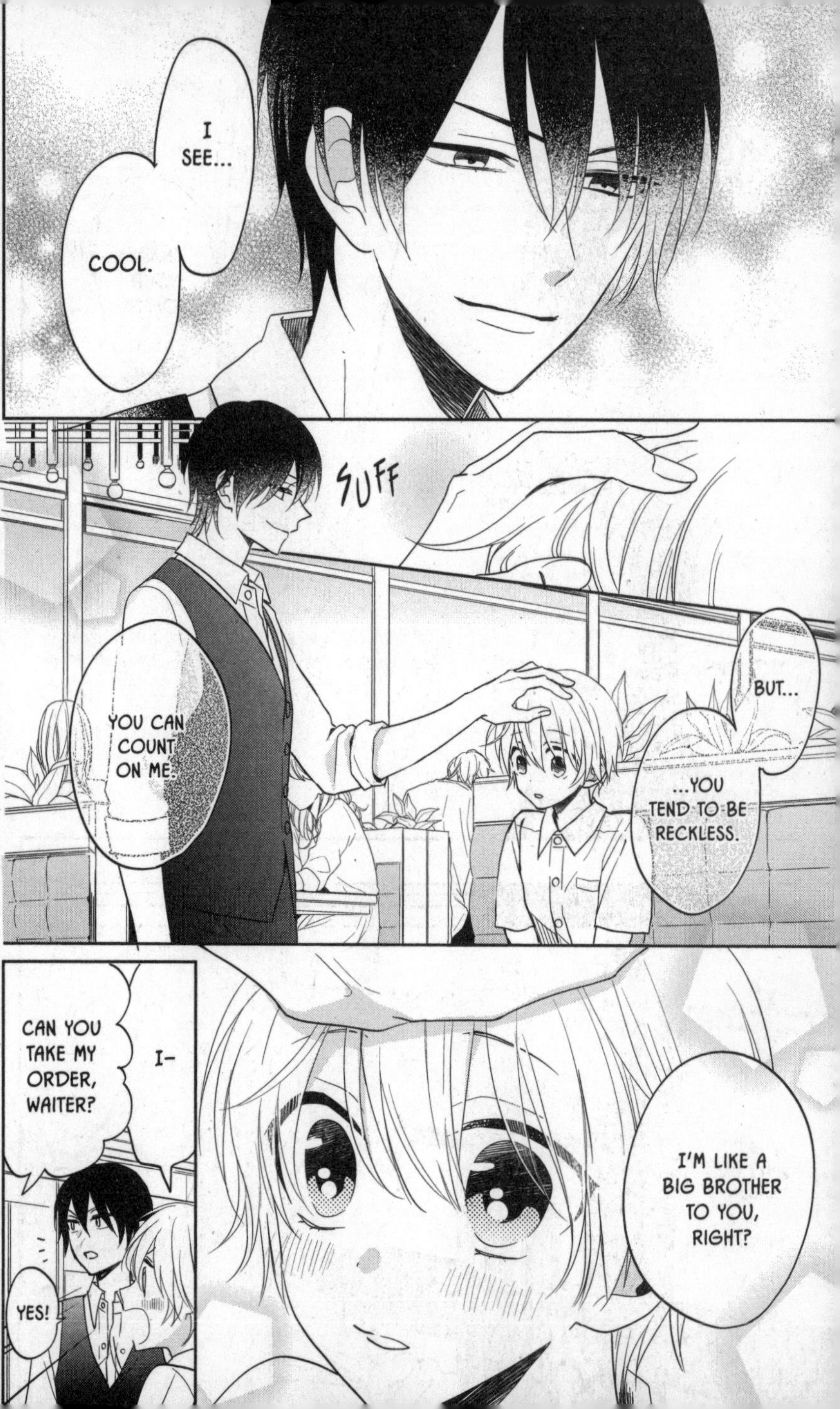
I SEE...
COOL.
SUFF
BUT...
...YOU TEND TO BE RECKLESS.
YOU CAN COUNT ON ME.
I'M LIKE A BIG BROTHER TO YOU, RIGHT?
I-
CAN YOU TAKE MY ORDER, WAITER?
YES!

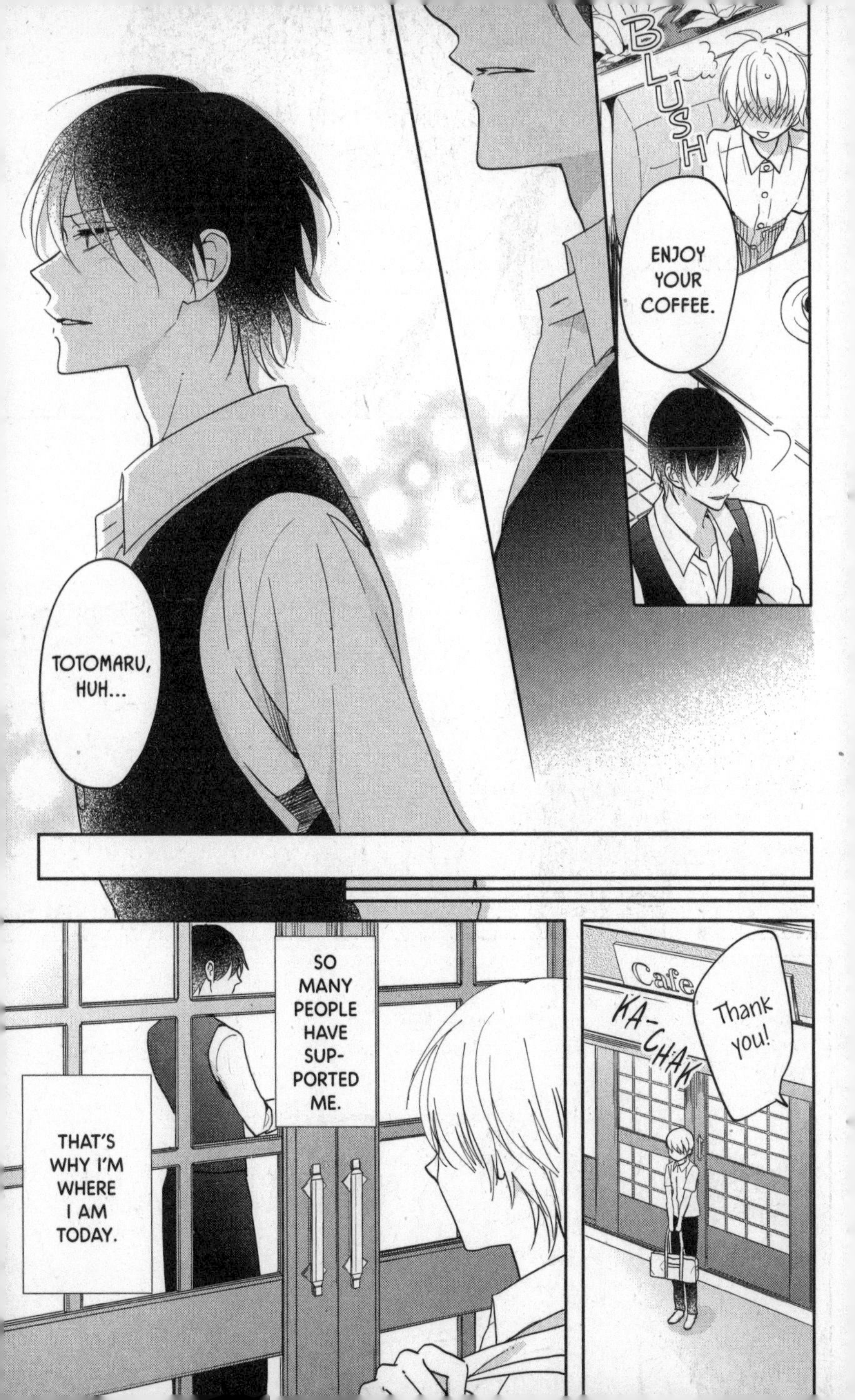
BLUSH
ENJOY YOUR COFFEE.
TOTOMARU, HUH...
Cafe
KA-CHAK
Thank you!
SO MANY PEOPLE HAVE SUP-PORTED ME.
THAT'S WHY I'M WHERE I AM TODAY.

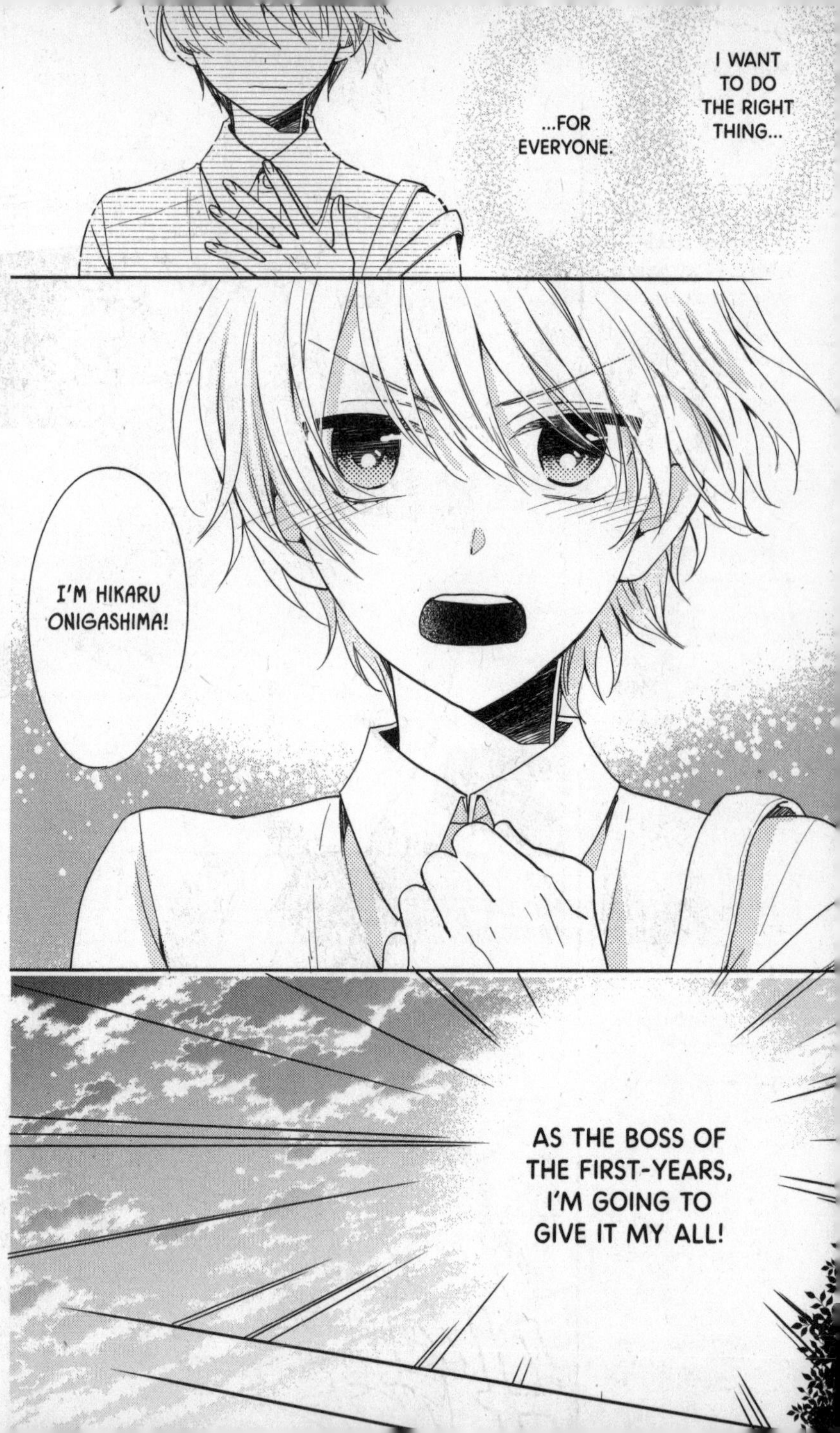
I WANT TO DO THE RIGHT THING...
...FOR EVERYONE.
I'M HIKARU ONIGASHIMA!
AS THE BOSS OF THE FIRST-YEARS, I'M GOING TO GIVE IT MY ALL!

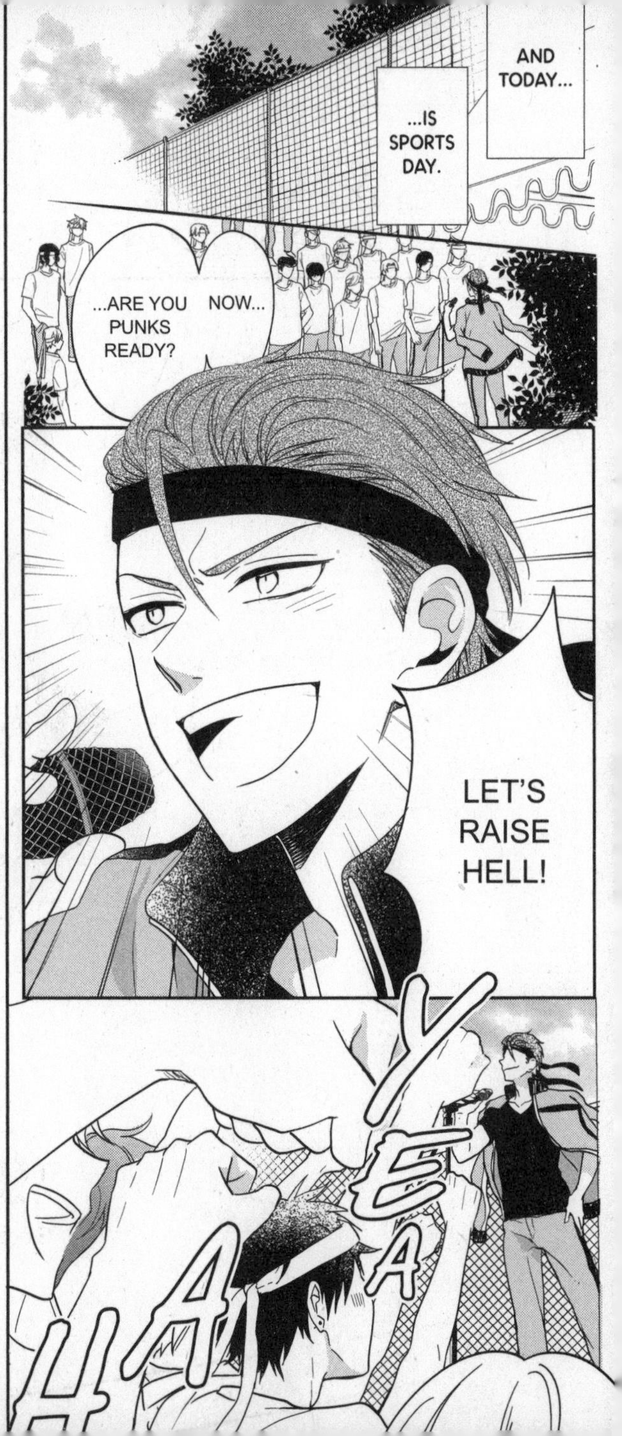
AND TODAY...
...IS SPORTS DAY.
NOW...
...ARE YOU PUNKS READY?
LET'S RAISE HELL!
YEAH

Men Can Be Brave and Apologize!!

The three radio hosts apologize for the listeners who couldn't apologize. Each pretends to be a female listener.

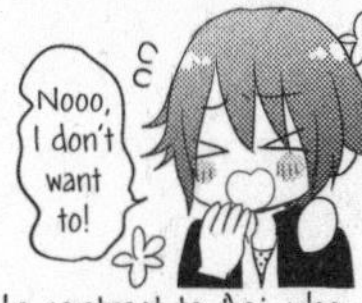
Nooo, I don't want to!

In contrast to Aoi, who can maximize femininity and put on a perfect performance as a girl...

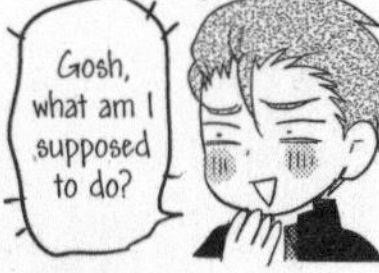
Gosh, what am I supposed to do?

Maeno is pushing it, to be honest. (He has a deep voice.)

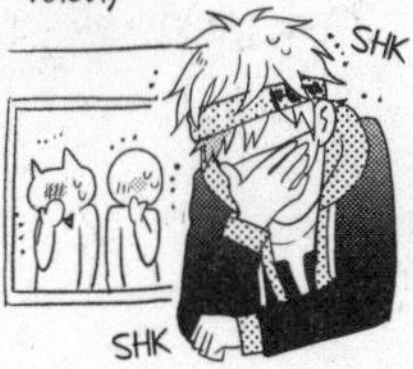
SHK
SHK

KENN found it so hilarious that he could barely speak.

It was like a crazy comedy act performed by three people. It was so funny to listen to. Please check out the CD of the radio program if you want to listen to the entire series. ✿

Highly recommended!

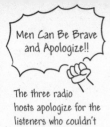

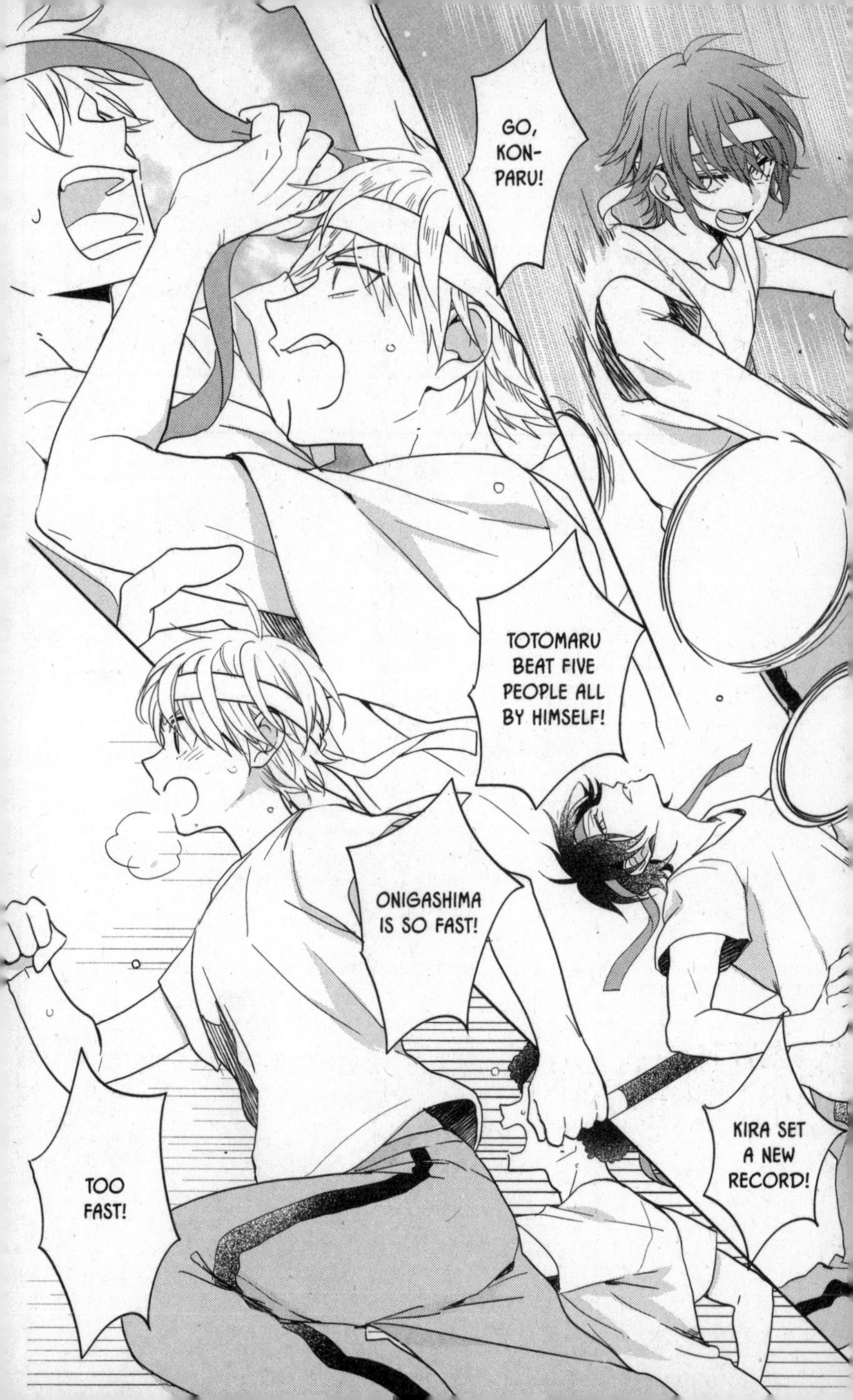
GO, KON-PARU!
TOTOMARU BEAT FIVE PEOPLE ALL BY HIMSELF!
KIRA SET A NEW RECORD!
ONIGASHIMA IS SO FAST!
TOO FAST!

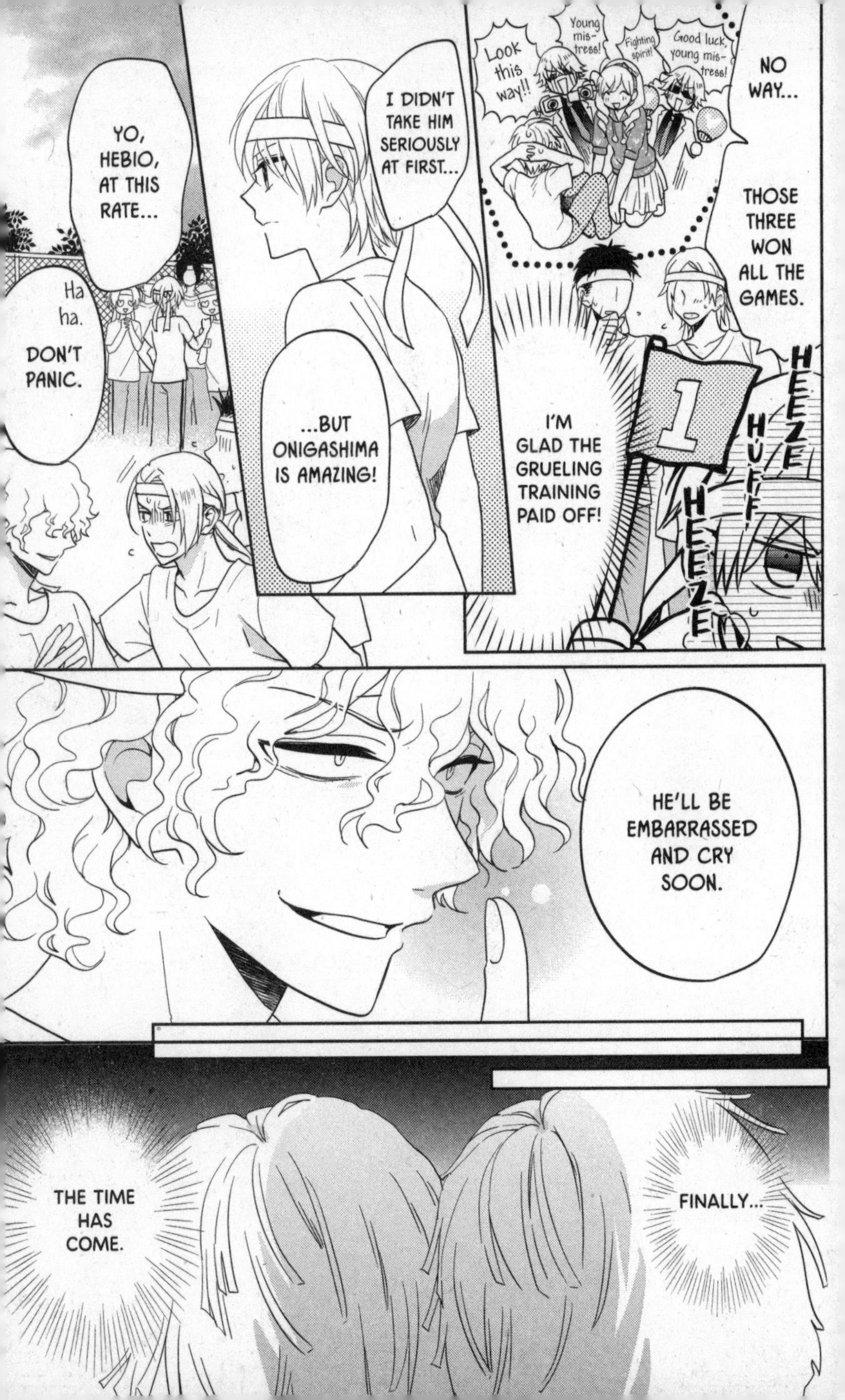
NO WAY...
Good luck, young mistress!
Fighting spirit!
Young mistress!
Look this way!!
THOSE THREE WON ALL THE GAMES.
HEEZE
HUFF
HEEZE
I'M GLAD THE GRUELING TRAINING PAID OFF!
I DIDN'T TAKE HIM SERIOUSLY AT FIRST...
...BUT ONIGASHIMA IS AMAZING!
YO, HEBIO, AT THIS RATE...
Ha ha.
DON'T PANIC.
HE'LL BE EMBARRASSED AND CRY SOON.
FINALLY...
THE TIME HAS COME.

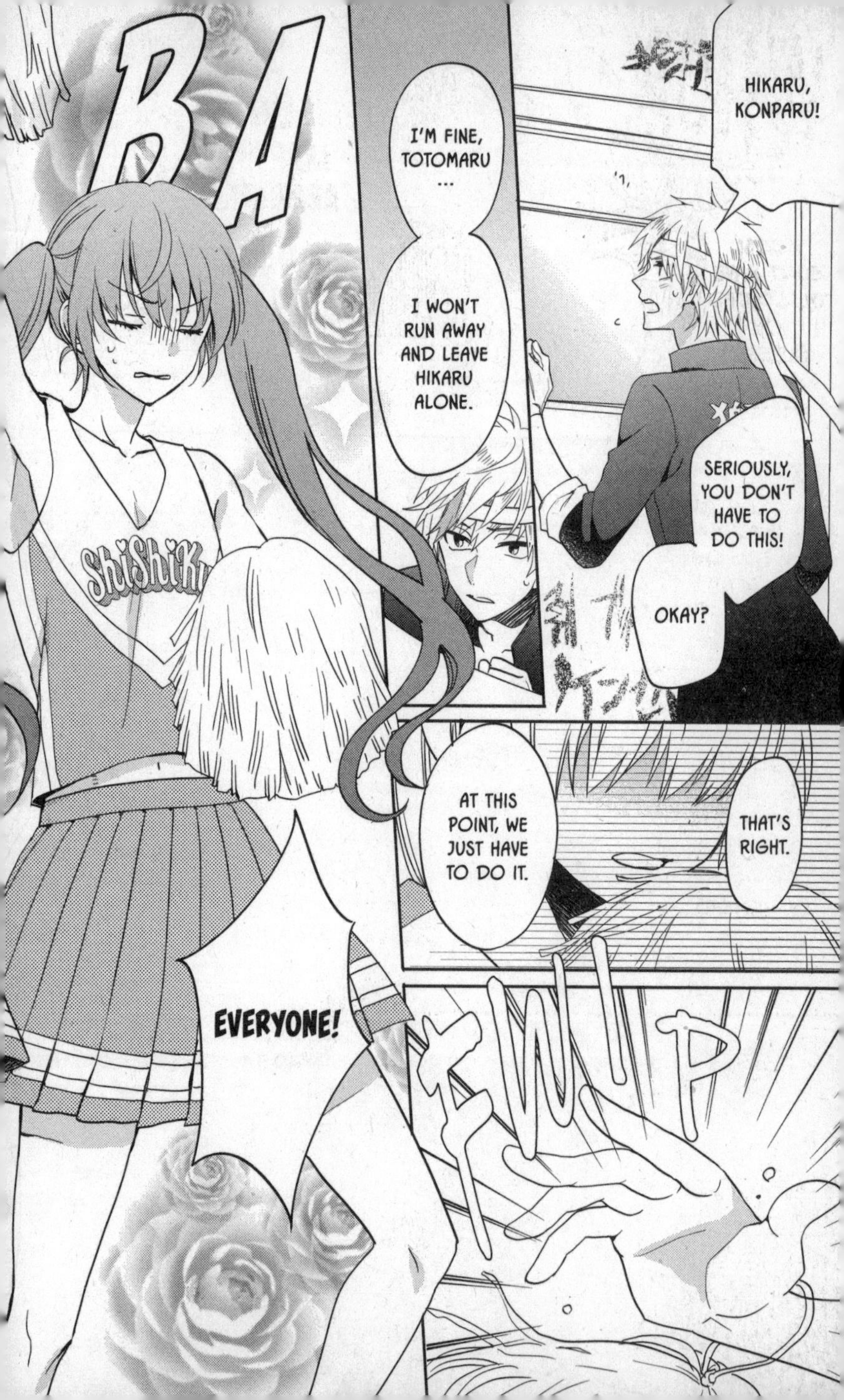

HIKARU, KONPARU!
SERIOUSLY, YOU DON'T HAVE TO DO THIS!
OKAY?
I'M FINE, TOTOMARU ...
I WON'T RUN AWAY AND LEAVE HIKARU ALONE.
THAT'S RIGHT.
AT THIS POINT, WE JUST HAVE TO DO IT.
WHIP
BA
EVERYONE!

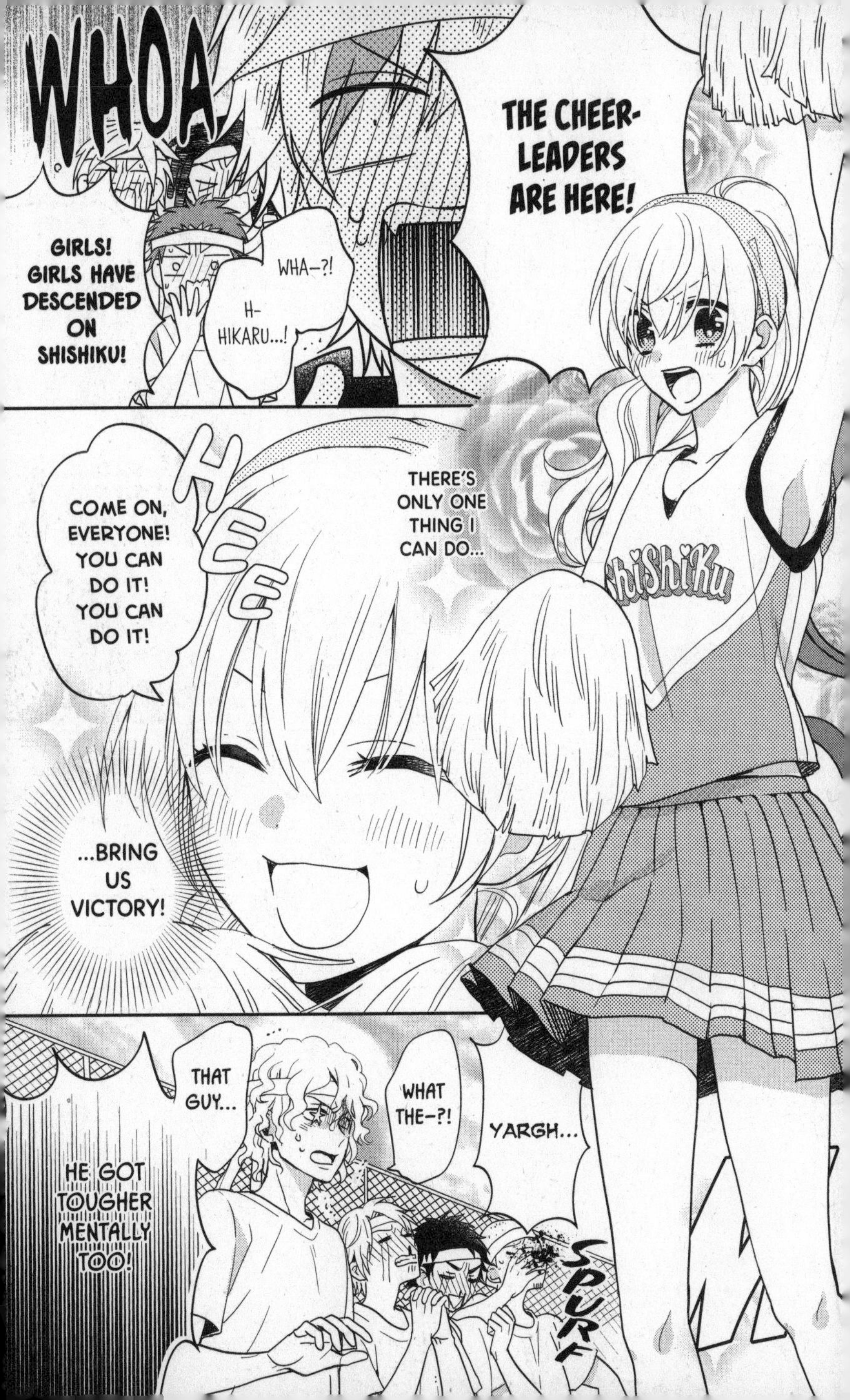
THE CHEER-LEADERS ARE HERE!
WHOA
WHA-?!
H-HIKARU...!
GIRLS! GIRLS HAVE DESCENDED ON SHISHIKU!
THERE'S ONLY ONE THING I CAN DO...
HEE
COME ON, EVERYONE! YOU CAN DO IT! YOU CAN DO IT!
...BRING US VICTORY!
ShiShiKu
YARGH...
SPURF
WHAT THE-?!
THAT GUY...
HE GOT TOUGHER MENTALLY TOO!

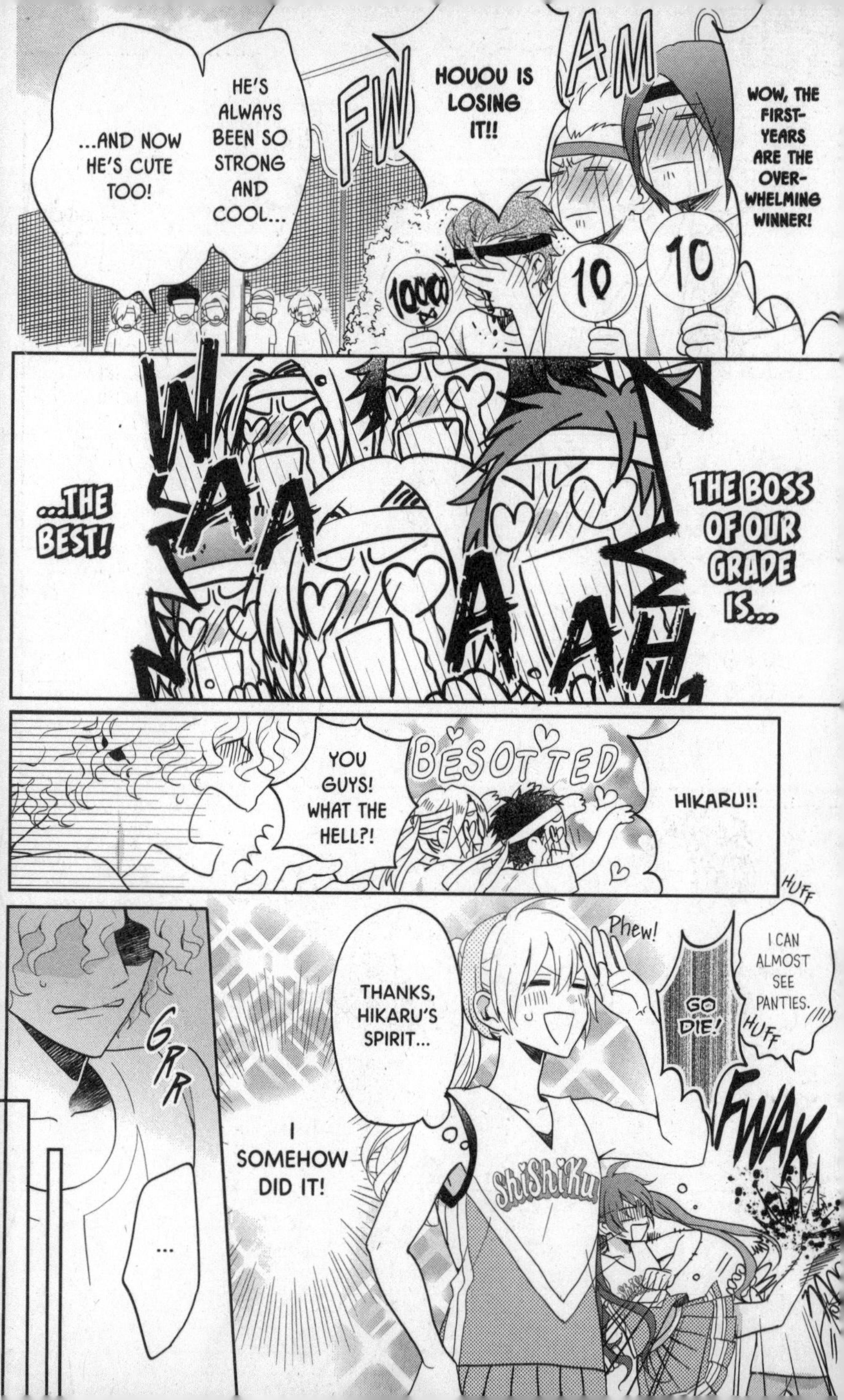
WOW, THE FIRST-YEARS ARE THE OVERWHELMING WINNER!
AM
10
10
HOUOU IS LOSING IT!!
FW
HE'S ALWAYS BEEN SO STRONG AND COOL...
...AND NOW HE'S CUTE TOO!
THE BOSS OF OUR GRADE IS...
WAAAAAH
...THE BEST!
HIKARU!!
BESOTTED
YOU GUYS! WHAT THE HELL?!
HUFF
I CAN ALMOST SEE PANTIES.
HUFF
GO DIE!
FWAK
Phew!
THANKS, HIKARU'S SPIRIT...
I SOMEHOW DID IT!
ShiShiKu
GRR
...

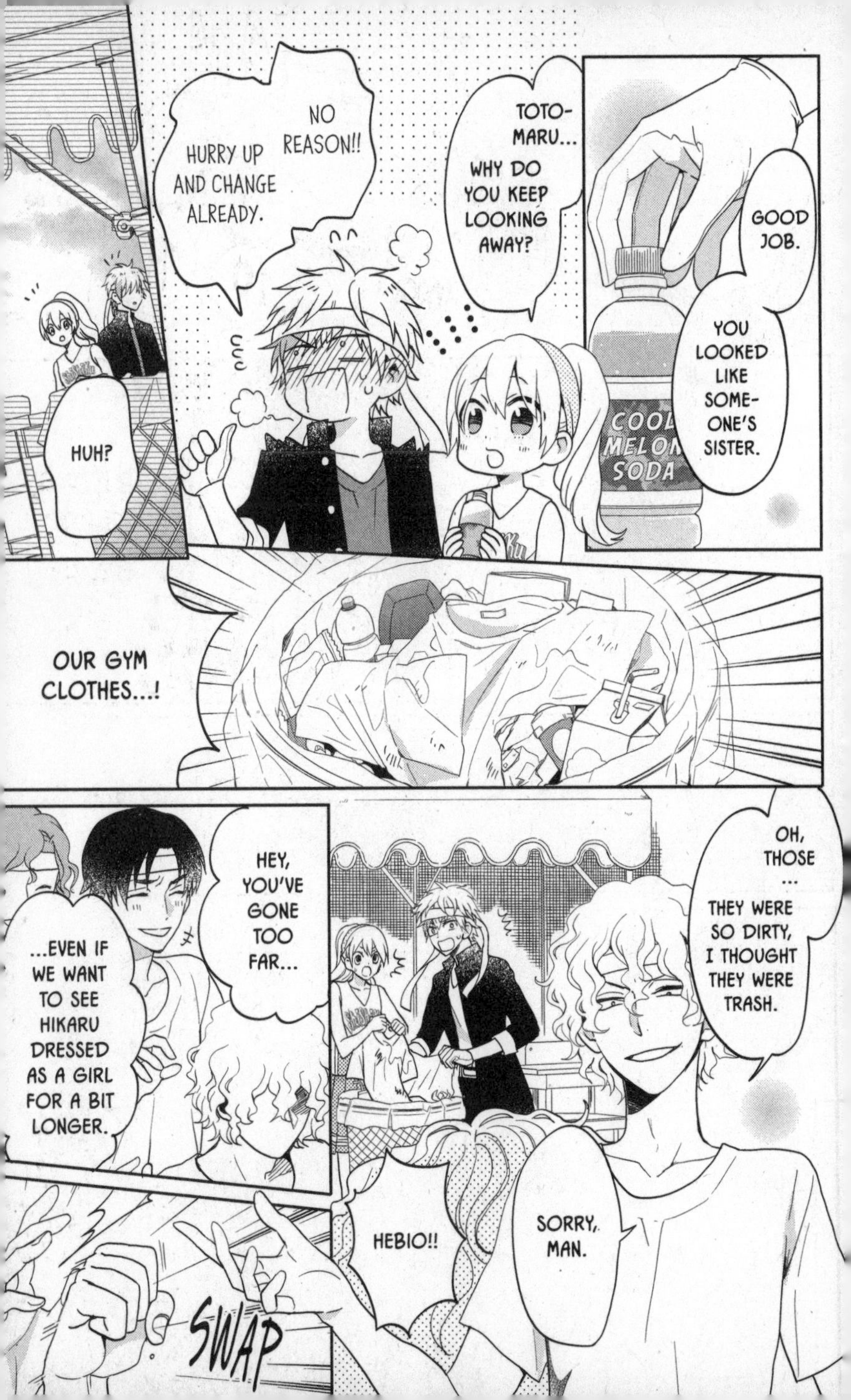
GOOD JOB.
YOU LOOKED LIKE SOME-ONE'S SISTER.
COOL MELON SODA
TOTO-MARU...
WHY DO YOU KEEP LOOKING AWAY?
NO REASON!!
HURRY UP AND CHANGE ALREADY.
HUH?
OUR GYM CLOTHES...!
OH, THOSE... THEY WERE SO DIRTY, I THOUGHT THEY WERE TRASH.
HEY, YOU'VE GONE TOO FAR...
...EVEN IF WE WANT TO SEE HIKARU DRESSED AS A GIRL FOR A BIT LONGER.
SORRY, MAN.
HEBIO!!
SWAP

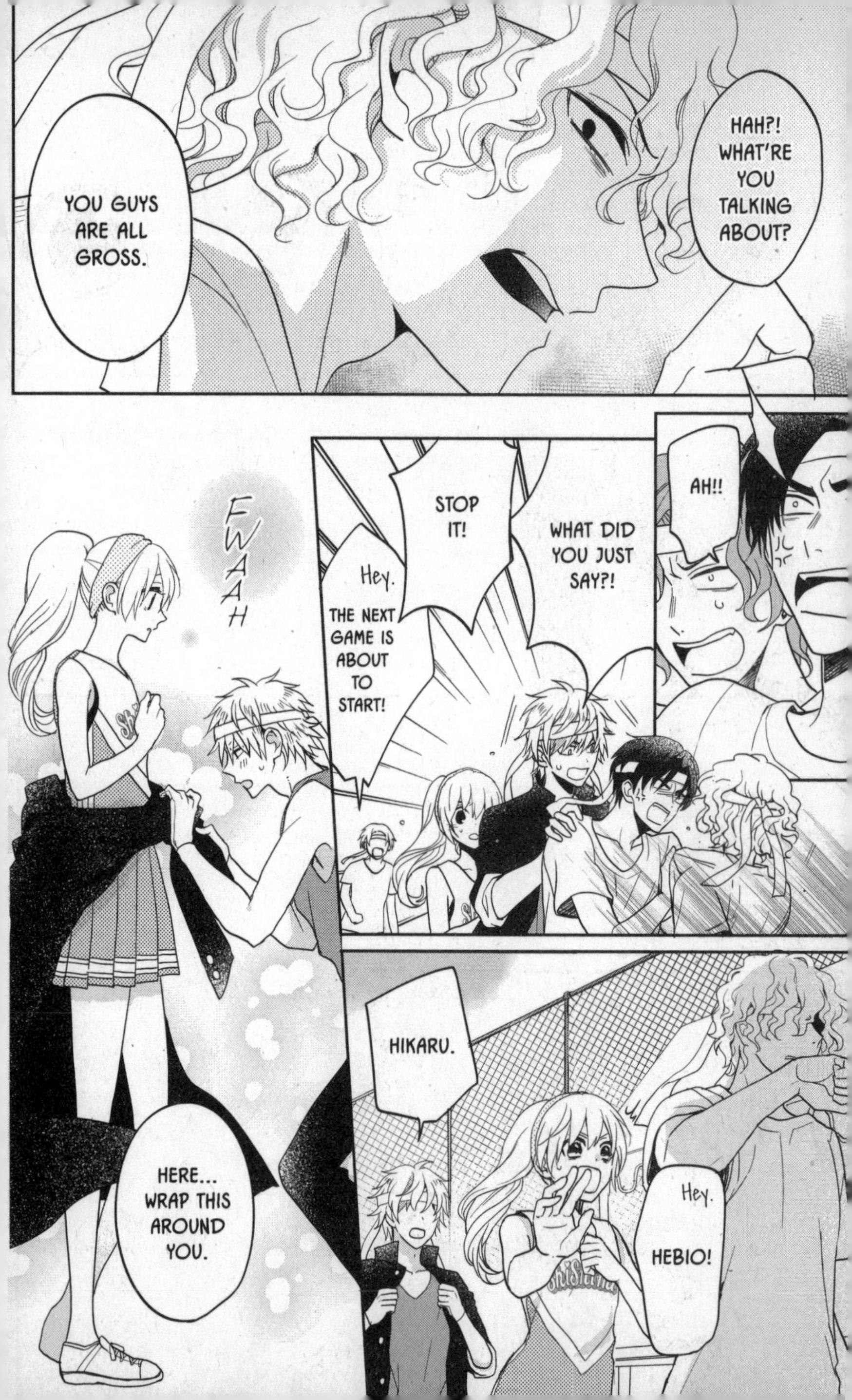
HAH?! WHAT'RE YOU TALKING ABOUT?
YOU GUYS ARE ALL GROSS.
AH!!
WHAT DID YOU JUST SAY?!
STOP IT!
Hey.
THE NEXT GAME IS ABOUT TO START!
Hey.
HEBIO!
HIKARU.
FWAAH
HERE... WRAP THIS AROUND YOU.

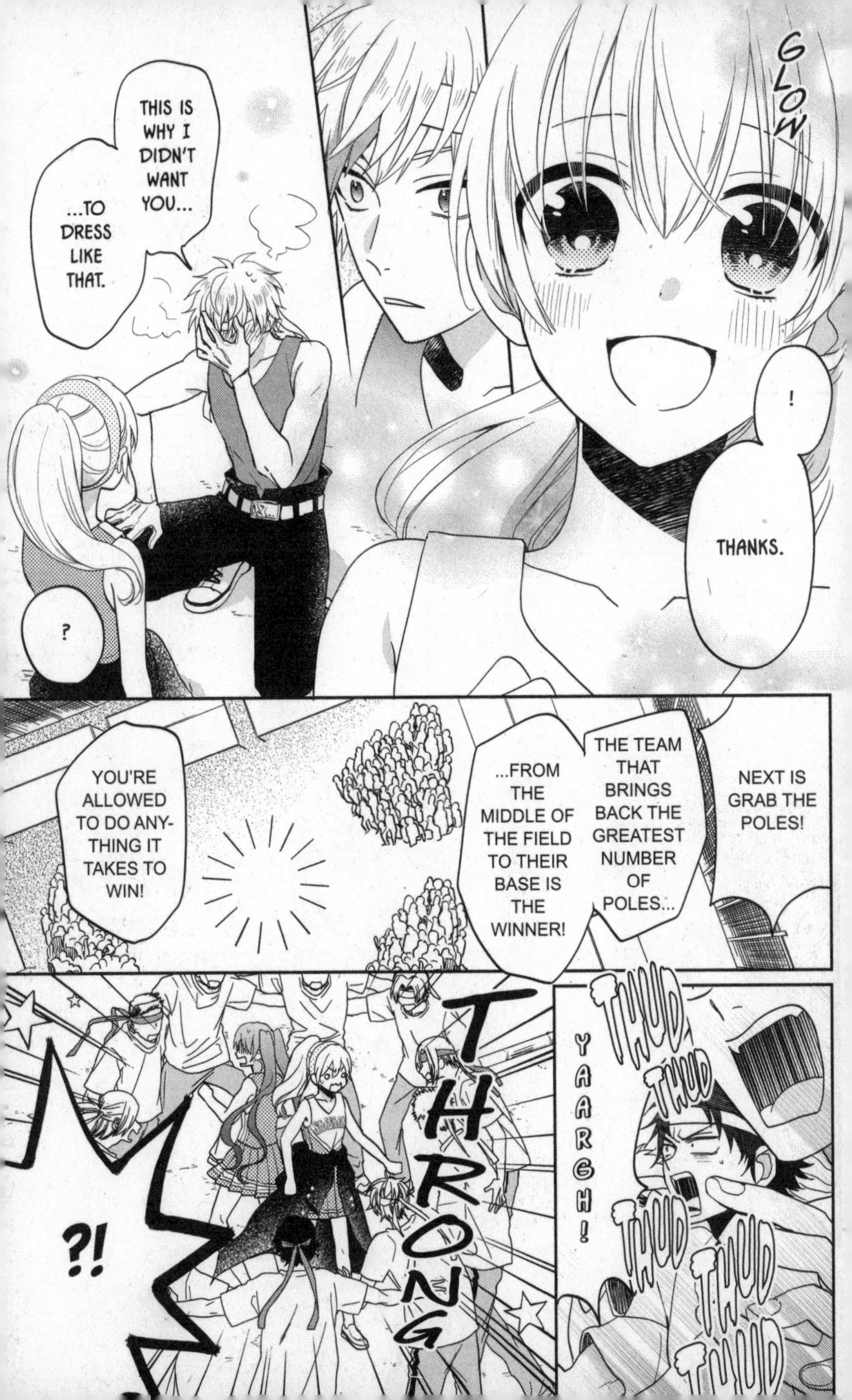
GLOW
!
THANKS.
THIS IS WHY I DIDN'T WANT YOU...
...TO DRESS LIKE THAT.
?
NEXT IS GRAB THE POLES!
THE TEAM THAT BRINGS BACK THE GREATEST NUMBER OF POLES...
...FROM THE MIDDLE OF THE FIELD TO THEIR BASE IS THE WINNER!
YOU'RE ALLOWED TO DO ANY-THING IT TAKES TO WIN!
THUD
THUD
YAARGH!
THUD
THUD
THUD
THUD
THRONG
?!

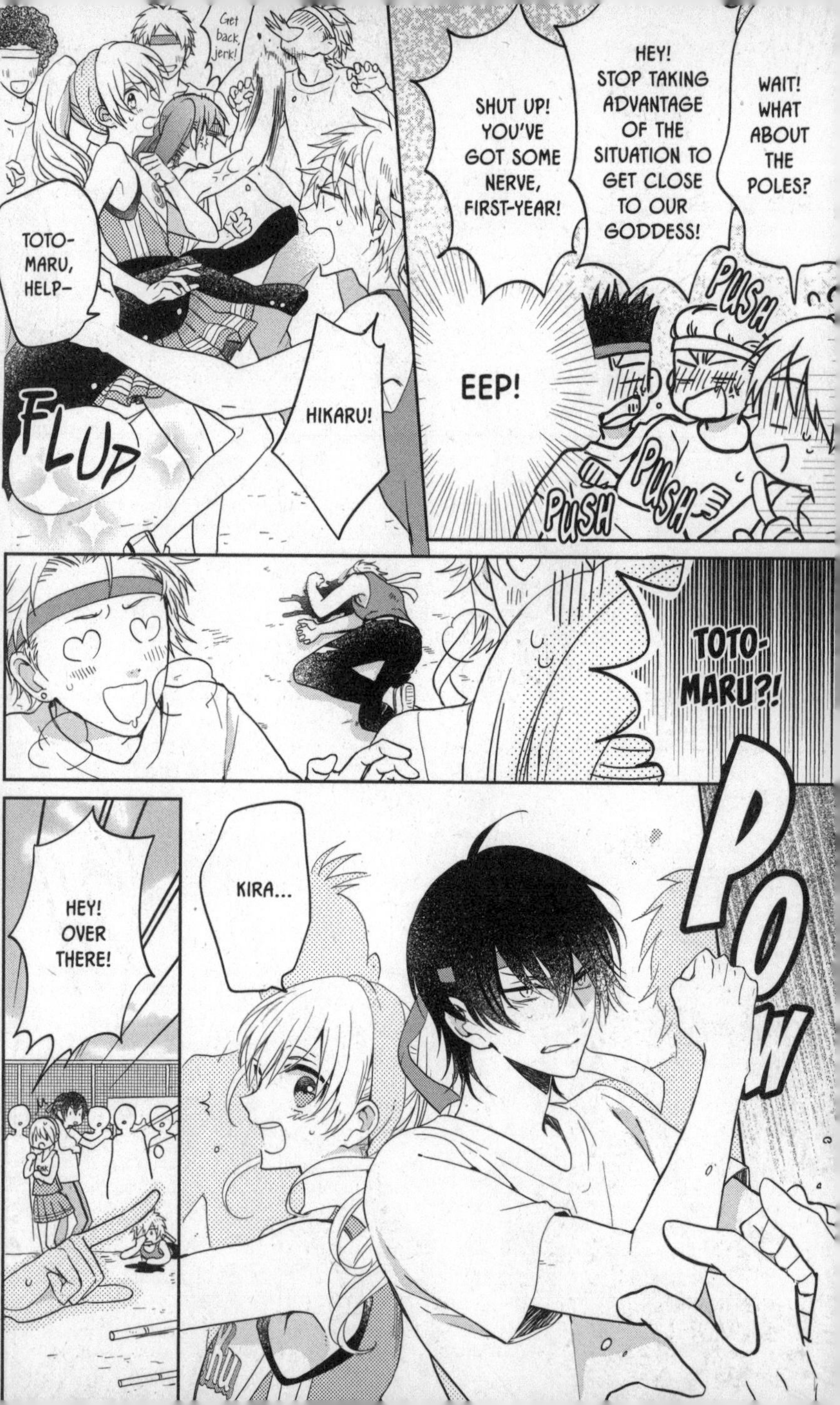
WAIT! WHAT ABOUT THE POLES?
HEY! STOP TAKING ADVANTAGE OF THE SITUATION TO GET CLOSE TO OUR GODDESS!
SHUT UP! YOU'VE GOT SOME NERVE, FIRST-YEAR!
PUSH
EEP!
PUSH
PUSH
Get back, jerk!
TOTO-MARU, HELP–
HIKARU!
FLUP
TOTO-MARU?!
POW
KIRA...
HEY! OVER THERE!

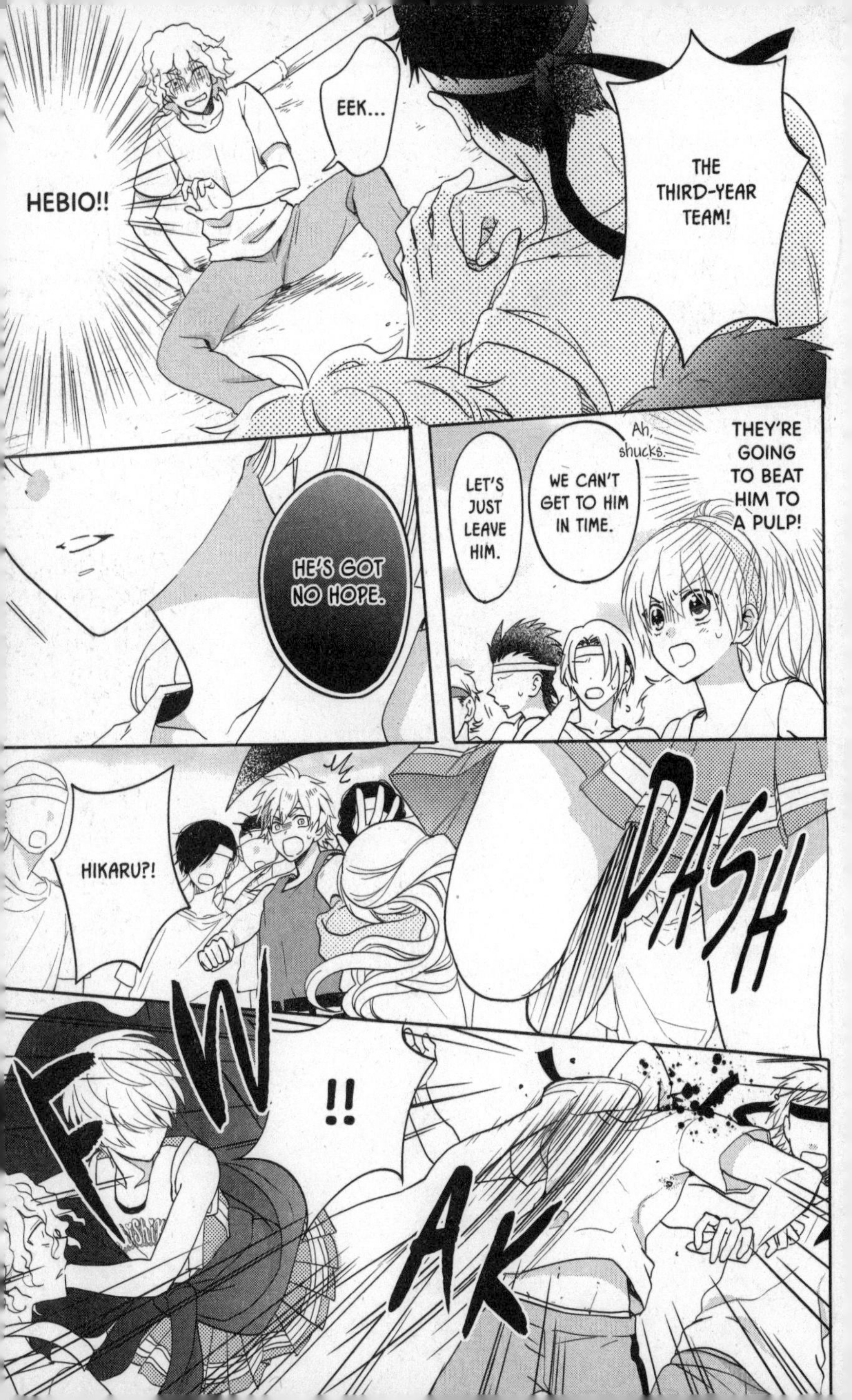
THE THIRD-YEAR TEAM!
EEK...
HEBIO!!
THEY'RE GOING TO BEAT HIM TO A PULP!
Ah, shucks.
WE CAN'T GET TO HIM IN TIME.
LET'S JUST LEAVE HIM.
HE'S GOT NO HOPE.
DASH
HIKARU?!
THWAK
!!

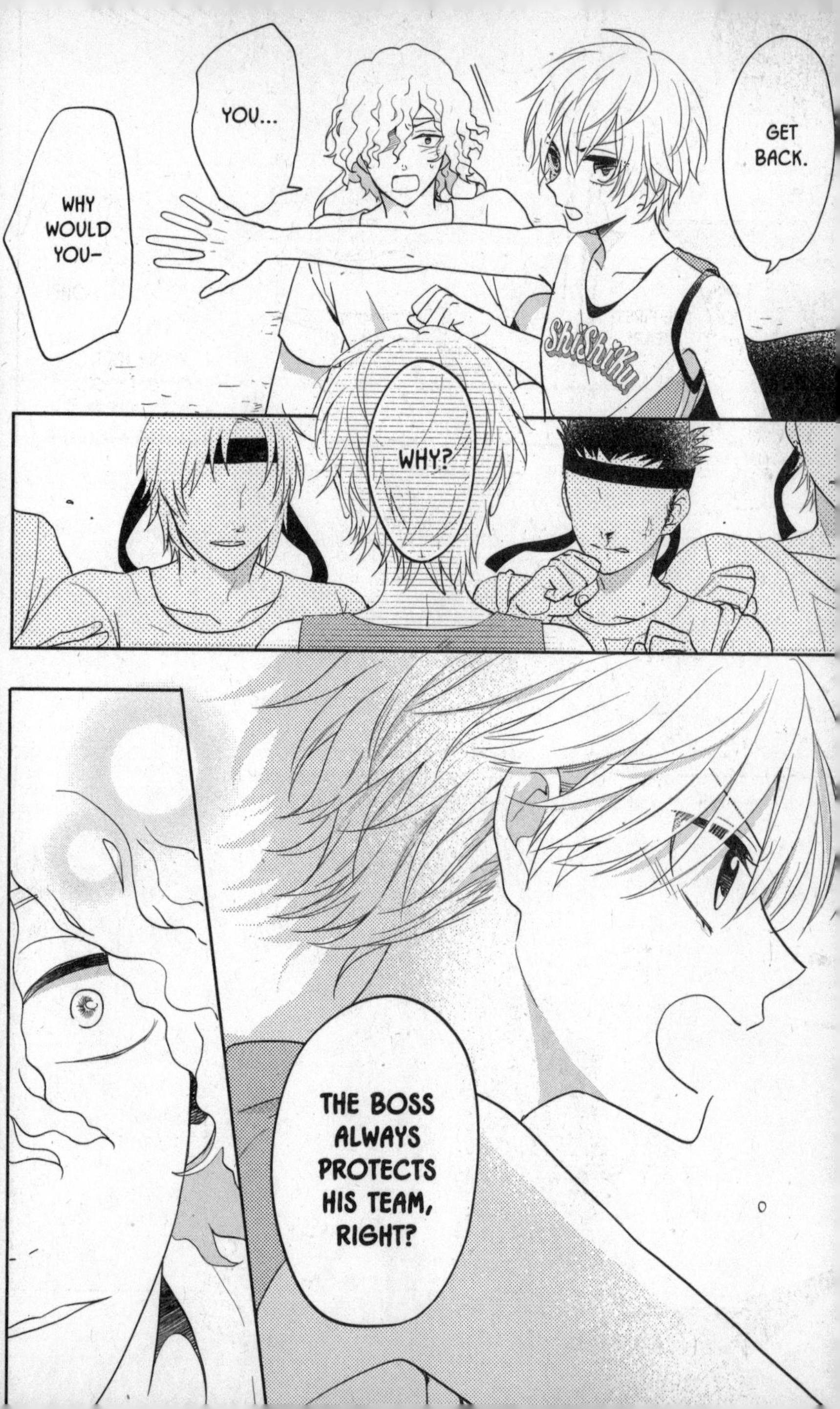
GET BACK.
ShiShiKu
YOU...
WHY WOULD YOU-
WHY?
THE BOSS ALWAYS PROTECTS HIS TEAM, RIGHT?

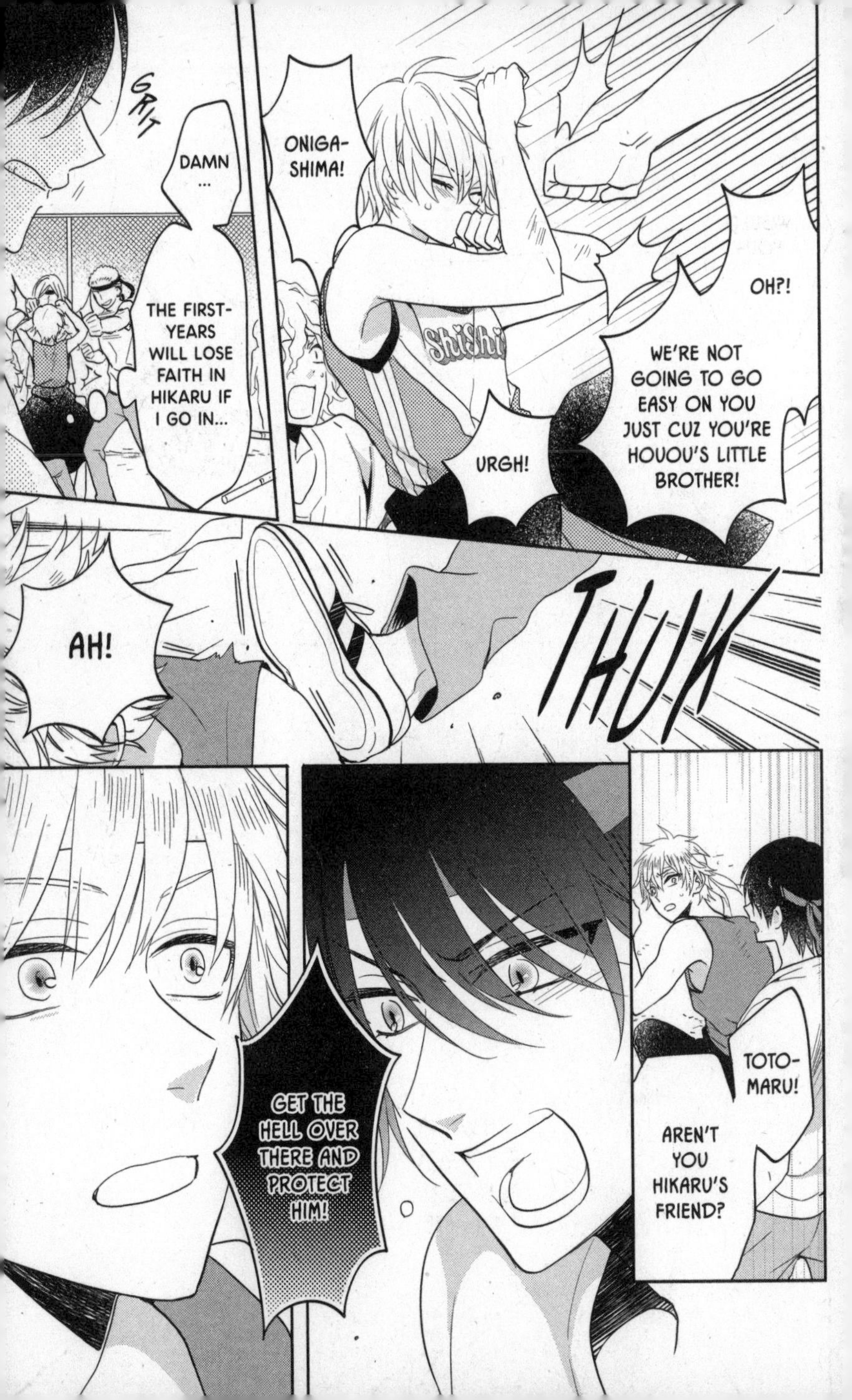
OH?!
WE'RE NOT GOING TO GO EASY ON YOU JUST CUZ YOU'RE HOUOU'S LITTLE BROTHER!
URGH!
ONIGA-SHIMA!
GRIT
DAMN...
THE FIRST-YEARS WILL LOSE FAITH IN HIKARU IF I GO IN...
THUK
AH!
TOTO-MARU!
AREN'T YOU HIKARU'S FRIEND?
GET THE HELL OVER THERE AND PROTECT HIM!

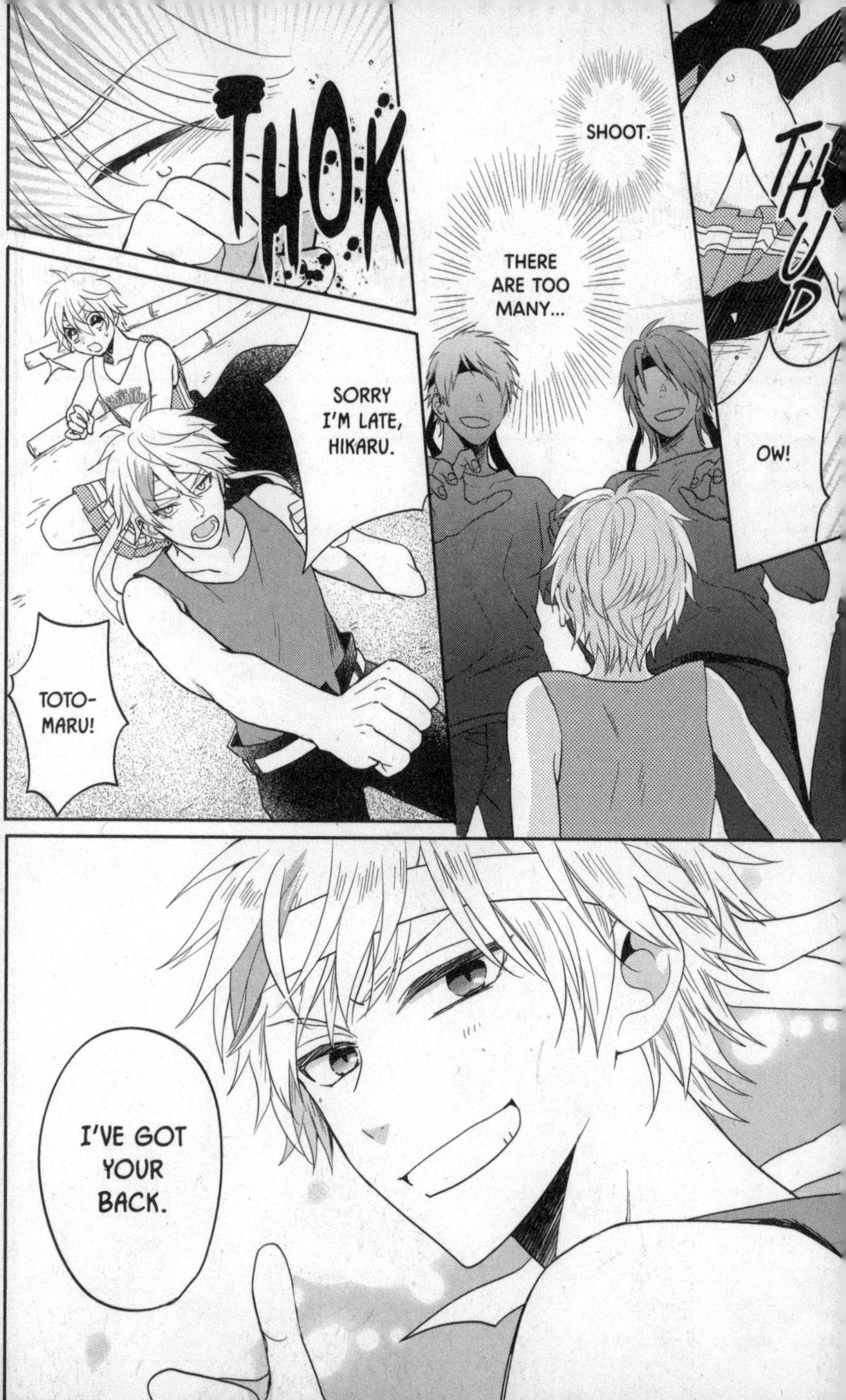
THUD
OW!
THOK
SHOOT.
THERE ARE TOO MANY...
SORRY I'M LATE, HIKARU.
TOTO-MARU!
I'VE GOT YOUR BACK.

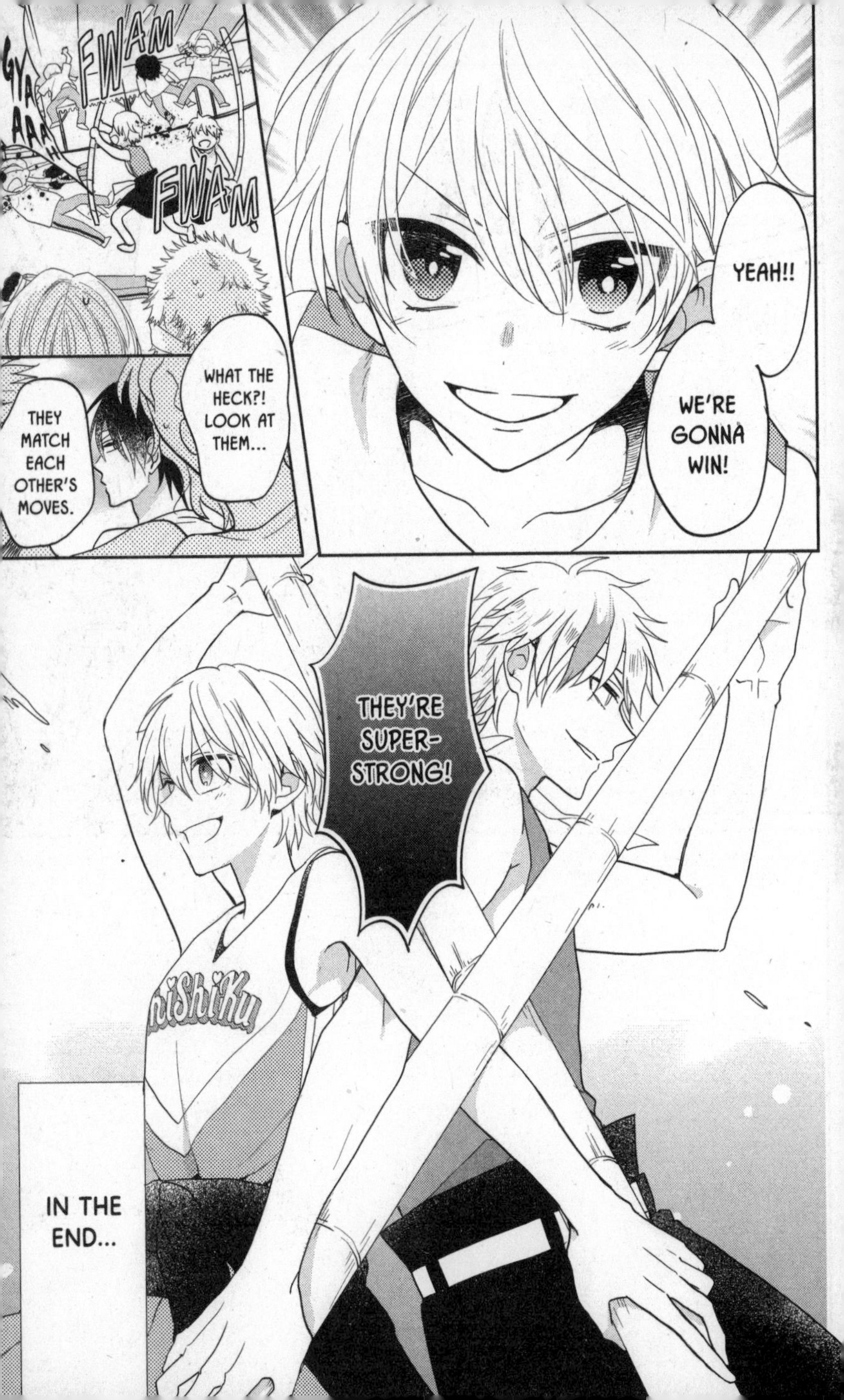
YEAH!!
WE'RE GONNA WIN!
GYAAAAH
FWAM
FWAM
WHAT THE HECK?! LOOK AT THEM...
THEY MATCH EACH OTHER'S MOVES.
THEY'RE SUPER-STRONG!
IN THE END...

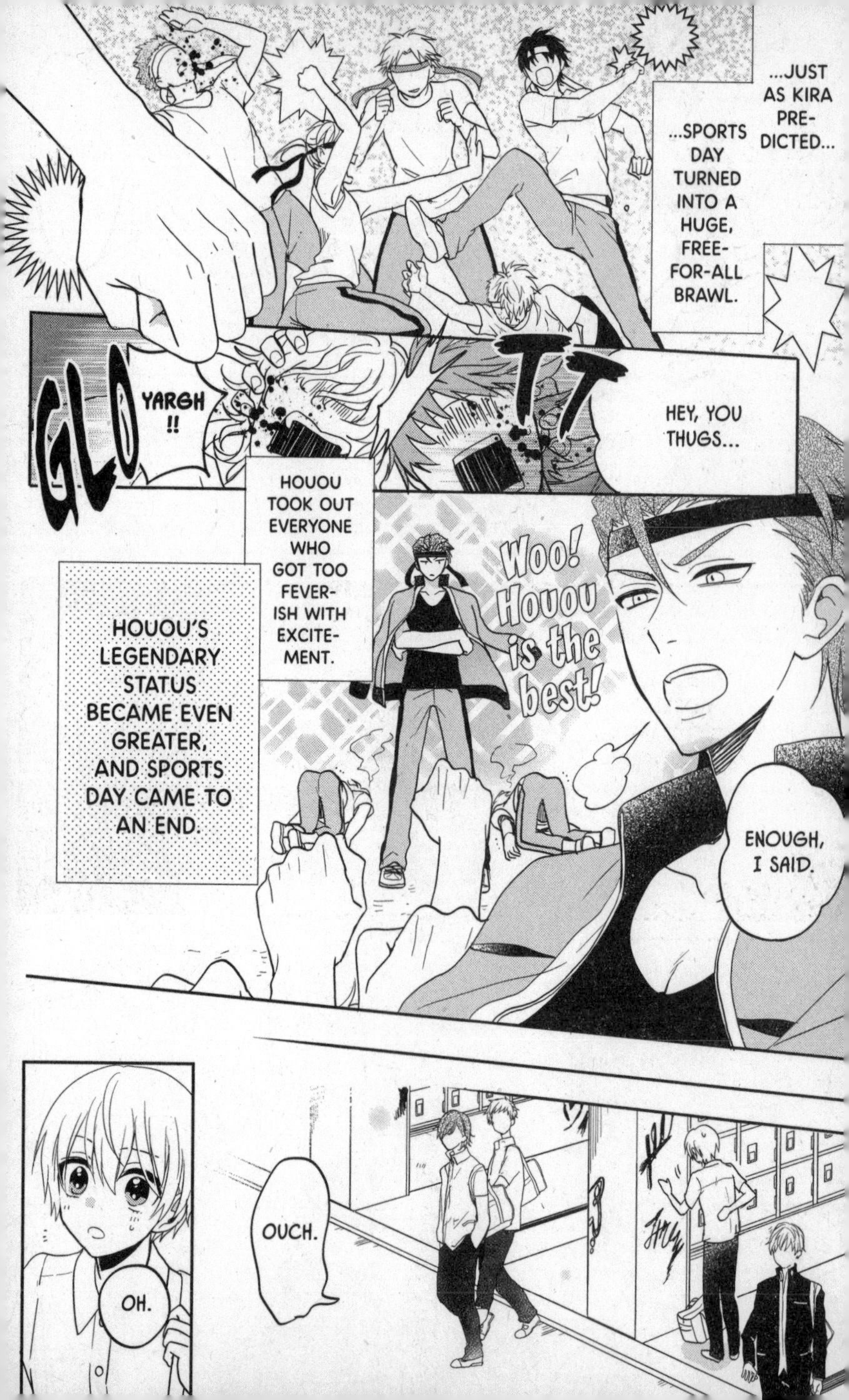
...JUST AS KIRA PREDICTED...
...SPORTS DAY TURNED INTO A HUGE, FREE-FOR-ALL BRAWL.
HEY, YOU THUGS...
YARGH!!
ENOUGH, I SAID.
Woo! Houou is the best!
HOUOU TOOK OUT EVERYONE WHO GOT TOO FEVERISH WITH EXCITEMENT.
HOUOU'S LEGENDARY STATUS BECAME EVEN GREATER, AND SPORTS DAY CAME TO AN END.
OUCH.
OH.

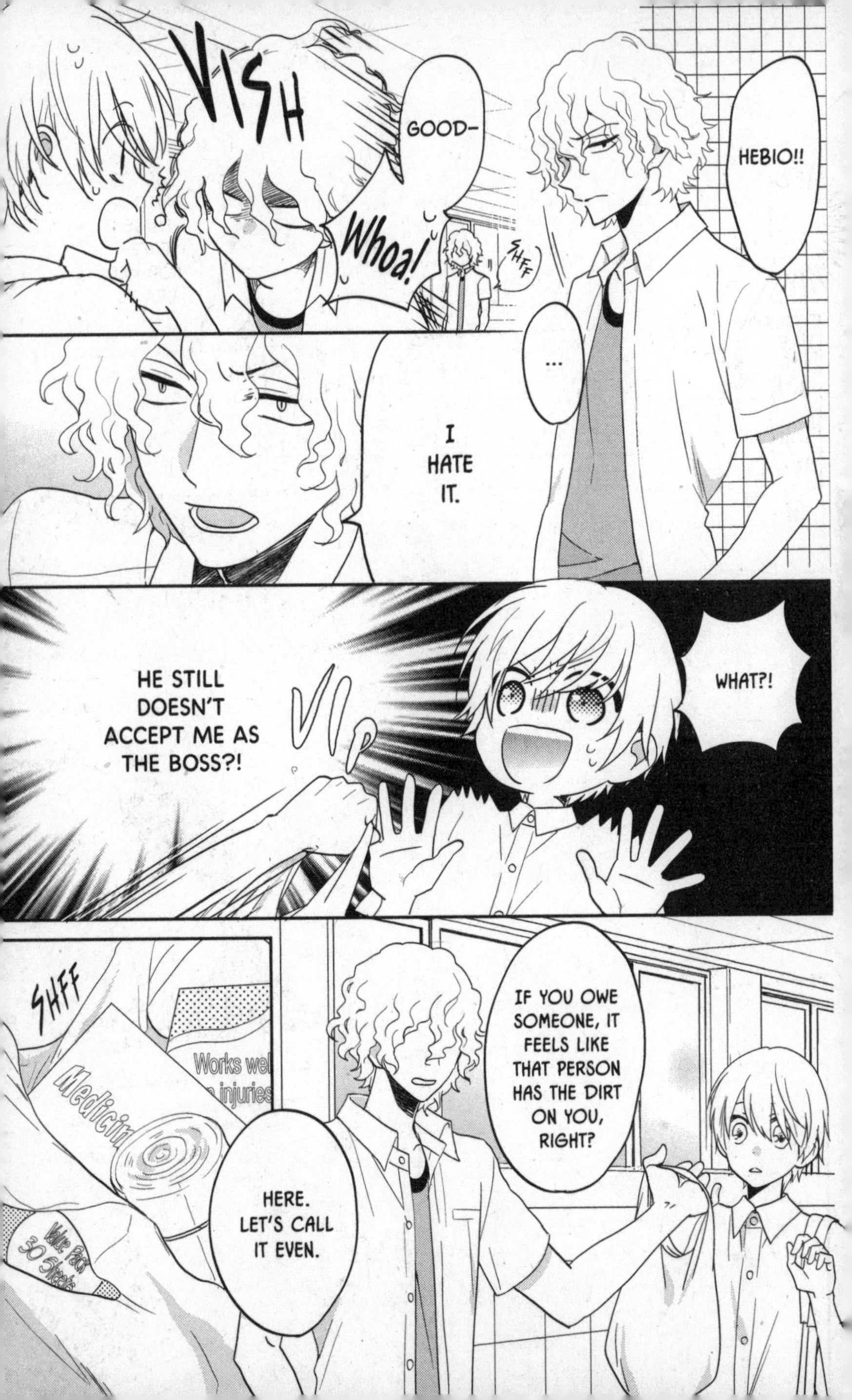
HEBIO!!
...
VISH
GOOD-
Whoa!
SHFF
I HATE IT.
WHAT?!
HE STILL DOESN'T ACCEPT ME AS THE BOSS?!
VI
IF YOU OWE SOMEONE, IT FEELS LIKE THAT PERSON HAS THE DIRT ON YOU, RIGHT?
HERE. LET'S CALL IT EVEN.
SHFF
Works wel
injuries
Medicin
Value Pack 30 Sheets

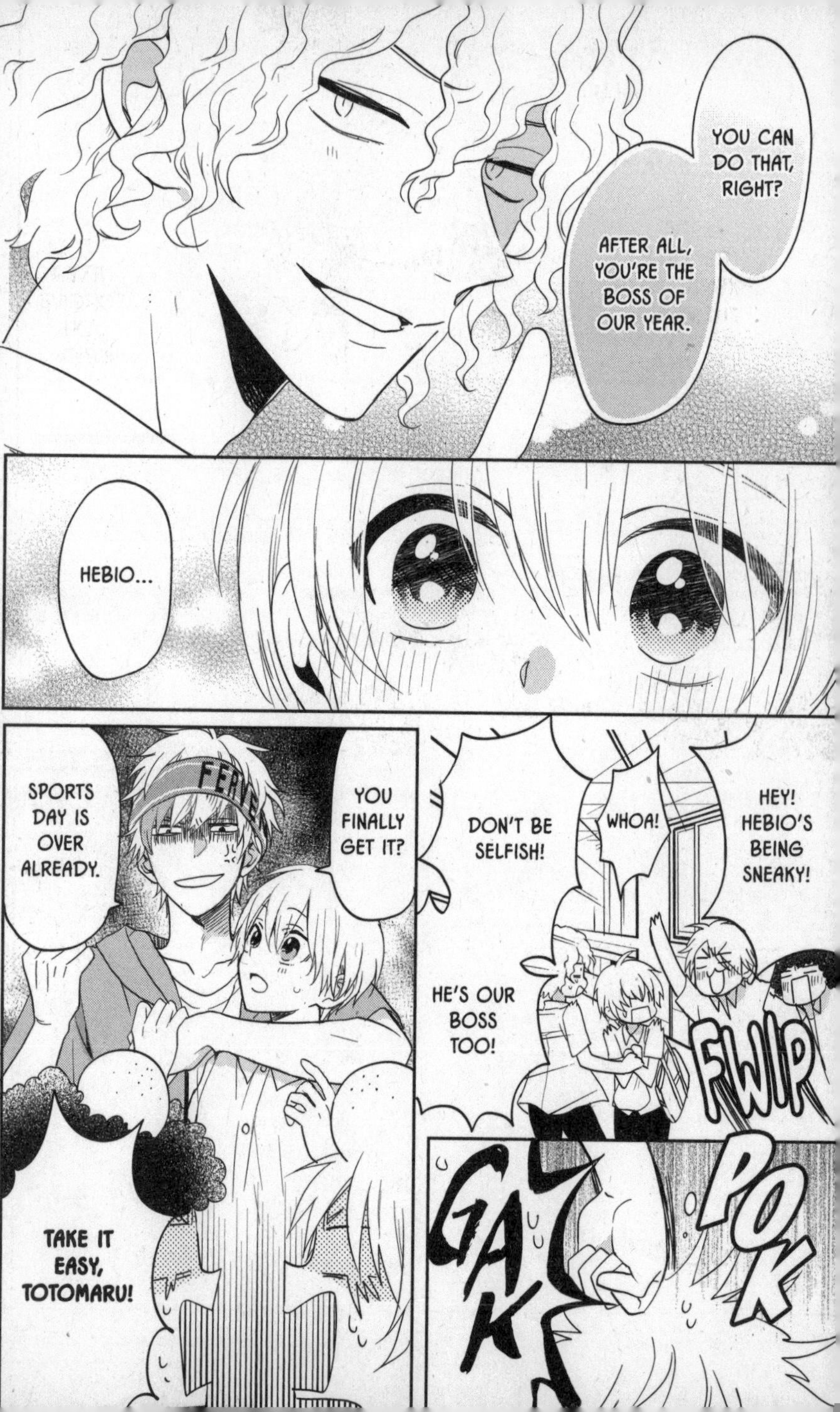
YOU CAN DO THAT, RIGHT?
AFTER ALL, YOU'RE THE BOSS OF OUR YEAR.
HEBIO...
HEY! HEBIO'S BEING SNEAKY!
WHOA!
DON'T BE SELFISH!
HE'S OUR BOSS TOO!
FWIP
POK
GAK
YOU FINALLY GET IT?
SPORTS DAY IS OVER ALREADY.
TAKE IT EASY, TOTOMARU!

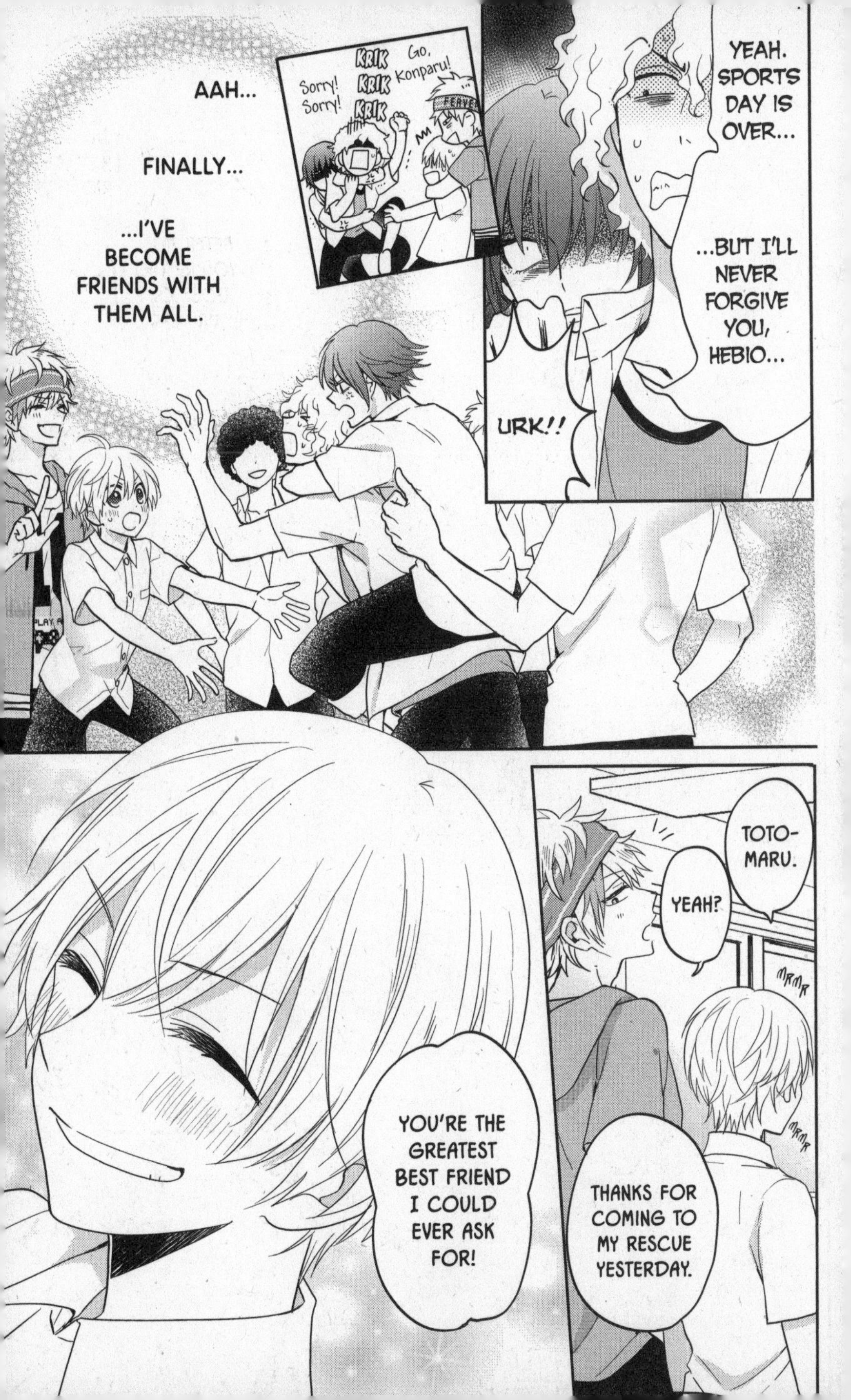
YEAH. SPORTS DAY IS OVER...
...BUT I'LL NEVER FORGIVE YOU, HEBIO...
URK!!
Go, Konparu!
KRIK KRIK KRIK
Sorry! Sorry!
AAH...
FINALLY...
...I'VE BECOME FRIENDS WITH THEM ALL.
TOTO-MARU.
YEAH?
MRMR
MRMR
THANKS FOR COMING TO MY RESCUE YESTERDAY.
YOU'RE THE GREATEST BEST FRIEND I COULD EVER ASK FOR!

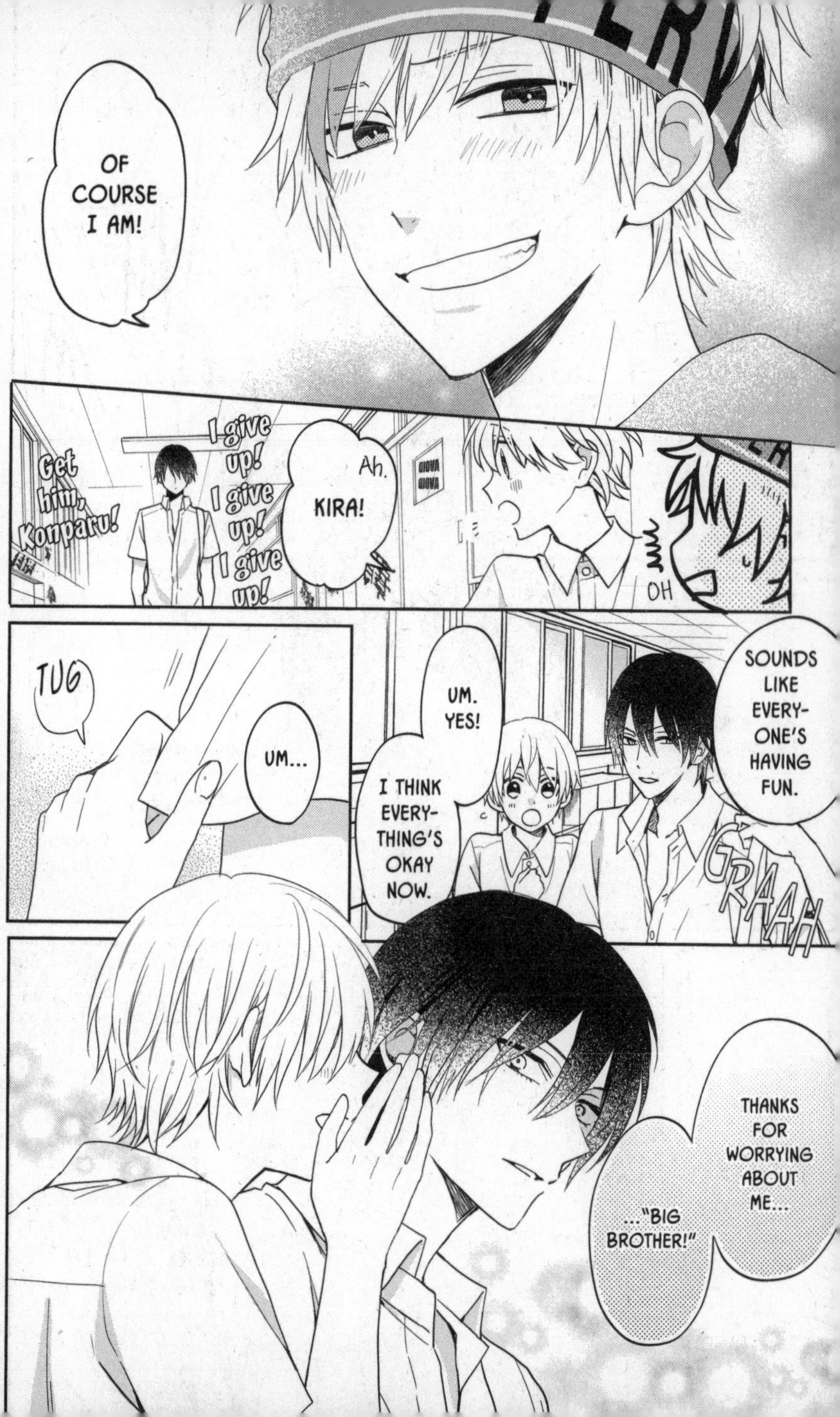

OF COURSE I AM!
OH
Ah. KIRA!
I give up! I give up! I give up!
Get him, Konparu!
SOUNDS LIKE EVERY-ONE'S HAVING FUN.
UM. YES!
I THINK EVERY-THING'S OKAY NOW.
GRAAAH
UM...
TUG
THANKS FOR WORRYING ABOUT ME...
..."BIG BROTHER!"

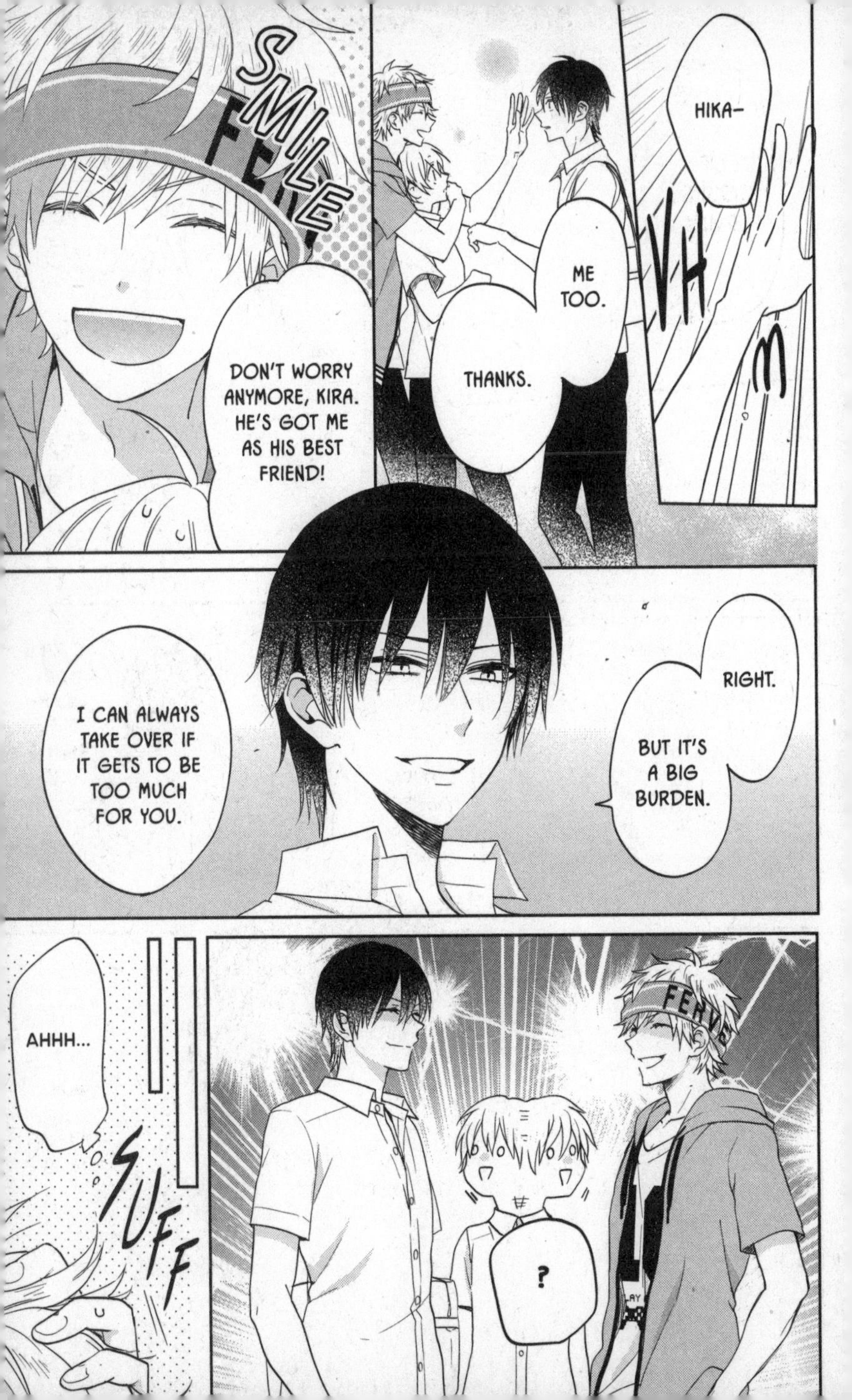
HIKA—
VHm
ME TOO.
THANKS.
SMILE
DON'T WORRY ANYMORE, KIRA. HE'S GOT ME AS HIS BEST FRIEND!
RIGHT.
BUT IT'S A BIG BURDEN.
I CAN ALWAYS TAKE OVER IF IT GETS TO BE TOO MUCH FOR YOU.
?
AHHH...
SUFF

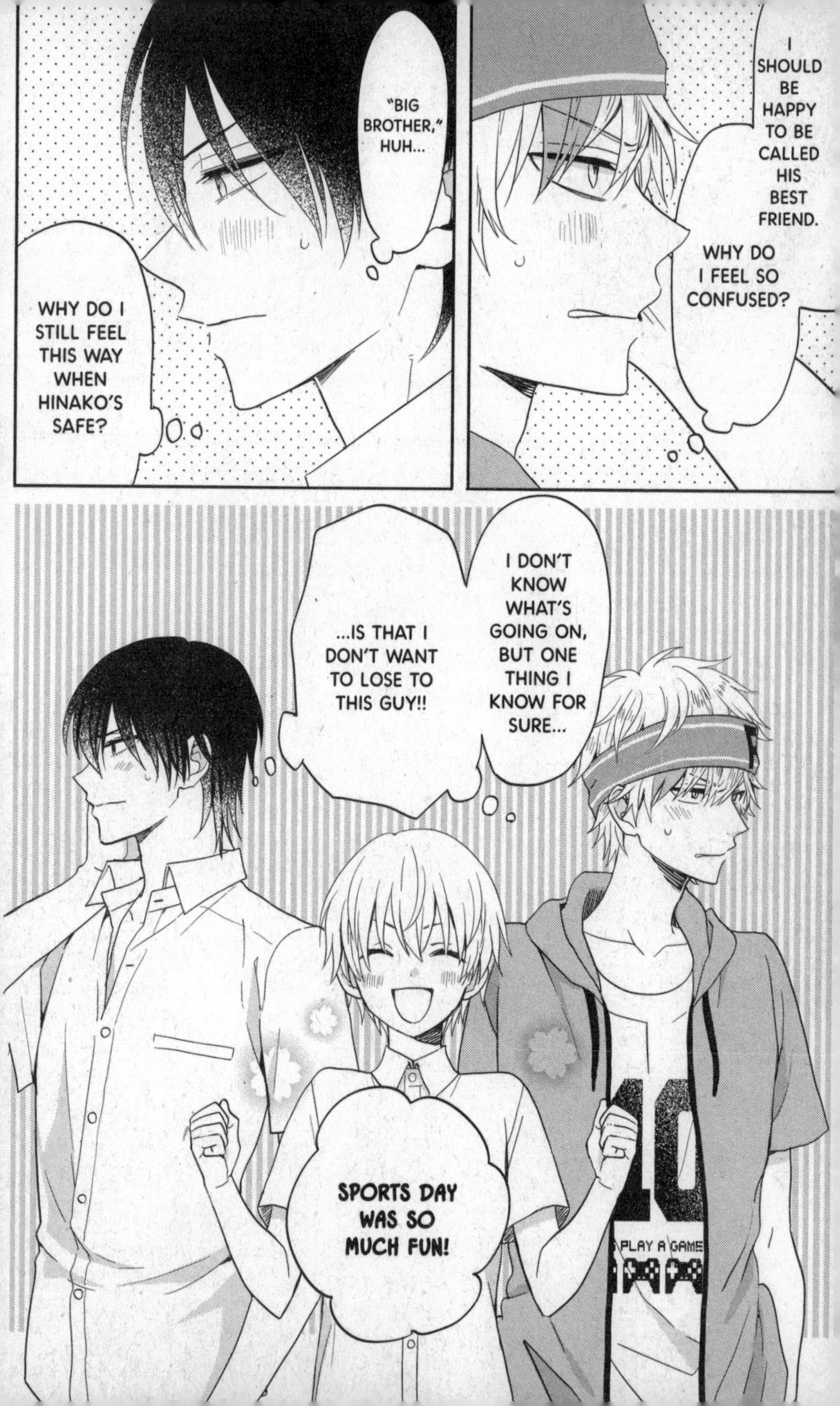
I SHOULD BE HAPPY TO BE CALLED HIS BEST FRIEND.
WHY DO I FEEL SO CONFUSED?
"BIG BROTHER," HUH...
WHY DO I STILL FEEL THIS WAY WHEN HINAKO'S SAFE?
I DON'T KNOW WHAT'S GOING ON, BUT ONE THING I KNOW FOR SURE...
...IS THAT I DON'T WANT TO LOSE TO THIS GUY!!
SPORTS DAY WAS SO MUCH FUN!
PLAY A GAME

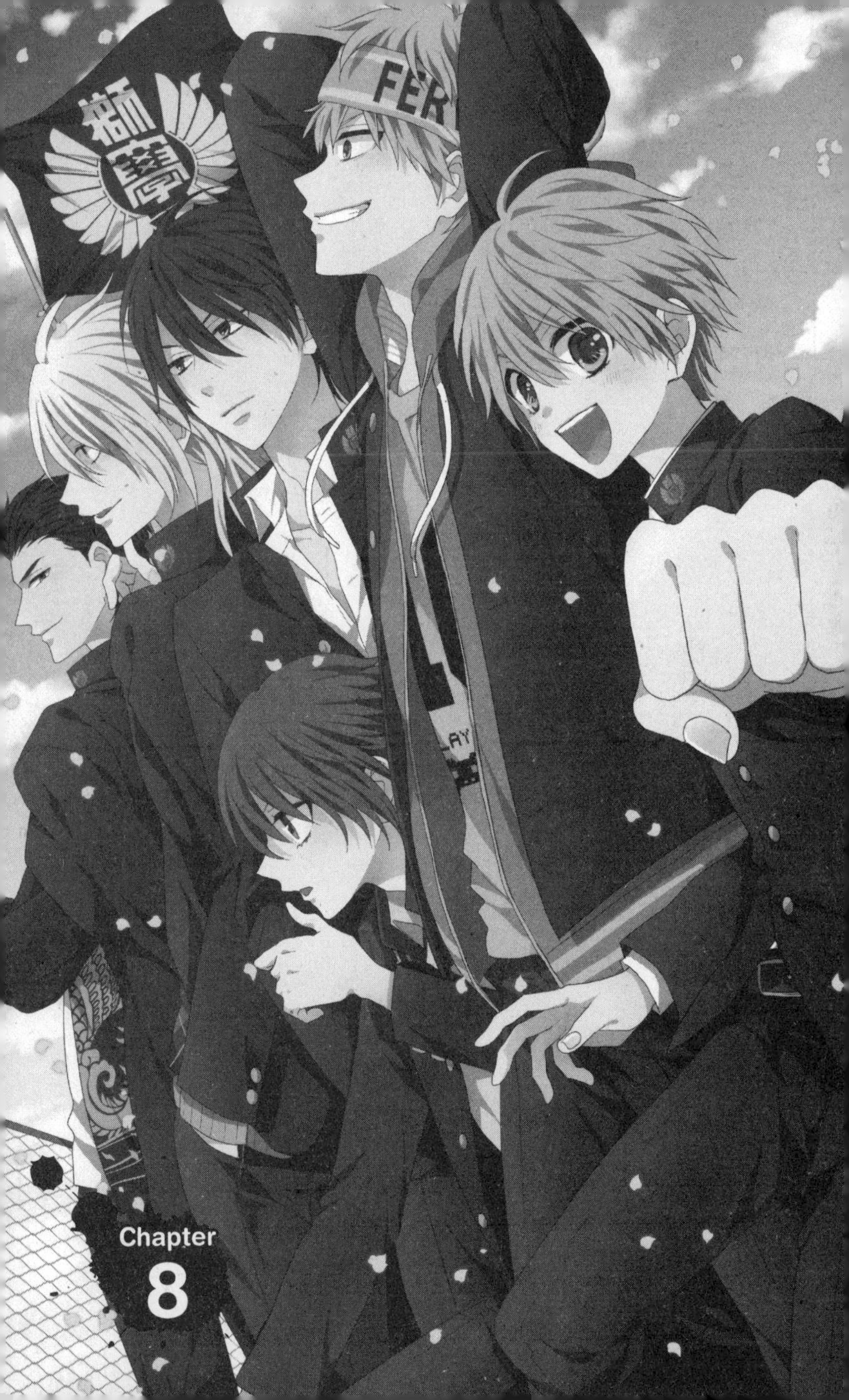
FER
Chapter
8

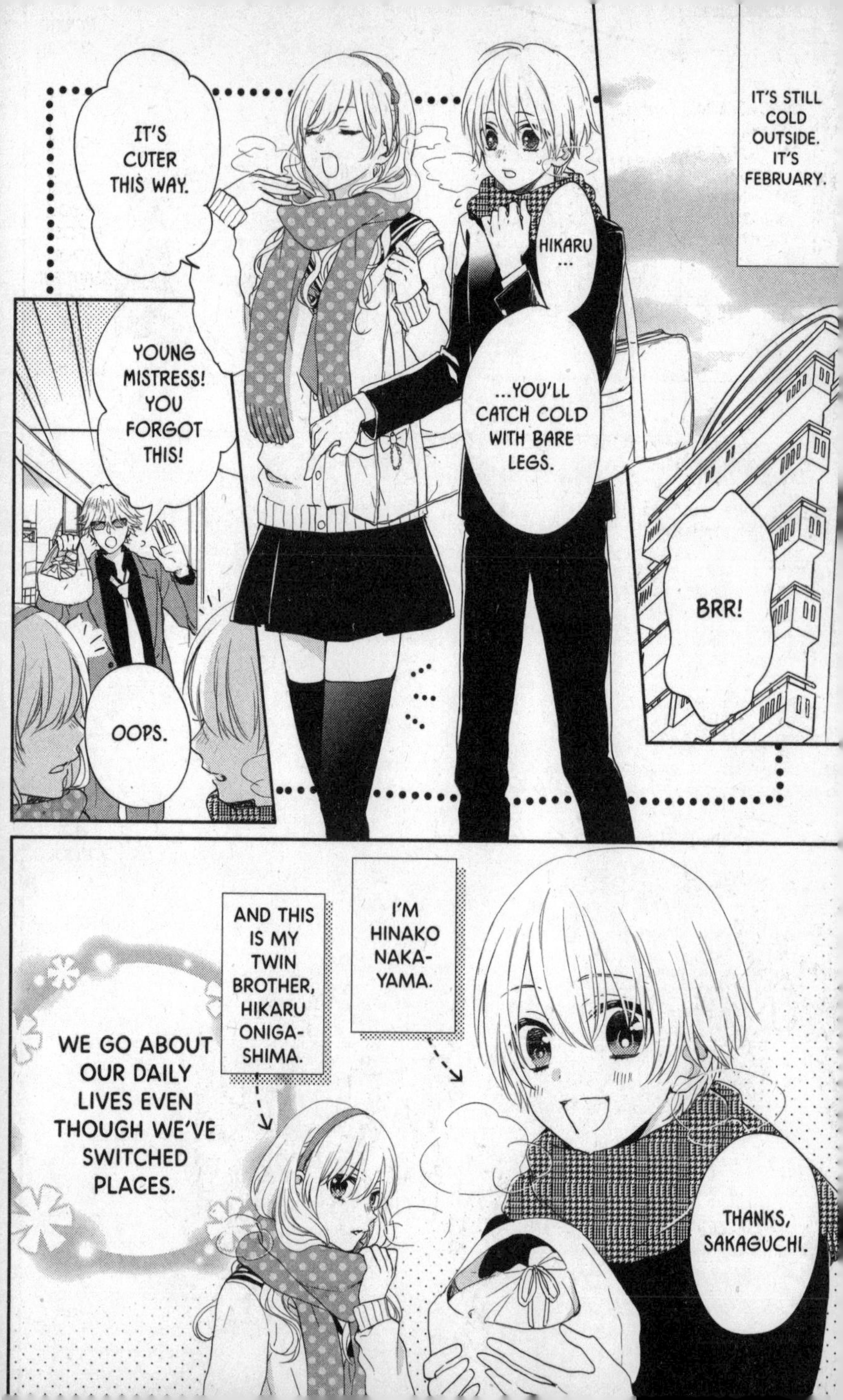
IT'S STILL COLD OUTSIDE. IT'S FEBRUARY.
BRR!
HIKARU...
...YOU'LL CATCH COLD WITH BARE LEGS.
IT'S CUTER THIS WAY.
...
YOUNG MISTRESS! YOU FORGOT THIS!
OOPS.
I'M HINAKO NAKA-YAMA.
AND THIS IS MY TWIN BROTHER, HIKARU ONIGA-SHIMA.
THANKS, SAKAGUCHI.
WE GO ABOUT OUR DAILY LIVES EVEN THOUGH WE'VE SWITCHED PLACES.

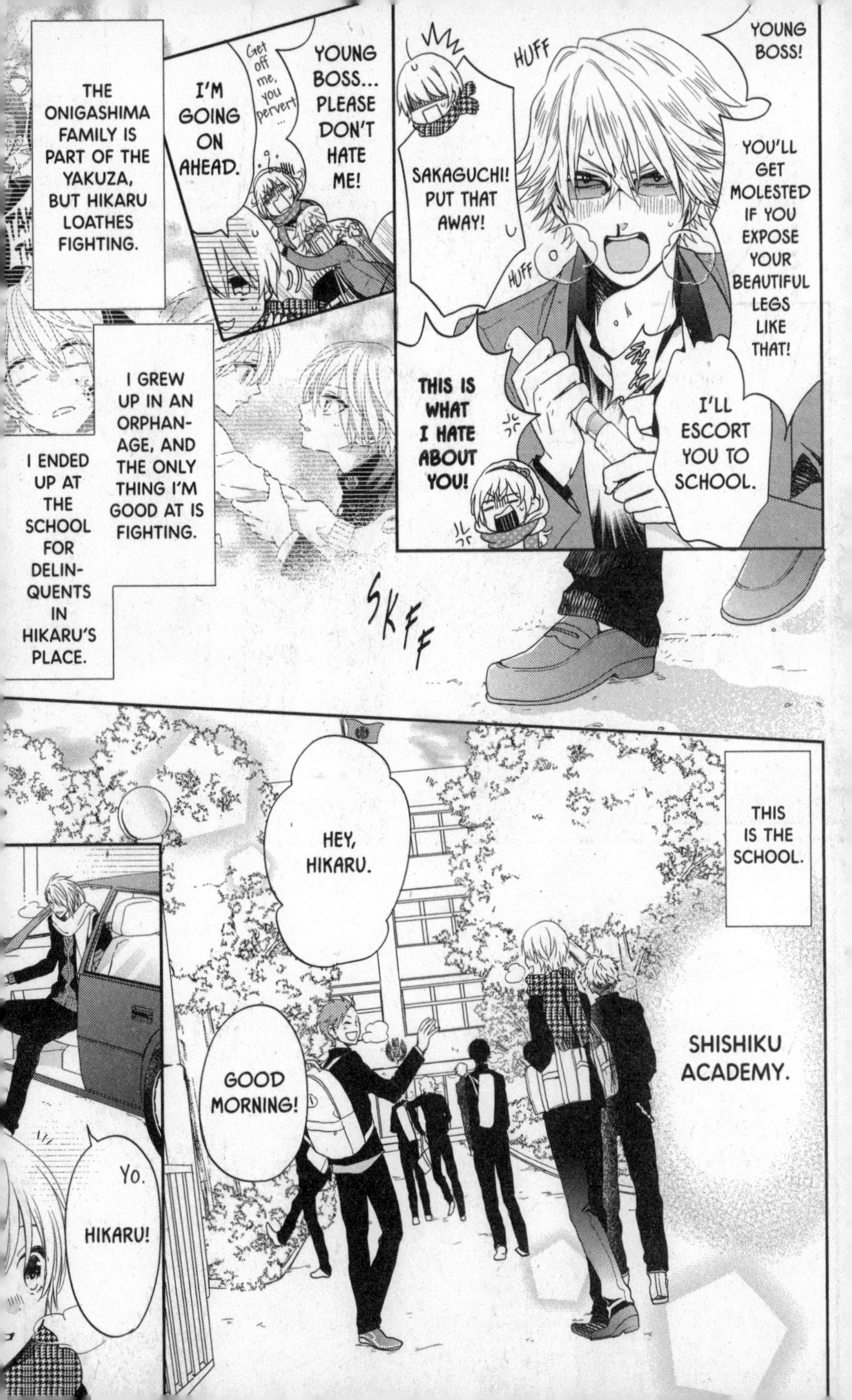
YOUNG BOSS!
HUFF
YOU'LL GET MOLESTED IF YOU EXPOSE YOUR BEAUTIFUL LEGS LIKE THAT!
SAKAGUCHI! PUT THAT AWAY!
HUFF
I'LL ESCORT YOU TO SCHOOL.
THIS IS WHAT I HATE ABOUT YOU!
YOUNG BOSS... PLEASE DON'T HATE ME!
Get off me, you pervert...
I'M GOING ON AHEAD.
THE ONIGASHIMA FAMILY IS PART OF THE YAKUZA, BUT HIKARU LOATHES FIGHTING.
I GREW UP IN AN ORPHAN-AGE, AND THE ONLY THING I'M GOOD AT IS FIGHTING.
I ENDED UP AT THE SCHOOL FOR DELIN-QUENTS IN HIKARU'S PLACE.
SKFF
THIS IS THE SCHOOL.
SHISHIKU ACADEMY.
HEY, HIKARU.
GOOD MORNING!
Yo.
HIKARU!

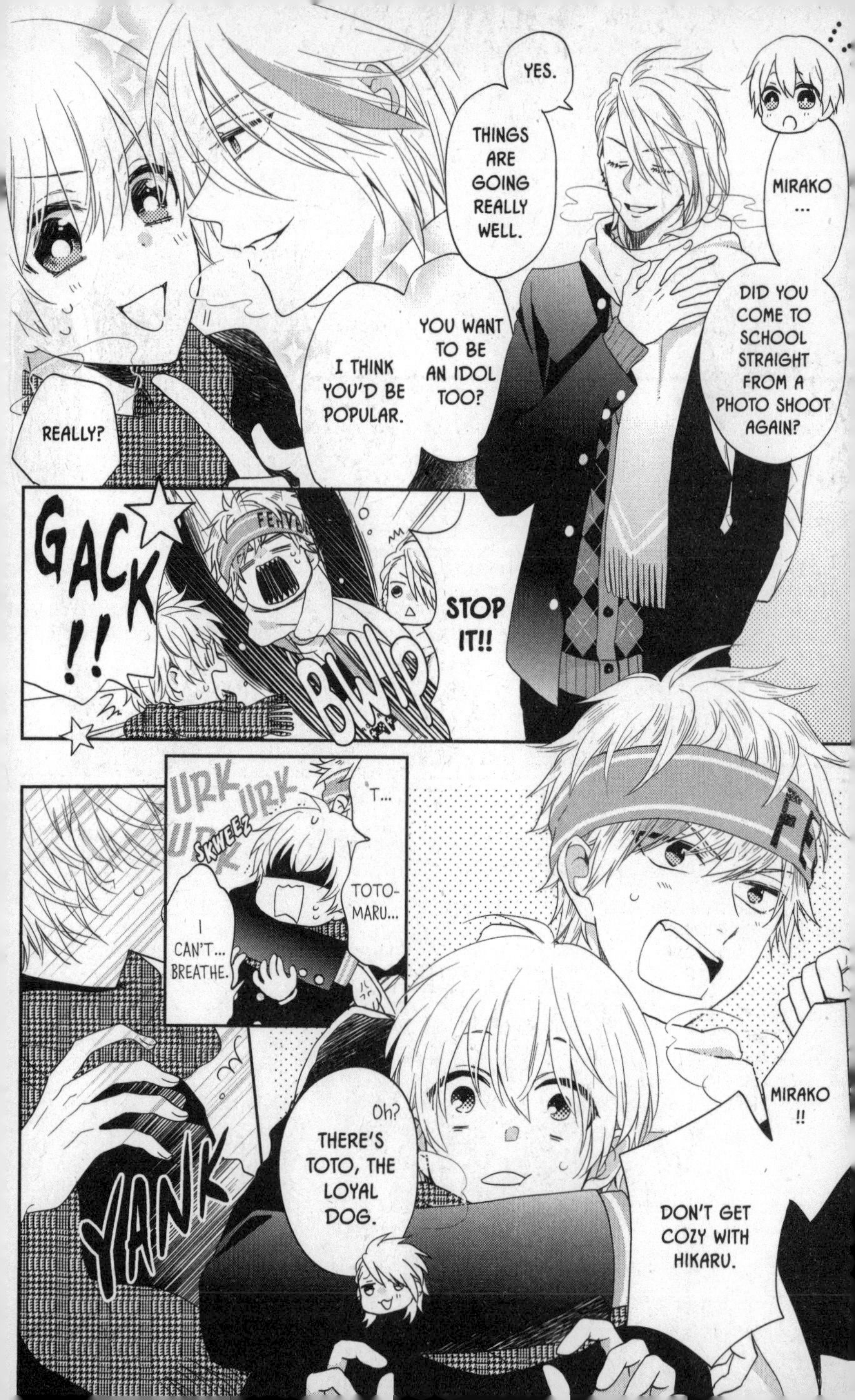
MIRAKO...
DID YOU COME TO SCHOOL STRAIGHT FROM A PHOTO SHOOT AGAIN?
YES.
THINGS ARE GOING REALLY WELL.
YOU WANT TO BE AN IDOL TOO?
I THINK YOU'D BE POPULAR.
REALLY?
STOP IT!!
BWIP
GACK!!
MIRAKO!!
DON'T GET COZY WITH HIKARU.
Oh?
THERE'S TOTO, THE LOYAL DOG.
YANK
T...
TOTO-MARU...
I CAN'T... BREATHE.
URK URK URK
SKWEEZ

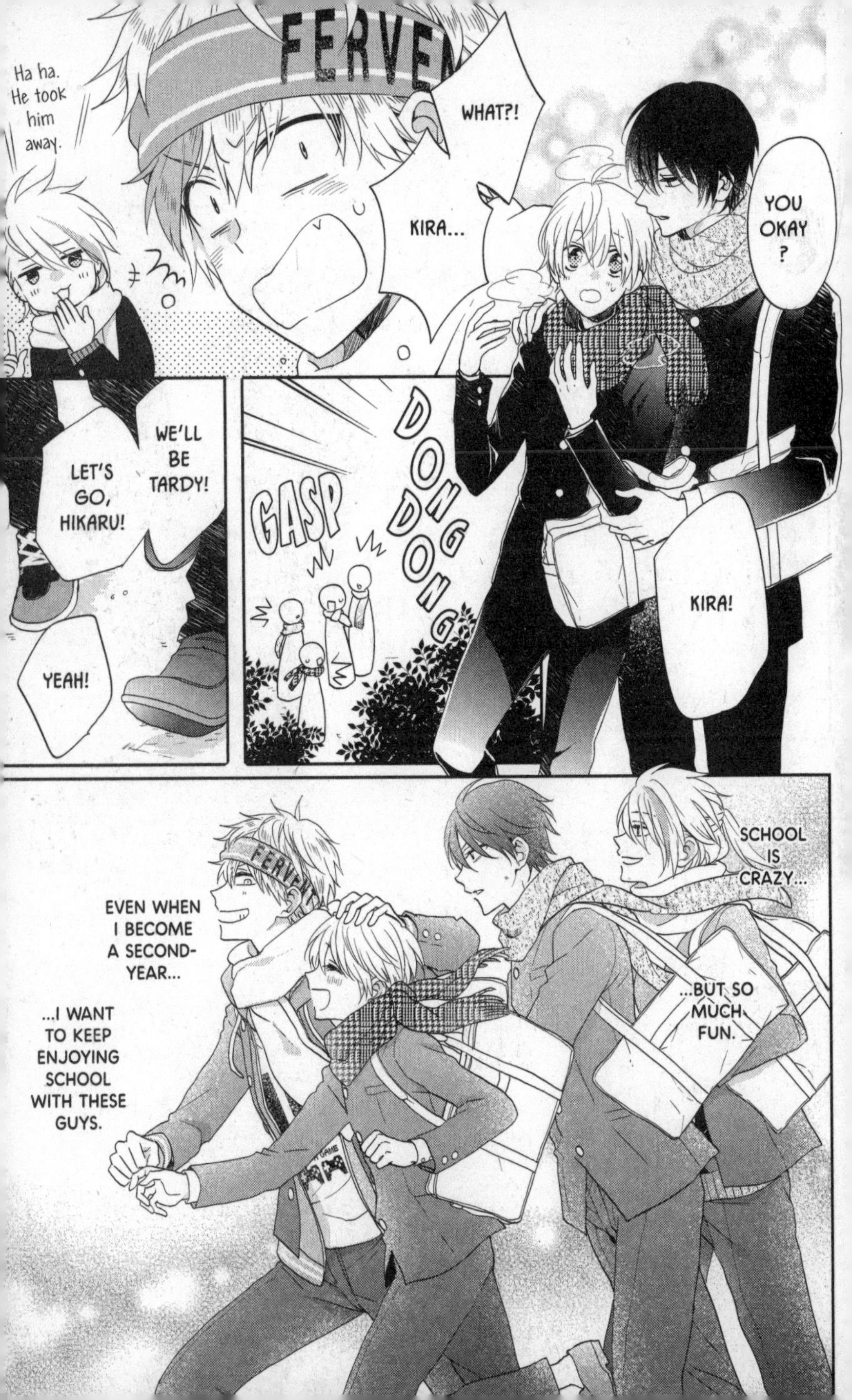
YOU OKAY?
KIRA...
WHAT?!
Ha ha. He took him away.
KIRA!
DONG DONG
GASP
WE'LL BE TARDY!
LET'S GO, HIKARU!
YEAH!
SCHOOL IS CRAZY...
...BUT SO MUCH FUN.
EVEN WHEN I BECOME A SECOND-YEAR...
...I WANT TO KEEP ENJOYING SCHOOL WITH THESE GUYS.

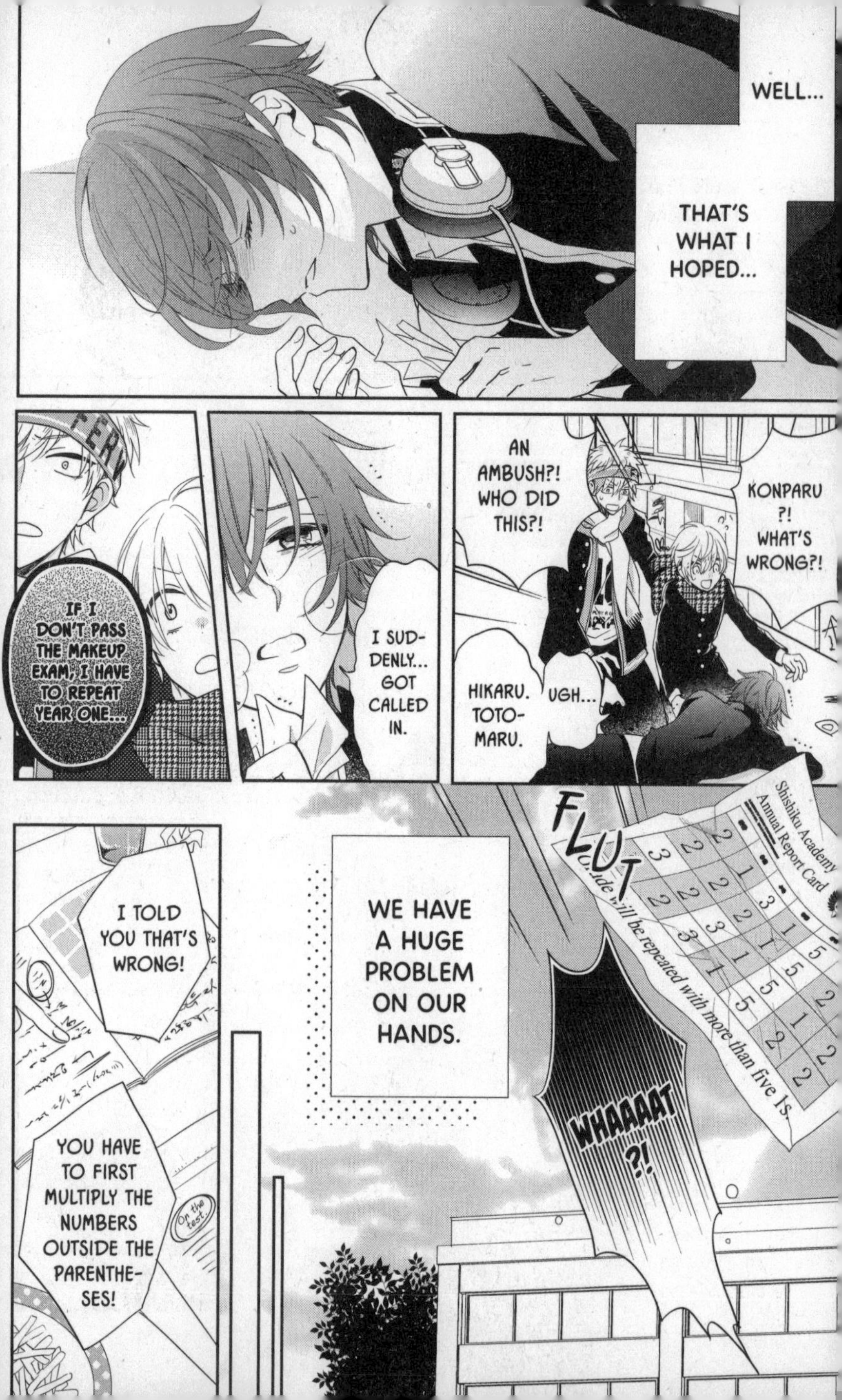
WELL...
THAT'S WHAT I HOPED...
KONPARU?! WHAT'S WRONG?!
AN AMBUSH?! WHO DID THIS?!
UGH...
HIKARU. TOTOMARU.
I SUDDENLY... GOT CALLED IN.
IF I DON'T PASS THE MAKEUP EXAM, I HAVE TO REPEAT YEAR ONE...
Shishiku Academy Annual Report Card
de will be repeated with more than five 1s.
FLUT
WHAAAAT?!
WE HAVE A HUGE PROBLEM ON OUR HANDS.
I TOLD YOU THAT'S WRONG!
YOU HAVE TO FIRST MULTIPLY THE NUMBERS OUTSIDE THE PARENTHESES!
On the test.

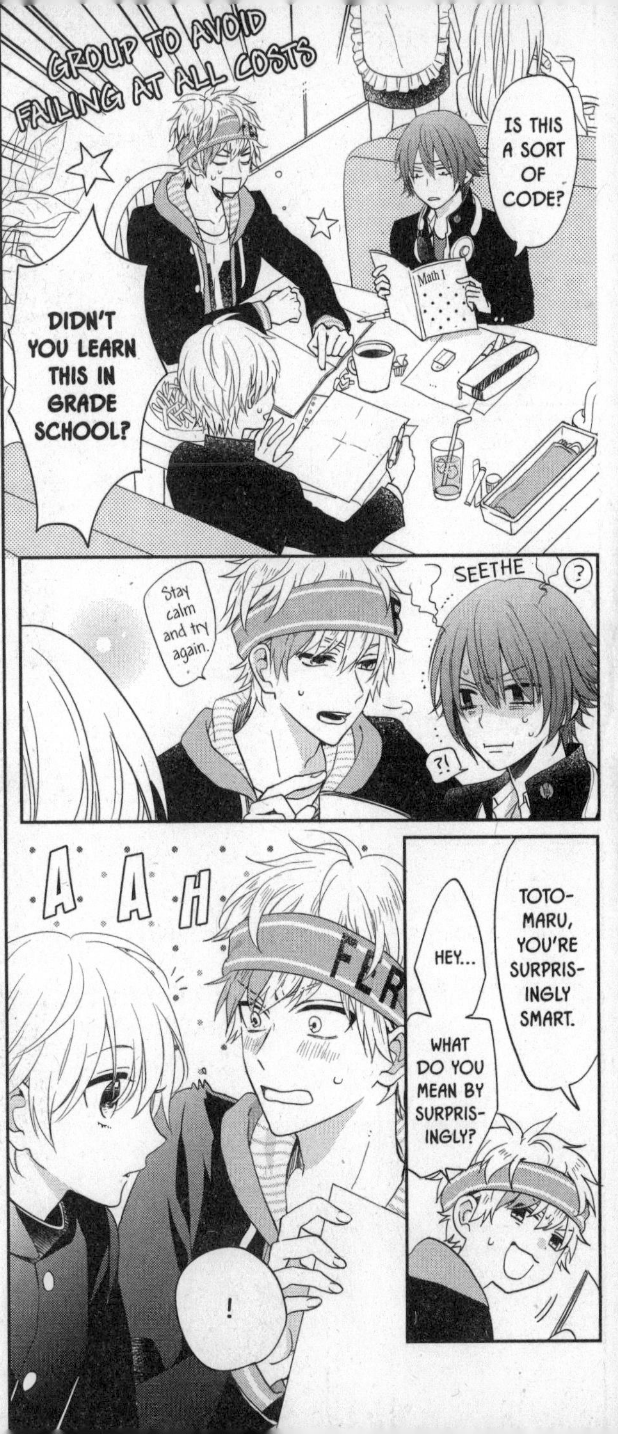
GROUP TO AVOID FAILING AT ALL COSTS
IS THIS A SORT OF CODE?
Math I
DIDN'T YOU LEARN THIS IN GRADE SCHOOL?
SEETHE
?
Stay calm and try again.
?!
TOTO-MARU, YOU'RE SURPRIS-INGLY SMART.
HEY... WHAT DO YOU MEAN BY SURPRIS-INGLY?
AAH
FLR
!

While drawing *Bancho*...

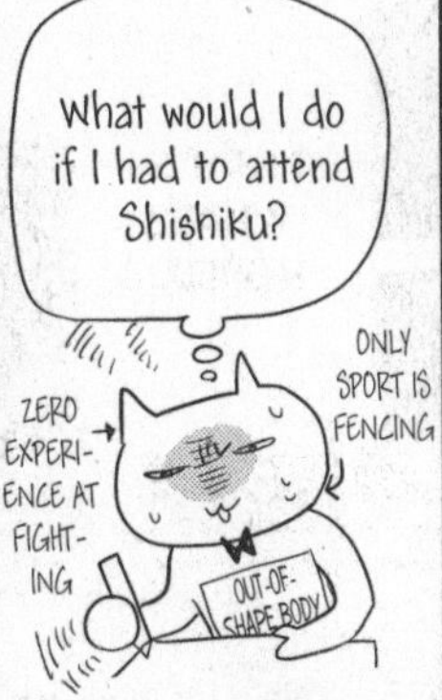
What would I do if I had to attend Shishiku?
ZERO EXPERI-ENCE AT FIGHT-ING
ONLY SPORT IS FENCING
OUT-OF-SHAPE BODY

I thought about this seriously. As a result...

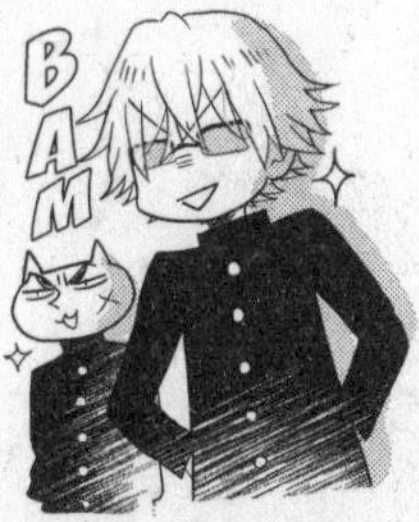
BAM

The best way is to get Sakaguchi to somehow attend too so he can protect me!

STRONGEST!!

What do you think? What? Would that be against the rules? I see... It made me realize how amazing Hinako is because she's just as strong as all the delinquents (if not stronger). If I were to use my fist to fight, I'd break bones. The ones in my hands, that is.

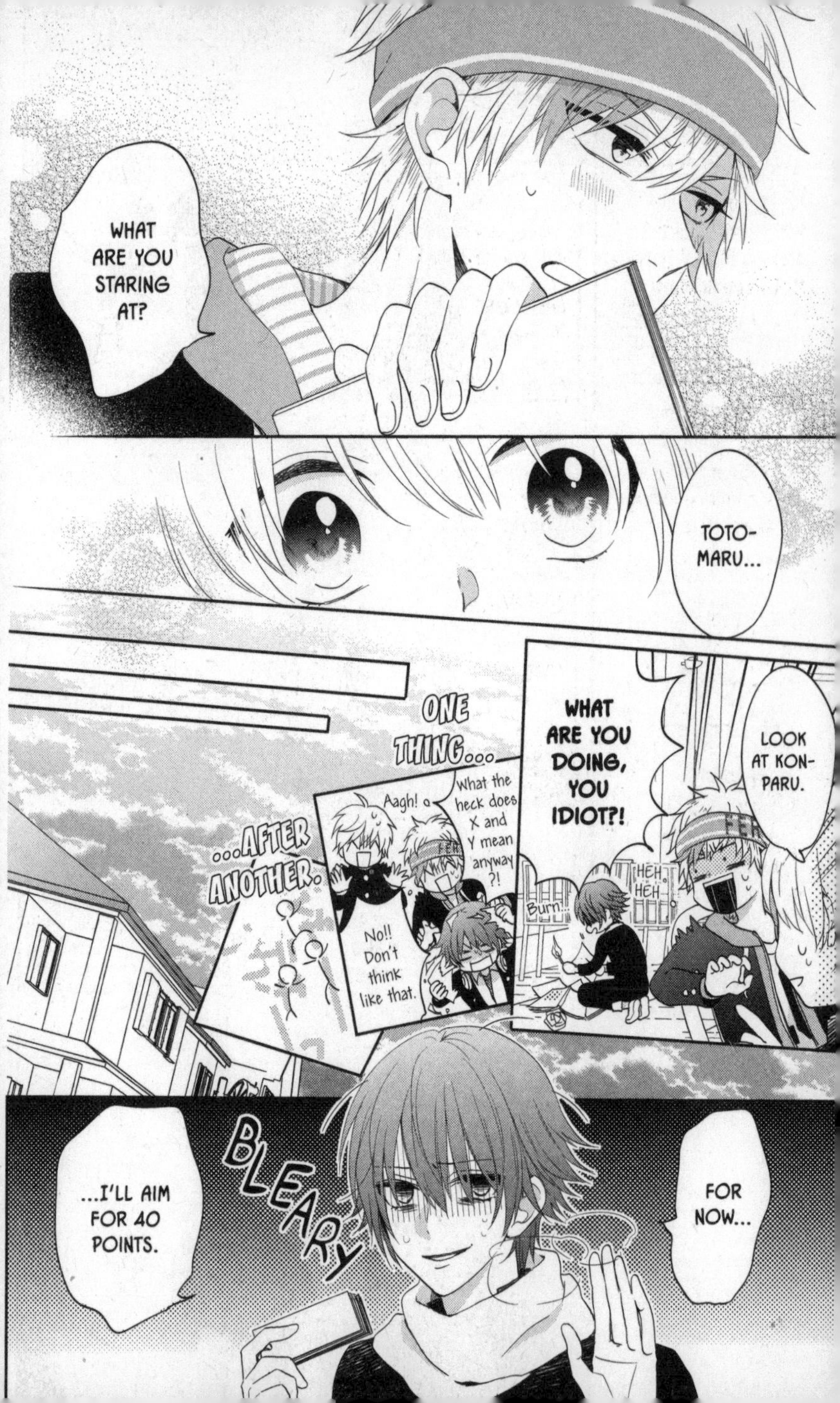
WHAT ARE YOU STARING AT?
TOTO-MARU...
ONE THING...
LOOK AT KON-PARU.
WHAT ARE YOU DOING, YOU IDIOT?!
HEH, HEH
Burn...
What the heck does X and Y mean anyway?!
Aagh!
No!! Don't think like that.
...AFTER ANOTHER.
FOR NOW...
BLEARY
...I'LL AIM FOR 40 POINTS.

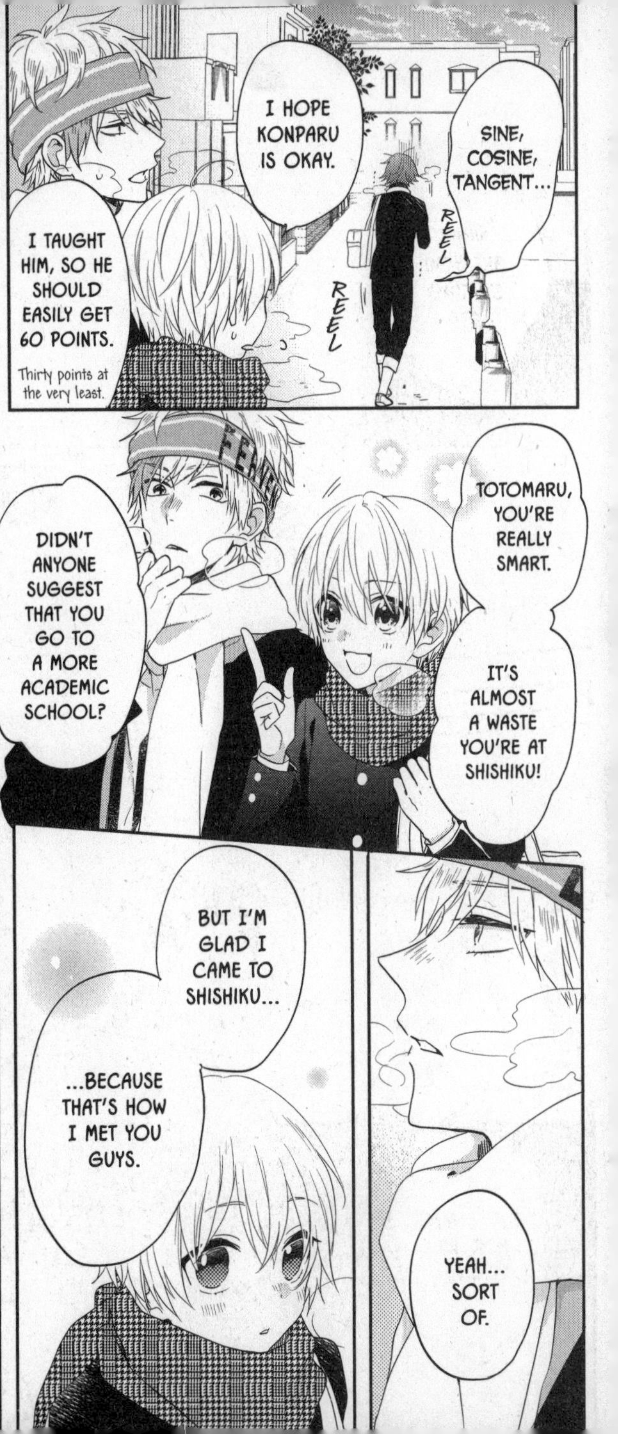
SINE, COSINE, TANGENT...
REEL
REEL
I HOPE KONPARU IS OKAY.
I TAUGHT HIM, SO HE SHOULD EASILY GET 60 POINTS.
Thirty points at the very least.
TOTOMARU, YOU'RE REALLY SMART.
IT'S ALMOST A WASTE YOU'RE AT SHISHIKU!
DIDN'T ANYONE SUGGEST THAT YOU GO TO A MORE ACADEMIC SCHOOL?
YEAH... SORT OF.
BUT I'M GLAD I CAME TO SHISHIKU...
...BECAUSE THAT'S HOW I MET YOU GUYS.

This is the last sidebar. All the characters in "Love's Battle Royale" are wild yet compassionate, so I enjoyed drawing them. I hope I'll be able to draw them again soon...

There's a lot more in the works—an anime and more manga—and I'd be really happy if you'll continue to enjoy the world of *Kenka Bancho Otome*.

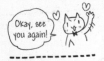

Okay, see you again!

To my editor
Everyone at RED
Everyone at Spike
Chunsoft
All the voice actors
Anzai
Gondahara
My publisher
And every single reader

Thank you very much!!

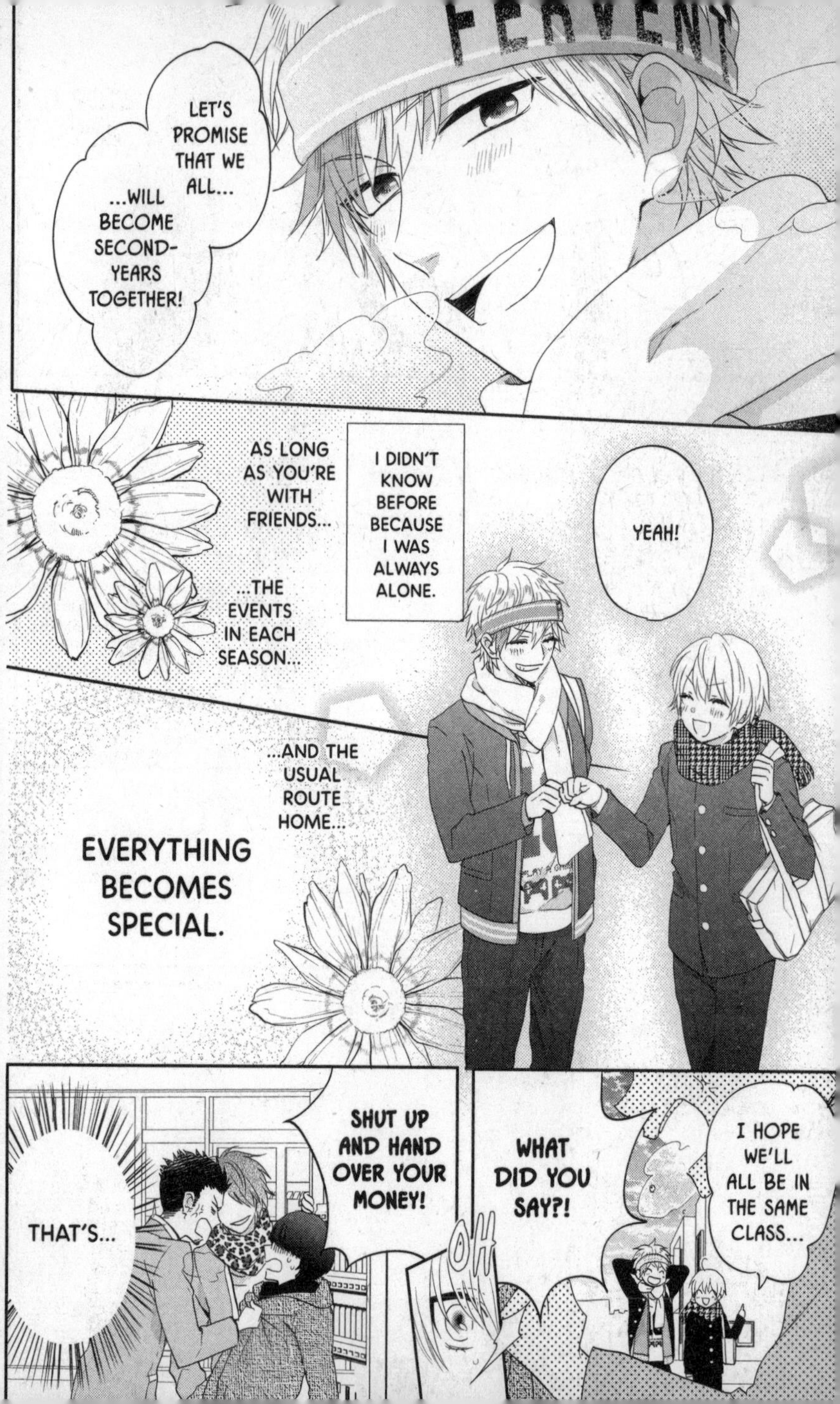
LET'S PROMISE THAT WE ALL...
...WILL BECOME SECOND-YEARS TOGETHER!
YEAH!
I DIDN'T KNOW BEFORE BECAUSE I WAS ALWAYS ALONE.
AS LONG AS YOU'RE WITH FRIENDS...
...THE EVENTS IN EACH SEASON...
...AND THE USUAL ROUTE HOME...
EVERYTHING BECOMES SPECIAL.
I HOPE WE'LL ALL BE IN THE SAME CLASS...
OH
WHAT DID YOU SAY?!
SHUT UP AND HAND OVER YOUR MONEY!
THAT'S...

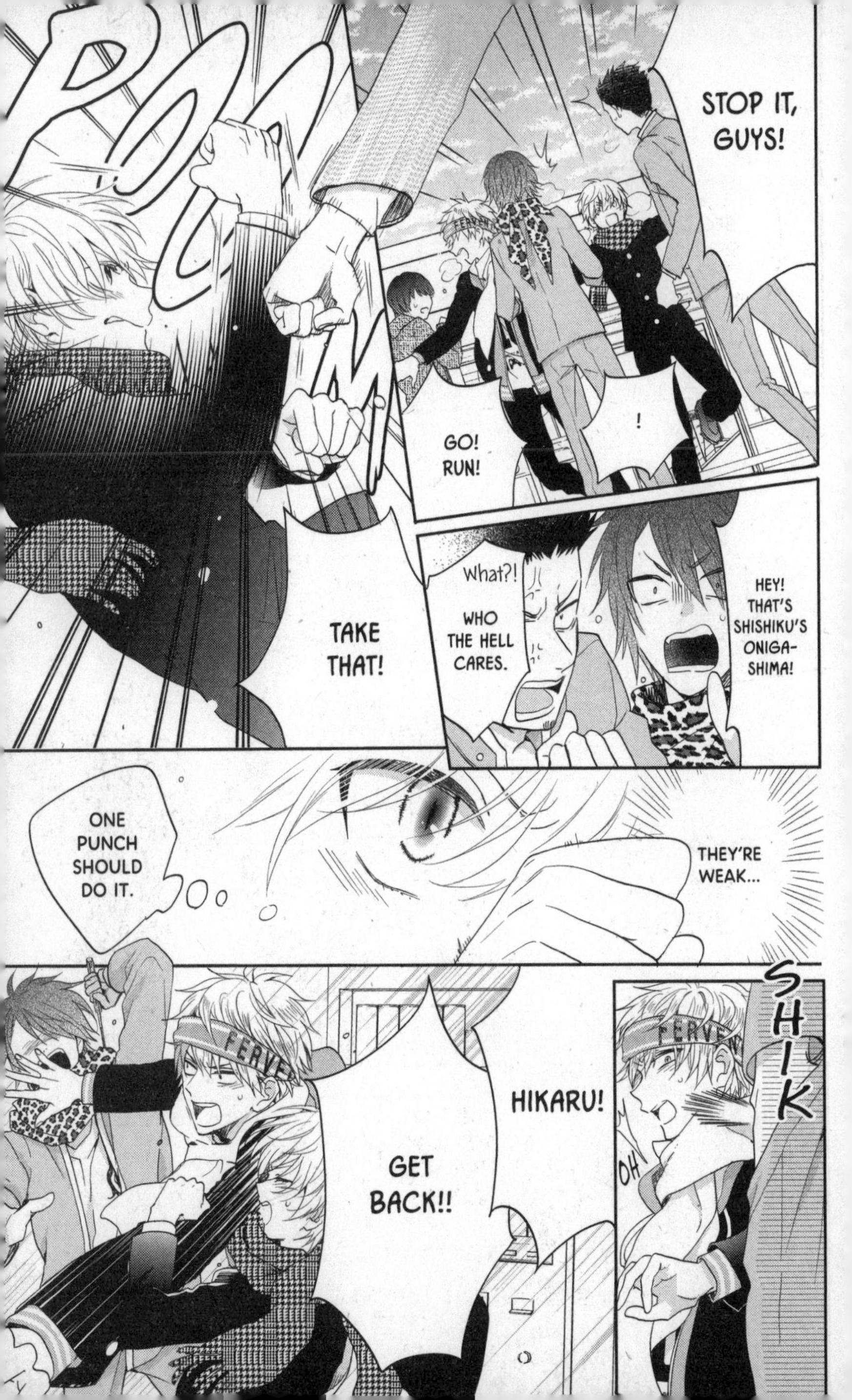
STOP IT, GUYS!
!
GO! RUN!
HEY! THAT'S SHISHIKU'S ONIGA-SHIMA!
What?!
WHO THE HELL CARES.
TAKE THAT!
THEY'RE WEAK...
ONE PUNCH SHOULD DO IT.
SHIK
OH
HIKARU!
GET BACK!!

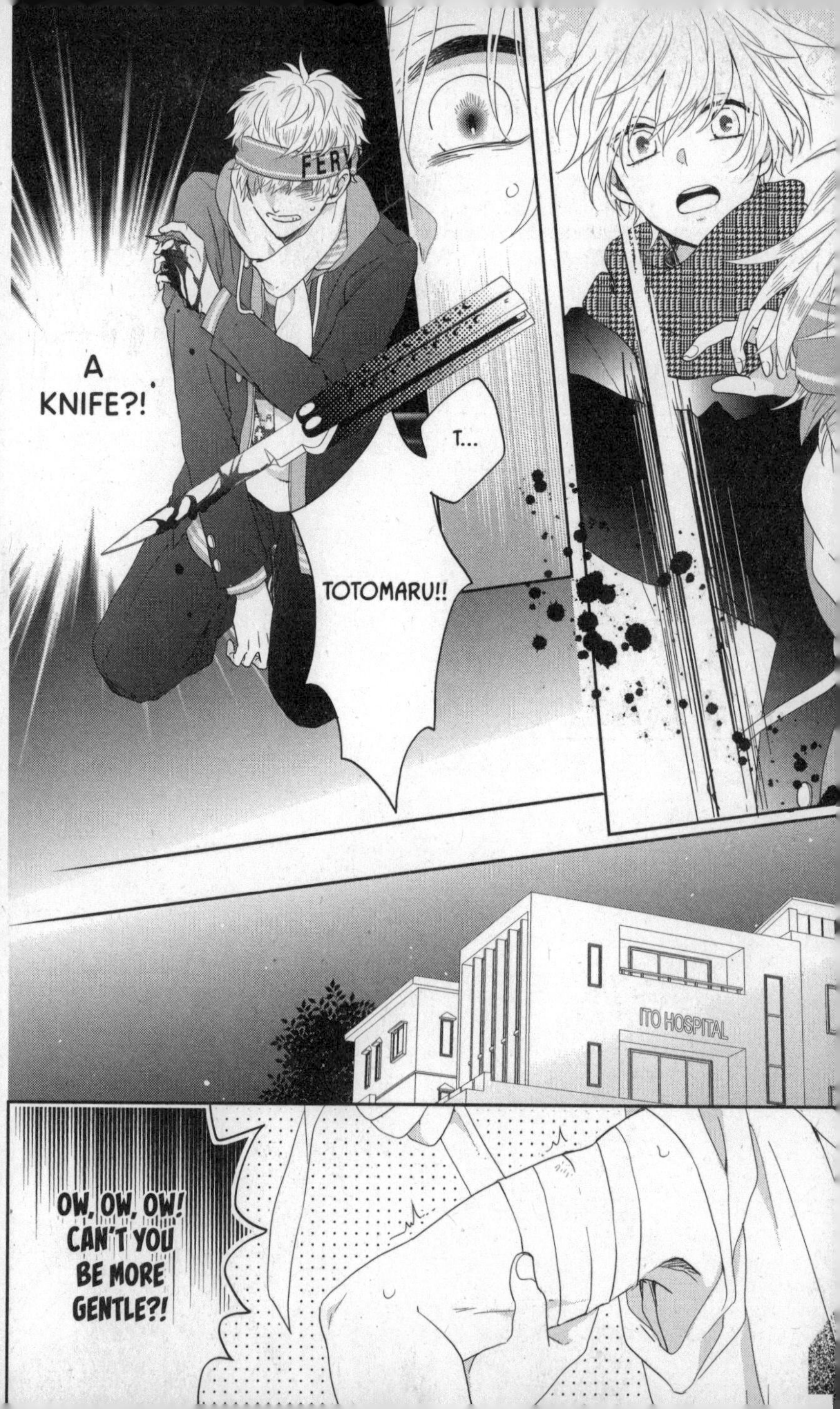
T...
TOTOMARU!!
A KNIFE?!
ITO HOSPITAL
OW, OW, OW! CAN'T YOU BE MORE GENTLE?!

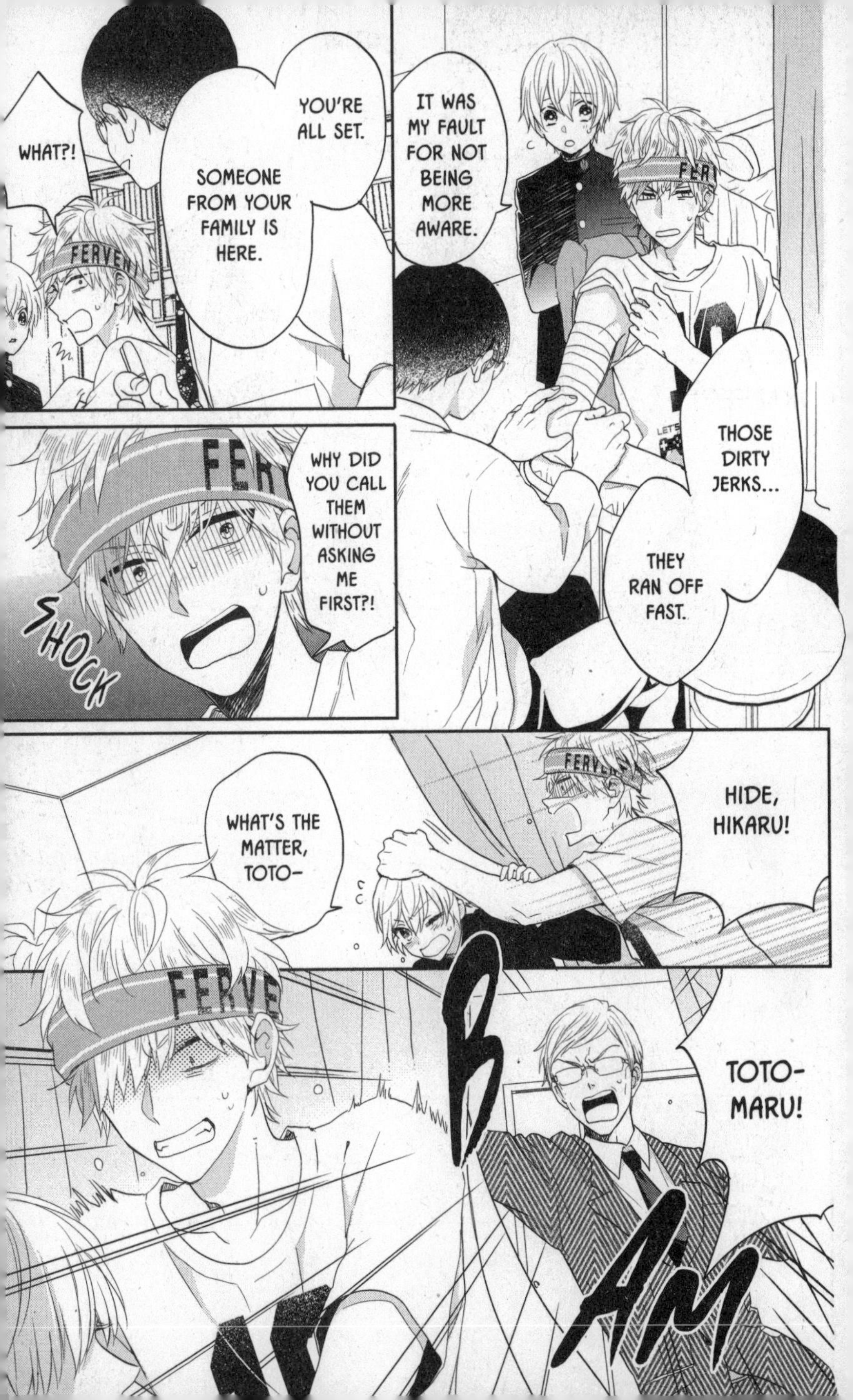
THOSE DIRTY JERKS...
THEY RAN OFF FAST.
IT WAS MY FAULT FOR NOT BEING MORE AWARE.
YOU'RE ALL SET.
SOMEONE FROM YOUR FAMILY IS HERE.
WHAT?!
WHY DID YOU CALL THEM WITHOUT ASKING ME FIRST?!
SHOCK
HIDE, HIKARU!
WHAT'S THE MATTER, TOTO-
TOTO-MARU!
BAM

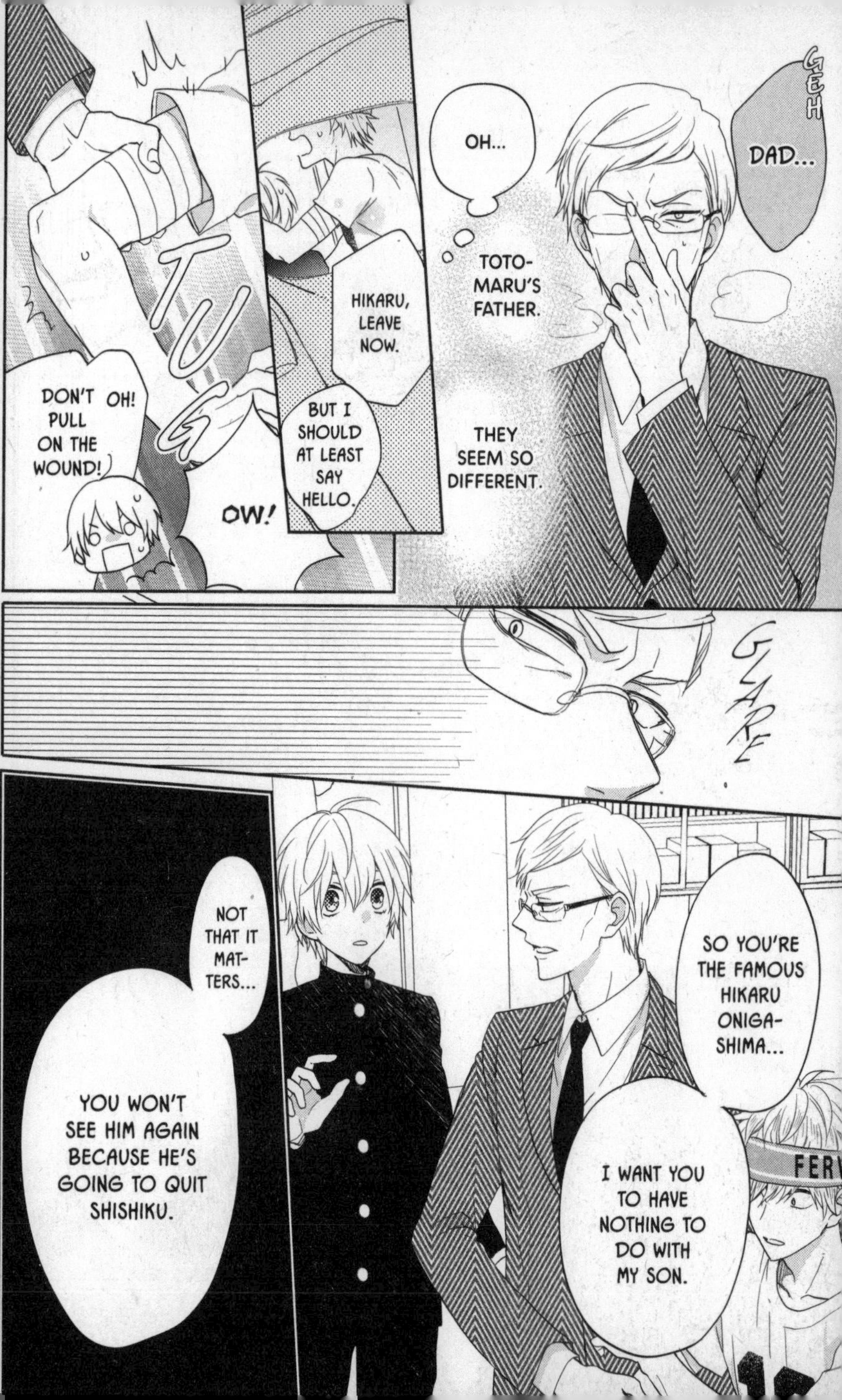
GEH
DAD...
OH...
TOTO-MARU'S FATHER.
THEY SEEM SO DIFFERENT.
HIKARU, LEAVE NOW.
BUT I SHOULD AT LEAST SAY HELLO.
TUG
OH!
DON'T PULL ON THE WOUND!
OW!
GLARE
SO YOU'RE THE FAMOUS HIKARU ONIGA-SHIMA...
I WANT YOU TO HAVE NOTHING TO DO WITH MY SON.
NOT THAT IT MATTERS...
YOU WON'T SEE HIM AGAIN BECAUSE HE'S GOING TO QUIT SHISHIKU.

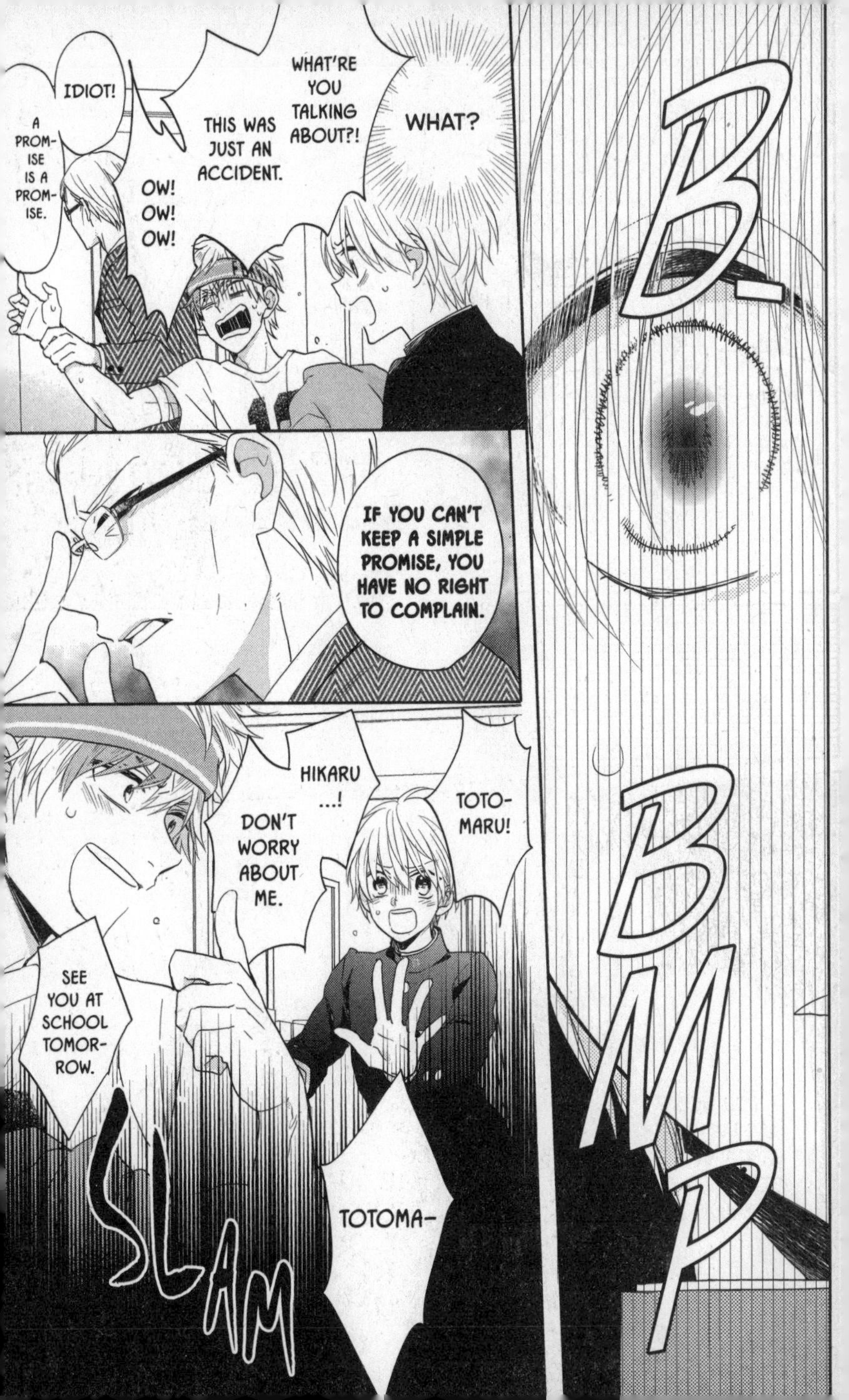
B-
BMP
WHAT?
WHAT'RE YOU TALKING ABOUT?!
THIS WAS JUST AN ACCIDENT.
OW! OW! OW!
IDIOT!
A PROM-ISE IS A PROM-ISE.
IF YOU CAN'T KEEP A SIMPLE PROMISE, YOU HAVE NO RIGHT TO COMPLAIN.
TOTO-MARU!
HIKARU ...!
DON'T WORRY ABOUT ME.
SEE YOU AT SCHOOL TOMOR-ROW.
TOTOMA-
SLAM

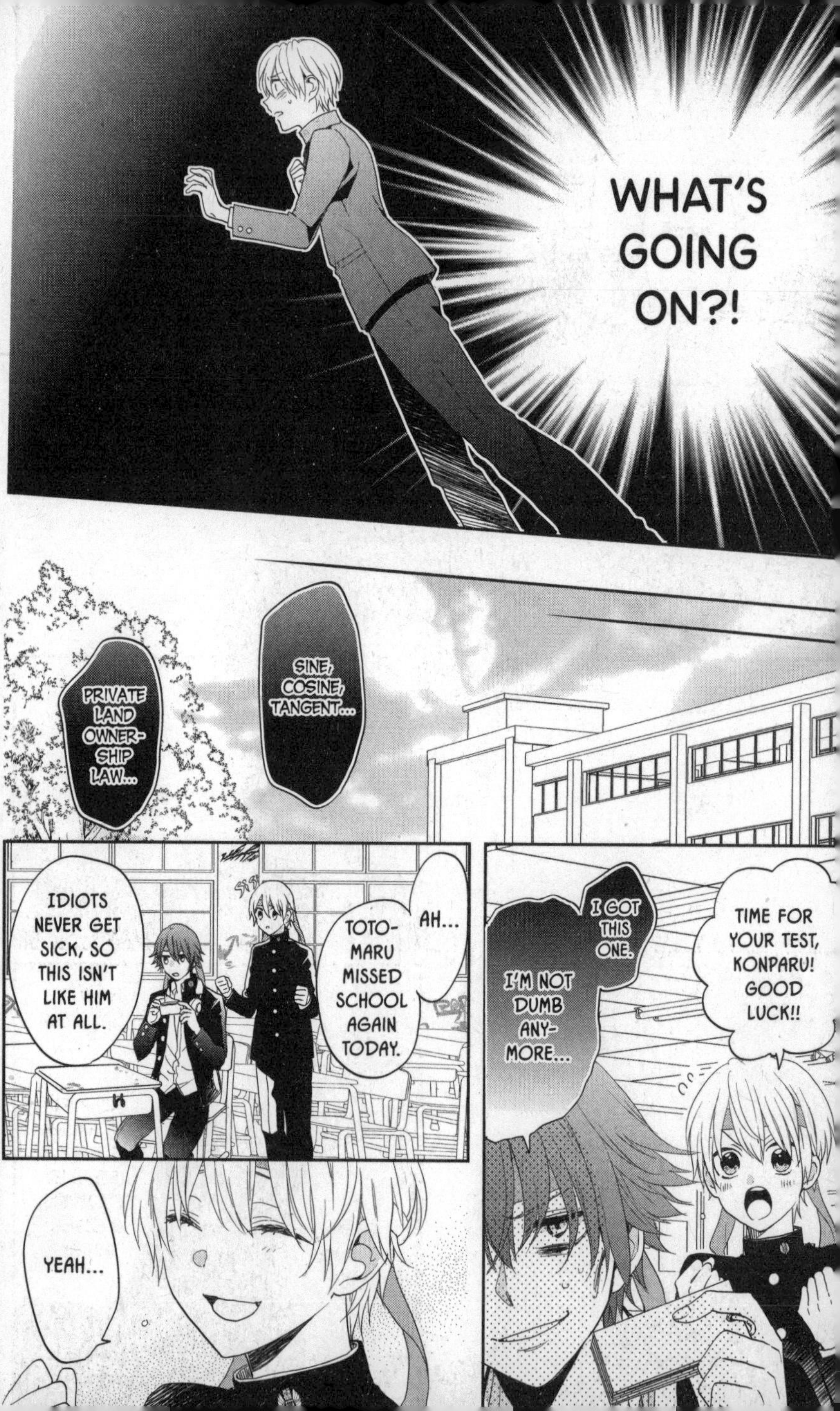
WHAT'S GOING ON?!
SINE, COSINE, TANGENT...
PRIVATE LAND OWNERSHIP LAW...
TIME FOR YOUR TEST, KONPARU! GOOD LUCK!!
I GOT THIS ONE.
I'M NOT DUMB ANYMORE...
AH...
TOTOMARU MISSED SCHOOL AGAIN TODAY.
IDIOTS NEVER GET SICK, SO THIS ISN'T LIKE HIM AT ALL.
YEAH...

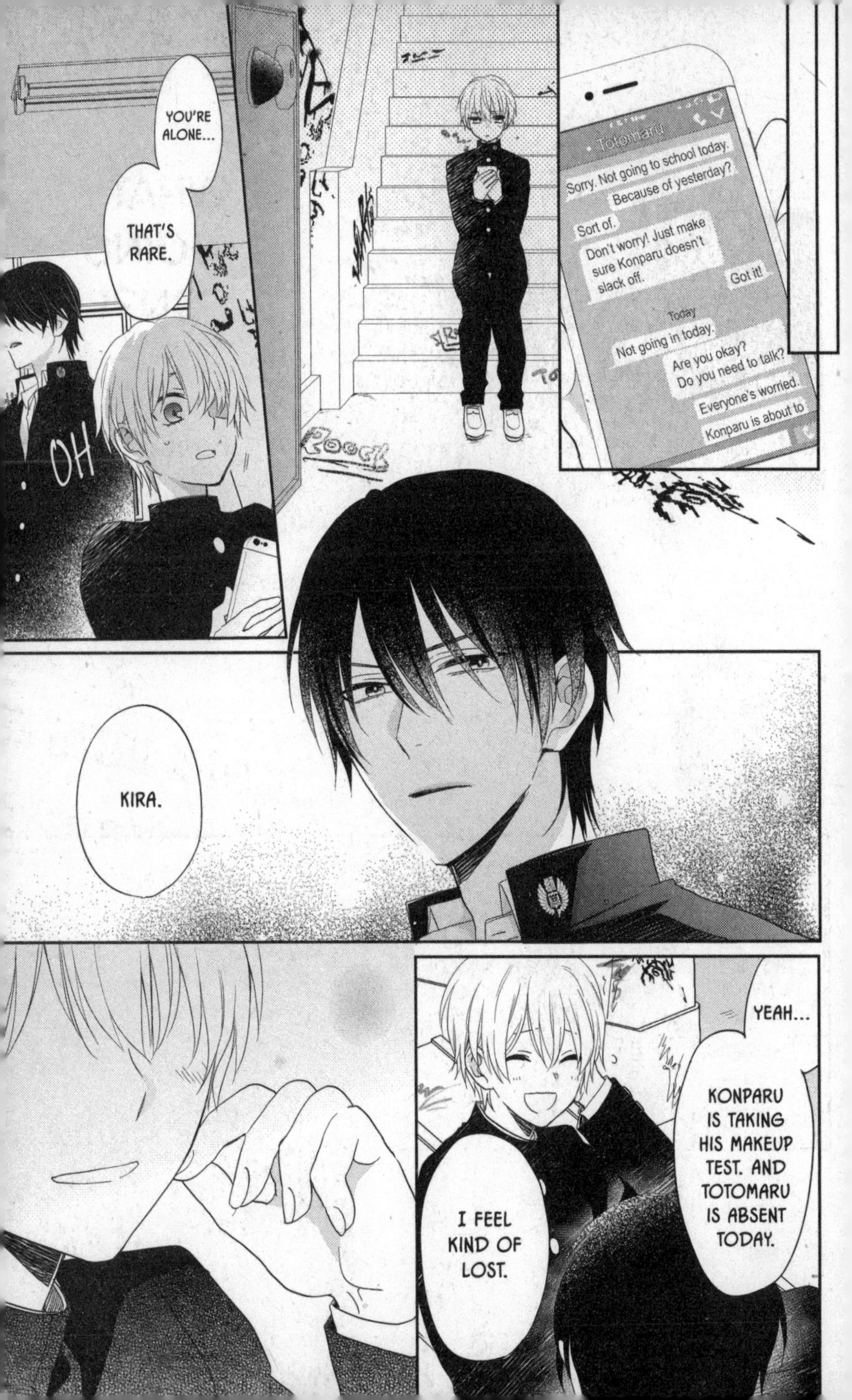

Totomaru
Sorry. Not going to school today.
Because of yesterday?
Sort of.
Don't worry! Just make sure Konparu doesn't slack off.
Got it!
Today
Not going in today.
Are you okay? Do you need to talk?
Everyone's worried.
Konparu is about to
YOU'RE ALONE...
THAT'S RARE.
OH
KIRA.
YEAH...
KONPARU IS TAKING HIS MAKEUP TEST. AND TOTOMARU IS ABSENT TODAY.
I FEEL KIND OF LOST.

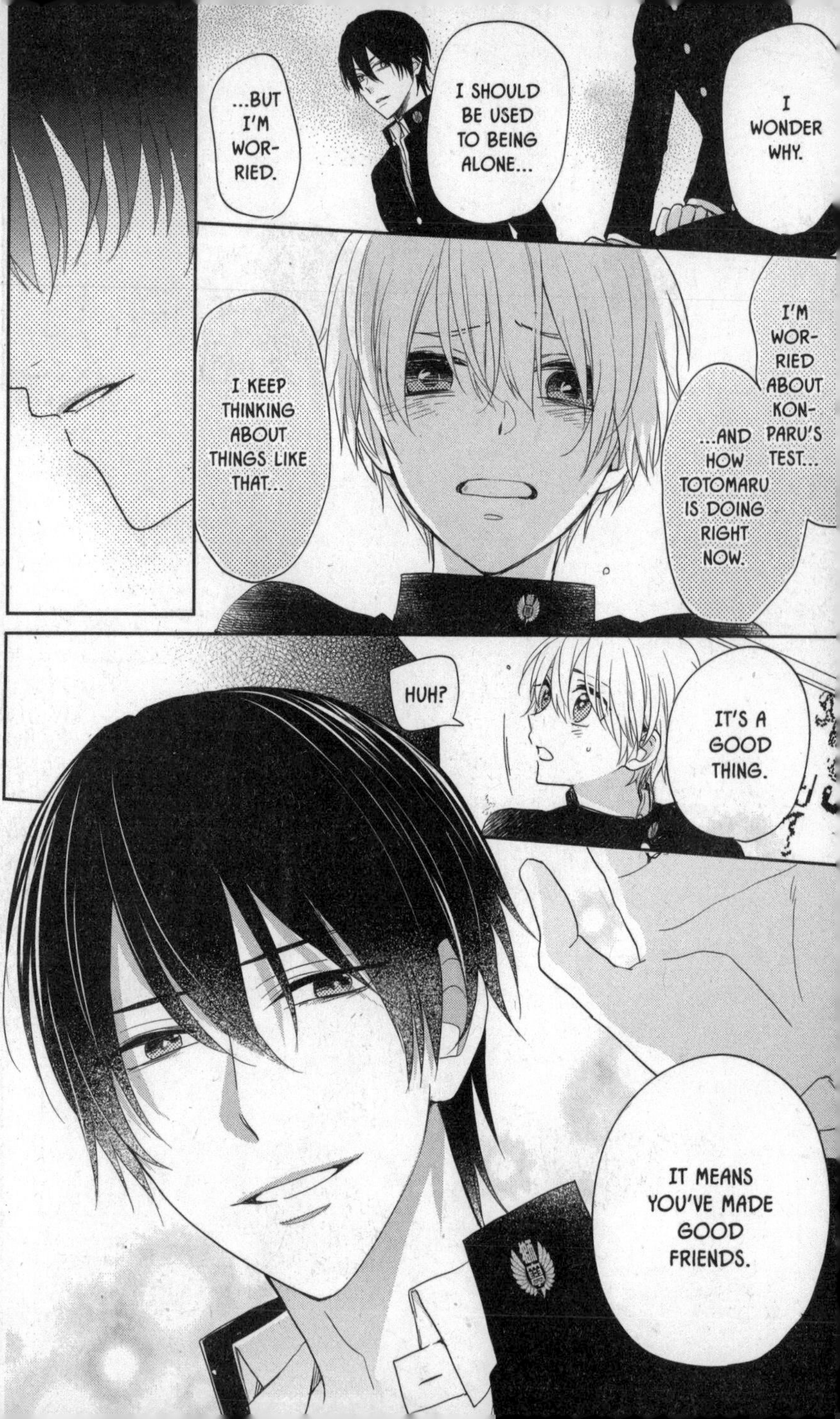
I WONDER WHY.
I SHOULD BE USED TO BEING ALONE...
...BUT I'M WOR-RIED.
I'M WOR-RIED ABOUT KON-PARU'S TEST...
...AND HOW TOTOMARU IS DOING RIGHT NOW.
I KEEP THINKING ABOUT THINGS LIKE THAT...
IT'S A GOOD THING.
HUH?
IT MEANS YOU'VE MADE GOOD FRIENDS.

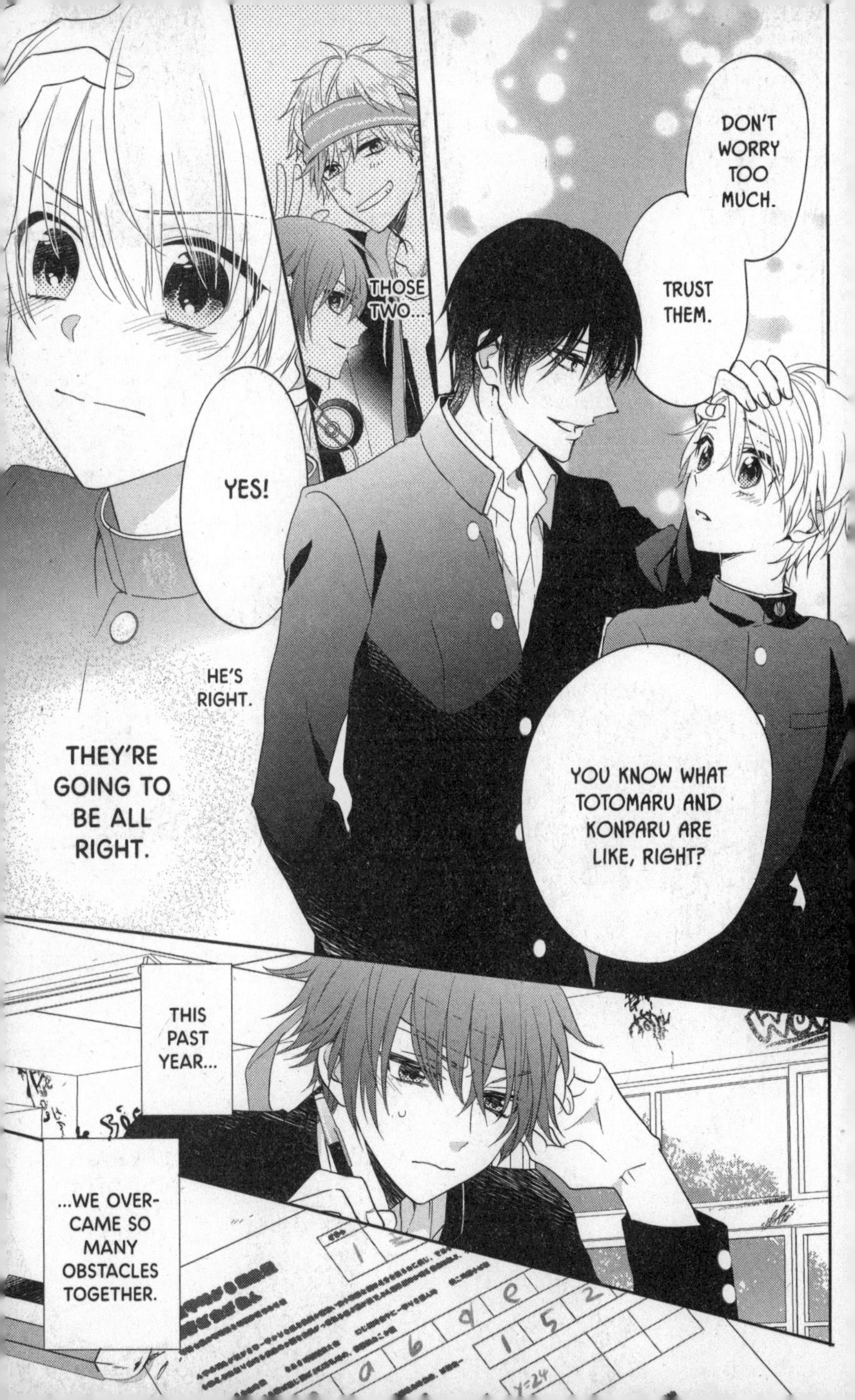
DON'T WORRY TOO MUCH.
TRUST THEM.
YOU KNOW WHAT TOTOMARU AND KONPARU ARE LIKE, RIGHT?
THOSE TWO...
YES!
HE'S RIGHT.
THEY'RE GOING TO BE ALL RIGHT.
THIS PAST YEAR...
...WE OVER-CAME SO MANY OBSTACLES TOGETHER.

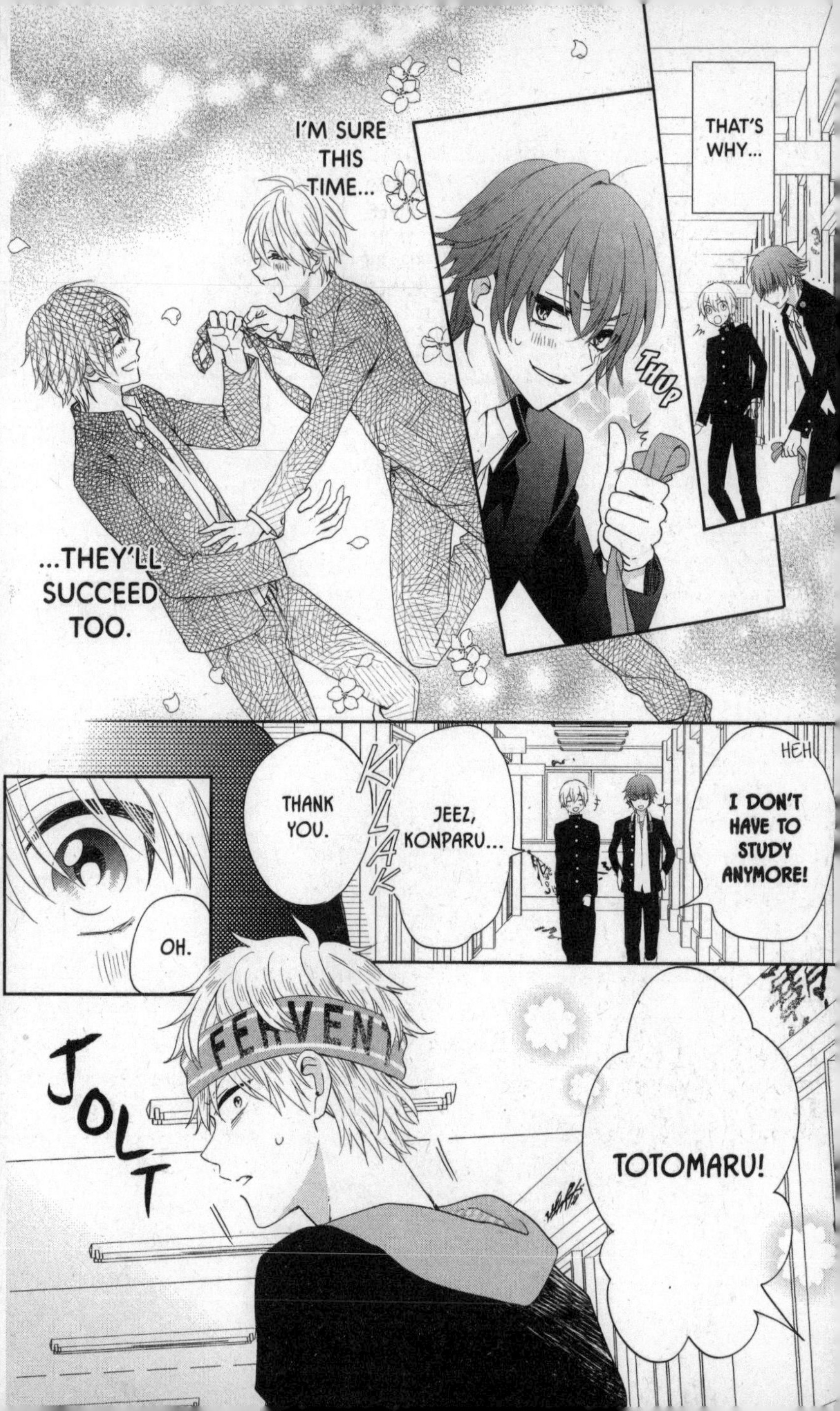
THAT'S WHY...
THUP
I'M SURE THIS TIME...
...THEY'LL SUCCEED TOO.
HEH
I DON'T HAVE TO STUDY ANYMORE!
JEEZ, KONPARU...
KLAK
THANK YOU.
OH.
TOTOMARU!
FERVENT
JOLT

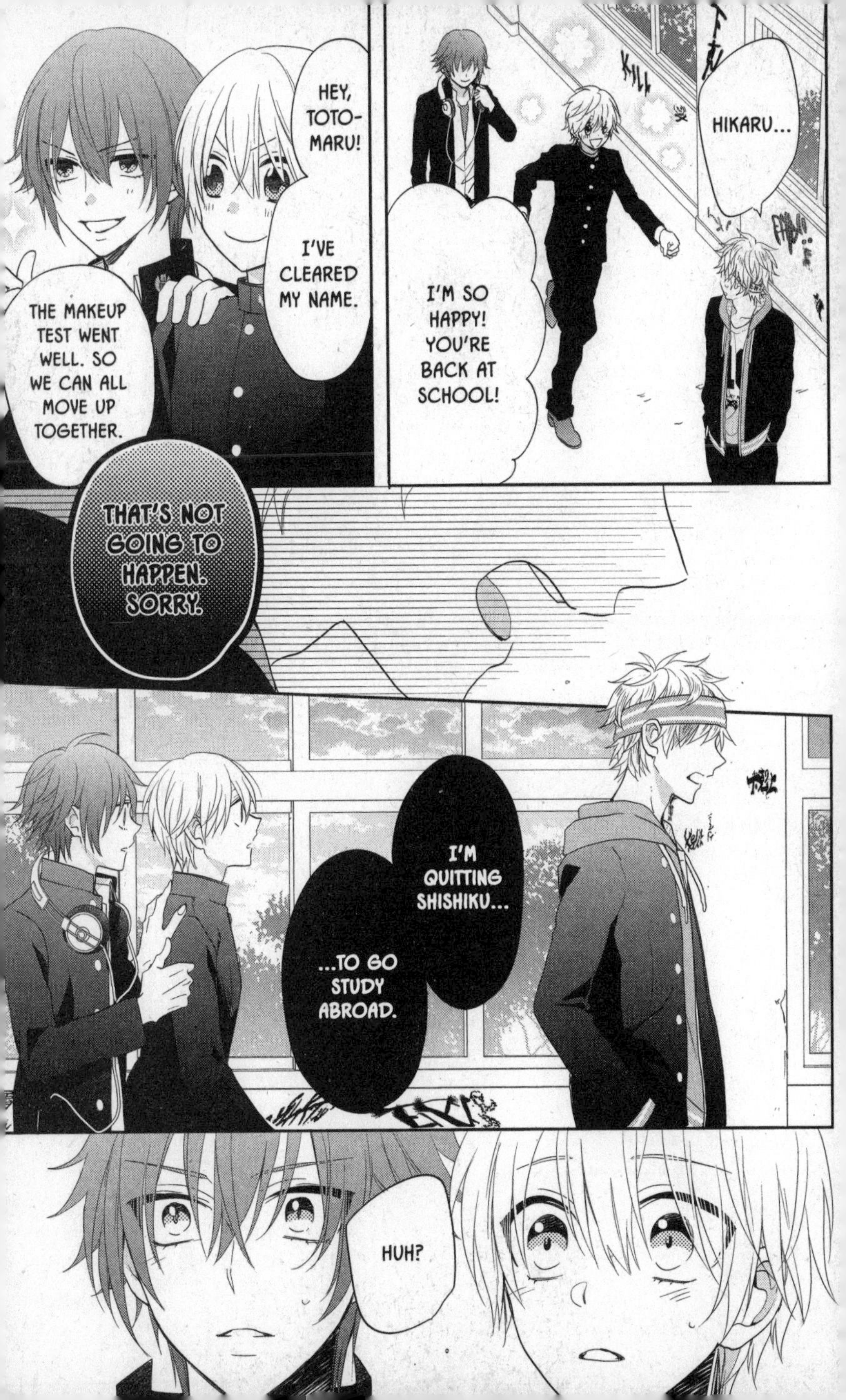
HIKARU...
I'M SO HAPPY! YOU'RE BACK AT SCHOOL!
HEY, TOTO-MARU!
I'VE CLEARED MY NAME.
THE MAKEUP TEST WENT WELL. SO WE CAN ALL MOVE UP TOGETHER.
THAT'S NOT GOING TO HAPPEN. SORRY.
I'M QUITTING SHISHIKU...
...TO GO STUDY ABROAD.
HUH?

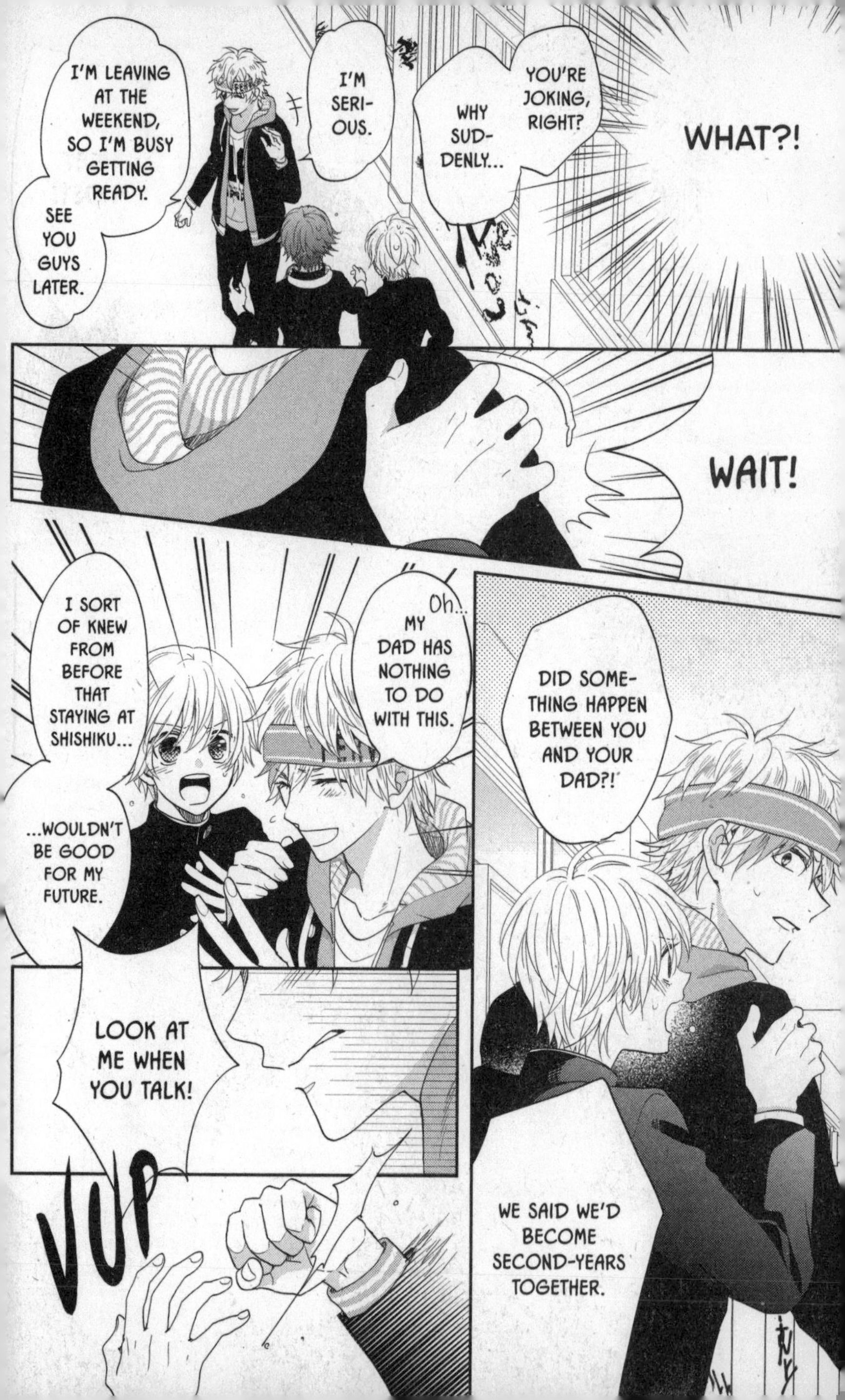
WHAT?!
YOU'RE JOKING, RIGHT?
WHY SUDDENLY...
I'M SERIOUS.
I'M LEAVING AT THE WEEKEND, SO I'M BUSY GETTING READY.
SEE YOU GUYS LATER.
WAIT!
DID SOMETHING HAPPEN BETWEEN YOU AND YOUR DAD?!
WE SAID WE'D BECOME SECOND-YEARS TOGETHER.
Oh...
MY DAD HAS NOTHING TO DO WITH THIS.
I SORT OF KNEW FROM BEFORE THAT STAYING AT SHISHIKU...
...WOULDN'T BE GOOD FOR MY FUTURE.
LOOK AT ME WHEN YOU TALK!
VUP

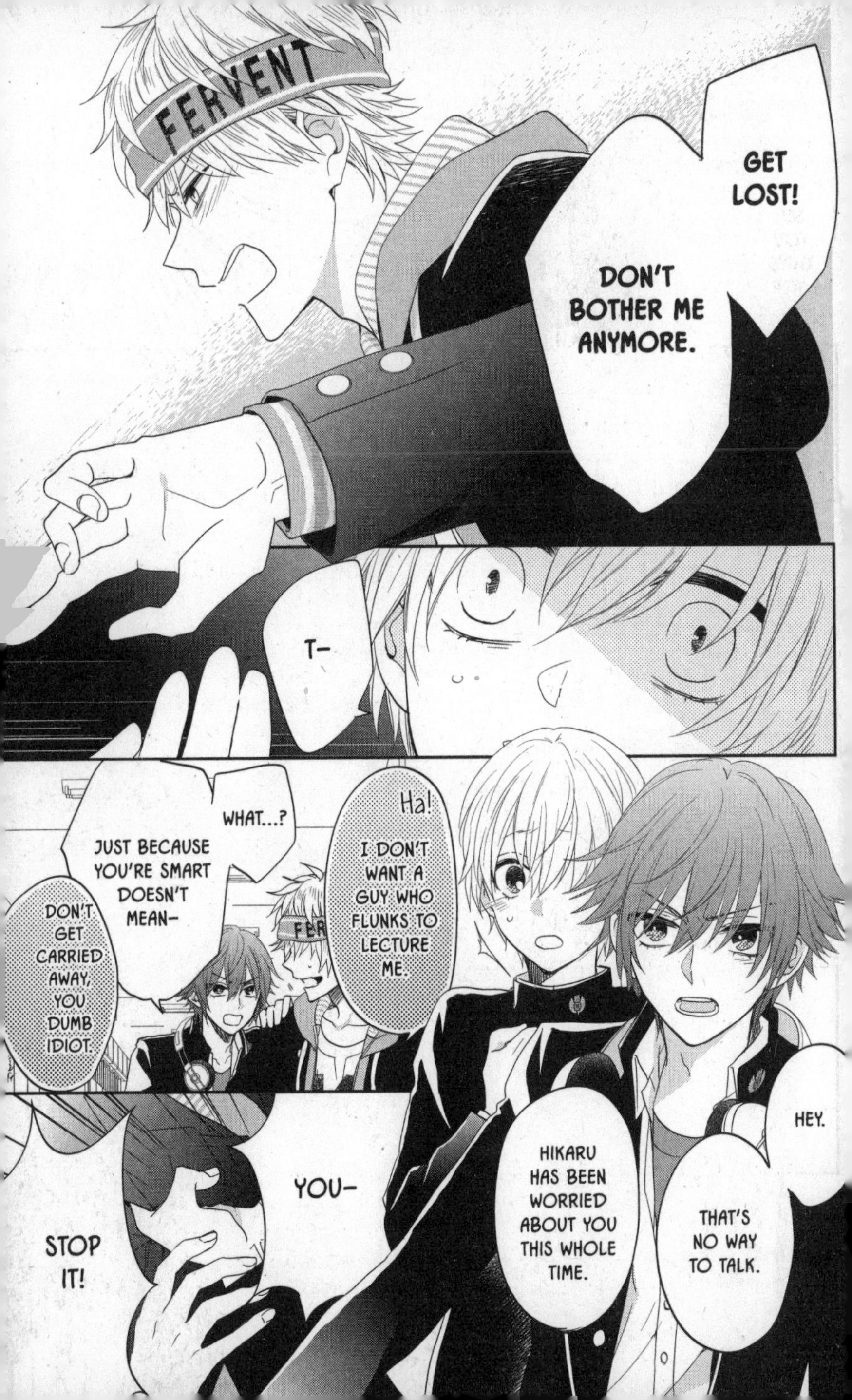
FERVENT
GET LOST!
DON'T BOTHER ME ANYMORE.
T-
Ha!
I DON'T WANT A GUY WHO FLUNKS TO LECTURE ME.
WHAT...?
JUST BECAUSE YOU'RE SMART DOESN'T MEAN-
DON'T GET CARRIED AWAY, YOU DUMB IDIOT.
HEY.
THAT'S NO WAY TO TALK.
HIKARU HAS BEEN WORRIED ABOUT YOU THIS WHOLE TIME.
YOU-
STOP IT!

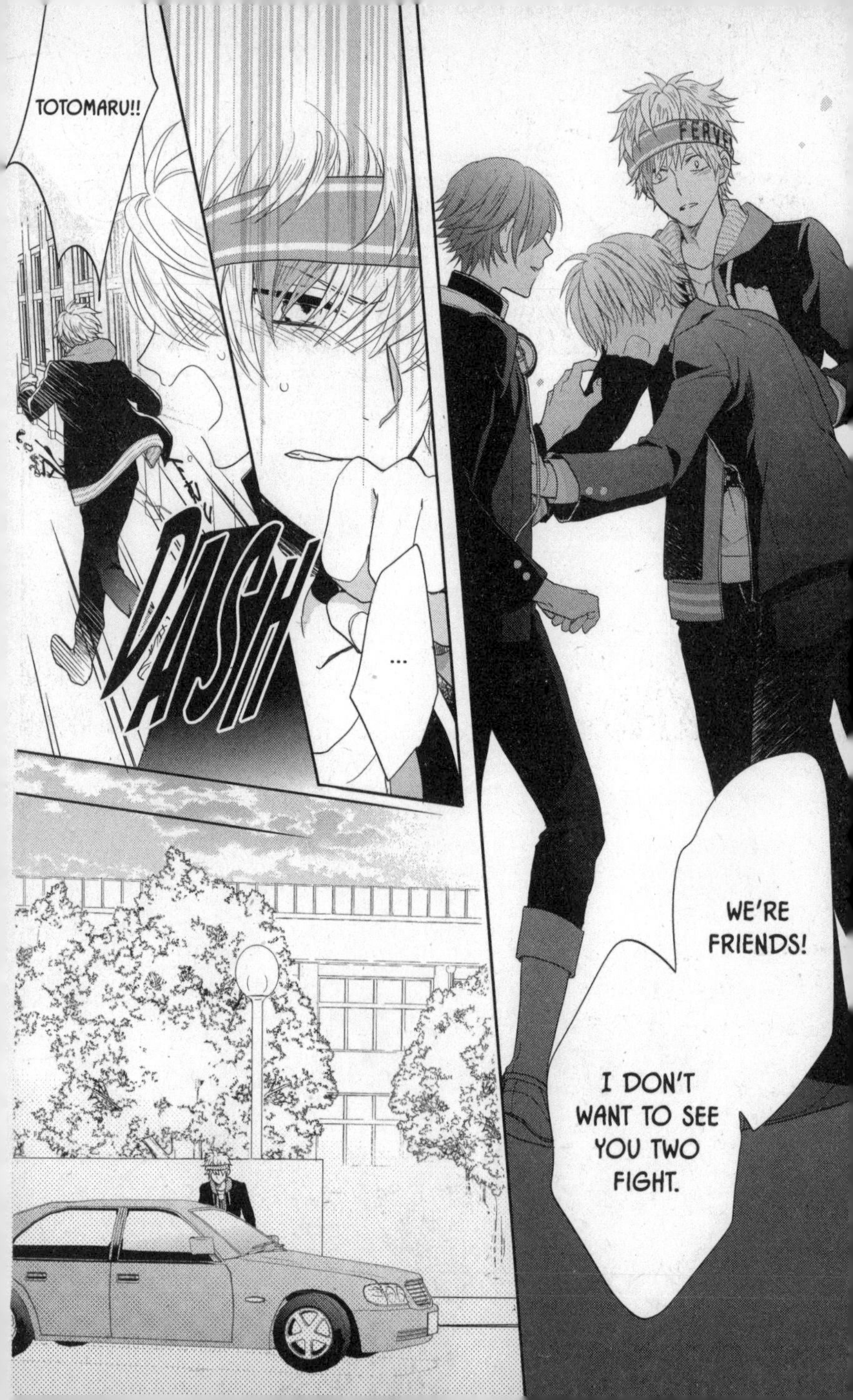
WE'RE FRIENDS!
I DON'T WANT TO SEE YOU TWO FIGHT.
...
TOTOMARU!!
DASH

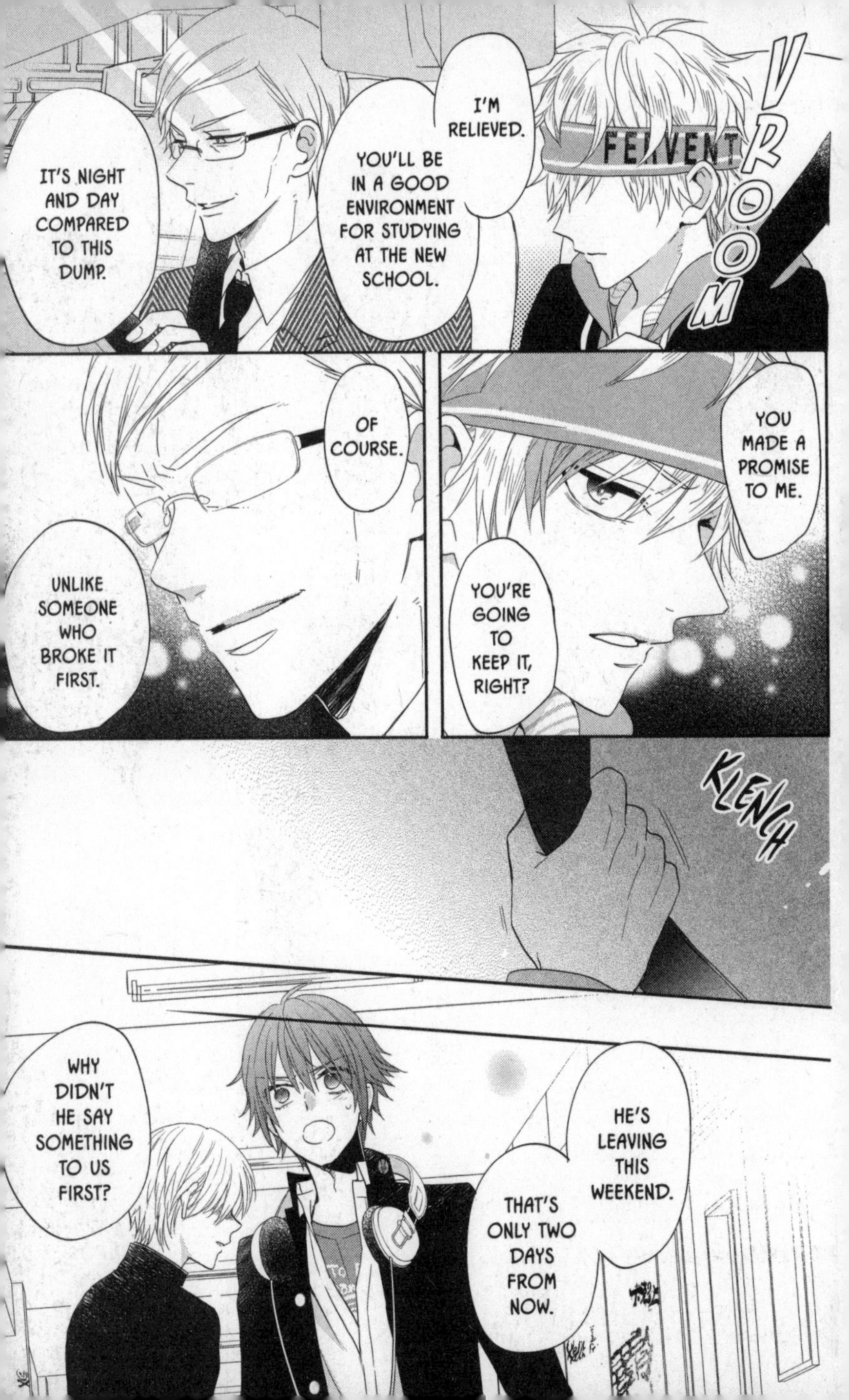
VROOOM
I'M RELIEVED.
YOU'LL BE IN A GOOD ENVIRONMENT FOR STUDYING AT THE NEW SCHOOL.
IT'S NIGHT AND DAY COMPARED TO THIS DUMP.
YOU MADE A PROMISE TO ME.
YOU'RE GOING TO KEEP IT, RIGHT?
OF COURSE.
UNLIKE SOMEONE WHO BROKE IT FIRST.
KLENCH
HE'S LEAVING THIS WEEKEND.
THAT'S ONLY TWO DAYS FROM NOW.
WHY DIDN'T HE SAY SOMETHING TO US FIRST?

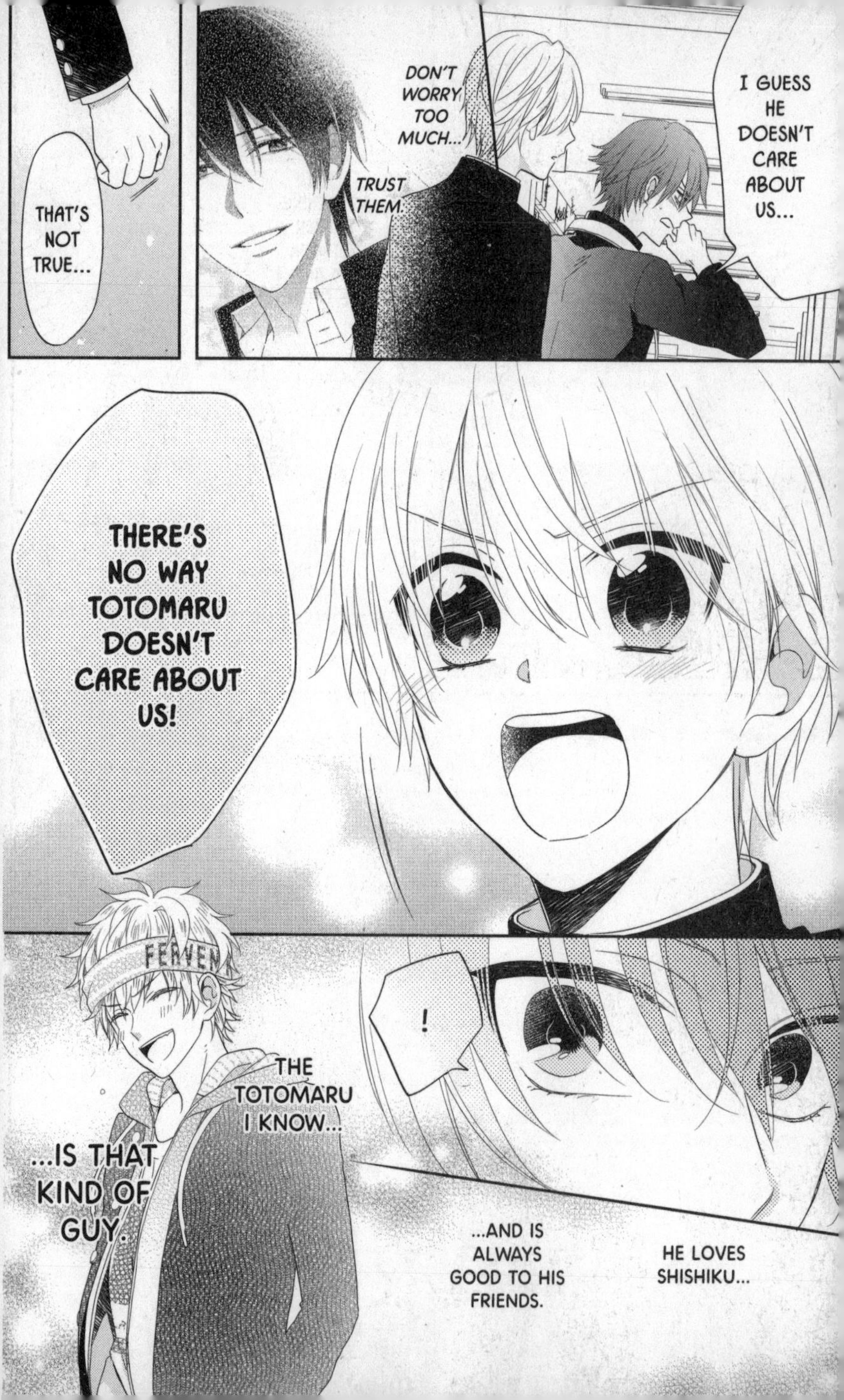
I GUESS HE DOESN'T CARE ABOUT US...
DON'T WORRY TOO MUCH...
TRUST THEM.
THAT'S NOT TRUE...
THERE'S NO WAY TOTOMARU DOESN'T CARE ABOUT US!
!
HE LOVES SHISHIKU...
...AND IS ALWAYS GOOD TO HIS FRIENDS.
THE TOTOMARU I KNOW...
...IS THAT KIND OF GUY.

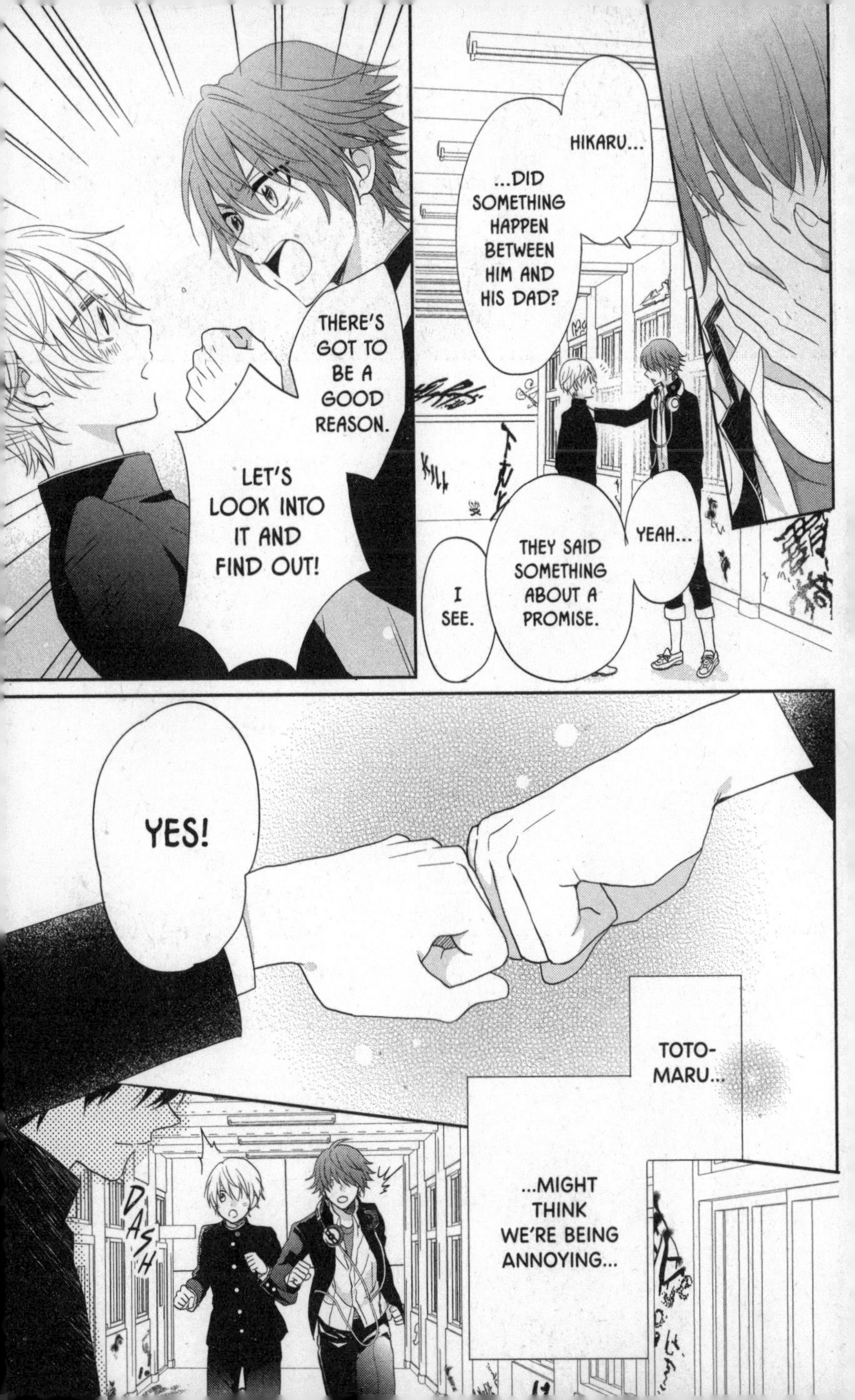
HIKARU...
...DID SOMETHING HAPPEN BETWEEN HIM AND HIS DAD?
YEAH...
THEY SAID SOMETHING ABOUT A PROMISE.
I SEE.
THERE'S GOT TO BE A GOOD REASON.
LET'S LOOK INTO IT AND FIND OUT!
YES!
TOTO-MARU...
...MIGHT THINK WE'RE BEING ANNOYING...
DASH

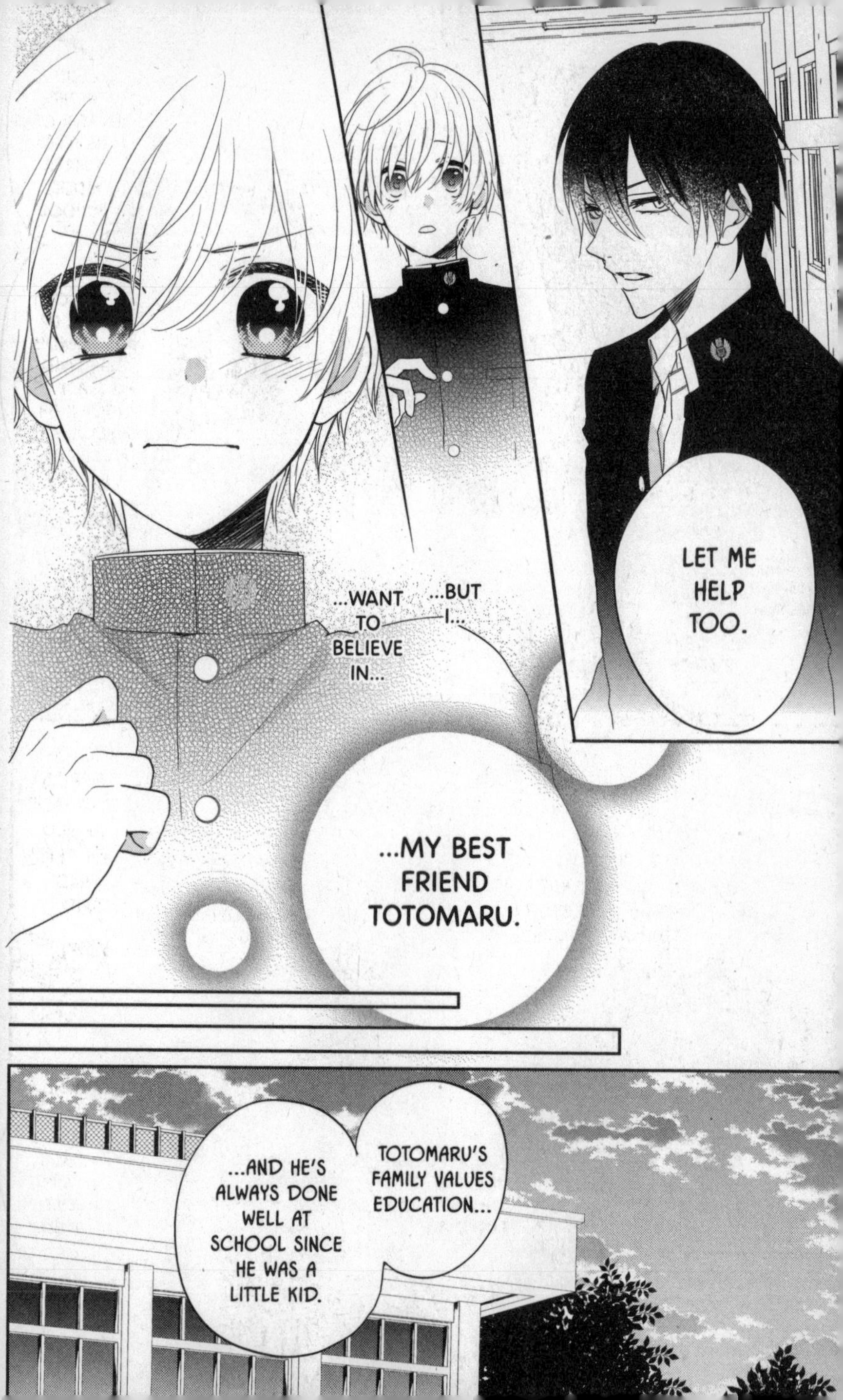
LET ME HELP TOO.
...BUT I...
...WANT TO BELIEVE IN...
...MY BEST FRIEND TOTOMARU.
TOTOMARU'S FAMILY VALUES EDUCATION...
...AND HE'S ALWAYS DONE WELL AT SCHOOL SINCE HE WAS A LITTLE KID.

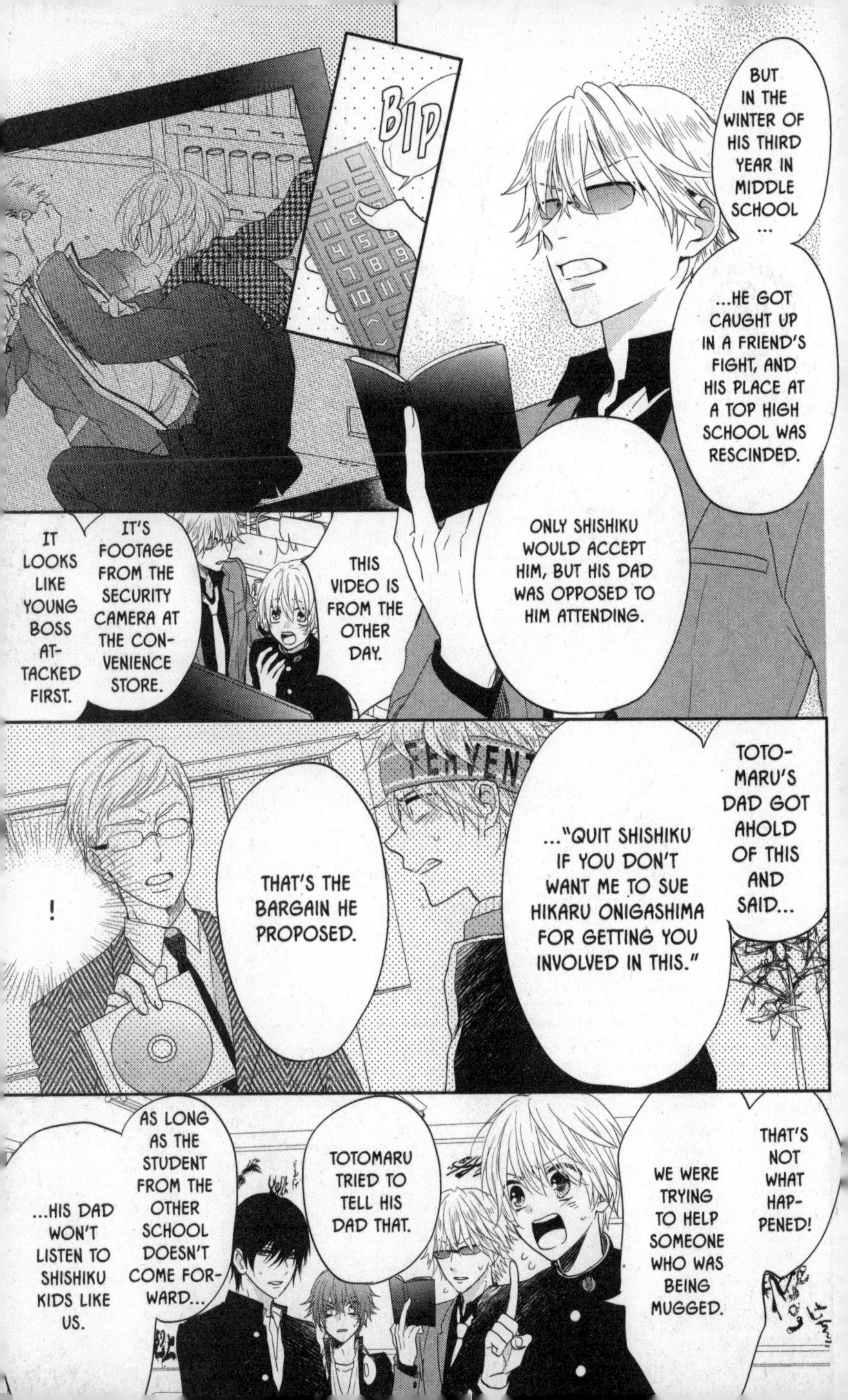
BUT IN THE WINTER OF HIS THIRD YEAR IN MIDDLE SCHOOL ...
...HE GOT CAUGHT UP IN A FRIEND'S FIGHT, AND HIS PLACE AT A TOP HIGH SCHOOL WAS RESCINDED.
ONLY SHISHIKU WOULD ACCEPT HIM, BUT HIS DAD WAS OPPOSED TO HIM ATTENDING.
BIP
THIS VIDEO IS FROM THE OTHER DAY.
IT'S FOOTAGE FROM THE SECURITY CAMERA AT THE CON-VENIENCE STORE.
IT LOOKS LIKE YOUNG BOSS AT-TACKED FIRST.
TOTO-MARU'S DAD GOT AHOLD OF THIS AND SAID...
..."QUIT SHISHIKU IF YOU DON'T WANT ME TO SUE HIKARU ONIGASHIMA FOR GETTING YOU INVOLVED IN THIS."
THAT'S THE BARGAIN HE PROPOSED.
!
THAT'S NOT WHAT HAP-PENED!
WE WERE TRYING TO HELP SOMEONE WHO WAS BEING MUGGED.
TOTOMARU TRIED TO TELL HIS DAD THAT.
AS LONG AS THE STUDENT FROM THE OTHER SCHOOL DOESN'T COME FOR-WARD...
...HIS DAD WON'T LISTEN TO SHISHIKU KIDS LIKE US.

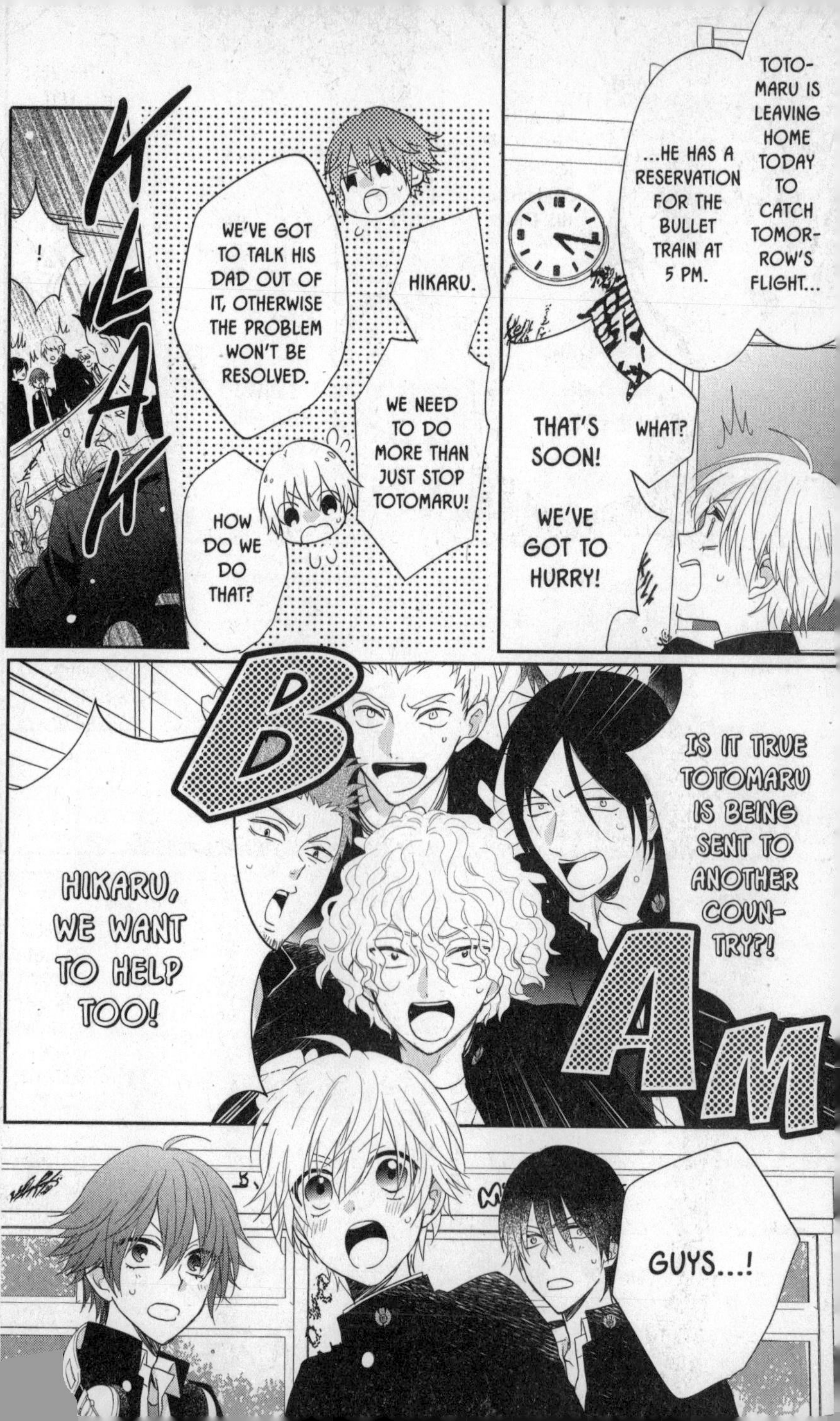
TOTOMARU IS LEAVING HOME TODAY TO CATCH TOMORROW'S FLIGHT...
...HE HAS A RESERVATION FOR THE BULLET TRAIN AT 5 PM.
WHAT?
THAT'S SOON!
WE'VE GOT TO HURRY!
HIKARU.
WE'VE GOT TO TALK HIS DAD OUT OF IT, OTHERWISE THE PROBLEM WON'T BE RESOLVED.
WE NEED TO DO MORE THAN JUST STOP TOTOMARU!
HOW DO WE DO THAT?
KLAK
!
IS IT TRUE TOTOMARU IS BEING SENT TO ANOTHER COUNTRY?!
BAM
HIKARU, WE WANT TO HELP TOO!
GUYS...!

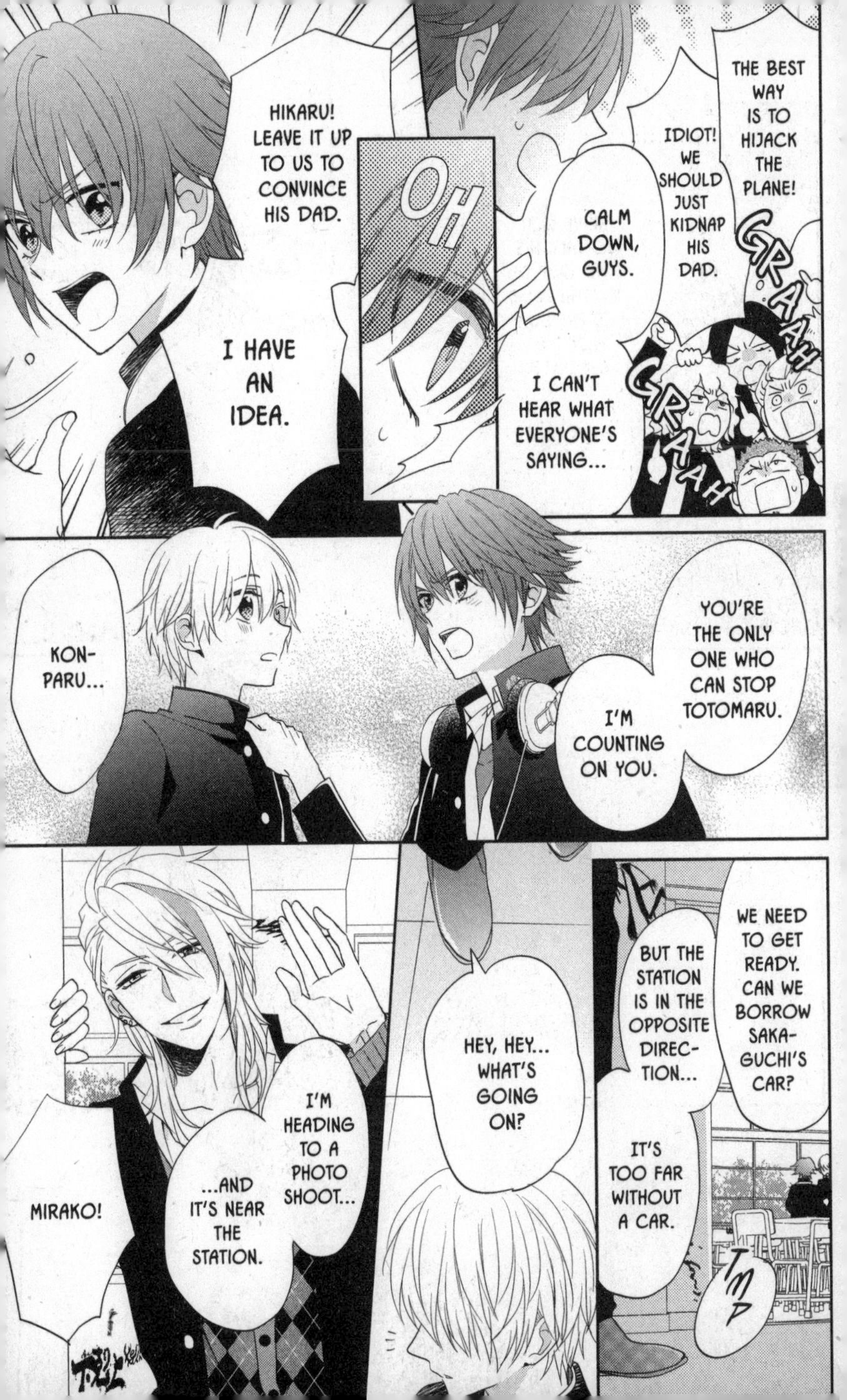
THE BEST WAY IS TO HIJACK THE PLANE!
IDIOT! WE SHOULD JUST KIDNAP HIS DAD.
GRAAH
GRAAAH
CALM DOWN, GUYS.
I CAN'T HEAR WHAT EVERYONE'S SAYING...
OH
HIKARU! LEAVE IT UP TO US TO CONVINCE HIS DAD.
I HAVE AN IDEA.
YOU'RE THE ONLY ONE WHO CAN STOP TOTOMARU.
I'M COUNTING ON YOU.
KON-PARU...
WE NEED TO GET READY. CAN WE BORROW SAKA-GUCHI'S CAR?
BUT THE STATION IS IN THE OPPOSITE DIREC-TION...
IT'S TOO FAR WITHOUT A CAR.
TMP
HEY, HEY... WHAT'S GOING ON?
I'M HEADING TO A PHOTO SHOOT...
...AND IT'S NEAR THE STATION.
MIRAKO!

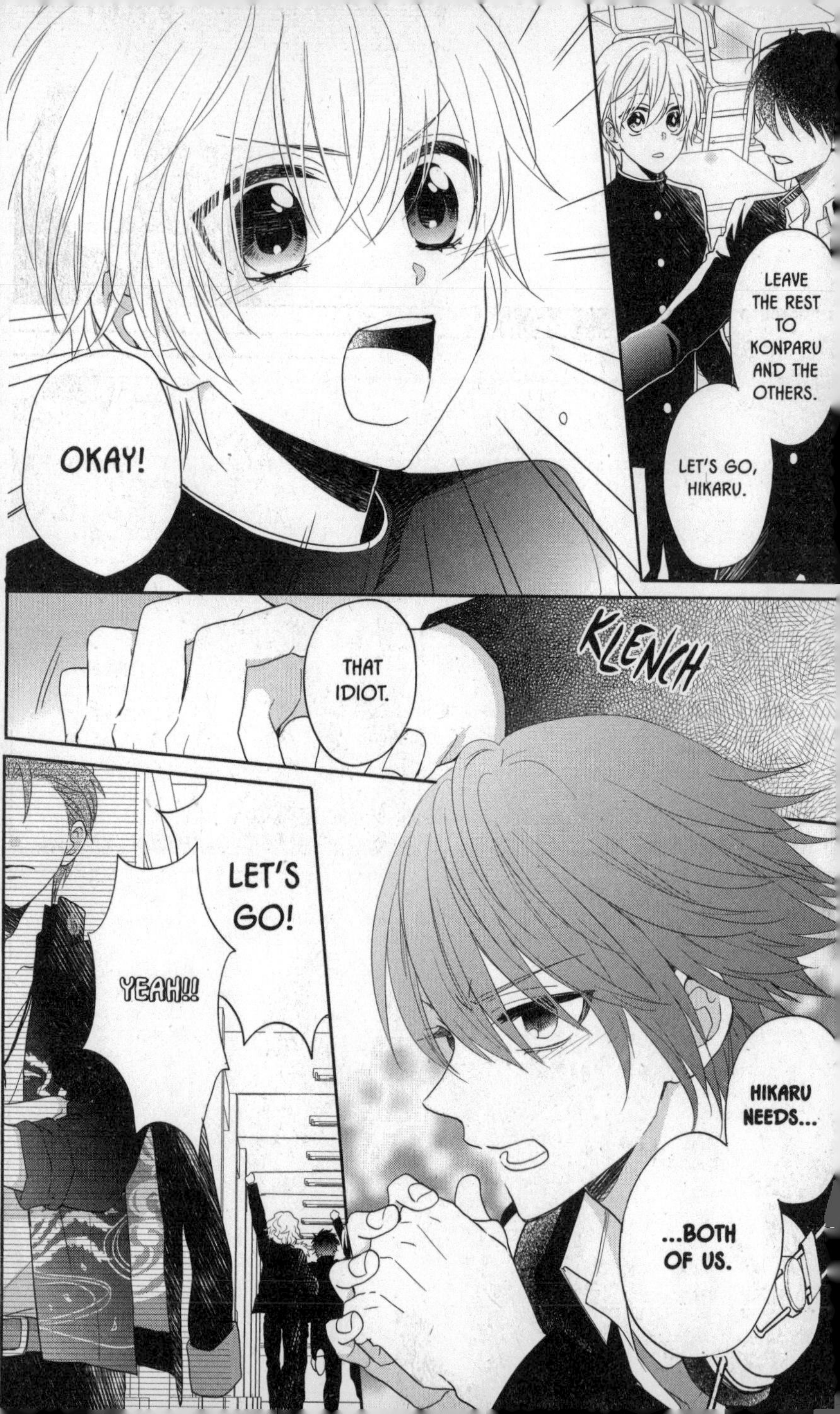
LEAVE THE REST TO KONPARU AND THE OTHERS.
LET'S GO, HIKARU.
OKAY!
KLENCH
THAT IDIOT.
HIKARU NEEDS...
...BOTH OF US.
LET'S GO!
YEAH!!

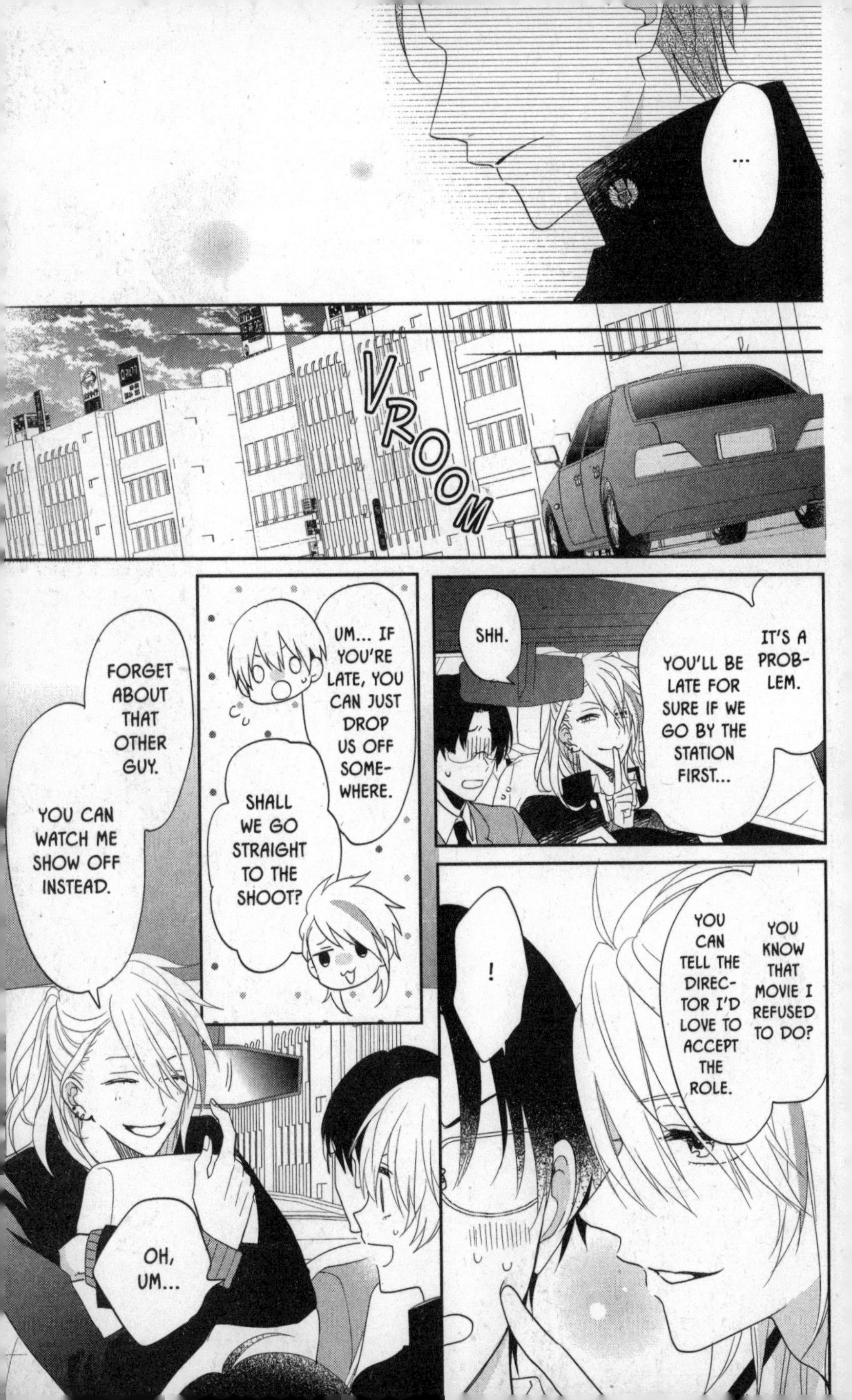
...
VROOM
IT'S A PROB-LEM.
YOU'LL BE LATE FOR SURE IF WE GO BY THE STATION FIRST...
SHH.
YOU KNOW THAT MOVIE I REFUSED TO DO?
YOU CAN TELL THE DIREC-TOR I'D LOVE TO ACCEPT THE ROLE.
!
UM... IF YOU'RE LATE, YOU CAN JUST DROP US OFF SOME-WHERE.
SHALL WE GO STRAIGHT TO THE SHOOT?
FORGET ABOUT THAT OTHER GUY.
YOU CAN WATCH ME SHOW OFF INSTEAD.
OH, UM...

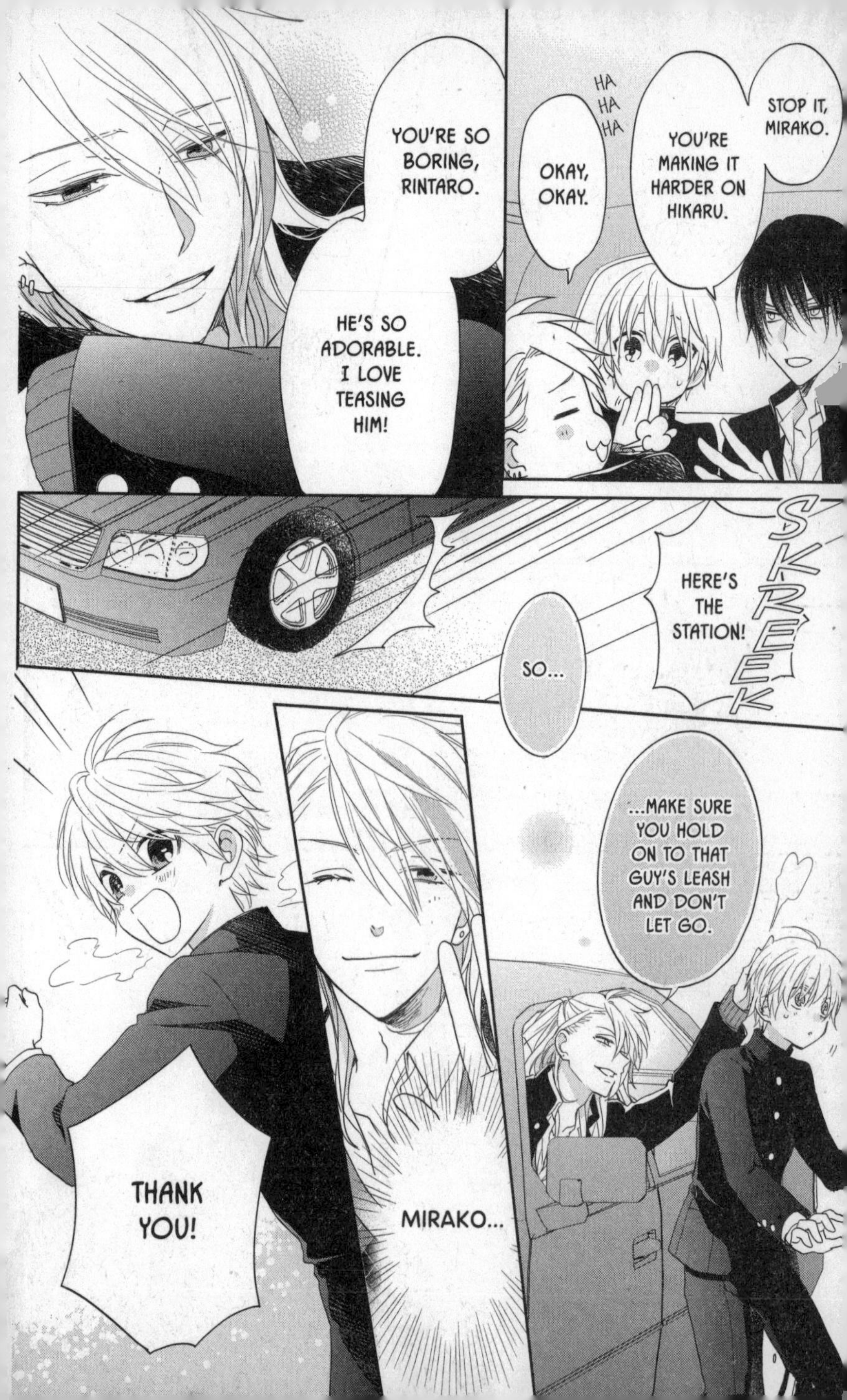
STOP IT, MIRAKO.
YOU'RE MAKING IT HARDER ON HIKARU.
HA HA HA
OKAY, OKAY.
YOU'RE SO BORING, RINTARO.
HE'S SO ADORABLE. I LOVE TEASING HIM!
SKREEK
HERE'S THE STATION!
SO...
...MAKE SURE YOU HOLD ON TO THAT GUY'S LEASH AND DON'T LET GO.
MIRAKO...
THANK YOU!

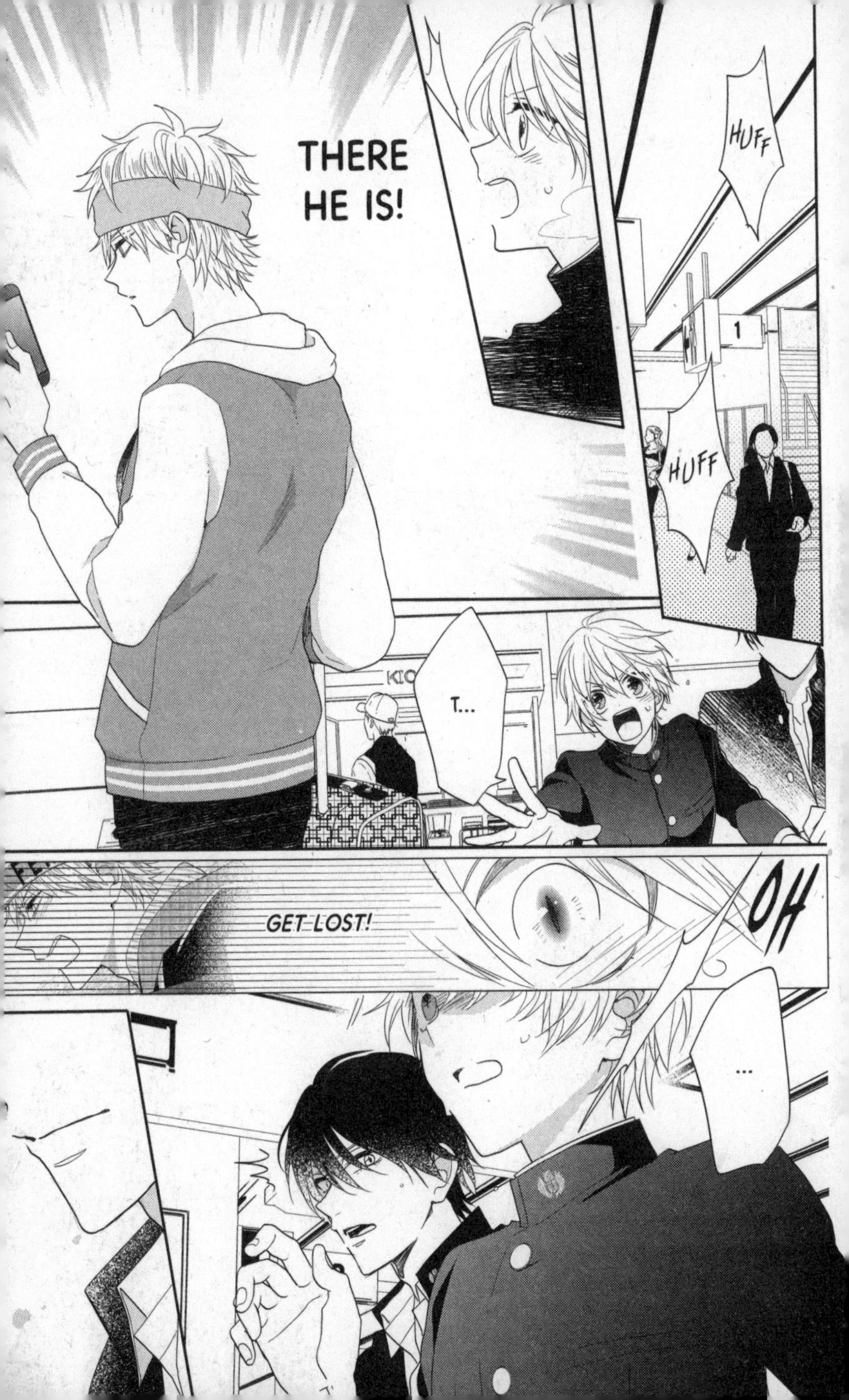
HUFF
HUFF
T...
THERE HE IS!
OH
GET LOST!
...

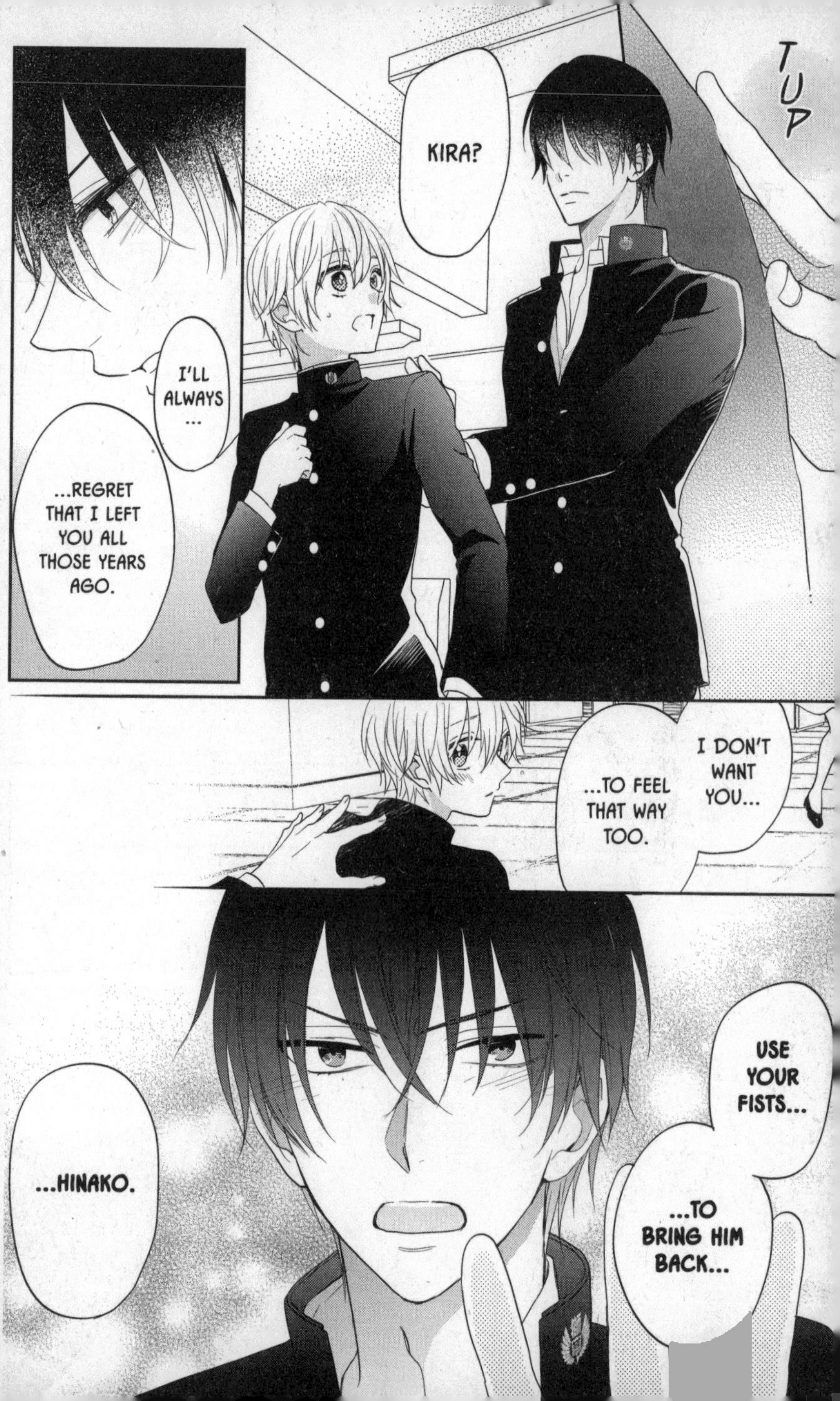
TUP
KIRA?
I'LL ALWAYS ...
...REGRET THAT I LEFT YOU ALL THOSE YEARS AGO.
I DON'T WANT YOU...
...TO FEEL THAT WAY TOO.
USE YOUR FISTS...
...TO BRING HIM BACK...
...HINAKO.

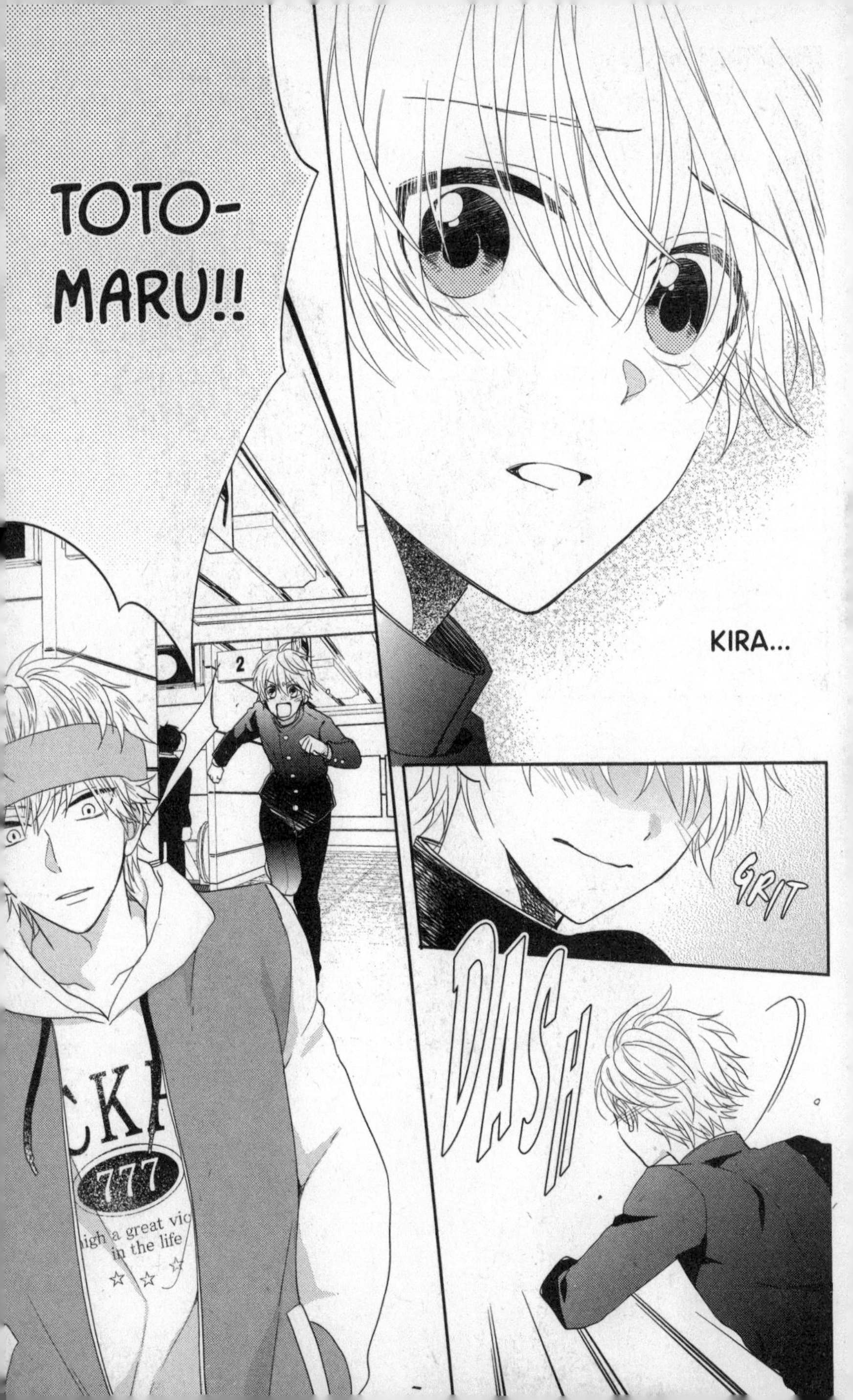
KIRA...
GRIT
DASH
TOTO-
MARU!!

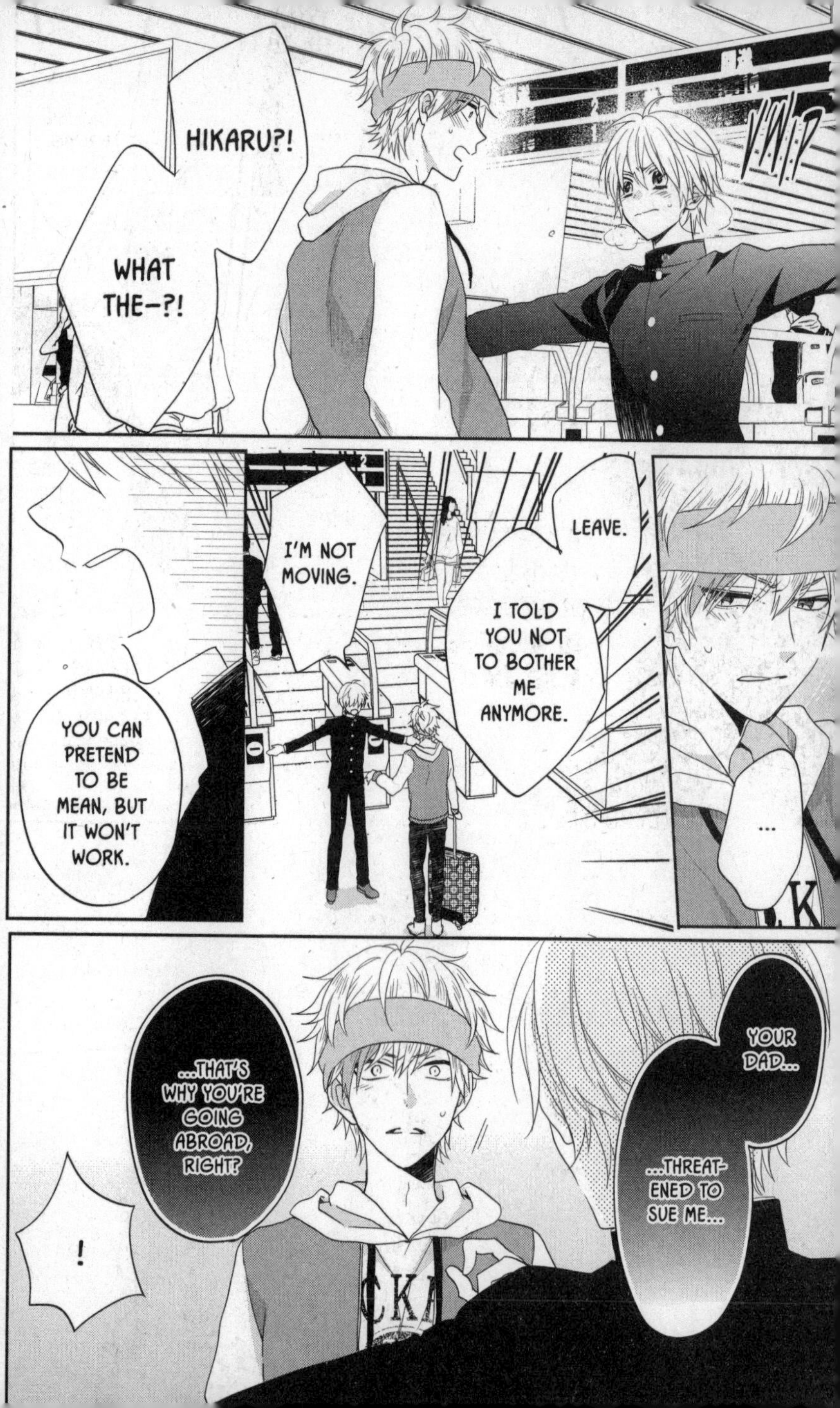
VWIP
HIKARU?!
WHAT THE-?!
...
LEAVE.
I TOLD YOU NOT TO BOTHER ME ANYMORE.
I'M NOT MOVING.
YOU CAN PRETEND TO BE MEAN, BUT IT WON'T WORK.
YOUR DAD...
...THREAT-ENED TO SUE ME...
...THAT'S WHY YOU'RE GOING ABROAD, RIGHT?
!

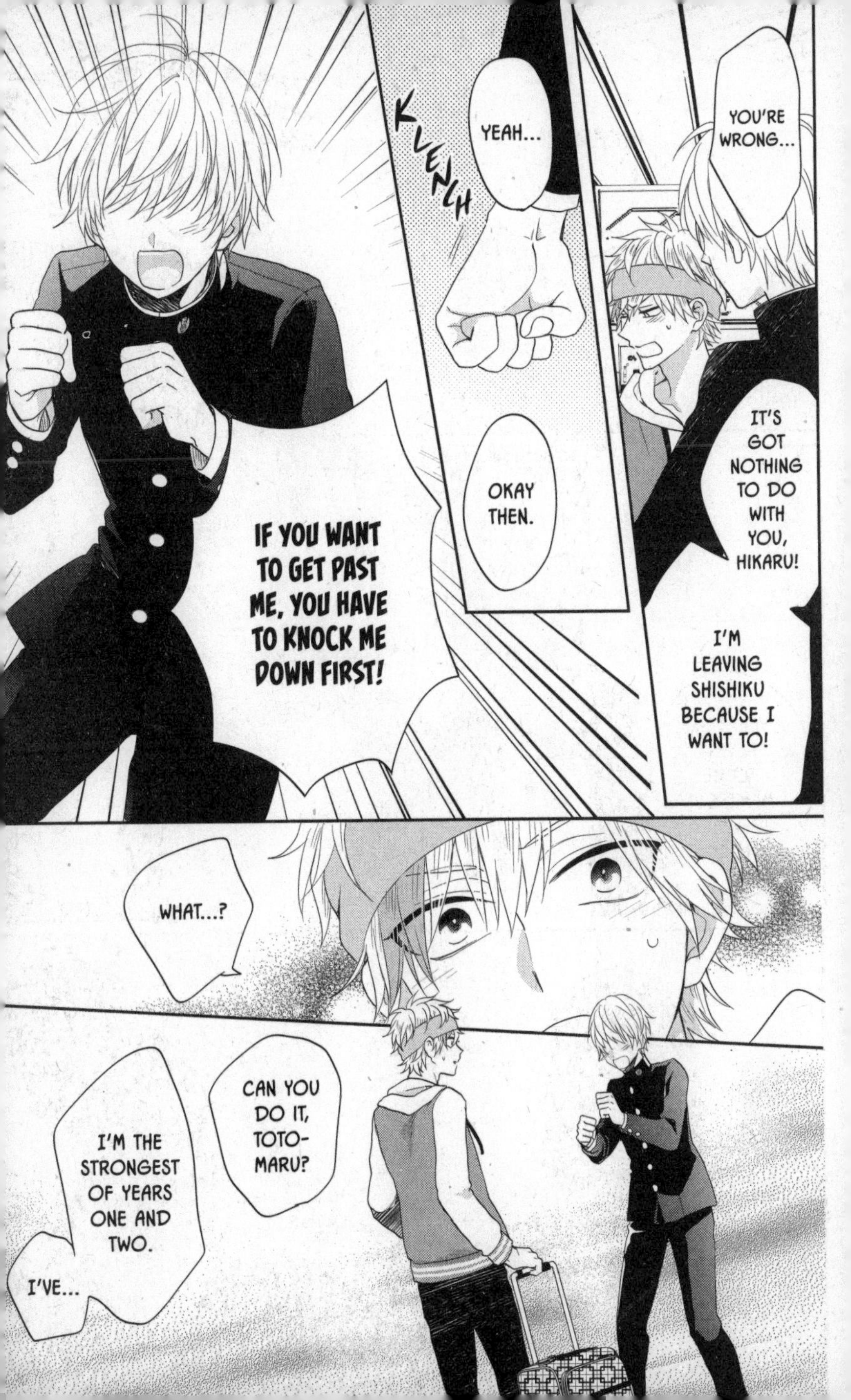
YOU'RE WRONG...
IT'S GOT NOTHING TO DO WITH YOU, HIKARU!
I'M LEAVING SHISHIKU BECAUSE I WANT TO!
KLENCH
YEAH...
OKAY THEN.
IF YOU WANT TO GET PAST ME, YOU HAVE TO KNOCK ME DOWN FIRST!
WHAT...?
CAN YOU DO IT, TOTO-MARU?
I'M THE STRONGEST OF YEARS ONE AND TWO.
I'VE...

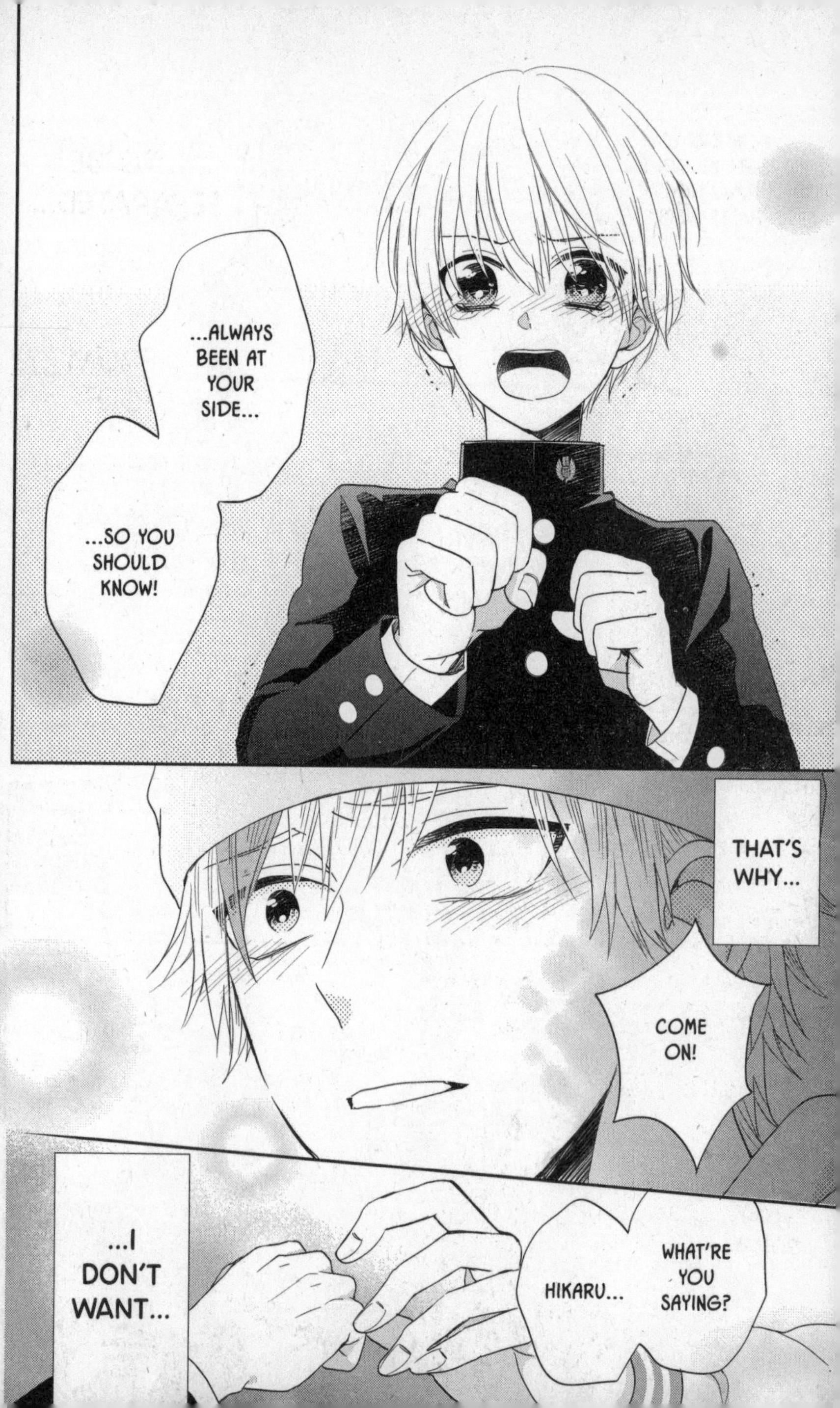
...ALWAYS BEEN AT YOUR SIDE...
...SO YOU SHOULD KNOW!
THAT'S WHY...
COME ON!
HIKARU... WHAT'RE YOU SAYING?
...I DON'T WANT...

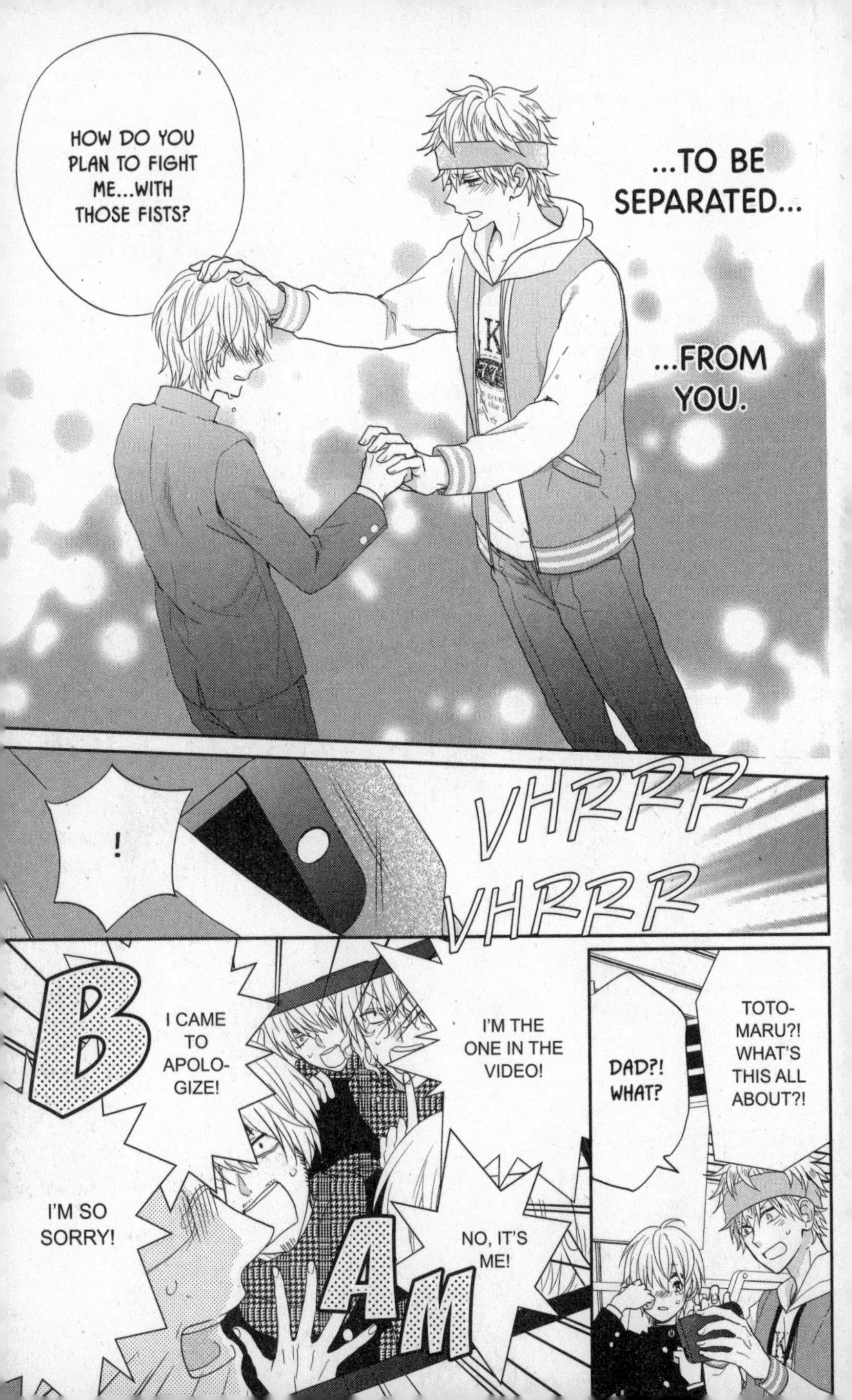
...TO BE SEPARATED...
...FROM YOU.
HOW DO YOU PLAN TO FIGHT ME...WITH THOSE FISTS?
!
VHRRR
VHRRR
TOTO-MARU?! WHAT'S THIS ALL ABOUT?!
DAD?! WHAT?
I'M THE ONE IN THE VIDEO!
I CAME TO APOLO-GIZE!
BAM
NO, IT'S ME!
I'M SO SORRY!

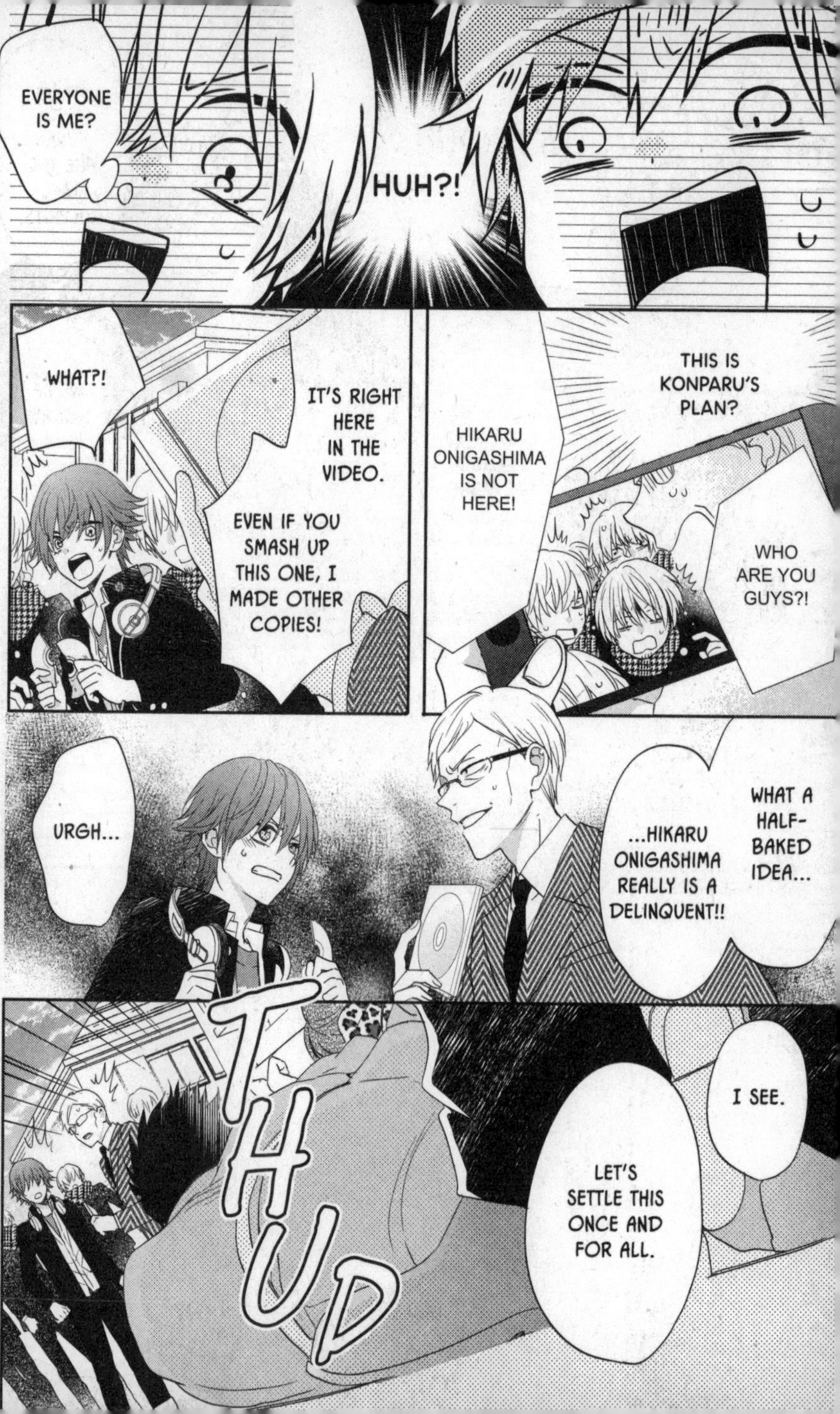
EVERYONE IS ME?
HUH?!
THIS IS KONPARU'S PLAN?
WHO ARE YOU GUYS?!
HIKARU ONIGASHIMA IS NOT HERE!
WHAT?!
IT'S RIGHT HERE IN THE VIDEO.
EVEN IF YOU SMASH UP THIS ONE, I MADE OTHER COPIES!
WHAT A HALF-BAKED IDEA...
...HIKARU ONIGASHIMA REALLY IS A DELINQUENT!!
URGH...
I SEE.
LET'S SETTLE THIS ONCE AND FOR ALL.
THUD

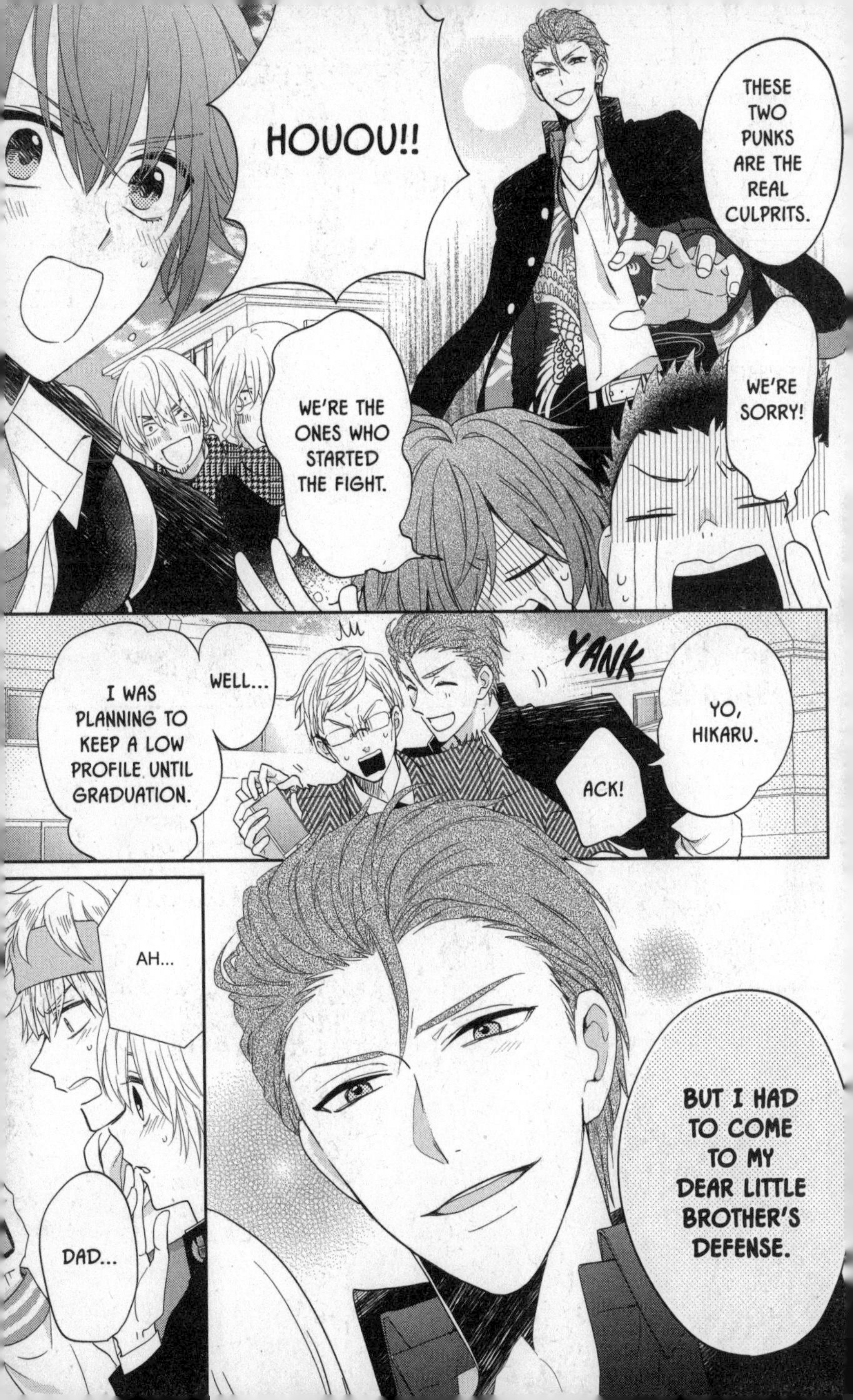
THESE TWO PUNKS ARE THE REAL CULPRITS.
HOUOU!!
WE'RE SORRY!
WE'RE THE ONES WHO STARTED THE FIGHT.
YO, HIKARU.
YANK
ACK!
WELL...
I WAS PLANNING TO KEEP A LOW PROFILE UNTIL GRADUATION.
BUT I HAD TO COME TO MY DEAR LITTLE BROTHER'S DEFENSE.
AH...
DAD...

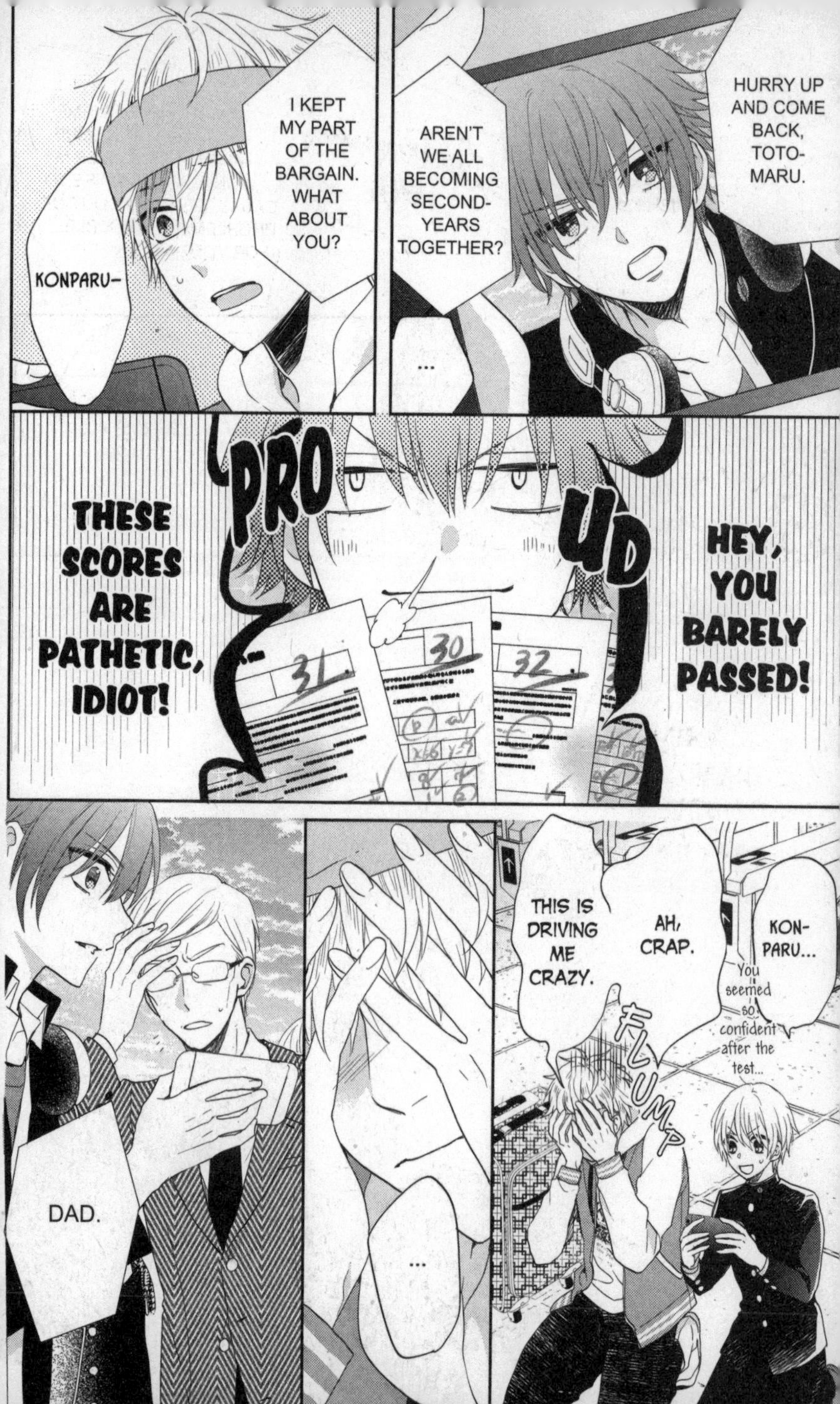
HURRY UP AND COME BACK, TOTO-MARU.
AREN'T WE ALL BECOMING SECOND-YEARS TOGETHER?
...
I KEPT MY PART OF THE BARGAIN. WHAT ABOUT YOU?
KONPARU–
HEY, YOU BARELY PASSED!
PROUD
32
30
31
THESE SCORES ARE PATHETIC, IDIOT!
KON-PARU...
You seemed so confident after the test...
AH, CRAP.
THIS IS DRIVING ME CRAZY.
FLUMP
...
DAD.

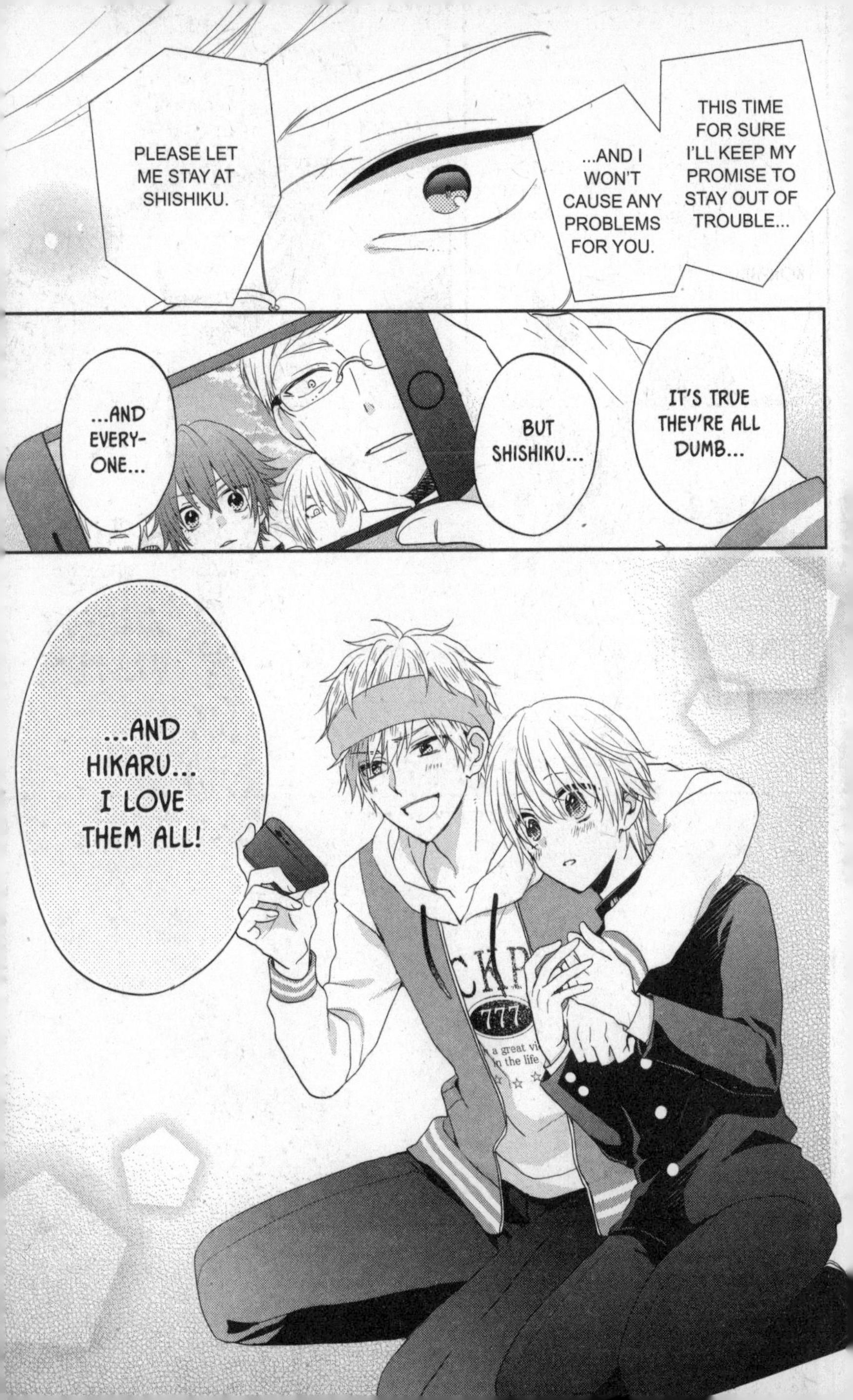
THIS TIME FOR SURE I'LL KEEP MY PROMISE TO STAY OUT OF TROUBLE...
...AND I WON'T CAUSE ANY PROBLEMS FOR YOU.
PLEASE LET ME STAY AT SHISHIKU.
IT'S TRUE THEY'RE ALL DUMB...
BUT SHISHIKU...
...AND EVERY-ONE...
...AND HIKARU... I LOVE THEM ALL!

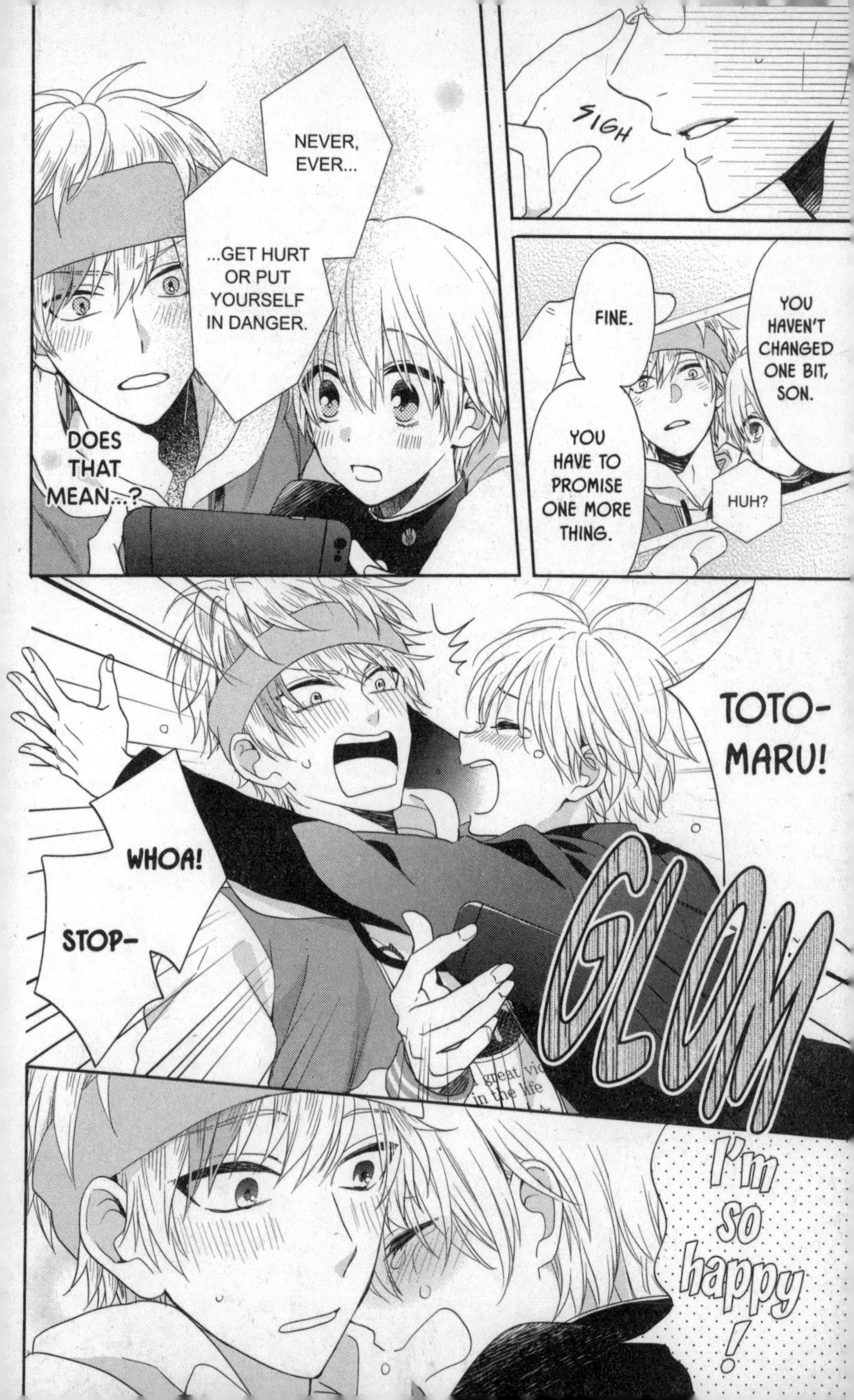
SIGH
YOU HAVEN'T CHANGED ONE BIT, SON.
HUH?
FINE.
YOU HAVE TO PROMISE ONE MORE THING.
NEVER, EVER...
...GET HURT OR PUT YOURSELF IN DANGER.
DOES THAT MEAN...?
TOTO-MARU!
WHOA!
STOP-
GLOM
I'm so happy!

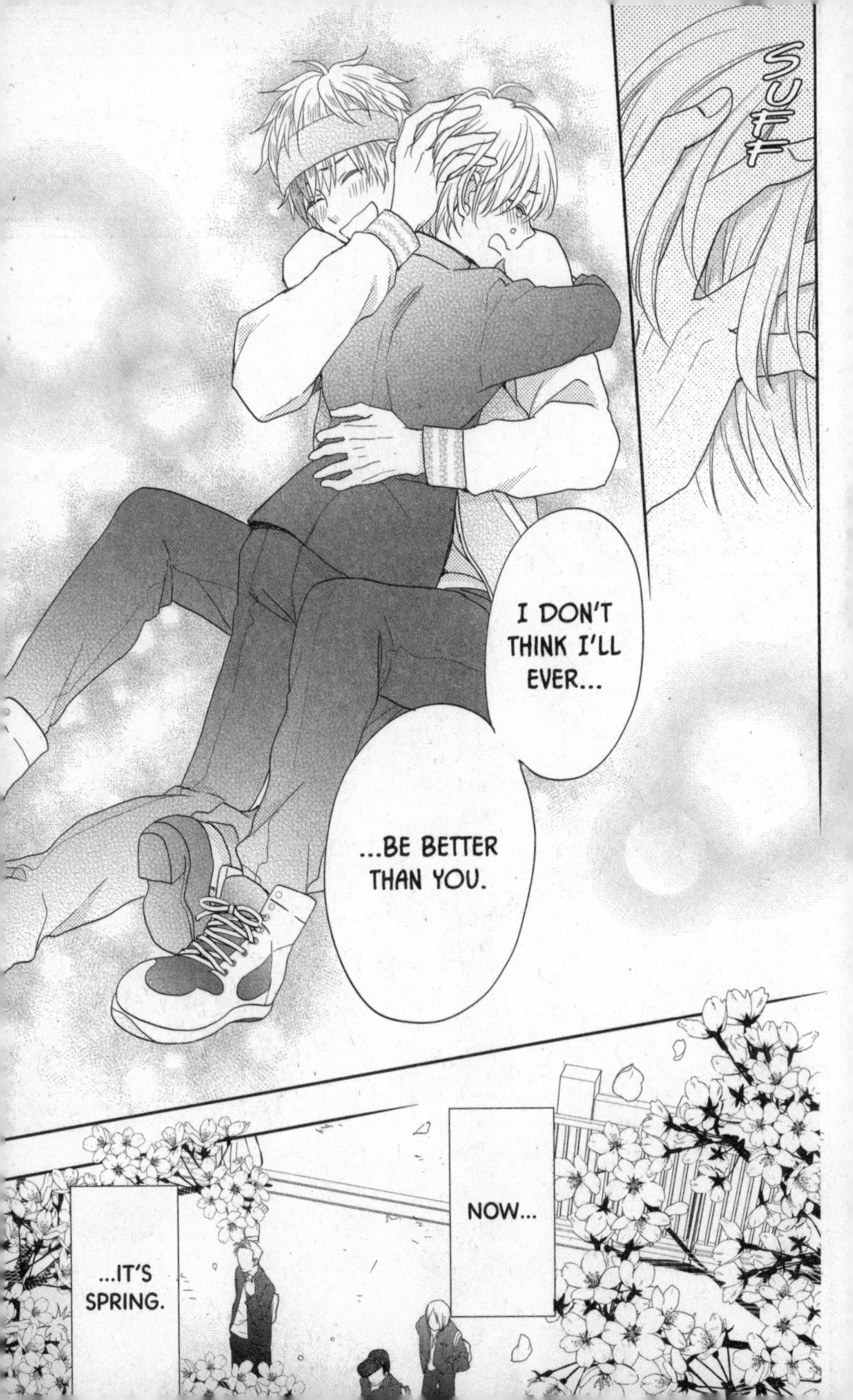
SUFF
I DON'T THINK I'LL EVER...
...BE BETTER THAN YOU.
NOW...
...IT'S SPRING.

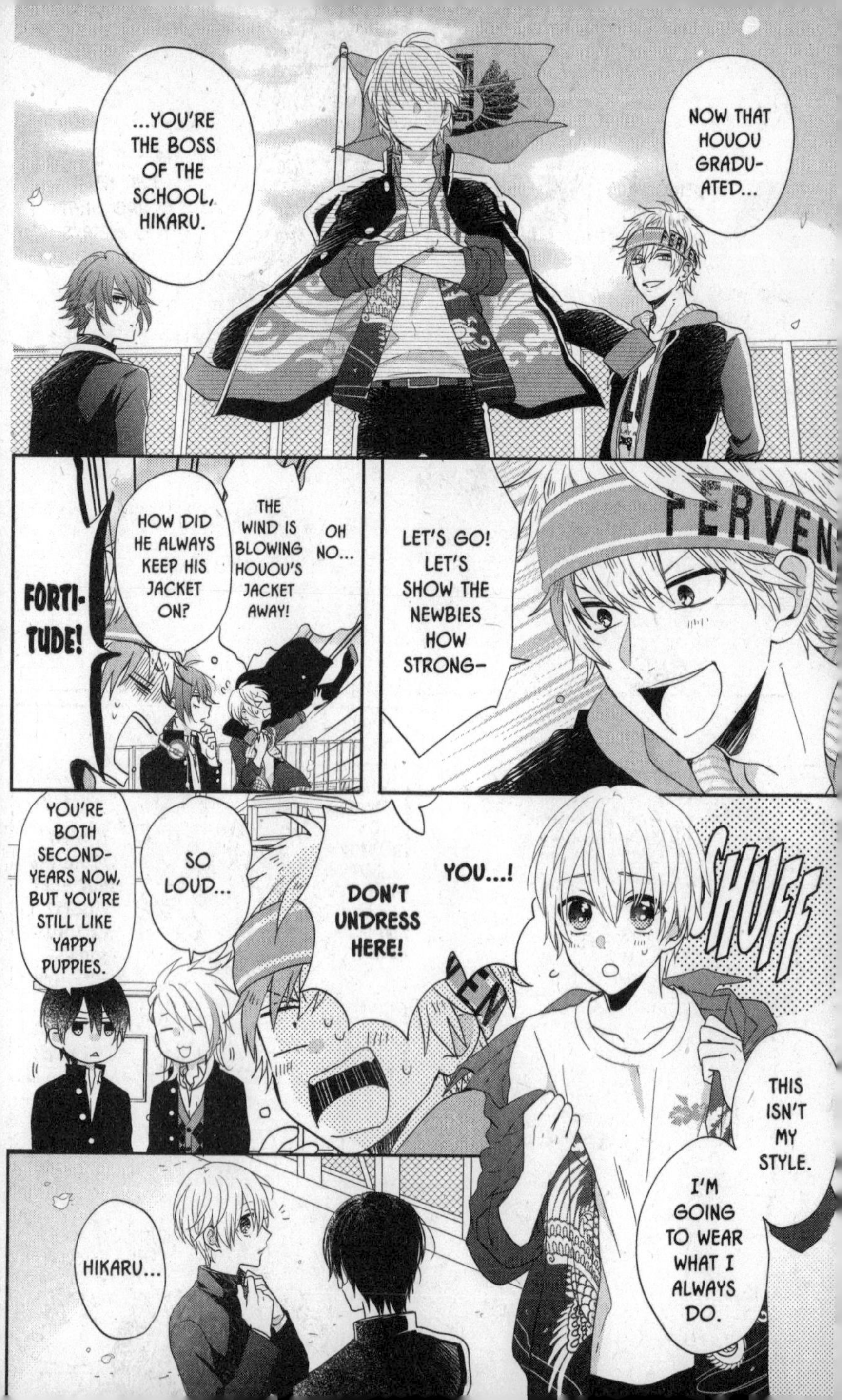
NOW THAT HOUOU GRADUATED...
...YOU'RE THE BOSS OF THE SCHOOL, HIKARU.
LET'S GO! LET'S SHOW THE NEWBIES HOW STRONG–
OH NO...
THE WIND IS BLOWING HOUOU'S JACKET AWAY!
HOW DID HE ALWAYS KEEP HIS JACKET ON?
FORTITUDE!
SHUFF
YOU...!
DON'T UNDRESS HERE!
SO LOUD...
YOU'RE BOTH SECOND-YEARS NOW, BUT YOU'RE STILL LIKE YAPPY PUPPIES.
THIS ISN'T MY STYLE.
I'M GOING TO WEAR WHAT I ALWAYS DO.
HIKARU...

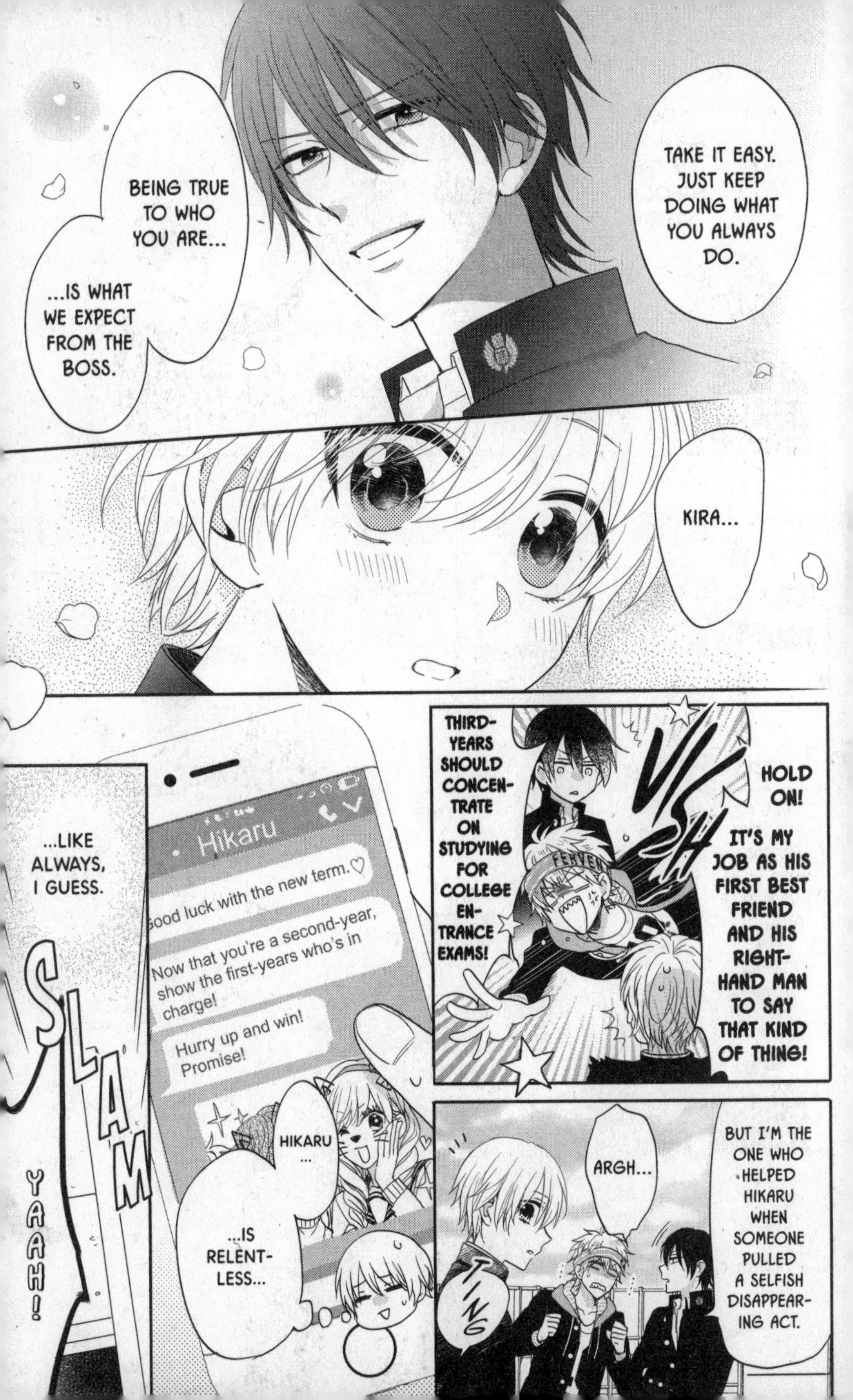
TAKE IT EASY. JUST KEEP DOING WHAT YOU ALWAYS DO.
BEING TRUE TO WHO YOU ARE...
...IS WHAT WE EXPECT FROM THE BOSS.
KIRA...
HOLD ON! IT'S MY JOB AS HIS FIRST BEST FRIEND AND HIS RIGHT-HAND MAN TO SAY THAT KIND OF THING!
VISH
THIRD-YEARS SHOULD CONCENTRATE ON STUDYING FOR COLLEGE ENTRANCE EXAMS!
BUT I'M THE ONE WHO HELPED HIKARU WHEN SOMEONE PULLED A SELFISH DISAPPEARING ACT.
ARGH...
TING
Hikaru
Good luck with the new term.♡
Now that you're a second-year, show the first-years who's in charge!
Hurry up and win! Promise!
...LIKE ALWAYS, I GUESS.
HIKARU...
...IS RELENTLESS...
SLAM
YAAAH!

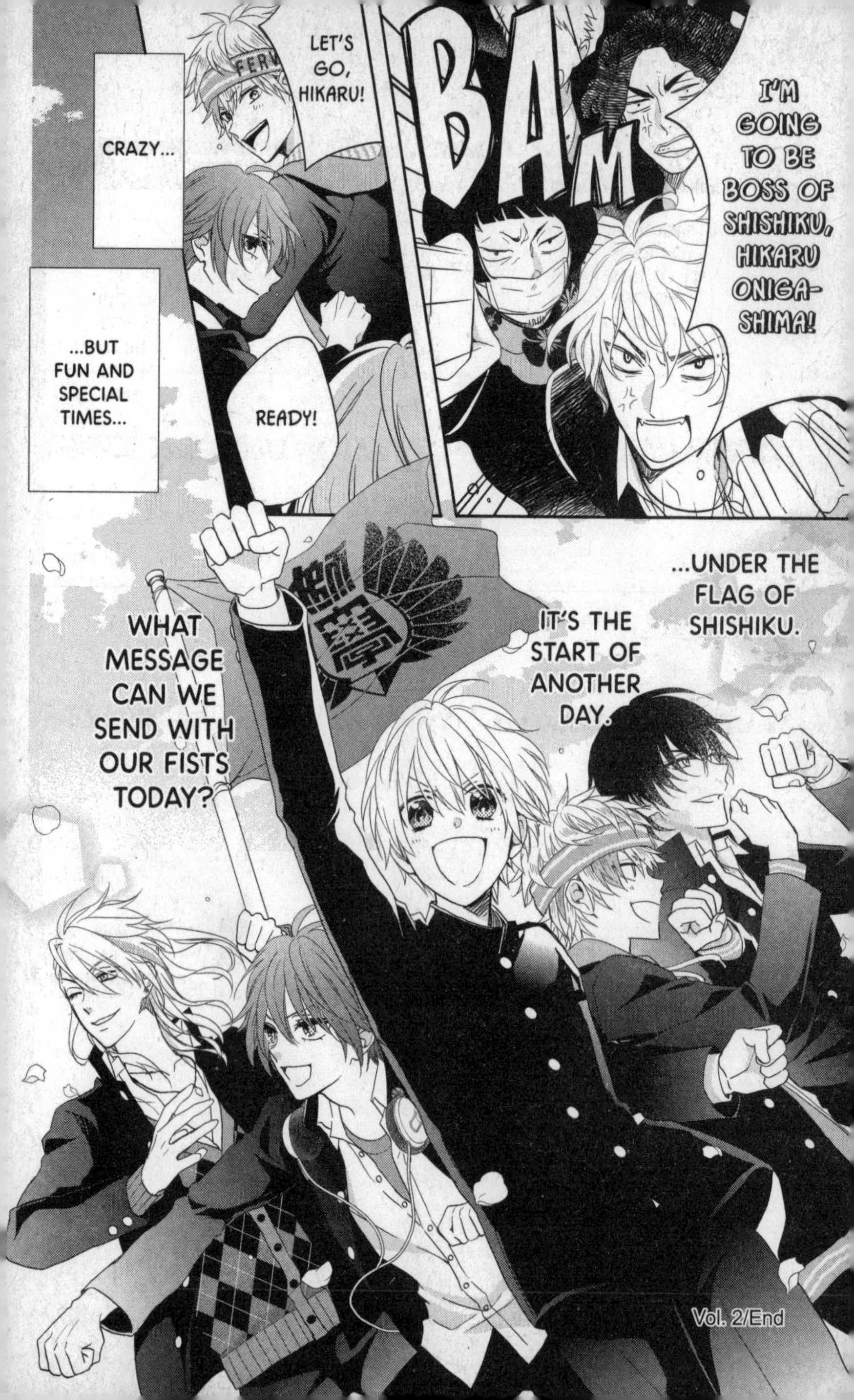
BAM
I'M GOING TO BE BOSS OF SHISHIKU, HIKARU ONIGA-SHIMA!
LET'S GO, HIKARU!
CRAZY...
READY!
...BUT FUN AND SPECIAL TIMES...
...UNDER THE FLAG OF SHISHIKU.
IT'S THE START OF ANOTHER DAY.
WHAT MESSAGE CAN WE SEND WITH OUR FISTS TODAY?
Vol. 2/End

GOT IN LINE AFTER CHANGING WIGS THREE TIMES

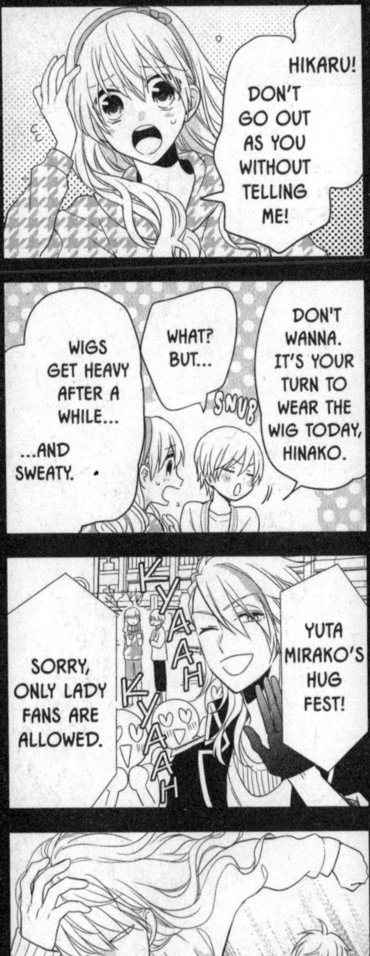
HIKARU! DON'T GO OUT AS YOU WITHOUT TELLING ME!
DON'T WANNA. IT'S YOUR TURN TO WEAR THE WIG TODAY, HINAKO.
SNUB
WHAT? BUT...
WIGS GET HEAVY AFTER A WHILE...
...AND SWEATY.
YUTA MIRAKO'S HUG FEST!
KYAAH
KYAAAH
SORRY, ONLY LADY FANS ARE ALLOWED.

A SCRAPBOOK THAT MAKES THE HEART FLUTTER

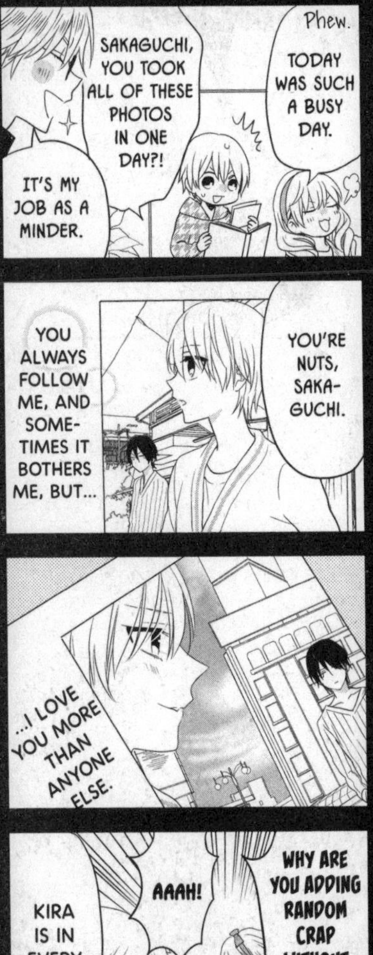
Phew.
TODAY WAS SUCH A BUSY DAY.
SAKAGUCHI, YOU TOOK ALL OF THESE PHOTOS IN ONE DAY?!
IT'S MY JOB AS A MINDER.
YOU'RE NUTS, SAKAGUCHI.
YOU ALWAYS FOLLOW ME, AND SOMETIMES IT BOTHERS ME, BUT...
...I LOVE YOU MORE THAN ANYONE ELSE.
WHY ARE YOU ADDING RANDOM CRAP WITHOUT PERMISSION?!
AAAH!
KIRA IS IN EVERY PHOTO...
Why?

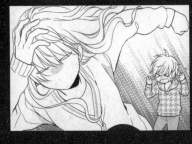

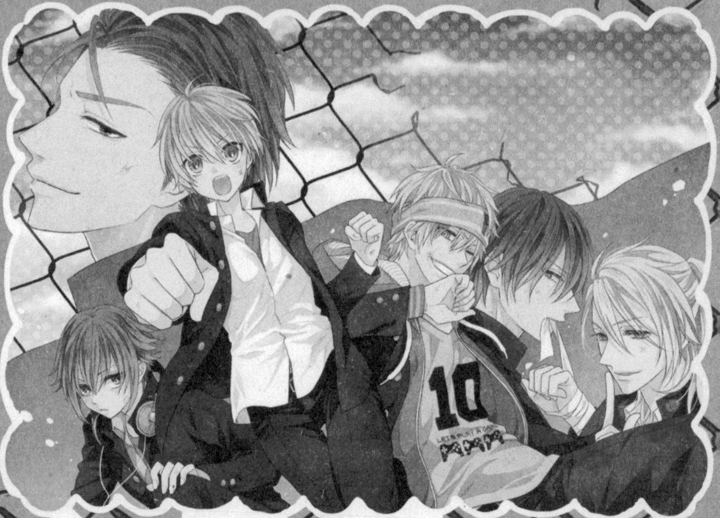

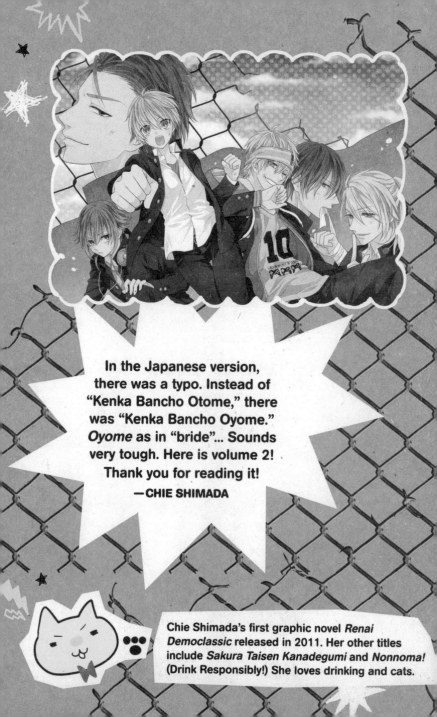

In the Japanese version, there was a typo. Instead of "Kenka Bancho Otome," there was "Kenka Bancho Oyome." *Oyome* as in "bride"... Sounds very tough. Here is volume 2! Thank you for reading it!

—CHIE SHIMADA

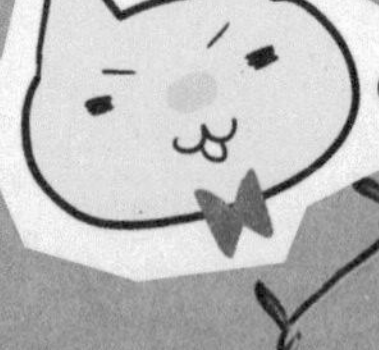

Chie Shimada's first graphic novel *Renai Democlassic* released in 2011. Her other titles include *Sakura Taisen Kanadegumi* and *Nonnoma!* (Drink Responsibly!) She loves drinking and cats.

Kenka Bancho Otome: Love's Battle Royale Vol. 2

SHOJO BEAT MANGA EDITION

STORY AND ART BY
Chie Shimada

ORIGINAL CONCEPT BY
Spike Chunsoft

VIDEO GAME DEVELOPED BY
Red Entertainment

TRANSLATION **JN Productions**
TOUCH-UP ART & LETTERING **Inori Fukuda Trant**
GRAPHIC DESIGN **Alice Lewis**
EDITOR **Nancy Thistlethwaite**

KENKABANCHO OTOME -KOI NO BATTLE ROYALE-
by CHIE SHIMADA / SPIKE CHUNSOFT / RED ENTERTAINMENT

First published in Japan in 2017 by HAKUSENSHA, Inc., Tokyo.
English language translation rights arranged with HAKUSENSHA, Inc., Tokyo.

Printed in Canada

Published by VIZ Media, LLC
P.O. Box 77010
San Francisco, CA 94107

10 9 8 7 6 5 4 3 2 1
First printing, July 2018

ratings.viz.com RATED T TEEN

PARENTAL ADVISORY
KENKA BANCHO OTOME is rated T for Teen and is recommended for ages 13 and up. This volume contains more fighting!!

VIZ MEDIA
viz.com

Shojo Beat
shojobeat.com

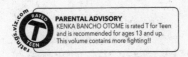

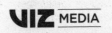

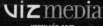

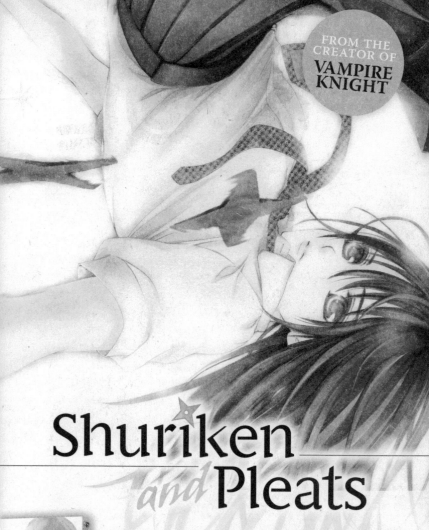

Shuriken *and* Pleats

When the master she has sworn to protect is killed, Mikage Kirio, a skilled ninja, travels to Japan to start a new, peaceful life for herself. But as soon as she arrives, she finds herself fighting to protect the life of Mahito Wakashimatsu, a man who is under attack by a band of ninja. From that time on, Mikage is drawn deeper into the machinations of his powerful family.

www.viz.com

STOP!

You may be reading the wrong way!

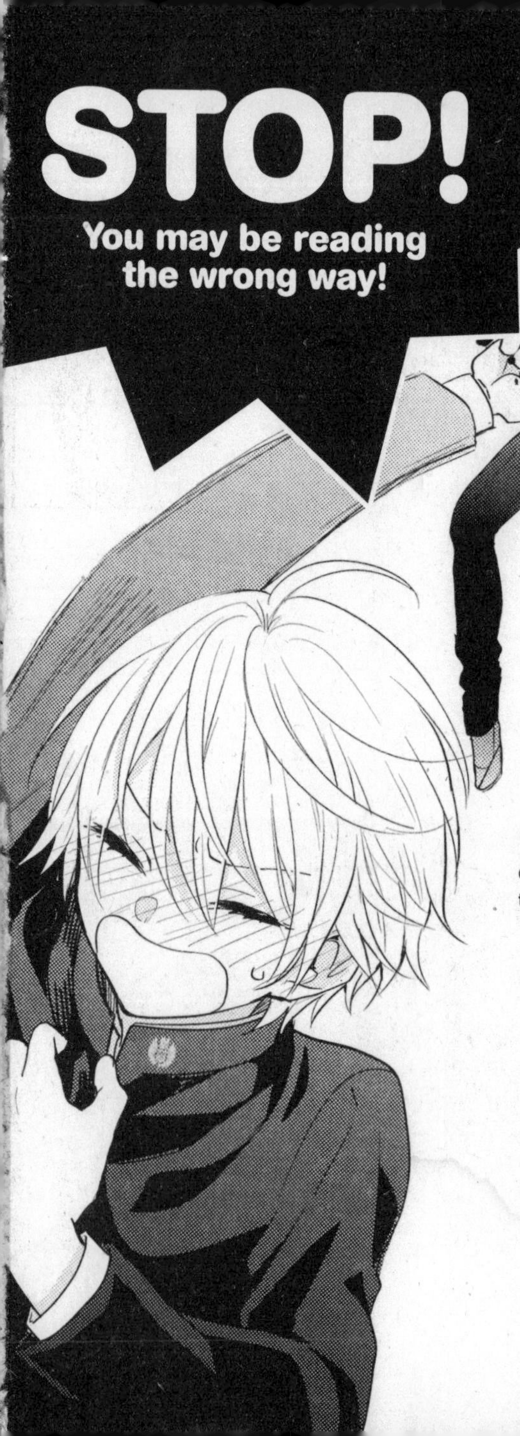

In keeping with the original Japanese comic format, this book reads from right to left—so action, sound effects and word balloons are completely reversed to preserve the orientation of the original artwork.

Check out the diagram shown here to get the hang of things, and then turn to the other side of the book to get started!

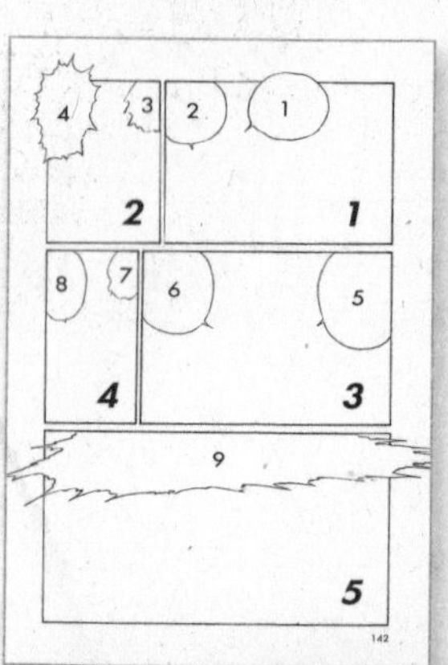
1
2
3
4
1
2
5
6
7
8
3
4
9
5
142